FAT
and
MEAN

The Corporate Squeeze of Working Americans
and the Myth of Managerial "Downsizing"

DAVID M. GORDON

MARTIN KESSLER BOOKS

THE FREE PRESS

New York   London   Toronto   Sydney   Singapore

THE FREE PRESS
A Division of Simon & Schuster Inc.
1230 Avenue of the Americas
New York, NY 10020

Designed by Carla Bolte

Manufactured in the United States of America

10 9 8 7 6 5 4 3 2 1

Library of Congress Cataloging-in-Publication Data

Gordon, David M.
    Fat and mean : the corporate squeeze of working Americans and the myth of managerial
"downsizing" / David M. Gordon.
        p.   cm.
    Includes bibliographical references and index.
    ISBN 0–684–82288–1
    1. Industrial management—United States.   2. Bureaucracy—United States.
3. Corporations—United States.   4. Downsizing in organizations—United States.
5. Wages—United States.   6. Labor productivity—United States.   I. Title.
HD70.U5G58   1996
658.4—dc20   96-2145
                                                                            CIP

For Dinni

CONTENTS

LIST OF FIGURES

LIST OF TABLES

ACKNOWLEDGMENTS

Morethan usually, this book could not have been completed without the help of superb research assistants—often working under unreasonable time pressures. Special thanks to Ellen Houston for her care, resourcefulness, efficiency, and good humor. Many thanks as well to David Kucera and Heather Boushey for exemplary service in a pinch.

A number of people also kindly supplied me with data and references which might otherwise have taken ages to trace. I am grateful to the staff of the Government Documents Division of the Bobst Library, New York University; to Erik Olin Wright and Michael Hout for help in obtaining their survey on the United States; to Margaret Duncan for scouting and providing sources; to Maury Gittelman of the Bureau of Labor Statistics on a number of fronts; and to William Janeway for helping steer me toward a useful case study.

As numerous mentions in the text indicate, I was stimulated to work on many of these issues through my continuing involvement and contact with the staff and projects of the Labor Institute; many thanks to all, and especially to Les Leopold.

I am heavily indebted to friends and associates for comments on the manuscript. Once again demonstrating that best friends can also be best (and most stringent) critics, Sam Bowles and Tom Weisskopf gave me a real run for my money on the bulk of a first draft; their reservations and suggestions were very useful in subsequent revisions. Ben Harrison also provided some useful reactions to several chapters, while David Howell continuously fed me materials and references and helped keep me pointed in the right direction on the analytic chapters. Michael Reich and Margaret Duncan helped me track down some useful sources. Colleagues David Plotke, Lance Taylor, and John Eatwell gave me some interesting feedback on my public lecture introducing some of these themes.

I also want to thank my medical supporters—Keith Aaronson, John Fisher, Debbie Johnston, Stuart Katz, especially Mark Lipton, and their staffs—for helping me meet my deadline more or less on time, without too many untoward interruptions.

This book would not have appeared without Martin Kessler's interest, curiosity, support, and insistence; many of us will long treasure his contributions to serious trade publishing in the United States. Peter Dougherty provided excellent editorial suggestions and support—far beyond the call of his sudden conscription. Abigail Strubel helped throughout and displayed considerable patience with my persistent and sometimes pesky inquiries. Special thanks to Adam Bellow for taking on and helping guide the book through the final stages of publication.

Diana R. Gordon provided her usual close and ruthless editing help. We waded through some tough times together during this book's gestation and completion; there's no way I can thank her enough for her involvement and love.

INTRODUCTION

In the 1992 presidential campaign, Bill Clinton's advisers focused increasingly on a simple maxim: "It's the economy, stupid." And the strategy seemed to work. One of the keys to Clinton's plurality was the swing of working- and lower-middle-class voters from the Reagan-Bush coalition back to the Democrats, voters who had grown increasingly angry about the recession and the longer-term erosion of their living standards, voters who came to believe that a Clinton Administration could do more for their economic problems than the incumbent regime.[1]

Then the Democrats got pasted in the 1994 congressional elections. There were no doubt many reasons for the Republicans' resurgence at the polls and their seizure of power in the House and Senate. Gingrichians pointed to the "Contract with America" for their success. The Christian right highlighted the heavy voter participation of their core constituencies and the social issues that are said to have moved them. Many across the political spectrum lambasted Clinton and his Administration for their political spinelessness and their opportunism on key issues of policy and principle.

Any or all of these interpretations may be correct; they are not mutually exclusive. But when we turn to the actual voting patterns, another kind of lesson virtually catapults from the data. According to exit polls, at least two dramatic switches in voter allegiance seem to explain much if not most of the Democrats' collapse in 1994.[2]

• One involved the economically ravaged: In the 1992 elections for the House of Representatives, voters who said their living standards were "getting worse" supported the Democrats by a margin of 72 to 28 percent. By 1994, this same group of voters—those who had been taking it on the chin economically—supported the Republicans by a nearly mirror margin of 63 to 37—*a loss for the Democrats with this bloc of thirty-five percentage points over the 1992 results.*

• Another featured the notoriously "angry" white males: Between the two elections, according to the same set of exit polls, the Republicans gained eleven percentage points among white males, winning in 1994 by a massive 62–38 margin. Poor, working- and lower-middle-class males, indeed, had

1

been the groups whose economic fortunes had been sagging most severely over the previous fifteen years.

These were the voters who had pulled their levers in 1992 betting that the Democrats would do something, almost anything to salve their financial wounds. And these were now the voters who felt abandoned, left twisting in the winds, by an Administration which had done almost nothing to address their economic anxieties and even less to improve their living standards.[3]

Another two years have passed. For all the rhetorical flourishes and political gambits, all the strategic posturing and tactical maneuvering between the Democrats in the White House and the Republicans controlling Congress, all the talk of new "values" and "renewed leadership," all the slick television and packaged commercials defining this year's election campaign, a core economic issue still runs through American politics like a subterranean stream. The American economy has been growing for fifteen years but the vast majority of Americans have not been sharing in the harvest. Most U.S. families have been struggling to make ends meet and many have failed. "Who gets what is the issue of the 90s," political analyst Kevin Phillips declared at the beginning of the decade.[4] And the vast majority of workers and citizens in the United States—roughly the bottom 80 percent of the income distribution—are still waiting for theirs.

In Fall 1994, observing the Virginia Senate campaign featuring soldier-turned-politician Oliver North, philosopher Richard Rorty smelled the fears in the breeze:[5]

> the suburban middle class . . . is scared stiff, and has every reason to be. Its sacrifices to pay college tuition will not necessarily be rewarded by comfortable white collar jobs for its children. Its hard work is probably not going to pay off in rising income. Its moral uprightness may go entirely unrewarded.

White House pollster Stanley Greenberg echoed Rorty when returning after the 1994 electoral Democratic debacle to Macomb County, Michigan—a district of largely working- and middle-class communities—where he had been tracking voters' moods since the mid-1980s.[6]

> Macomb County, Michigan, is not just a place. It represents the ordinary citizenry of America trying to make a better life and hold on to its dreams. [Through the late '80s and early '90s] the Macomb Counties across the land fell into revolt.
>
> Yet the people of Macomb are not in search of a rebellion. They want a new contract, one they can trust and rely on, one that binds both the leaders and the citizenry, one that ensures a rising prosperity. They know little of what is happening in Canada, Europe, and Asia. They know something about corporate restructuring and a new world economy. They still want to know that

America can create its own moment for its own people. . . . These voters are waiting for a new contract and a better day.

Influential Wall Street economist Stephen Roach recently warned his financial clients:[7]

Worker backlash could be one of the key issues of the 1996 presidential campaign. . . . The so-called majority of public opinion in favor of deficit reduction—and its associated dismantlement of entitlement spending—is about to be drowned out by a groundswell of worker backlash. Workers want more—not less.

"The frustrations run deep," R. W. Apple Jr. concluded from the results of a *New York Times*/CBS News poll in August 1995, "perhaps deeper than at any other time in modern American history."[8]

THE AMERICAN ECONOMY has been failing most of its people. Why?

Every pundit, politician, and professor has his or her favorite diagnosis. Some claim that our moral values have decayed, that we've lost the will to compete in the global economy, that our spines have softened. Some argue that we are failing to equip our present and future generations with the sophisticated skills they need for the twenty-first century, that we need smarter and savvier workers to restore American economic leadership. Others complain that the powerful and greedy have been let loose to feed at the trough—sucking up our resources for their soaring salaries, leveraged buyouts, golden parachutes, and rich and famous lifestyles. Still others blame our political leadership—their indifference, their arrogance, their addiction to lobbyists' largesse and bureaucratic booty. Some of these explanations get combined—as, for example, in Kevin Phillips' trenchant recent analysis in *Arrogant Capital* of the entwined interests and power of those feasting on Wall Street and those wheeling and dealing inside the Beltway.[9]

Some of these diagnoses contain useful insights. But I argue in this book that all of them have badly missed the mark. *I contend that we have been ignoring a major source of our economic problems over the last twenty years: the way most U.S. corporations maintain bloated bureaucracies and mistreat their workers.* Until and unless we apprehend and begin to transform those corporate practices, we shall continue to witness the frustration of ordinary Americans' dreams and the tragic shackling of our economic future. Contrary to the argument being made by business leaders and scholars who contend that American corporations are trimming their managerial operations in the interests of revitalization and competitiveness, the opposite is true: Corporations are still fat in the 1990s, and no prosperity explosion is coming around the corner. The losers are working Americans, ordinary citizens, and our broader society. We must begin to attend to this basic fault in our economic geology.

This book does not address all of the problems of the U.S. economy—automation and joblessness, for example, or the problem, however misdefined, of the federal budget deficit. Rather than raining shotgun pellets all over the economic landscape, I focus my sights on two basic problems in the U.S. economy and their single, fundamental, under-girding source in the structure of corporate America. U.S. corporations are both *fat* and *mean*, I argue, and the economic anxieties shared by scores of millions of Americans flow fundamentally from this source. My argument is fairly simple, but it confounds some of the conventional wisdom at nearly every turn.

I begin with the two basic problems, corporate bloat and falling wages. I call them the *bureaucratic burden* and the *wage squeeze* and show that they are two sides of the same coin.

Many have noted the wage squeeze. It has become commonplace to observe that millions of Americans have suffered declining hourly earnings. My characterization of these trends is probably the least controversial argument of the book, though some technical and definitional quibbles will remain. The bottom line is clear: over the past twenty years, real hourly take-home pay for production and nonsupervisory workers—representing more than 80 percent of all wage-and-salary employees—has declined by more than 10 percent. The economy has grown massively since the mid-1960s, but workers' real spendable wages are no higher now than they were almost thirty years ago. The American Dream is fading for most who have dared to dream it—fading not just for the poor and unskilled but for the vast majority of U.S. workers, for steelworkers and secretaries; bank tellers, burger flippers; and boiler makers; stock-handlers and statistical clerks. Most recently, even those with a college degree have begun to feel the pinch. This first problem does not primarily concern the rising gap between the rich and the poor, although income and wealth inequality has indeed increased dramatically over the past fifteen years. Much more centrally, the wage squeeze is crunching both the bottom *and* the vast middle, not just the disadvantaged but almost everybody else.

The second problem is much less widely noted and will be shocking to many. U.S. corporations run their affairs with bloated, top-heavy managerial and supervisory bureaucracies. The bureaucratic burden weighs heavily upon both our corporations and our economy. How big is it? Depending on the definition, between 15 and 20 percent of private nonfarm employees in the United States work as managers and supervisors. In 1994 we spent $1.3 trillion on the salaries and benefits of nonproduction and supervisory workers, almost one-fifth of total gross domestic product, almost exactly the size of the revenues absorbed by the entire federal government.

The burdens of bloated corporate management have grown steadily over the postwar period, taking an extra ratchet-jump upward as corporations grew increasingly aggressive toward their workers in the 1970s. By the 1980s, many observers were beginning to note the obesity of U.S. managerial structures—their top-heaviness, their inertia, their flab, their redundancies.

And these critics were right. It is possible to compare the bureaucratic burden in U.S. corporations with those in the leading competing economies. In the 1980s, by common measures, the proportion of managerial and administrative employment was more than three times as high in the United States as in Germany and Japan. Those economies were handing us our lunch in international competition. Did we really need to spend so much on the managers and supervisors of our private corporations?

Here I experience my first close encounter with the conventional wisdom. Every time I've talked with people about this book, or shown them early drafts, I've been greeted with an immediate response. Isn't top-heavy corporate bureaucracy a problem of the past? What about "downsizing"? Aren't corporations paring their managerial fat like Lizzie Borden with her ax? Welcome to the 1990s. Welcome to the world of the *lean* and mean corporation.[10]

Scores of thousands of managers have been sent packing in the 1990s. But our corporations are still *fat*. Despite all the headlines, despite all the personal tragedies, as I show in Chapter 2, the proportion of managers and supervisors in private nonfarm employment *has grown during the 1990s*, not shrunk. The conventional wisdom is wrong. The bureaucratic burden remains.

I then turn to the central argument of the book. *Fat* and *mean* go together. I argue in Chapter 3 that the wage squeeze and the bureaucratic burden, these two central features of our economic landscape—conventionally either ignored or treated as entirely separate phenomena—are integrally connected as key elements of an underlying corporate approach to management and production in the United States. I call it the Stick Strategy: U.S. corporations rely on the stick, not the carrot.

The connection between the wage squeeze and the bureaucratic burden runs in both directions.

• In one direction, stagnant or falling wages create the need for intensive managerial supervision of frontline employees. If workers do not share in the fruits of the enterprise, if they are not provided a promise of job security and steady wage growth, what incentive do they have to work as hard as their bosses would like? So the corporations need to monitor the workers' effort and be able to threaten credibly to punish them if they do not perform. The corporations must wield the Stick. Eventually the Stick requires millions of Stick-wielders.

• In the other direction, once top-heavy corporate bureaucracies emerge, they acquire their own, virtually ineluctable expansionary dynamic. They push for more numbers in their ranks and higher salaries for their members. Where does the money come from? It can't come from dividends, since the corporations need to be able to raise money on equity markets. It can't come from interest obligations, since the corporations need to be able to borrow from lenders as well. One of the most obvious targets is frontline workers' compensation. The more powerful the corporate bureaucracy becomes, and the weaker the pressure with which employees can counter, the greater the downward pressure on production workers' wages. The wage squeeze intensifies.

This connection seems clearest when we compare different styles of labor management across the advanced countries. Those with the most cooperative approaches feature *both* the most rapid wage gains *and* the smallest corporate bureaucracies. Those with the most adversarial approaches to labor relations, notably including the United States, manifest *both* much slower wage growth *and* much top-heavier corporate structures.

In short, I argue that both the wage squeeze and the bureaucratic burden build upon a common foundation in the United States—our corporate reliance on the Stick Strategy for managing production. If we want to begin addressing the economic anxieties shared by scores of millions of U.S. workers and their families, we need to confront this basic feature of our economic topography.

But here I immediately run into a second strand of the conventional wisdom. Many believe that U.S. corporations have abandoned the Stick Strategy and are embracing the "high-performance workplace"—providing new incentives to their workers, involving them in production, sharing decision-making, promoting "quality circles" and "flexible production." As with top-heavy bureaucracies, many believe that oppressive labor relations are a thing of the past.

There is no question that some U.S. corporations have moved in a more cooperative direction. In his recent book *Rethinking America* Hedrick Smith insightfully reports on some of what he calls the American Innovators. "In industry," he observes, "a daring minority has found certain keys to a winning strategy: that trust is their most powerful motivator, that people rise to the level of the responsibility they are given, and that learning is the engine of continuous growth."[11]

The problem is precisely that this is a minority—a small minority. Many firms have been experimenting, I argue at the end of Chapter 3, but very few have actually committed themselves to the kind of full transformation that a switch from the Stick Strategy would require. Among other requirements, fully involved workers need clear promises of job security and clear rewards from shared productivity gains. In the United States, from year to year, job security is eroding and fewer of the gains from technology and workplace reorganization are being shared with the workforce. This is not the way to run a "high-performance workplace" with the carrot. Think of it as the "high-pressure workplace" still driven by the Stick.

These differences in perception matter. U.S. corporations continue to be fat and mean, I contend, and we pay a massive price for their enduring commitment to the Stick Strategy. In Part II of this book, I turn to the consequences for working Americans and their families, for our communities, and for our economy.

The consequences for Americans' lives and livelihoods extend far beyond the obvious. Some respond to stories about rising inequality by worrying about the poor and disadvantaged. But the reality is that, beyond the suffering of the poor and disadvantaged, the *average working household* has found its cupboards increasingly bare, enduring the constant pressure to get by on too little, to stretch a little into something. In Chapter 4 I trace a ripple of effects of the Stick Strategy purling outward from the wage squeeze. Falling wages have pushed members of many U.S. households to work longer hours—often for *both* parents in married-couple households. Longer hours and spreading job insecurity have eroded job satisfaction and exacerbated pressures on the job. Longer hours and job stress have spilled over into the family, causing strain, breakup, even domestic violence.

And here we face our third encounter with prevailing views. Conservatives are determined to argue, with more and more assent from the center, that a whole host of social problems can be traced to the decay of our moral fabric: family breakup and the crisis of "family values," teen pregnancy and illegitimate births, welfare "dependency," the "underclass," crime in the streets. The scourges are tearing us apart as a nation.

We would understand these problems in our communities much better, I argue in Chapter 5, if we properly understood their roots in the deepening reliance of U.S. corporations on the Stick. Many of the "social problems" about which the right rants, I contend, are better explained by the kinds of limited and corroding job opportunities that millions of Americans face. In his eagerness to dismiss the importance of "the economy, stupid," columnist and commentator Ben J. Wattenberg argues in his recent, widely cited book that "values matter most." As sources of social strain, morals matter, surely, but jobs matter more.

The price we pay for our fat and mean corporations is higher still. Not only do millions pay the costs directly in their lives and livelihoods, but we all bear the burden through the effects of U.S. corporate practice on our macroeconomy's performance—on our ability to build for the future and our competitiveness in the broadening global economy. Many who compare the advanced economies refer to two different avenues to economic growth—the "low road" and the "high road."[12] We in the United States are stuck following the low road, squeezing and scolding our workers, cheapening labor costs, trying to compete economically through intimidation and conflict. Other leading economies such as Japan and Germany take the high road, fueling their growth with cooperation and trust.

The costs of the low road are considerable. It would appear from the evidence I review in Chapter 6 that, when we compare relatively cooperative and conflictual economies, those driving the high road enjoy more rapid productivity growth, more buoyant investment, and a better combination of inflation, unemployment, and trade performance. There may be many reasons for their greater macroeconomic successes over the past twenty years, but at least one of them appears to be that their approach to labor-management pays off not merely for their workers but also for their entire economy. The Carrot Strategy, as I call it for contrast, pays macroeconomic dividends as well.

A fourth skirmish with the conventional wisdom: Hasn't the U.S. economy recovered strongly in recent years, reviving its productivity performance, diversifying its industrial structure, producing millions of jobs, managing a stable recovery through a delicate combination of "soft landings" and buoyant take-offs? Haven't many other leading economies begun to stumble, facing rising unemployment and slower growth? Hasn't the U.S. economy begun to reap the rewards of its greater "flexibility"? Haven't some of the European economies, perhaps even Japan, begun to stagger from economic sclerosis?

Some of these characterizations about the recent past are accurate, most aren't. More importantly, these recent developments do not provide evidence that the U.S. production system has advantages over others, that we should preserve it rather than reject it. The more cooperative of the European economies are still outperforming us, despite their recent bad press. Most important, we could do better in the United States—and millions more could share in the fruits of our macroeconomic performance—if we began to transform our fat and mean corporations.

In the final part of the book I make policy recommendations which could begin to push us toward the high road—toward a future of relatively more cooperative managerial and labor relations based on rising wages, job security, and real worker involvement in production and investment decisions. They would also help us take the first steps, if my analysis here is correct, toward building stronger communities, more inclusive politics, and a more promising economic future.

These proposals are not the standard fare of political discourse in the United States, especially in the heat of electoral passion. It would be premature to put my recommendations on the table before first considering more conventional analyses of the problems addressed in this book. The analysis presented here is not the language in which most people talk about the forces driving falling wages and rising inequality. Where is the discussion of skills and training, of foreign competition and low-wage workers abroad? If so unfamiliar, can my arguments about the foundations of the wage squeeze have any merit? Is there not the danger that I'm looking entirely in the wrong direction?

I turn in Chapters 7 and 8 to a more detailed examination of alternative explanations for the wage squeeze and the consequent hardships millions have been facing. Two main kinds of explanations dominate prevailing discourse.

One refers to the "skills mismatch." It argues that many workers' wages have fallen, while others' have risen, because of bad matching between the skills workers bring to the labor market and the technology requirements that employers have on the job. Get ready for the twenty-first century, workers are told. If your wages have been falling, it's because you haven't acquired the skills and training that modern corporations now demand. There are too many unskilled workers and too few with sufficient skills. The wages of the former group have been driven down. Wages too low? Go to college. Get computer literate. When the going gets tough, the tough get trained.

The second principal prevailing explanation focuses on the global economy. Capital now roams the world, bringing advanced technology into every corner of the globe. Wages are far lower in the developing world than here. Unless wages continue to decline here, according to this second view, corporations would be crazy not to locate their production operations abroad. And low wages are pushing more and more immigrants across our borders, creating gluts in low-wage labor markets. The logic of increasingly intense international competition is as simple as short division.

Both of these views are plausible. They fit with many workers' direct experiences. And we hear them so often they acquire a patina of legitimacy from constant repetition.

But now comes the fifth encounter with prevailing views: I argue that the evidence supporting both of these conventional explanations is relatively unpersuasive, despite their plausibility and widespread acceptance. Neither appears to explain very much of the wage squeeze. Skill mismatches have made much less difference than commonly believed, and global competition— though obviously present and important—has had far less wrenching effects than many suppose.

What then? I turn in Chapter 8 to a crystallization of the explanation that flows from the core arguments of the first part of the book. I call it the "low road" hypothesis. I argue that a critically important source of falling wages has been U.S. corporations' increasingly aggressive stance with their employees, their mounting power to gain the upper hand in those struggles, and the shifts in the institutional environment that this mounting power has helped foster. The management offensive since the 1970s has driven three important institutional changes in labor relations and the political environment affecting them—the decline in the real value of the minimum wage, the erosion of union reach and power, and the emergence of "disposable" employment. These three changes appear to underlie much if not most of the wage squeeze. If we care about the lives and livelihoods of millions of Americans, we need to attend to the kinds of labor structures and practices that our corporations pursue.

Could we conceivably cross over to the high road in the United States? Could we plausibly pressure our corporations to pursue an American version of the Carrot Strategy instead?

In the final chapter of the book I turn to policy prescription. I do not aim at a comprehensive program to address all of our economic problems. Still focusing my aim narrowly, I suggest five policies which could support movement in the United States onto the high road toward economic prosperity and a more balanced distribution of its benefits. The policy proposals are purposefully simple, designed to illustrate the possibilities, rather than drafting the detailed language, for legislative initiatives. I propose that we substantially increase the minimum wage; dramatically reform U.S. labor law to ease the path toward unionization; amend the Fair Labor Standards Act to make "contingent" employment less tempting for employers; establish an investment bank to reward firms that embrace more democratic and cooperative approaches to labor management; and substantially expand the education and training we provide to management and employees who embark on this transformational path.

And now we have a close encounter of a sixth and final kind. Each of these proposals is technically practicable: each can be framed legislatively, and each could be implemented fairly quickly—certainly within 100 days. But skeptics will immediately raise three kinds of objections.

First, they will argue that at least some of the proposals will do more harm than good. Won't an increase in the minimum wage, for example, simply eliminate many jobs and exacerbate our competitive problems in the global economy? I try to show in Chapter 9 that these conventional and often shopworn objections are misplaced and that in fact the economic benefits from these initiatives would substantially outweigh their costs.

The second and third kinds of objections go together. One tells me to get serious: The conservatives are on the offensive in U.S. politics, the center is chasing the right, liberals are retreating faster than greased lightning, and progressives have little more political impact than a mosquito bite on an elephant. These sorts of proposals swim against currents that are far too powerful; they'll simply be washed out to sea.

The other, which is a close correlate, says that U.S. business is not in the mood to accept these kinds of proposals. Whether or not they might be in the long-run interest of the economy and even of business, they're nowhere to be found on the short-run corporate agenda. And if they're not on the corporate agenda, they're off the table of acceptable political discourse and debate.

Both of these objections are on target. But both are too fatalistic. A sensible program that addresses popular anxieties, points plausibly to the sources of those problems, and could move us in promising directions can have potentially transformative impact. Much about U.S. politics is currently unsettled. If established political interests are likely to ridicule the kinds of analysis and proposals with which I close this book, that may be a strike *for* those proposals—not against them—with the citizenry. If I were a betting man about politics, I wouldn't want to place my bets right now on the reigning political forces in the United States. Citizens are too angry, and with good reason. A little courage, clear headedness, forthrightness, and above all common sense may go a long way as we gird for the twenty-first century. If nothing else, they would enliven and refresh U.S. policy debates.

Which brings us to the final problem—the likely opposition of business. One would hope that many if not most corporations would recognize we could all enjoy not only a more decent but also a stronger and more vibrant economy and society if they abandoned the Stick Strategy. "We're partners with labor," Nation Steel Corporation has proclaimed in some of its ads, "because we can't imagine a future without them."[13] Questions of morality and self-interest are intertwined. Do the waste and meanness engendered by the Stick Strategy represent the kinds of virtues U.S. business prefers and admires? And can they imagine continuing to prosper over the longer run, even from the narrow vantage point of their own bottom lines, if the wage squeeze and bureaucratic burden continue to exact such a heavy price for ordinary Americans and for our economy? "Corporations are not vehicles for realizing the ideal society," political scientist James Q. Wilson recently observed. "But they . . . cannot for long command the loyalty of their members if their standards of collective action are materially lower than those of their individual members."[14]

Unfortunately, for many reasons that I discuss throughout this book, most U.S. corporations are not prepared to embrace either the high road or the kinds of proposals that might potentially push us toward the high road. Should that close the book on political debate?

We in the United States have long been in the political habit of accommodating, catering to and sometimes even groveling before big business interests. It would take some serious twelve-step programs to begin to break us of that addiction. But we may have little choice. I argue in this book both structurally and historically that U.S. corporations bear much of the blame for the squeeze on working Americans and for our suffocating economy. They are unlikely to change their ways voluntarily, without some serious pressure. In other countries that seem to have pursued successfully more cooperative labor relations, businesses originally dragged their heels and sometimes kicked and screamed during the construction and consolidation of those labor-management systems. We can hope for enlightened business self-interest, but we cannot expect business to solve our problems for us and we can't expect to solve those problems ourselves without at least a little stepping on corporate toes.

The public has few illusions about U.S. corporations. In 1993, only 16 percent of poll respondents expressed "confidence" in "major companies," down from 29 percent in 1973 and much higher levels still in the mid-1960s.[15] In

1995, 79 percent agreed that "the Government is run by a few big interests looking out for themselves"—a cynicism which has increased dramatically since the early 1970s.[16]

The public is not cowed, but our major political parties and their leaders have toed the corporate line for some time. That can change. And it should change. Unless it does, the arguments in this book suggest, we will probably be spinning our wheels in the United States for years to come. U.S. corporations are fat and mean. We could begin to push them in leaner and gentler directions. We could and we must.

Part I

CORPORATE BLOAT AND FALLING WAGES

Chapter 1

THE WAGE SQUEEZE

For years Craig Miller had been a sheet-metal worker at a major airline. After he lost his job in 1992, he and his wife—parents of four kids—had to scramble. Craig took on two lower-paying jobs and started a small sideline business. His wife worked nights as a stock clerk. They were patching together, counting his business, four part-time jobs and they were still earning less than half Craig's previous paycheck.

"Sure we've got four jobs," Craig told a reporter. "So what? So you can work like a dog for $5 an hour?"[1]

The Miller family saga is hardly unique. Since the mid-1970s, more and more U.S. workers and their families have been suffering the *wage squeeze*, enduring steady downward pressure on their hourly take-home pay. The wage squeeze has afflicted not merely the unskilled and disadvantaged but the vast majority of U.S. households, not merely the poor and working class but the middle class as well. Most people in the United States used to be able to look forward to a future of steadily rising earnings. Now they have to race merely to stay in place.

The wage squeeze has even broader consequences. It not only pinches workers and their immediate families. It sends tremors through entire communities, eroding their stability, ripping their social fabric. The frustration and anger it provokes begins to attack the body politic like a plague, spreading virulent strains of cynicism and discontent, of disaffection from government and hatred toward "others" like immigrants who are often blamed for the scourge. Many observers in the United States are inclined to turn their heads, viewing falling wages as somebody else's problem. But the effects are too far-reaching, too extensive. It won't work to play the ostrich, sticking one's head in the sand. The sand is eroding all around us.

Back to the 1960s

The public receives mixed signals about the wage squeeze. On the one hand, more and more observers have taken note of the vise closing around workers' earnings—citing the pressure to work longer hours, the "disappearing middle class," the increasingly elusive American Dream, the mounting gap between the rich and the poor. Personal stories of declining fortunes abound. Statistical studies of stagnant earnings and soaring inequality have become a growth industry. In my research for this book, finding journalistic accounts and scholarly analyses of the wage squeeze was as easy as following the trail of Newt Gingrich's newfound notoriety.

By late 1995, as I was completing the manuscript, the issue was becoming inescapable. *Business Week,* often a leader in tracking changes in the economic climate, devoted a cover story to "The Wage Squeeze" in July 1995. Surveying the atmospheric conditions they reported: [2]

> Four years into a recovery, profits are at a 45-year high, unemployment remains relatively low, and the weak dollar has put foreign rivals on the defensive. Yet U.S. companies continue to drive down costs as if the economy still were in a tailspin. Many are tearing up pay systems and job structures, replacing them with new ones that slice wage rates, slash raises, and subcontract work to lower-paying suppliers.

"Although the problem [of slumping wages] has been plaguing Americans for years," wrote *New York Times* economics reporter Louis Uchitelle that same summer, "it is just now rising to the level of a major campaign issue."[3] "Nearly everyone by now knows the situation," economic columnist William Greider wrote in November 1995, "either from the headlines or from their own daily lives: the continuing erosion of wage incomes for most American families."[4] Commenting on yet another twelve months of stagnant wage growth, Robert D. Hershey Jr. wrote in late 1995: "The frustration and insecurity that have resulted are expected to play a major role in shaping next year's Presidential race as politicians of both parties try to portray themselves as the best choice to provide economic growth that will benefit the middle class."[5]

On the other hand, many pundits, economists and business leaders seem not to lament the wage squeeze but rather to praise it. Instead of wringing their hands about working households' living standards, many express relief about the moderation of wage pressure on prices and profits—a trend they hope will dampen inflationary pressure, keep U.S. firms competitive in global markets, and protect small enterprises against business failure. When journalists report monthly data on workers' hourly earnings, they are much more likely to celebrate wage moderation or decline than to worry about its consequences for the millions who depend on that labor income.

Take the *New York Times'* report in April 1994 on real wage trends in the first quarter of the year. Noting that nominal wages and prices had grown at roughly the same rates, leaving real wages flat, the story appeared to welcome this "relatively benign reading on wages and benefits . . .": "American workers are obtaining less in pay and benefit increases from employers these days . . . ," with the result that ". . . price pressures remained subdued." The reporter observed hopefully that "bond prices rallied at the news." Nowhere in the story did he wonder how workers themselves might regard these "relatively benign" developments.[6]

So there are, indeed, two sides to the news about wages. "The good news is labor costs are under control," economic forecaster Michael Evans put it in 1992. "The bad news is that employees are broke."[7]

More often than not, however, the good news for business seems to blot out the bad for nearly everyone else. I was recently struck by the prevalence of these priorities at a conference about macroeconomic policy in Washington, D.C. in the spring of 1994. At lunch we heard from a Presidential economic adviser. A distinguished scholar, the speaker had been an economic liberal, more to the left than to the right of the mainstream of economic discourse. In a recent policy book, he had expressed concern about a polarized society in which the economic extremes of the 1980s had made the rich richer and set the rest adrift.

The economist lauded the progress of the economy in the spring of 1994 and the continuing signs, in the Administration's view, of a decent economic recovery. He noted with approval the evidence of (modest) growth in consumer spending, investment, and exports. He applauded the Federal Reserve's and the markets' continuing restraint in interest rates and pointed proudly to the tepid pace of inflation. He projected 1994 real wage growth at zero percent.

What is notable about this presentation is what was *not* said. A projection of zero real wage growth, but no reflections on the hardships experienced by ordinary working people. No lament about the twenty-year decline in real earnings. And this from a key economic adviser to the president who had promised, in his initial economic message to Congress, that "our economic plan will redress the inequities of the 1980s."[8]

This widespread inattention to workers' living standards even shows up in the preferences of government data collectors. For decades, since the end of the Depression and the spread of the union movement, the U.S. Bureau of Labor Statistics had kept track of the living standards of the average American worker with published data on *spendable earnings*.[9] The series measured the real after-tax value of workers' weekly take-home pay. But in 1981 the Reagan Administration discontinued the index, citing conceptual and measurement problems. They proposed no replacement, leaving us without any official series intended specifically to monitor the effective purchasing power of workers' earnings.

Had the government data apparatchiki actually cared about illuminating the trends in workers' income, the statistical problems they cited would not have been especially difficult to overcome—hardly so vexing that they warranted dropping this kind of series altogether. But their priorities lay elsewhere. At more or less the same time as the discontinuation of the weekly spendable earnings series, the Bureau of Labor Statistics, reflecting the Reaganites' ever-extending solicitude for the needs of business, was expanding the range and variety of its *employment cost indices*, tracking the hourly costs to corporations of their wage-and-salary employees. As a result, in recent years, corporations need merely dial the phone to get up-to-date data about changes in labor costs faced by them and their competitors.

More than a decade ago, in response to this change in priorities, my collaborators Samuel Bowles, Thomas E. Weisskopf, and I proposed an alternative version of the spendable earnings index, with modifications designed to address each of the specific problems raised about the traditional indicator.[10] Where the traditional series on *weekly* earnings had conflated movements in hourly earnings and changes in hours worked per week, we proposed relying on a much simpler index of *hourly* earnings. Where the traditional series had relied on a somewhat implausible adjustment for the taxes paid by the "average" worker, we suggested a much more immediate and direct calculation. We called our proposed alternative an index of *real spendable hourly earnings*.

Our proposal was graciously published in the Bureau of Labor Statistics official journal, but, hardly to our surprise, the Reagan Administration ignored our advice, persisting in providing no official record of trends in workers' take-home pay.[11] So we have continued ourselves to maintain and update what we consider to be the most salient indicator of workers' earnings.

Our index of *real spendable hourly earnings* provides a straightforward measure of the real value of the average production or nonsupervisory worker's take-home pay. "Production and nonsupervisory" workers, as they're defined in the official BLS surveys of business establishments, comprised 82 percent of total employment in 1994.[12] They represent that group in the labor force that is most clearly dependent on wage and salary income. They include both blue-collar and white-collar workers, both unskilled and skilled. They cover not only laborers and machinists but also secretaries, programmers and teachers.

I focus primarily on these "production and nonsupervisory" employees at least partly to avoid distortions in the data from the huge increases during the 1980s in the salaries of top management—a group covered by the earnings data for the other fifth of employees excluded from our measure, a category called "nonproduction or supervisory" employees. In further discussion in this chapter and throughout the rest of the book, in order to avoid the cumbersome terminology used by the BLS, I shall refer to the "production and nonsupervisory" category in the establishment data as *production* workers and to the other grouping as *supervisory* employees, respectively.[13]

Spendable hourly earnings measure the average production worker's hourly wage-and-salary income minus personal income taxes and Social Security taxes. These earnings are then expressed in constant dollars in order to adjust for the effects of inflation on the cost of living. They measure how much per hour, controlling for taxes and inflation, the average production worker is able to take home from his or her job.

Figure 1.1 charts the level of average real hourly spendable earnings for private nonfarm production employees in the United States from 1948 to 1994.[14]

The data show a clear pattern. The average worker's real after-tax pay grew rapidly through the mid-1960s. Its growth then slowed, with some fluctuation, until the early 1970s. After a postwar peak in 1972, this measure of

FIGURE 1.1

The Wage Squeeze

Real spendable hourly earnings ($1994), production/nonsupervisory employees, private non-farm sector, 1948–94

Source: See text and notes; series maintained by author.

earnings declined with growing severity, with cyclical fluctuation around this accelerating drop, through the rest of the 1970s and 1980s. The average annual growth of real spendable hourly earnings reached 2.1 percent a year from 1948 to 1966, slowed to 1.4 percent between 1966 and 1973, and then dropped with gathering speed at a shade less than *minus* one percent per year from 1973 to 1989.[15]

Despite the recovery from the recession of 1990–91, real spendable hourly earnings were lower in 1994 than they had been in the business-cycle trough of 1990. Even though the economy had been growing steadily for three years from the bottom of the recession, they continued to decline at an average annual rate of –0.6 percent from the peak in 1989 through 1994.

By 1994, indeed, real hourly take-home pay had dropped by 10.4 percent since its postwar peak in 1972. More dramatically still, *real spendable hourly earnings had fallen back to below the level they had last reached in 1967.* Growing massively over those nearly three decades, the economy's real gross output per capita in 1994 was 53 percent larger than it had been in 1967, but real hourly take-home pay was four cents lower.[16] Referring to these trends since the early 1970s as "the wage squeeze" is polite understatement. Calling it the "wage collapse" might be more apt.

These harsh winds have continued to blow through the recent recovery. Most economic meteorologists have described them in similarly cloudy terms. But a few have recently tried to present a sunnier weather report.

In one highly visible piece in late 1994, for example, the *New York Times* published a long news story beginning on its front page. Sylvia Nasar, the *Times* reporter, broadcast a considerably more sanguine view about wage trends: "it is practically gospel that the growing American economy cannot deliver the higher pay that American workers want," she wrote. But she claimed that wage changes during the early 1990s appeared to suggest a turnaround, with the majority of new jobs paying above-average wages. "As a result," she concluded, "average hourly pay for all employees, adjusted for inflation, is slowly rising."[17]

The source of Nasar's discrepant conclusions was not hard to find. Unlike all the data reviewed thus far in this chapter, which cover production employees—accounting for roughly four-fifths of the wage-and-salary workforce—Nasar was looking at wage trends for *all* workers. These data cover those at the top of the earnings distribution, including top-level executives whose total compensation has continued to soar straight through the mid-1990s. Those who have long pointed to the wage squeeze have never denied that the top 10 to 20 percent of the earnings distribution has fared much better than everyone else. If you mix together those in the middle and bottom with those at the top, you're bound to get a different and ultimately misleading story. Nasar's story was effectively demonstrating a penetrating glimpse into the obvious—that supervisory employees have continued to enjoy rising real hourly compensation.

In his recent book *Values Matter Most*, commentator Ben J. Wattenberg makes the same mistake. Hoping to create the space for his argument that we should concentrate on social values, not the economy, he seeks to cast doubt on the economic pressures cited by many. He notes that many highlighting the wage squeeze focus on real earnings series for production and nonsupervisory workers. He argues that this series gives an "inaccurate" picture because it "concerns cash only, ignoring benefits."[18] Then, almost quicker than the eye can blink, he shifts our attention to the same series Nasar reported, the index for total employee compensation per hour. "That line," he observes hopefully, "is clearly trending *upward* . . . ," lending support to his ultimate conclusion that "our economic situation is somewhat less than grievous."[19] But while the eye was blinking, Wattenberg switched to a series that differed from the first in *two* respects, not just one: including benefits, it traced total compensation; *and*, tracking all workers, it included those at the top who have been feeding at the trough. As I show in the Appendix to this chapter, just including benefits in our series, while continuing to focus on production and nonsupervisory workers, tells almost exactly the same story as earnings without benefits. Whether we look at earnings or full compensation, the wage squeeze for production workers remains severe.

For the vast majority of workers, then, these have been hard times indeed. In 1994, the average production employee working thirty-five hours a week and fifty-two weeks a year was able to take home about $16,833 after taxes, barely above the official poverty standard for a family of four.[20] An earlier generation had expected that their earnings would rise over their working lifetimes and that their children could anticipate higher living standards than their own. For the past two decades, however, more and more workers have had to adjust their expectations, reconciling themselves to toil at what are sometimes derisively called "McJobs."[21]

One Michigan woman, talking in a pollster's focus group in the early 1990s about deflated expectations, lamented:[22]

> I think about when I was married, a week of groceries cost me $13 and my husband thought that was entirely too much money to spend for a week's groceries. Now I spend $150. I feel like I'm always running—and this big snowball is behind me getting bigger and bigger—and just trying to keep it from running over me.

Another focus group participant talked about shifting expectations across generations. "[Our kids]'ll have to be good to us if they want to have a home to live in, because the only way they'll get one is if we will them ours. They're never going to be able to buy a house."[23]

You don't have to organize your own focus groups to get a strong whiff of these kinds of economic concerns. Recent national polls repeatedly reveal such fears about economic pressure and the cloudy future for this and future generations. In a 1992 Gallup poll, for example, more than three-fifths said they were dissatisfied with "the opportunity for the next generation of Americans to live better than their parents"; 58 percent were dissatisfied with the "opportunity for a poor person in this country to get ahead by working hard."[24] In a June 1993 *LA Times*/CNN poll, 39 percent of participants described their personal finances as "shaky," while more than half—51 percent—said they "expect the next generation of Americans will have a worse standard of living than the one we have now."[25] Even though the economy was well into its recovery, in a November 1993 *LA Times*/CNN poll two-thirds reported that job security was "worse for Americans now, compared to two years ago" and 53 percent that they felt this "greater job insecurity will occur over the long term, for many years."[26] Even further into the recovery, a March 1994 *New York Times* poll found that two-fifths of respondents expressed "worry" that during the next two years they might be laid off, required to work reduced hours, or forced to take pay cuts. Nearly two-fifths also reported that in order "to try to stay even financially" during the last two years they had had to work overtime or take on extra jobs.[27] In a March 1995 *Business Week*/Harris poll, people were asked whether "the American Dream . . . has become easier or harder to achieve in the *past* 10 years." Two-thirds answered that it has become "harder." Participants were also asked if it

would be "easier or harder to achieve in the *next* 10 years." Three-quarters chose "harder."[28]

A Crowded Boat

Andrew Flenoy, a twenty-one-year-old living in Kansas City, did better in 1994 than many, holding down a steady job paying a cut above the minimum wage. In fact, he had even enjoyed some recent promotions, rising at a food catering firm from dishwasher to catering manager. Through that sequence of promotions, however, his earnings had increased from $5.50 an hour to only $6.50 an hour—the equivalent of only about $12,000 a year working full-time year-round. Whatever satisfaction he had enjoyed from his promotions had quickly paled. "Now he is tired of the burgundy and black uniform he must wear," a reporter concluded, "and of the sense that he works every day from 6 A.M. to 2 P.M. just to earn enough money so that he can come back and work some more the next day." "My resolution for 1994," Flenoy remarked, "is that if nothing comes along, I'll relocate and start from scratch somewhere else."[29]

Flenoy attended only a semester of community college after high school and suffered the additional employment disadvantage of being African American. Many are inclined to assume, indeed, that the wage squeeze has mostly afflicted the young, the unskilled, and the disadvantaged.

Although some have suffered more than others, however, a much wider band of the working population has been caught in the vise. For most Americans, the wage squeeze has been a profoundly democratizing trend.

Indeed, the data on the breadth of the wage squeeze seem finally to have persuaded skeptics not normally known for their empathy with workers. Recently confronted with some of these data, for example, Marvin Kosters, a well-known conservative economist at the American Enterprise Institute who had earlier challenged reports about trends toward growing inequality, admitted surprise at the variety of subgroups affected by wage erosion. "It's really quite amazing," he acknowledged.[30] The data would scarcely seem "amazing," of course, to those who've been directly feeling the pinch.

In order to assess the breadth of the wage squeeze, we need to turn to data from household surveys, which unlike the establishment surveys afford considerable detail on workers' personal characteristics. We can look at trends in real hourly earnings between 1979 and 1993 for a variety of different groups in the private nonfarm workforce, since it is trends in the private sector with which I am most concerned in this book.[31]

Looking at this universe, we find that real hourly earnings for *all* private nonfarm employees, including those at the top, remained essentially flat from 1979 to 1993—barely rising from $11.62 to $11.80 (in 1993 prices). (Government workers did somewhat better.)

But we know that those at the top did fairly well. The more telling comparison looks at real wage trajectories for the bottom four-fifths of the real wage distribution and for the top fifth. As anticipated from the data for production workers reviewed in the previous section, it was the bottom 80 percent that experienced actual real wage decline, with the 1993 level dropping by 3.4 percent below the 1979 figure. For the top 20 percent times were not so harsh; they enjoyed a healthy rate of increase, with their real hourly earnings rising by 1993 to almost three times those for the bottom four-fifths.

We can also compare workers by race and ethnic origin. Looking at workers in the bottom 80 percent of the overall wage distribution, it is true, not surprisingly, that African Americans and Hispanics fared less well than whites. But even among whites in the bottom 80 percent, real hourly earnings dropped by nearly 3 percent. (Of course, a much larger percentage of African Americans and Hispanics were situated in the bottom four-fifths of the wage distribution than of whites.) Not just the disadvantaged but the advantaged racial group joined the wake.

Looking at wage trends by gender, we find a major difference in the impact of the wage squeeze. While male workers in the bottom 80 percent of the distribution experienced devastating declines in their real hourly earnings—facing a decline of close to 10 percent—women workers in the bottom 80 percent enjoyed modest real wage growth, with a total increase over the full period of 2.8 percent. Despite these gains, however, women's wages still lagged substantially behind men's. In 1993, the median female hourly wage had reached barely more than three-quarters of the median male wage, at 78 percent. Women were gaining on men, to be sure, but their gains occurred primarily because real male wages were plummeting, not because real female earnings were themselves growing rapidly. Indeed, almost three-quarters of the decline in the wage gap between men and women from 1979 and 1993 can be attributed to the decline in male earnings—a trend which undoubtedly contributed to the widespread frustration which many males have apparently been feeling and venting.[32]

A final comparison looks at the experience of workers with different levels of education. It was the bulk of workers on the bottom, those with less than a college degree, who experienced actual wage decline. Only those with a college degree or better were able to gain some measure of protection against the unfriendly winds. And the most recent trends have been harsh even for a large number in that group. From 1989 to 1993, for example, even male workers with just a college degree, but no postgraduate education, were hit with declining real earnings.

Table 1.1 pulls together these separate tabulations for different groups of workers. The wage squeeze has caught a huge proportion of U.S. workers in its grip.

TABLE 1.1
The Wage Squeeze Across the Work Force
Real hourly earnings, nonfarm private sector ($1993)

	1979	1993	% Change
All workers	$11.62	11.80	1.5%
Bottom 80 percent	8.93	8.59	–3.4
Top 20 percent	22.41	24.66	10.04
White workers, bottom 80 percent	9.03	8.77	–2.9
Black workers, bottom 80 percent	8.28	7.98	–3.6
Hispanic workers, bottom 80 percent	8.53	7.86	–7.9
Male workers, bottom 80 percent	9.94	9.05	–9.0
Female workers, bottom 80 percent	7.94	8.16	2.8
High school dropout	10.31	8.19	–20.6
High school graduate	11.11	10.05	–9.5
Some college education	13.12	11.03	–15.9
College graduate	16.01	16.57	3.5
Postgraduate	19.84	21.59	8.8

Sources and Notes: Based on author's own tabulations from data samples extracted from Current Population Survey.

Hourly earnings for all nonfarm private workers and all subgroupings defined as usual weekly earnings divided by usual weekly hours worked. Hourly earnings deflated by CPI-U-X1 price deflator.

In better times, of course, workers in a pinch often pulled up stakes and migrated in search of greener pastures—in Andrew Flenoy's words, "to relocate and start from scratch somewhere else." But the greener pastures have mostly turned brown. *New York Times* reporter Louis Uchitelle tells the story about workers in Peoria, Illinois, where layoffs and givebacks at Caterpillar had cast long shadows over the local economy:[33]

Today the adventurous search for opportunity is no longer rewarding. For generations, Americans migrated—going West, so to speak—when jobs in their communities became scarce or failed to pay well. But income stagnation is a nationwide phenomenon. Migration has become futile. Peorians, for example, uprooted themselves by the thousands in the early 1980's, when recession and then massive layoffs at Caterpillar and the numerous local companies that supply Caterpillar pushed the unemployment rate here above 16 percent. By the late 1980's, they were trickling home again.

"When they got to Oklahoma and Texas, they found that the promise of good wages was a lot of talk; they worked hard and had little to show for it," said David Koehler, executive director of the Peoria Area Labor Management Council. "Now, many have come home to jobs that pay less than they once earned, but they have returned because this is where their families are to help them."

Slipping Behind

Some readers may be inclined to view the wage squeeze as par for the course at the twilight of the twentieth century. The world economy is becoming more and more tightly integrated. Developing countries, where wages are much lower than the advanced economies, have been expanding their exports. Low-wage import competition has been intensifying. Isn't wage pressure in the advanced economies to be expected?

There is no denying that import competition from lower-wage developing countries has grown more intense over the past twenty years or more. But it does not necessarily follow, for a variety of reasons we shall explore in later chapters, that workers in the advanced economies must inexorably face the wage crunch as a result.

Quite to the contrary. In fact, the most striking conclusion that emerges from comparing wage trends in the advanced countries is how isolated, how relatively unique has been the U.S. experience.

Careful compilations by the U.S. Bureau of Labor Statistics allow us to compare wage trends across twelve of the leading advanced economies—including the G-7 powers of the United States, Germany, Japan, France, Italy, the United Kingdom, and Canada as well as five other smaller European countries (Belgium, Denmark, Norway, the Netherlands, and Sweden). Their data provide comparable information on trends in real hourly compensation for all manufacturing employees, with compensation deflated by the consumer price index for each country to provide an insight into trends directly affecting workers' living standards.[34] I look here at the period from 1973 to 1993, the most recent year for which the data were available at the time of writing.

This measure matches the series for real spendable hourly earnings in the United States, presented above in Figure 1.1, with three differences. The comparative numbers are before-tax rather than after-tax, and focus just on compensation in *manufacturing*, rather than the much larger nonfarm private sector. And they include all employees, not merely production workers.

By this measure, real hourly compensation for all manufacturing employees in the United States was flat rather than collapsing in the period between 1973 and 1993. It barely changed over that period, rather than declining substantially as for the data presented in Table 1.1. The principal reason that this index of hourly wages does not show decline is that it includes nonproduction workers as well as production employees and this group at the top, as the data on the top 20 percent in the previous section suggest, was the one group whose wages stayed ahead of inflation over the past two decades. (The difference in coverage between the manufacturing and private nonfarm sectors matters less since trends in the two sectors were roughly comparable over this period; and Appendix A shows that before-tax and after-tax measures move closely together.)

If by this measure, real hourly compensation in manufacturing was roughly flat in the United States between 1973 and 1993, how did workers fare in the other eleven advanced economies?

Figure 1.2 allows us to pursue this comparison. It presents the average annual percent change in real hourly compensation for all manufacturing employees in the United States (on the far right) and in eleven other advanced economies (arranged in alphabetical order). Wage stagnation in the United States stands out like a sore thumb. It is the only country with wage change close to zero. Only two other countries—Canada, which feels the wage competition from its near North American neighbor, and Denmark—feature

FIGURE 1.2
U.S. Wages Lagging Behind
Percent change, real hourly compensation, all manufacturing employees, 1973–93

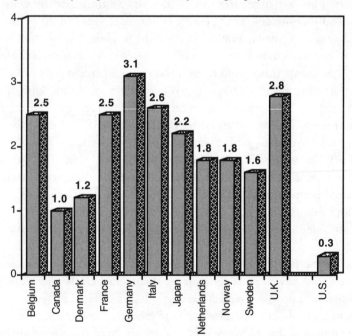

Source: U.S. Bureau of Labor Statistics data; see text note #34.

wage growth rates less than 1.5 percent a year. Workers in Japan and Germany, our two major trading competitors, fared markedly better than U.S. workers, with real wage growth at 2.2 percent and 3.1 percent respectively.

Indeed, the average for the other eleven countries altogether is 2.1 percent per year, seven times more rapid than for the United States over the same period. Import competition from low-wage developing countries may have been intensifying, but workers in other advanced economies seem to have escaped its wrath much more effectively than workers in the United States.

Later chapters will explore some of the reasons for this huge discrepancy in wage growth between the United States and most other advanced countries and will consider the possibility that many of the other advanced economies paid a substantial price for their more rapid wage growth with relatively higher unemployment rates.

But one possible explanation deserves immediate attention. Perhaps wage growth in the United States has been relatively slow because U.S. wages have historically been so high compared to our advanced competitors and, therefore, competition with those other advanced economies has forced U.S. corporations into tough bargaining with their employees.

That factor may once have weighed heavily in the United States, but it no longer applies. By 1994, compared to the other countries featured in Figure 1.2, the United States no longer paid its employees top dollar. When we look at average hourly compensation for production workers in manufacturing, converted by exchange rates to U.S. dollars, we find that the United States ranked only eighth among the twelve countries featured in the graph, and was ahead of only Canada, France, Italy, and the United Kingdom among the twelve. Japanese manufacturers, which have competed so successfully against their U.S. competitors, paid their employees 25 percent more than did U.S. manufacturing firms. Average hourly compensation in the United States in 1994 was $17.10, while, for example, the average for the countries of the European Union, weighted by their share of U.S. trade, was $19.47.[35] Figure 1.3 provides a graphic view of this comparison.

Nor is this an especially recent phenomenon. In 1980, hourly compensation for U.S. manufacturing workers was lower than in six of the other twelve advanced economies; in 1975, it was lower than in four others.[36]

More dramatically still, although the comparisons are difficult to make with precision, the United States appears to be the only advanced country in which lower paid workers have actually suffered *absolute declines* in real earnings over the past couple of decades. Harvard labor economists Richard B. Freeman and Lawrence F. Katz survey the data carefully and "conclude that less educated and lower-paid American workers suffered the largest erosion of economic well-being among workers in advanced countries."[37] The result of this erosion was that U.S. workers on the bottom of the wage distribution hit rock bottom. Based on his own assessment of the data, Freeman reports that

FIGURE 1.3
U.S. Wages No Longer Top Dollar
Real hourly compensation in U.S. dollars, all manufacturing employees, 1994

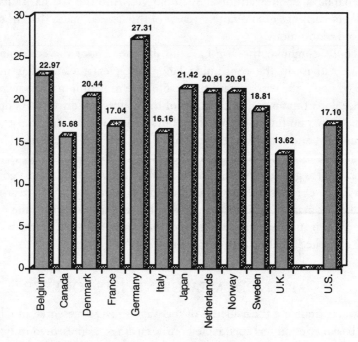

Source: U.S. Bureau of Labor Statistics data; see text note #35.

"low-paid Americans have lower real earnings than workers in all advanced countries for which there are comparable data—which is due largely to the fall in their real earnings."[38]

One might imagine that the United States gained competitive advantage over the past twenty years because its real wages grew so much more slowly than in the other leading economies. Not so lucky. Between 1973 and 1989, real hourly manufacturing compensation in Japan grew eight times more rapidly than in the United States, but this did not prevent Japanese firms from knocking the socks off their U.S. competitors in global markets. In 1973, both countries enjoyed roughly balanced trade, with exports approximately equal to imports and the net balance of trade in goods and services close to zero. By 1989, however, the United States was running a trade deficit with the rest of the world of $77 billion while the Japanese were enjoying a healthy trade surplus of $13 billion.[39] And this limp U.S. trade performance was not limited to the comparison with the striking case of Japan; we have been running trade deficits with Western Europe, where wage growth has also been rapid, for many years as well.

MOST U.S. WORKERS have been experiencing a wage squeeze, with real hourly take-home pay in 1993 falling back to the levels of the mid-1960s. This wage collapse has affected not only the unskilled and disadvantaged but a remarkably wide swath of U.S. employees. And the vise has tightened on workers' earnings much more severely in the United States than in other advanced economies.

Those caught in the vise have no illusions about the consequences. A union activist in the continuing labor struggles at Caterpillar in Illinois looked down the road toward the turn of the millennium and saw hardship: "If we don't put an end to this drift of the country to drive wages down," he said, "there's no future for my three boys. There will be an upper class and a lower class, and I know where [my boys] will be."[40] A middle-class Michigan resident echoed this view: "Everybody is going to be either very rich or very poor. There's going to be the rich in their little towers, and there's going to be everybody else floundering around trying to survive."[41] A 48-year-old Milwaukee woman, laid off in June 1995 after seventeen years on the job, wondered when the wage pressure from corporations will end. "How far can this go," she asked, "before they ruin everything?"[42]

APPENDIX: MEASURING THE SQUEEZE

However dramatic the evidence of the wage squeeze presented in Chapter 1, the basic series on real spendable hourly earnings, as presented in Figure 1.1, remains unofficial. Is this measure somehow distorted in ways that might prompt readers to remain skeptical about either the existence or the extent of the wage squeeze? For ease of calculation and later comparisons, we can concentrate on the period from the business-cycle peak in 1979 through the most recent available data for 1994—the decade and a half, as Figure 1.1 shows, over which the bulk of this decline in real hourly take-home pay occurred.

One possible concern might involve our adjustment for the personal income and payroll taxes borne by the average production employee.[1] Suppose for the moment that we ignore taxes altogether and concentrate simply on *real before-tax hourly earnings* with a simple correction for the toll exacted by inflation. We can calculate the after-tax and before-tax measures for 1979 and 1994 and judge how crucial our tax estimates are in shaping the underlying trends in the series.

The level of the series estimated before taxes is obviously higher in both benchmark years—for example, $11.13 in 1994 compared with an after-tax estimate of $9.36—since taxes are not yet deducted from real earnings. But the rate of decline in 1979–94 was actually somewhat greater for the before-tax measure than for the after-tax measure. Tax rates, primarily payroll tax rates, increased enough over this period to add to the wage pressure which workers were already feeling before the tax man took his cut. Whether or not we take taxes into account, the wage squeeze remains severe. The first two rows of Table 1.A provide this comparison.

Another possible concern involves the measurement of earnings itself. The real spendable hourly earnings series builds on direct wage-and-salary payments to production employees. As such, it does not include indirect employer payments benefiting workers, such as health care premiums. Measuring full compensation, including these fringe benefits, might make more sense but government data do not directly provide this information for production workers. Could it be that these benefits increased enough over the past fifteen years to offset the collapse in earnings?

In order to assess this possibility, I have constructed an alternative estimate of production workers' *real hourly compensation* including an approximation of the value of indirect employee benefits covered by employers. The measure of real hourly earnings, measured before taxes, is adjusted by adding to it an estimate of the additional benefits provided for workers by employers but not directly paid to them as earnings.[2]

This adjustment makes only a minor difference, as the third row in Table 1.A makes clear. Now, the 1979–1994 decline in real (before-tax) hourly compensation is roughly 7.8 percent, compared with 8.6 percent in the measure ignoring benefits. This may surprise some readers; many assume that benefits

TABLE 1.A
Alternative Measures of the Wage Squeeze
Real earnings ($1994), production and nonsupervisory employees, private nonfarm sector, 1979–94

	1979	1994	%Change
1. Real spendable hourly earnings (after-tax)	$10.24	9.36	-8.6%
2. Real hourly earnings (before-tax)	12.34	11.13	-9.8
3. Real hourly compensation (before-tax)	14.70	13.57	-7.8

Sources and Notes:

Row [1]: Real spendable hourly earnings as explained in chapter text and notes. Data series available from author.

Row [2]: Real hourly earnings measured as private nonfarm production workers before-tax hourly earnings [*Employment and Earnings,* January 1995, Table B-2] deflated by consumer price index for urban consumers (CPI-U-X1) [*Economic Report of the President, 1995,* Table B-61].

Row [3]: Real hourly compensation measured as real hourly earnings (row [2]) multiplied by ratio of total employee compensation to total employee wages and salaries [*National Income and Product Accounts,* Tables 6.2C, 6.3C]. See note #2.

have recently been increasing substantially more rapidly than earnings, particularly because of soaring increases in health care costs. But during the 1980s, real hourly benefit payments also declined, indicating that many workers were being pressured to "give back" as much in benefits as they were in direct pay.[3] In their useful analyses of trends affecting working Americans, Economic Policy Institute economists Lawrence Mishel and Jared Bernstein highlight this feature of the 1980s:[4]

> Health insurance costs have indeed risen quickly. Apparently, however, the rapid growth of jobs with little or no employer-provided health benefits and the increased shift of employer health care costs onto employees has meant that average fringe-benefit costs did not rise over the 1977–89 period. In fact, they declined modestly.

In contrast to their increases in the 1960s and 1970s, indirect benefits were no longer providing even a modest shelter against the harsh winds of wage decline.

Chapter 2

THE BUREAUCRATIC BURDEN

M ore than a decade ago *The New York Times* hosted a small roundtable on "The Ailing Economy," subsequently publishing large ex-
tracts from the discussion.[1] Participants included Felix G. Rohatyn,
senior partner in the Wall Street firm Lazard Frères and a major economic
policy adviser in centrist Democratic Party circles; and Walter B. Wriston,
then chairman of Citicorp and Citibank and a member of President Reagan's
Economic Policy Advisory Board. I also joined in the conversation. Moder-
ated by the late *Times'* economics columnist Leonard Silk, we roamed widely
over the economy's problems in the early 1980s and various prescriptions for
their solution.

At one point in the discussion, talking about some of the structural sources
of stagnant productivity in the U.S. economy, we turned to the huge size of
U.S. corporate bureaucracies. I cited some recent management consultant
studies that had suggested that as many as 50 percent of corporate managerial
and supervisory personnel were redundant.[2] We could apparently trim huge
chunks of fat off the top and middle layers of those corporations, this seemed
to imply, and the corporations would be able to function just as effectively at
much lower cost.

One might have expected the participants from the business sector to rise
to the bait, defending the citadels of U.S. capitalism. But they scarcely batted
an eyelash. "I wouldn't know" if expenditures for executive personnel are
"wasted," Walter Wriston replied. "The chances are half of it is," he joked.
"[Figuring out] which half is the difficult problem."[3]

I call it the "bureaucratic burden"—the massive size and cost of the managerial and supervisory apparatus of private U.S. corporations. It's one of the
most stunning features of the U.S. economy.

The political right has mastered the rhetorical art of blaming the federal government for the size and wastefulness of its bureaucracies. Far less

attention is paid to the size and wastefulness of private corporate bureaucracies. The bureaucratic burden in the United States is gargantuan, especially when compared to other leading economies such as Germany and Japan. It's a huge mountain range in our economic landscape that has long been covered by clouds. This chapter attempts to penetrate the cloud cover and map the terrain. Having provided that mapping, it then explodes the widespread myth that in the 1990s, after a decade of "downsizing," U.S. corporations have pared their bureaucracies and are now slim and trim—free of fat and waste.

Top-Heavy Corporations

I got my first peek at this topography in the mid-1970s. Colleagues and I had just begun some outreach educational work with local union officials and rank-and-file workers. We were trying different ways of engaging workers about pressing economic issues. Since these first discussions came on the heels of the sharp recession of 1973–75 and in the throes of that strange new phenomenon called "stagflation," we expected that the workers in our classes would steer the conversations toward problems of job security and inflation.

Much to our surprise they were more interested in talking about problems they were constantly experiencing with their bosses on the job. They complained that their supervisors were always on their case, that bureaucratic harassment was a daily burden. They inveighed against speed-up, hostility, petty aggravations, capricious threats and punishments, and—perhaps most bitterly—crude, arrogant and often gratuitous exercises of power. Their catalogues of complaints were both eloquent and acute.

We were nonplussed. We had no idea whether these were the common and enduring laments of similarly situated workers at any time and place, or whether their urgency perhaps followed from a recent intensification of bureaucratic supervision on the job. I don't know to this day whether and when I might have paid attention to the bureaucratic burden if I hadn't been sitting in union halls in the mid-1970s, chewing on stale jelly doughnuts, listening to workers' grumbling about their continuing hassles with their employers.

The problem has remained hidden from public scrutiny for most of the intervening two decades. For at least some of the public, the first whiff of smoke came during the mid- and late-1980s when critics began to excoriate the soaring and often astronomic salaries of chief executives in U.S. corporations. During the 1980s, according to data developed by the British weekly *The Economist*, after-tax CEO annual salaries increased by two-thirds after adjusting for inflation—while production workers' real hourly take-home pay was declining by seven percent.[4] By 1994, taking it from the top, Michael D. Eisner of Walt Disney was reaping a total harvest of $203.0 million, including company stock gains, while second-ranked Sanford I. Weill of Travelers was earning a total remuneration of "only" $53.1 million.[5] Respondents to a 1991 *Industry Week* survey about soaring CEO salaries were not spare with their criticisms: according to the magazine's summary, respondents called top executive pay levels "way out of line," "baffling," "disgraceful," "embarrassing," "infuriating," and "sickening."[6] Sometime populist presidential candidate Bill Clinton charged in 1992 that "American CEOs were paying themselves 100 times more than their workers."[7] By the early 1990s, writes Derek Bok, former president of Harvard University, "almost everyone seemed to agree that executive pay had reached unseemly heights."[8]

But CEO salaries are only the tip of the iceberg. We need to peer below the surface and assess the size and cost of the entire corporate administrative apparatus—not just the millions paid to the top corporate guns. The key question, in the end, is the *relative* size of U.S. corporations' bureaucracies, in comparison to the numbers of employees they control. We need to gauge how much of that bureaucracy is dedicated to bossing people and whether that's an efficient or effective allocation of resources. And we need to be more than a little skeptical about the widespread impression that corporations have recently pared their managerial ranks, that through "downsizing" they have sliced away at the layers of flab at the top and middle of their bureaucratic hierarchies. "Downsizing" has certainly been taking place since the 1980s in many U.S. corporations. *But the weight of the bureaucratic burden has actually been growing, not contracting, through the mid-1990s.*

The easiest gauge of the size of this corporate behemoth—partly because the data are consistently available back to World War II—comes from official government surveys of business establishments. In 1994, according to the U.S. Bureau of Labor Statistics, 17.3 million private nonfarm employees worked in nonproduction and supervisory jobs[9]—mostly, as we shall see, as managers and supervisors at all levels of the corporate hierarchy. (Remember from Chapter 1 that I am adopting the expositional convention of referring to this category of "nonproduction and supervisory" employees as "supervisory.") This was almost as many employees as those working in the entire public sector, in all occupations at all levels of government including federal, state, and local. It was close to as many people living in the states of either Texas or New York. It roughly equaled the national populations of Australia, Ghana, or Saudi Arabia.[10] Stretched out head-to-toe, all these supervisory employees would reach more than three-quarters of the way around the earth's equator.[11]

At least as imposing is the amount of money we pay to cover the salaries and benefits of these millions of employees. In 1994 supervisory employees in the private nonfarm sector were paid $1.3 trillion in total compensation.[12] This accounted for almost a quarter of all national income received by all income recipients. Twenty cents of every dollar we paid for goods and services went to cover the salaries and benefits of supervisory employees. This is as if, when we pay $5.00 for a sixpack of beer, $1.00 goes to cover the costs of the bureaucratic burden. Or when we pay $20,000 for a new car, we are pouring $4,000 into the managerial tank.

And this doesn't even include the costs of supporting these supervisory employees. Think of all the equipment and supplies purchased to provision these armies of bureaucratic employees. And think of the secretaries and assistants whose sole function is to serve this officer corps of 17 million. If we can assume that at least some of these bureaucratic personnel are unnecessary, then some of the desk chairs and paper clips and computers and secretaries mobilized to support them may constitute unnecessary expenditures as well.

Even ignoring these additional support costs, the tithe we pay for supervisory compensation dwarfs many other expenditure categories about which various groups have been publicly wringing their hands in recent years.[13] In 1994, for example, supervisory compensation was *four* times the total federal bill for Social Security payments—a tab which critics like Wall Street investment banker Peter Peterson have charged is bankrupting our future.[14] It was more than *four* times as large as total federal expenditures for national defense, a burden on which the peace movement has aimed its non-violent ire for decades. It was more than *fifty* times the payments providing Aid for Dependent Children (AFDC), or welfare, the scapegoated public assistance program over which Republicans and Democrats alike have been sharpening their scalpels.

Perhaps the most salient comparison, given the continuing right-wing cacophony about the costs of government, is with the tax burden. The taxpayers' revolt continues to spread, impelled by anger at the weight of all those taxes paid in different forms to different levels of government. What about the weight of the bureaucratic burden?

In 1994 private nonfarm supervisory compensation cost almost *seven* times as much as all property taxes paid to state and local governments. Its burden was almost *twice* as weighty as all personal income taxes paid to all levels of government. It was more than *twice* as high as all payroll taxes paid in contributions to social insurance to all levels of government.

Rush Limbaugh wishes the federal government would sink of its own weight, disappearing without a trace into the Potomac River—except for the Pentagon and the FBI, of course. But the total size of the entire federal government tax bill, including not only personal taxes and payroll taxes but also profits taxes and indirect taxes, was $1.34 trillion in 1994, almost exactly equal to the $1.31 trillion price tag of the corporate hierarchy. Yo, Rush, you old populist devil, you. Doesn't the vast scope, size, and potential waste of private corporate bureaucracies deserve at least some of your bile?

Who are all these millions of managers and supervisors?

The name of the statistical grouping itself—"nonproduction and supervisory" employees—tells us very little. When I talk about the bureaucratic burden with a wide variety of audiences, many balk at my assertion that the preponderance of employees in this category are managers and supervisors. Popular discussions pay much more attention to high-tech employees, the "symbolic analysts" in Labor Secretary Robert B. Reich's vision of late twentieth-century capitalism, the architects, engineers and toll-keepers of the information superhighway.[15] And so, many suspect that a large portion of my supervisory category must actually be performing professional and technical functions. Images flash of lawyers and systems programmers and lab technicians dancing with their notebook computers.

It is difficult to be very precise about the specific jobs performed by these more than 17 million supervisory employees. The surveys of business establishments from which these figures are drawn provide no further detail about occupation, allowing no breakdown within the nonproduction/supervisory classification. We are simply told from the instructions for the establishment surveys that enterprise respondents should include in this grouping all employees "engaged in the following activities: executive, purchasing, finance, accounting, legal, personnel, cafeteria, medical, professional and technical activities, sales, advertising, credit collection, and in the installation and servicing of own products, routine office functions, and factory supervision (above working supervisor's level)."[16] These instructions make it sound, indeed, as if a wide variety of occupational functions may be covered, especially including professional and technical activities.[17]

But some quick detective work suggests otherwise, appearing to confirm this initial reckoning of the scale of the bureaucratic burden. We can look to the Bureau of Labor Statistics' surveys of households, which provide much more detailed occupational breakdowns, for some important clues. Data for 1993 were the most recent raw data available to me at the time of writing.

In 1993, according to the same establishment data we've already plumbed, 17.1 million supervisory employees worked in the private nonfarm sector. According to the household surveys for the same year, there were 16.6 million private nonfarm employees who worked as wage-and-salary employees in various occupations labeled as either "managers" or "supervisors."[18] (These totals exclude the self-employed, those who work for themselves rather than for a corporation.) So when we count "supervisory" workers from the establishment surveys or "managers" and "supervisors" from the household surveys, we arrive at roughly comparable measures of the size of the bureaucratic burden. Some who are tallied as "nonproduction and supervisory" employees in the establishment surveys, given the survey instructions, are obviously not managers and supervisors. At the same time, however, those surveys do not include those "at the working supervisor's level." These two effects seem roughly to cancel each other out. When we get a more direct tally of managers and supervisors from the detailed occupational definitions of the household surveys, the totals are almost exactly equivalent.

And what did these 16.6 million managerial and supervisory employees do? Somewhat more than three-fifths worked as managers and a little less than two-fifths as supervisors.

Among the managers, the bulk—4.1 million out of 10.7 million—were all-purpose managers in the catch-all "not elsewhere classified" category. More than six million worked as "supervisors" in one sector or another. About 1.3 million worked as supervisors of blue-collar "production occupations," for example, and another 340,000 worked as clerical supervisors.

Still, even these tabulations from the household surveys are only estimates, based on approximate categories from government surveys. They could potentially be off the mark as measures of the full extent of managerial and supervisory employment in either of two possible directions. They could *over*estimate the extent of supervision if large numbers of employees categorized as managers are not actually and actively involved in supervision. Or they could *under*estimate the bureaucratic burden if many other kinds of employees, not officially categorized in these government data as managers or supervisors, *also* engage in substantial supervision as an important part of their activities.

We have one important body of data that can help us assess these possible distortions in the official series. Through some pioneering studies spearheaded by Wisconsin sociologist Erik Olin Wright, we can glimpse the actual extent of supervision by U.S. employees regardless of their primary occupational categorization. In nationally representative surveys conceived and organized by Wright and replicated in the United States in both 1980 and 1991, respondents were asked directly about their positions and roles on their jobs. Several different questions aimed at highlighting occupational responsibilities from a number of different angles. Referring to their present or most recent jobs, participants were asked whether or not they were engaged in supervising others, whether or not their position was considered to be managerial or supervisory, and what kinds of authority they exercised over others. We can compare impressions from these data—afforded by what I shall be labeling for short as the Class Structure Surveys—with estimates from the official government sources already reviewed. The more recent data from the 1991 survey are the most relevant for this discussion.[19]

• In 1991, according to government establishment surveys, 19.1 percent of private nonfarm employees worked in nonproduction or supervisory jobs. But in the 1991 Class Structure Survey, almost exactly double this proportion—fully 38.9 percent of all private nonfarm workers—reported that they "supervise the work of other employees or tell other employees what work to do." This would amount to roughly 35 million employees in the private nonfarm sector who report direct supervisory responsibility.

• In the 1991 household surveys, 18.7 percent of private nonfarm workers were categorized as in either managerial or supervisory occupations. But in the 1991 Class Structure Survey, 36.3 percent report that their position within their business or organization was "managerial" or "supervisory." Of these 36 percent, roughly half worked in "supervisory" jobs and the other half at various levels of the "managerial" hierarchy.

• One of the main tests of how many "bosses" are sprinkled through the occupational category is how many employees can discipline or even fire another employee. In the 1991 Class Structure Survey, 27.7 percent of private nonfarm employees reported that they had the authority directly to "discipline a subordinate because of poor work or misconduct."

Why are these estimates of managerial and supervisory employment so much higher than the estimates we derive from official government sources? The Class Structure Surveys were carefully structured and weighted so that they were effectively representative of the characteristics of the population revealed in other official government surveys.[20] Consequently the differences do not appear to flow from biases in the construction of the actual surveys.

One possibility, of course, is that when asked direct questions about their role on the job, people might tend to exaggerate their importance and attribute greater authority to their own positions than they actually have. This source of bias is probably relatively minor in the Class Structure Survey, however, because estimates of managerial and supervisory responsibilities based on very different kinds of questions within the survey fall within a fairly narrow range—and all considerably higher than the estimates from official government sources.

More important as an explanation of the discrepancy between the two kinds of information, apparently, is precisely that many people besides those working in jobs officially categorized as "managers" and "supervisors" *also* have substantial supervisory responsibilities.

Table 2.1 compiles the percent of private nonfarm employees in different occupational categories in the 1991 U.S. Class Structure Survey—as those categories are conventionally defined in standard government censuses—who report that their present (or most recent) job is best described as a "managerial or supervisory position." As the table shows, substantial numbers of workers outside the explicit occupational categories of managers and supervisors also have such responsibilities within their firms' hierarchies. Someone trained as a lawyer who is running a corporate division, for example, may get tabulated in the government surveys as a "professional" but would be captured in the Class Structure Survey as someone who also exercises managerial responsibility.

This would suggest, in short, that we can rely on the kinds of official government sources reported initially—such as the percent of employees in supervisory jobs estimated from the establishment data—as *minimum* estimates of the scope of the bureaucratic burden in the United States. It would appear that there are many more people in other occupational categories than

TABLE 2.1

Supervisory Responsibilities Across the Occupations, 1991

Percent in various private nonfarm occupations with "managerial" or "supervisory" responsibilities

Managers	79.6%
Technicians or supervisors	59.0
Professionals	29.1
Clerical or sales workers	16.4
Skilled workers	12.0
Semiskilled workers	8.1
Unskilled workers	2.2
All employees	35.5

Sources and Notes: Author's own calculations from the Class Structure Survey for the United States, 1991. Sample is for all nongovernment employees not in farm occupations.

"managers" and "supervisors" *who have direct supervisory responsibility* than there are people in jobs categorized as "managers" and "supervisors" *who do not actually perform such supervisory roles.* Yes it is certainly true that many, perhaps most of these cadres do not spend every working hour directly supervising others. But the fact that they spend at least some of their time directing subordinates means that the corporate structures in which they work are predicated upon those supervisory functions, that their supervisory and managerial responsibilities are an essential aspect of their jobs. We shall apparently not be engaged in false advertising if we conclude that the legions of bosses and supervisors in the United States corporations are plenteous indeed—even if we rely on the relatively more restrictive occupational data which tabulate only managers and supervisors and ignore those in other occupational categories who also have supervisory responsibilities.

How is it possible that so many people spend at least some of their time directing others? The basic principle is simple. If a labor-management system relies on hierarchical principles for managing and supervising its front-line employees on the shop and office floors—as does that in the United States—then it needs more than just the front-line supervisors who directly oversee these production and nonsupervisory workers. Who keeps the supervisors honest? What guarantees that those supervisors won't be in cahoots with their charges? In such a hierarchy, you need supervisors to supervise the supervisors . . . and supervisors above them . . . and managers to watch the higher-level supervisors . . . and higher-level managers to watch the lower-level managers. A pyramid takes shape in which every level of supervision from the bottom on up is essential to the operations of the entire enterprise.

We get some feel for this pyramiding effect from a classic article in 1970 by Elinor Langer about her brief career as a customer sales representative in the New York Telephone Company:[21]

> [My supervisor] is the supervisor of five women. She reports to a Manager who manages four supervisors (about twenty women) and he reports to the District Supervisor along with two other managers. . . . A job identical in rank to that of the district supervisor is held by four other men in Southern Manhattan alone. They report to the Chief of the Southern Division, himself a soldier in an army of division chiefs.

And thus is the bureaucratic burden formed. Layer upon layer rises from the base of the corporation, each layer spread with officers checking on their subordinates. In the Class Structure Survey for 1991, for example, we find that of those employees with supervisory responsibilities, roughly one quarter supervise someone who *also* has "people working under them"—suggesting an average span of supervision within the supervisory ranks of something like one to three or four. In his study of the size and structure of corporate management for the American Management Association, business analyst Robert M. Tomasko infers from his own case studies an estimate that is consistent with this mapping of the managerial hierarchy. Although front-line supervisors oversee larger numbers, he writes, "in middle-management ranks, the pyramid commonly narrows to 3, 4, or 5 people reporting to a manager, and [as a result] the number of management layers increases."[22]

Robert H. Hayes and Steven C. Wheelwright, from the Harvard and Stanford business schools respectively, analyze this general tendency in U.S. corporations organized on the basis of top-down authority:[23]

> As the scale of a production unit increases, so does the workforce required to operate it. The larger the workforce, the more supervisors, coordinators, and managers are required. Since managers usually feel that the number of people reporting to them ought to be less than some maximum number (generally 8 to 12), organizations tend to grow like pyramids: as the base of the pyramid (representing the number of workers) grows, so does the number of layers of managers—each of whom probably requires at least one support person (a secretary, assistant, etc.). As the number of layers in the management hierarchy grows, communication and coordination becomes more difficult, so additional support personnel are required. For example, whereas a 200–person workforce would normally have at most three organizational levels above the workers, a 2000–person workforce typically has four or five levels.

Tomasko echoes this analysis: "Big seems to breed bigger. As total employment increases, so does the number of management layers required to keep things under control."[24]

The pattern is quite general. No one can be trusted. Everyone must be watched. And everyone must be paid more than those below them on the hierarchical ladder. For this, we spent $1.3 trillion in 1994.

Who's Fat and Who's Not

It could be, of course, that this massive bureaucratic burden is part of the cost of doing business in a sophisticated, increasingly globalized economy. Perhaps it is inevitable that we need legions of managers and supervisors to oversee complex production systems, spur product and process innovations, conquer markets at home and abroad, and plan for the future. Maybe we need such a large corps of corporate officers if we are to win the war for global economic supremacy.

When I first started studying the bureaucratic burden in the late 1970s, I didn't know how seriously to take the kinds of consultant reports of redundant managers to which I alluded at the beginning of the chapter. Some observers seemed to find layers of fat in U.S. management, but fat is partly in the eye and mind of the beholder. What kinds of effective standards should one use to judge whether a corporate bureaucracy is too small, too big, or just the right size?

One obvious approach would be to compare the size of the bureaucratic burden across U.S. firms, stacking relatively more successful firms up against their less successful competitors, an approach I pursue somewhat later on. Another obvious strategy would essay international comparisons. By the early 1980s, it was widely perceived that large corporations in other leading economies such as Germany and Japan were competing at least as effectively in global markets as U.S. firms. Were their bureaucratic armies as massive as ours?

It is this kind of international standard, indeed, which has helped fuel spreading public anger about stratospheric CEO salaries in the United States. Many observers have noted that top-level managers in the United States earn far more than they do abroad. A 1991 survey found, for example, that chief executive officers in large U.S. corporations on average received almost exactly twice the total compensation of their counterparts in either Japan or Germany.[25] Are corporate honchos really twice as smart or productive or creative in the United States as corporate bosses elsewhere?

It turns out that international comparisons of the bureaucratic burden reveal similar patterns.

There are no direct analogues for other economies to the U.S. data on nonproduction and supervisory employment. But the International Labour Organization (ILO) has made possible some direct cross-country explorations of a similar kind of category. ILO compilations provide international data for the number and relative proportions of employees in "administrative and managerial" occupations.[26] Although individual countries' definitions of oc-

cupational categories vary substantially, the ILO has devoted considerable effort to fitting the respective nations' census data into standardized occupational definitions across countries. Overlaying the ILO figures with U.S. data,
we find that "administrative and managerial" occupations in the ILO data
correspond precisely to the category of "executive, administrative, and managerial" occupations in the BLS household surveys, or the group I've been
calling "managers" for short.[27] The ILO data therefore allow us to compare
the relative proportions of managers across countries but not the relative
numbers of other employees in job slots called "supervisors." This will provide at least a start in gauging the relative size of the managerial armies in the
United States.

Let's return to the same set of twelve countries for which we compared
wage growth in Chapter 1. And because the employment share of supervisory
workers is highly sensitive to the business cycle, let's focus on 1989, the most
recent year in which these advanced economies were more or less at their
business cycle peaks. With the ILO data, we can compare nine of those twelve
countries; data for 1989 are not available for France, Italy, and the United
Kingdom.

FIGURE 2.1

Comparing the Bureaucratic Burden

Managerial and administrative employees as percent of nonfarm employment, 1989

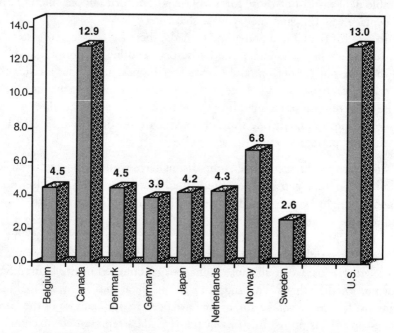

Source: ILO, *Yearbook of Labour Statistics,* 1994.

Figure 2.1 presents the percent of nonfarm employment in administrative and managerial occupations for the United States and for these other eight advanced economies.[28] The data in the graph suggest some fairly dramatic patterns.

- The bureaucratic burden in the United States was the highest among the nine countries. Thirteen percent of total nonfarm employment in the United States worked in administrative and managerial occupations in 1989.
- Canada also stands out as another economy weighted with a heavy proportion of managerial employees. As we shall see in some detail in Chapters 3 and 6, Canada and the United States along with the United Kingdom are considered the three advanced economies with the most "conflictual" systems of labor-management relations. This provides a first strong hint that among the developed countries top-heavy corporate bureaucracies are associated with adversarial labor relations.
- Following that lead further, we can look at the managerial proportions for three other economies that are widely regarded as representing much more "cooperative" approaches to corporate organization and labor management—Germany, Japan, and Sweden.[29] In 1989 the relative size of the U.S. bureaucratic burden had reached more than three times the levels in Japan and Germany and more than four times the percentage in Sweden. (This portrait would not differ markedly if we used the most recent available data instead of those for 1989. In 1993, for example, the U.S. percentage was 13.2 and the Japanese share was 4.1.)
- Except for the United States and Canada, there is a striking consistency in the size of the bureaucratic burden across the other economies. Sweden is the lowest at 2.6 percent and Norway the highest at 6.8, but all the others fall in a narrow band between 3.9 and 4.5 percent. The average for the seven economies not including the United States and Canada is 4.4 percent—almost exactly one-third of the U.S. proportion. By these standards, the U.S. pattern is obviously atypical.

Some who have seen these comparisons have wondered whether at least some of the huge gap between the United States and everyone else (except Canada) might be due to differences in the industry makeup of the various economies.

For example, if private corporations manage health insurance in the United States and the government oversees it in countries such as Sweden and the Netherlands, won't all those managers get counted in the United States but not for the others? This might be a consideration if we were looking at data just for the *private* sector, as we have been in our analyses of the United States up to this point. But in fact the ILO data represented in Figure 2.1 cover the *total* nonfarm economy including the government; a separate breakdown for just the private nonfarm sector is not available. So those health insurance managers are included in these figures regardless of whether they're employed by corporations or the government.

Or, if the United States has "de-industrialized" more than other economies, shedding manufacturing jobs like flies and shifting employment into sectors such as finance where the managerial proportions may be higher, might this be a reason that the U.S. burden is heavier? But this appears not to be a major factor affecting the comparisons either. For a few of the economies represented in the graph we can compare the percentage of managerial employees for specific industries. And the large differences reflected in the graph persist for individual sectors as well. In 1993, for example, 11.6 percent of manufacturing employment worked in administrative and managerial occupations in the United States and only 4.1 percent in Japan.[30] This almost exactly replicates the figures for the two countries for the nonfarm economy as a whole.

But could these differences reflect entirely different assumptions built into the occupational categories of the respective countries? For a few of the countries represented here, we can look more directly at the actual functions that employees perform on the job. The Class Structure Survey reported in the previous section allows for a comparison of actual employee responsibilities for the United States, Canada, Norway, and Sweden among the nine countries included in Figure 2.1.[31] Among the four, the rank order is exactly the same as with the ILO data: The United States once again features the highest percentage of employees identified as having "managerial" or "supervisory" responsibilities while Sweden exhibits the lowest; Canada ranks second and Norway third. In the United States, nearly 35 percent of all employees worked in "managerial" or "supervisory" positions. In Sweden, according to exactly the same definitions from the same survey instrument, only 22.5 percent worked in such jobs.[32]

Given that these estimates are uniformly higher in the Class Structure Survey than in the ILO data—since the former encompasses everyone with managerial and supervisory responsibilities, not just those called "managers"—the gap between the United States and Sweden is roughly comparable in the two sources. In the ILO data the difference between their percentages of "administrative and managerial" employees is slightly more than ten percentage points, while in the Class Structure Survey the interval between their shares of workers with "managerial" or "supervisory" responsibilities is roughly twelve points. As my own estimates presented earlier also indicate, one of the biggest sources of this gap is, in Wright's words, "the extent to which the supervisory aspect of managerial functions has been delegated to [other] positions" not normally categorized as managerial or supervisory.[33]

This should provide some confidence in the relative rankings revealed by the data in Figure 2.1. According to those data, there were 15 million managers and administrators in the nonfarm sector in the U.S. in 1989. If the

Japanese proportions had applied in the United States, there would have been less than 5 million in that occupational group. If the Swedish percentage had applied, only 3 million would have worked at that level. Almost 12 million workers would have been freed up to perform different kinds of tasks. This liberated army of employees would have been large enough virtually to treble the number of elementary and secondary teachers or almost to quadruple the number of doctors, dentists, nurses and other health technicians.[34]

Many speak about the possibility of a "peace dividend"—a huge fund that could accrue from cuts in unnecessary defense expenditures to help finance more socially productive activities. The international comparisons highlighted in Figure 2.1, by analogy, suggest that we might begin to imagine a "corporate bureaucratic dividend"—massive savings from reducing the bureaucratic burden to levels featured in other successful advanced economies.[35] Advocates of economic conversion gush about a prospective "peace dividend" of something like $150 billion. If Japanese or German managerial proportions applied to corporate bureaucracies in the United States, we might begin to project a "corporate bureaucratic dividend" at least four times more bounteous.

Gaining Weight

Why should U.S. corporations be so top-heavy compared to their major international competitors? Is there method to the fatness, a sound strategy behind the bloat? The answer to these questions is complex.

But one preliminary step toward such an answer is relatively straightforward. By placing the bureaucratic burden in historical perspective, we can at least determine whether U.S. corporations have always been so top-heavy or whether their massive scale is of relatively recent origin.

Let us return to the data for private nonfarm supervisory employees for the United States. One of the advantages of this measure of the bureaucratic burden is that we have continuous data, relying on fairly consistent definitions, since World War II.

In 1994, as we have already seen, there were somewhat more than 17 million supervisory employees in the private nonfarm sector. In 1948, there were only 4.7 million. In raw numbers, it would appear, there was tremendous growth in the cadres of managers and supervisors over the postwar period, an increase of roughly 360 percent.

Overall employment was increasing rapidly as well, of course, so just looking at the raw numbers doesn't tell us very much. It makes much more sense to look at the *relative* size of the bureaucratic burden, tracing the ratio of nonproduction and supervisory employment to total employment in the private nonfarm sector.

Figure 2.2 presents this measure of the bureaucratic burden. It shows that in 1948 it began at a postwar low of twelve percent of all private nonfarm

FIGURE 2.2
The Bureaucratic Burden Rises
Nonproduction and supervisory employees as percent of total, private nonfarm sector, 1948–94

Source: *Employment and Earnings,* various years.

TABLE 2.2
Taking on Weight
Administrative and managerial employees as percent of nonfarm employment

	1960	1970	1980	1989
Germany	2.6	2.5	2.8	3.9
Japan	3.9	5.9	5.2	4.2
Sweden	2.1	2.6	2.9	2.6
U.S.	6.6	8.7	11.4	13.0
Ratio, U.S. to average of other three	**2.3**	**2.4**	**3.1**	**3.6**

Sources and Notes: International Labour Organization, *Yearbook of Labour Statistics,* various years. Figure for 1960 for Germany is actually for 1961. See also text note #28.

employees working in supervisory jobs. It increased substantially as the post-war period progressed, leveling off at roughly 19 percent in the 1980s. At that point almost one in five private nonfarm wage-and-salary employees were employed in this category, working mostly, as we have already seen, as managers and supervisors of one sort or another.

The trends revealed by international comparisons show a similar pattern. Here, with the ILO data, we can only go back as far as 1960. Table 2.2 traces changes in the bureaucratic burden over the decades since 1960 for the United States and for Germany, Japan, Sweden—the three countries I listed earlier as representing relatively more cooperative approaches to labor relations—allowing us to glimpse when and how the huge gap between the United States and the other three countries, revealed above in Figure 2.1, actually emerged. The final row of the table calculates the ratio of the U.S. bureaucratic burden to the (unweighted) average of the other three economies.

In 1960 the United States had the highest share of administrative and managerial employees, but the gap was not particularly pronounced. Then the bureaucratic burden in the United States began to grow quite steadily and rapidly. At the same time, the administrative and managerial share in the other three countries remained relatively flat. In Sweden it scarcely changed; in Germany it remained quite low until a bit of growth in the 1980s; and in Japan it actually increased some through 1980 and then declined. In no other country do we find anything like the U.S. pattern of steady expansion, much less the massive levels to which the U.S. bureaucratic burden eventually expanded. The ratio between the U.S. share and the average for the other three grew consistently throughout, but increased most rapidly during the 1970s and 1980s.

A single slice of comparison helps underscore the story told by the data in the table. In 1960, the percentage of administrative and managerial employment in the United States was only about 1.5 times its level in Japan. By 1989, it had increased to more than three times the Japanese level. In 1960, by international standards, U.S. corporations were heavy. By 1989, they had become obese.

Can we be more precise about the trajectory along which U.S. corporations put on so much weight? If we look back at the trends portrayed for the United States in Figure 2.2 more closely, it appears that there are two phases in the general rise of the bureaucratic burden. The share of supervisory employees fluctuates fairly sharply with the business cycle, rising in recessions when relatively more production workers tend to be laid off. Taking those fluctuations into account, two fairly distinct periods emerge from the numbers.

In the first phase, the share of supervisory employees grew very rapidly through the late 1950s and then somewhat more slowly during the 1960s. This was the period during which the foundations of modern U.S. managerial structures were laid. Many corporations, especially in key manufacturing sectors such as auto and steel, had accommodated to life with labor unions by the early 1950s. But the entire premise of the postwar "accord" between corporations and their workers, as some of us have called it, was that corporations continued to control decisions about production and that workers, even if unionized, had no rights to interfere.[36] The corporations were running the show, they knew it, and they constructed a corporate bureaucracy to exercise their prerogatives. Having been strengthened in the 1940s and 1950s, the new managerial structures had begun to mature by the early 1960s and, as we can see from Figure 2.2, the growth of the bureaucratic burden began to ebb. After having grown by 1.8 percent a year during the long boom from 1948 to 1966, the supervisory employee share slowed to a rate of increase of only 0.4 percent a year from 1966 through 1973. The postwar system of corporate control was in place and, for a time, it was working.

Two features of this first phase were crucial. First, the instruments and structures of top-down corporate power were established, with managers and supervisors reasserting their control over basic investment and production decisions in a booming economy. Second, the very boom itself enabled workers to share at least partly in the harvest—with rising real wages, enhanced job security, and improving working conditions.[37] The labor-management system relied upon and reinforced corporate control over the workforce, but workers received a reward—reflected in their weekly paychecks—for their acquiescence to the new structures of control.

A second phase then appears to have emerged after the early 1970s. The growth of the bureaucratic burden accelerated once again. It increased from a ratio of 0.17 in 1973 to 0.19 in 1982 before leveling off in the 1980s. Its rate of growth climbed from 0.4 percent a year in 1966–73 to 1.0 percent in 1973–79 and then slowed again to 0.4 percent a year in the 1980s. These years were also the time in which the international data in Table 2.2 show the most rapid increase in the gap between the bureaucratic burden in the United States and in other leading economies. And it was also the period in which the proportion of nonproduction workers in manufacturing establishments—looking now at data not presented in the figures or tables but available from the *Census of Manufactures*—increased most rapidly, rising by almost one-quarter between 1973 and 1989.[38]

But we have already noted that the category of "nonproduction" workers is heterogeneous, something of a mixed bag. Did the acceleration of the growth of supervisory employees during the 1970s, by this measure of the bureaucratic burden, truly reflect increasingly intensive deployment of managers and supervisors, as I am suggesting, or of some other grouping within the "nonproduction and supervisory" category? Richard E. Caves and Matthew B. Krepps provide us with some important clues based on their detailed studies of occupations within manufacturing.[39] According to the establishment data, the share of nonproduction workers in manufacturing increased from

29.6 in 1970 to 32.6 in 1980, an increase of slightly more than 10 percent.[40] For the median firm during the 1970s, Caves and Krepps estimate (while controlling for changes in output across industries), the employment of "executive, administrative, and managerial personnel" increased by 20.6 percent while the employment of professional and technical workers declined by 10.5 percent. (Administrative support and service employees within manufacturing also declined.) The spurt we observe in Figure 2.2 does indeed appear to reflect an expansion of the managerial apparatus.

In this period the combination of the wage squeeze and the intensification of top-heavy systems of corporate control began to emerge with gathering force. In the previous phase, postwar prosperity had permitted rising real wages alongside the construction and consolidation of the top-heavy system of control. Now a variety of factors pressured corporations to push for both stagnant or declining wages *and* an intensification of their control. It was a time when many U.S. corporations began to adopt a much more aggressive stance toward their workers and toward trade unions, a period in which "an alternate nonunion system of industrial relations" was beginning to emerge much more "rapidly and visibly" than had been evident in the previous decades.[41] It was beginning in the early- to mid-1970s, indeed, that U.S. corporations grew more and more inclined to play hardball with their employees, to intimidate them with a stick. And for this strategy to work, the power of the stick-wielders had to be enhanced.

And this was the period, indeed, in which some observers began to note the bulge around the corporate middle. As the postwar boom commenced to sputter, Malcolm Baldridge, Secretary of Commerce under President Reagan, commented:[42]

> U.S. managers were sitting on their past laurels. In the 60s and 70s, we saw people fiddling around trying to have each quarter's earnings go up one increment over the last quarter. Our staffs got too big. We didn't put enough into research and development. We didn't get down to manage on the factory floor. Our quality stayed about the same, and everybody else's quality was coming up.

Through the 1970s, as we have already seen, the relative size of corporate bureaucracies continued to grow. By the mid-1980s, the paunch was protruding. Peter Drucker concluded in the 1980s: "Middle managements today tend to be overstaffed to the point of obesity. . . . A good many businesses, large and small, [have become] equally bureaucratic and equally suffer from gross overweight around the midriff."[43] Looking back at the same period, Barry Bluestone and Irving Bluestone concur: "by the beginning of the 1970s, and surely by the 1980s, bureaucratic firms were too bloated with middle-level managers to be efficient and much too burdened by rules and regulations to dance fast enough to keep up with foreign competition."[44] After John Welch became CEO of General Electric in the early 1980s, he observed that the company had reached the point "where we were hiring people [just] to read reports of people who had been hired to write reports."[45]

As we observe from Figure 2.2, the growth in the relative size of the corporate bureaucracy leveled off in the mid-1980s. The peak ratio of supervisory to total employment in the private nonfarm sector occurred in 1983. From then through the rest of the decade the share of managers and supervisors was essentially flat.

The Class Structure Survey shows roughly the same plateau for the 1980s. Comparing 1980 and 1990 using the same occupational categories and definitions, Wright estimates that 33.6 percent of employees worked as "managers" or "supervisors" in 1980. In 1990, the corresponding figure was 33.3 percent.[46] Over those ten years, the share of managers grew slightly and the share of supervisors declined by comparable amounts—leaving the total bureaucratic burden roughly constant.

If U.S. corporations were already suffering by the mid-1980s "from gross overweight around the midriff," in Drucker's words, should we conclude that they had solved their problems once the bureaucratic burden reached a more or less level plateau? Let's assume for the moment that the corporate world was indeed top-heavy. If so, concluding that they had solved their problems after 1983 would be like saying that a fat man of 350 pounds no longer suffered from obesity because he had stopped gaining weight. A fat corporation would still be a fat corporation.

What About "Downsizing"?

The story doesn't end with the 1980s. Corporate "downsizing" has become a watchword of the 1990s. We've read that corporations are becoming "lean and mean," that they're dramatically reducing their managerial staffs, that they've gone on a crash diet. Most astounding, as the news has been presented by the media, is that the scalpel has cut out managers as well as production workers. "After years of layoffs," *Business Week* reported in 1992, "the specter of downward mobility is haunting legions of once-secure managers and professionals. . . . As corporate stalwarts such as General Motors, United Technologies, and IBM join in a long list of downsizing companies, the economic trajectories of thousands of white-collar workers are plunging."[47] A relatively early study by the American Management Association sounded the theme: "There is a consensus that middle managers and technical professionals—the exempt employees who fill the boxes on the organization charts between line management and officers—are among the hardest hit in this leaner, meaner business climate."[48]

It is true that many managers and supervisors have been laid off in recent years, especially during the recent recession. Between 1990 and 1992, the total number of private nonfarm supervisory employees fell by 240,000—

hardly a trivial number. "Downsizing" as a term and phenomenon had become familiar to many by the mid-1980s—witness Robert Tomasko's book bearing that title, published in 1987.[49] And media reports—of the thousands laid off at IBM, the tens of thousands elsewhere—have continued since the 1990–91 recession. Typically, a new term was invented to refer to the victims of these excisions. "Just as the last decade was defined by yuppies and their flamboyant material excesses," *Business Week* wrote in 1992, "the 1990s may come to be the age of 'dumpies'—downwardly mobile professionals—and their struggle to stay in the upper end of the middle class."[50]

But all these stories do not by themselves establish that the problem of corporate top-heaviness is being addressed. They do not even establish, indeed, that the weight of the bureaucratic burden itself is being reduced. Hundreds of thousands of production employees have also been fired or laid off in recent years alongside the reductions at higher levels of the hierarchy. The story of the bureaucratic burden, as I've been recounting it in this chapter, is primarily a story of *relative* overweight, of the proportion of total employment in managerial and supervisory jobs and not simply their absolute mass.

What matters most, in short, is whether or not corporate "downsizing" in the past several years has actually reduced the bureaucratic burden itself.

In looking more closely at changes over a small number of years, the establishment data do not serve us as well as they did in Figure 2.2 because, as noted above, there are no further detailed occupational breakdowns within the category of nonproduction and supervisory employees. To explore the impact of "downsizing" since the late 1980s, we can get a more finely-grained picture if we concentrate on the occupational data in the household surveys, where specific tabulations of "executive, administrative, and managerial" employees as well as a range of supervisory occupations are provided.

Here, we can concentrate on employment changes from the business cycle peak of 1989 to 1994, the period during which stories of downsizing have been most widely reported. What happened to the managerial employment share over those years?

The household survey data suggest that the requiem for middle management has been premature. In 1989, according to the official published tabulations, "executive, administrative, and managerial" workers (excluding managers in public administration) accounted for 12.6 percent of total nonfarm employment. (This numbers includes only managers and does not yet consider the several million employees in various supervisory jobs.) Between 1989 and 1994, employment in this category accounted for almost one-quarter of total net employment growth, rising from 14.3 million in 1989 to 15.7 million in 1994.[51] As a result, the share of private managers in total nonfarm employment *increased over those five years by five percent over its 1989 level, from 12.6 percent to 13.2 percent,* rather than declining as the recurring and sometimes sensational stories have appeared to imply. During the recession there was some net reduction in managerial ranks, but since then, during the recovery, proportionately more managers have been hired back than other occupational groupings. Many managers have lost their jobs, but many have been rehired as managers and many others have joined the managerial ranks for the first time. For all of the talk of "downsizing," there were more managers in 1994 than there were in 1989 before the "downsizing" began.

And these trends appear to be continuing beyond 1994. As I write, the most recent available detailed occupational data cover the second quarter of 1995.[52] By then, the percent of private "executive, administrative and managerial" employees in total nonfarm employment had increased further still, from 13.2 percent in 1994 to 13.6 percent. Dating the recovery from 1991, total nonfarm employment had increased to the second quarter of 1995 by 7.4 million—a jobs expansion for which President Clinton wishes his economic policies would receive a little more credit. Growth of private managerial employment accounted for almost two million of these jobs. This surge in managerial employment amounted to more than a quarter of the total net jobs expansion during this period, *or more than double the managerial share at the beginning of the recovery.*

FIGURE 2.3

Did "Downsizing" Trim Bureaucratic Burden I?

Managers as percent of nonfarm employment in 1989 and 1995 2nd qtr.

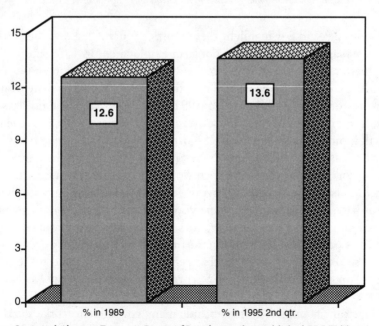

Sources: Statistical Abstract; Economic Report of President; and unpublished BLS Tables.

FIGURE 2.4
Did "Downsizing" Trim Bureaucratic Burden II?
Managers as percent of nonfarm employment in 1991 and as percent of 1991–95 nonfarm employment growth

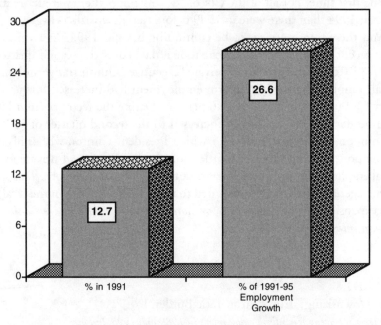

Sources: Statistical Abstract; Economic Report of President; and unpublished BLS Tables.

Figures 2.3 and 2.4 highlight these trends. Figure 2.3 shows the percentage of managers in total private nonfarm employment in 1989 and the second quarter of 1995. Figure 2.4 concentrates on the change in employment over the period of the recovery. The left-hand bar shows the share of managers in nonfarm employment in 1991. The right-hand bar displays the growth in managerial employment over the recovery as a percent of the total growth in nonfarm employment. If bloated corporate management has been put on a crash diet in the United States, you can't tell it from these scales.[53]

The story remains the same when we expand our focus not only to managers but also to those with supervisory responsibility. During the period of "downsizing" the percentage of supervisors in total nonfarm employment remained roughly constant. In 1989, 16.1 percent of total nonfarm employees worked as private managers and in the full range of supervisory occupations. By the second quarter of 1995, that percentage had increased to 16.8 percent.[54] Some may believe that U.S. corporations have become "leaner." In fact, they are even top-heavier than before.[55]

These official published data include many government workers and also include the self-employed. As a final check, we can use the underlying data samples from the Current Population Survey to look exclusively at wage-and-salary employees in the private nonfarm sector, targeting as closely as possible the composition of employment in private corporations. The story remains essentially the same. Between 1989 and 1993—the most recent year for which I was able to obtain the micro data samples at the time of writing—the percentage of managers and supervisors in private nonfarm wage-and-salary employment increased from 18.1 to 18.7 percent, once again suggesting that "downsizing" has not left private corporations any "thinner" at the top than before. Judging by the trends from 1993 through the second quarter of 1995 in the published data, indeed, we could expect the 1993 percentage of 18.7 percent to have increased even further as the recovery continued.

Nor, apparently, would we find a different story if we concentrated on the largest corporations. Here, we can turn to annual surveys by the American Management Association (AMA) of a sample of its membership, which is concentrated among "major" U.S. firms, especially those whose earnings place them in the top two percent of corporations.

The AMA has conducted surveys of what it calls "downsizing," of actual workforce reductions, since 1989. If the media reports were accurate, we would expect to find a rising percentage of managerial cutbacks over that period. But "middle management" reductions as a percent of total downsizing actually fell over the period, from 23.6 percent to 18.5 percent between 1989 and 1990 and 1993 and 1994. If we add supervisory jobs to middle management, then the proportion of the total reductions in those two categories remained about constant.[56]

The AMA argues that over the whole period of their surveys, workplace reductions have hit middle management disproportionately, that "middle managers in particular continue to bear the brunt of corporate reductions." This would be true if, as they claim, the share of middle managerial jobs in the recent layoffs was higher than their share of total employment in the corporate sample at the beginning of the period.

But they're looking *only* at reductions, not at net employment changes. Like many who have overreacted to the "downsizing" trends, the AMA fails in its study to keep track of the critical distinction between *net* and *gross* changes in employment. Lots of managers can be laid off, resulting in evidence of substantial *gross* job turnover, but lots of managers can also be rehired at similar positions in the same or other companies, potentially producing no *net* change or even a *net* increase in managerial employment. If workplace reductions at the middle managerial level are offset by job expansions in those same job categories, then the bureaucratic burden would not be affected. The aggregate numbers on the expanding managerial employment share cited above suggest that this is exactly what's been happening—that new managerial positions have been opening up to compensate for those eliminated.

And Labor Department studies of displaced workers precisely confirm this pattern. The most recent study, released in July 1995, allows us to look at workers displaced in 1991 and 1992 and to trace where they ended up as of February 1994.[57] In these studies, displaced workers are defined as those employees twenty years and older "who lost or left a job because their plant or company closed or moved, there was insufficient work for them to do, or their positions or shifts were abolished."[58] Their definition closely corresponds, in other words, to what most people have in mind when they write or talk about "downsizing."

According to their studies, to be sure, large numbers of displacements occurred among managers in 1991 and 1992. But for the bureaucratic burden to have been reduced displacement rates for managers would need to have been larger than for other occupational categories. And they weren't. "By the early 1990s," the BLS report concludes, "job loss had become more common among white-collar workers than it had been a decade earlier . . . ; however, even this higher figure was low relative to that for blue-collar workers."[59] Looking just at the category of managers rather than at all white-collar workers, we also find that the managerial displacement rate was lower than the average for all blue-collar workers.

But these data look only at the displacement side of the equation. What happened to all those managers after they lost their jobs? Two findings from the BLS study are especially useful in reconciling people's impressions of widescale managerial layoffs with the evidence of an actual increase in the managerial share of employment:

- Among those workers displaced in 1991 and 1992, managers had the highest rate of reemployment by February 1994 of *any* occupational grouping: Among managers displaced in 1991 and 1992, 80.6 percent were employed in February 1994 while, for example, only 74.8 percent of craft workers and 68.8 percent of other blue-collar workers had jobs in that month.
- Most of those reemployed managers landed on their feet as managerial or professional workers. (The data don't classify the occupation of reemployment for managers alone.) The rates of reemployment in the same occupational category were considerably higher for those with "managerial and professional specialty" and "technical, sales, and administrative support" workers than in most other categories. Almost three-fifths of managers and professionals were reemployed in February 1994 as managers and professionals, for example, while less than half of those in service occupations wound up in the same kinds of jobs.

If the reports of the decimation of corporate managerial ranks have been gravely exaggerated, why have they seemed so credible?

One possible explanation is that the media, and especially business journalists, report *about* and *for* the top strata of the occupational ladder. When managers are laid off, it's big news. When business eliminates the jobs of workers on the shop and office floor, it's small news. The media appear to pay disproportionate attention to downsizing toward the top rungs of the occupational hierarchy because these workers are disproportionately their friends and relatives and readers and listeners.

These kinds of exaggerated accounts have appeared before. In the sharp recession of 1979–82, hundreds of thousands of workers lost their jobs, including many middle-level managers and supervisors. It was widely reported, Mark Green and John F. Berry observed in their 1985 book, "that middle managers lost jobs in record numbers during the economic recessions of the early 1980s." Just like the more recent period. "But aside from the considerable anecdotal evidence in magazines and newspapers chronicling the gutting of middle management," they continued, "what statistical proof is there of this widespread cutback of middle managers? The answer is, there isn't any."[60] What they meant is that the bureaucratic burden hadn't declined, just as it hasn't declined during the more recent period.

A second possible reason that the effects of "downsizing" on managerial hierarchies have been exaggerated is that most observers, like the AMA, have failed to keep track of the distinction between *net* and *gross* changes in employment. They trumpet the announcements of managerial layoffs when they occur. But they fail even to notice the widespread hiring of managers in other firms. They wince when long-time managers lose their jobs. But they probably don't even know about the thousands of workers who previously had other kinds of jobs who have now climbed into the managerial ranks. Among displaced workers actually employed as managers and professionals in February 1994, for example, a total of 45 percent—close to 250,000 workers— came from occupational backgrounds outside the managerial and professional sphere.[61]

Another reason that "downsizing" stories have paid such disproportionate attention to the fates of mid-level managers, apparently, is that those who have fallen from the ranks have fallen hard. Columbia University anthropologist Katherine S. Newman traced the trajectories of many of these "fallen" managers during the mid-1980s. The personal stories are wrenching. "Middle-aged managers who have lost their jobs," she writes, "carry indelible memories of the day they were 'let go.' It is a central scene in the drama of downward mobility."[62]

"Downsized" managers, indeed, fall quite far. Managerial employment is a ticket to affluence in the U.S. economy. As a useful study by Stephen J. Rose of the National Commission for Employment Policy shows, those men who worked at least eight out of ten years as managers during the 1980s earned 68 percent more than the average earnings for all male workers. But, strikingly, those managers who were *unable* to maintain their position at that occupational rung, those who worked less than eight of the ten years as managers in the 1980s, suffered the biggest relative earnings dropoff, compared with those who stayed on the managerial ladder, of employees in any occupational grouping.[63] As Anthony Carnevale summarizes Rose's findings, "There is both more risk and more gain in managerial jobs."[64] And the risks involve more than just material losses. Newman concludes:[65]

> The distress that refugees from the managerial milieu feel is only partly a matter of income loss, or the destruction of a lifestyle. It is fundamentally the pain of being evaluated and found wanted. To be a downwardly mobile executive is first to discover that you are not as good a person as you thought you were and then to end up not sure who or what you really are.

The business pages have been especially sensitive to this distress.

You can only fool people for so long. Eventually, just as I was completing this manuscript, some in the business press were finally waking up and recognizing the facts. In Fall 1995 the *Wall Street Journal* published a front-page story which finally paid more attention to the facts than the fantasies of "downsizing." "Despite years of relentless downsizing, 'right-sizing' and re-engineering in corporate America, all aimed in part at shedding excess bureaucracy," the *Journal* acknowledged, "reports of middle management's demise are proving much exaggerated."[66] Even "corporate giants", among whom the most dramatic reports of managerial layoffs had been reported, "have more managers per 100 employees today than they did in 1993." And smaller companies appear to have been employing managers with a vengeance. Those running smaller, growing companies, according to one business analyst quoted by the *Journal*, "are some of the most control-oriented people out there. They add bureaucracy to their businesses in order to maintain control." Many managers have been laid off in corporate restructuring, the *Journal* concluded, but they've found managerial work elsewhere. "There is so much opportunity [for managers] in the marketplace," one "downsized" executive reported, "it's incredible."

There is one more reason not to take the widespread reports of "lean" corporations too seriously. If U.S. firms were actually addressing their problems of obesity in any kind of systematic way, we would find substantial evidence of *coherent strategies* underlying managerial cutbacks when and where they have actually occurred.

But the evidence seems to suggest the opposite. In general, U.S. corporations have been slicing their workforces in piecemeal and often shotgun fashion, rarely acting upon clear and considered strategies for changing their ways of doing business.

This was beginning to become evident, to some at least, from the start. In Tomasko's 1987 book, for example, he warned:

> The consequences of top-heavy organizational structures are already well known. . . . But the equally destructive consequences of deep, across-the-board

cutbacks, sometimes happening wave after wave, are only beginning to become apparent. These consequences include diminished employee commitment to their companies; bitter personal trauma inflicted when the reductions were implemented with concern only for their economic impact, ignoring their psychological impact; and creation of corporate environments that are risk-averse and innovation-fearing. These harder-to-quantify problems may return to haunt many businesses.

The pattern has continued. "Most organizations downsize poorly," contends Kim Cameron of the University of Michigan School of Business Administration, who has closely studied the phenomenon. "Productivity suffers, morale suffers, innovation gets squashed and companies get less flexible and less competitive."[67] In general, economists James R. Emshoff and Teri E. Demlinger report, downsizing has not been "part of a thoughtful strategy to redesign the whole corporate structure and culture. Instead it's an almost panicked reaction to pressures and problems, administered with the sheeplike justification that everyone else is doing the same thing."[68] In his recent study of restructuring corporations, former *New York Times* reporter Hedrick Smith concurs. "In corporate America today," Smith concludes from his travels around the country, "downsizing is like dieting: Everyone is doing it, so people try it again and again, even though few achieve the desired results. As one wag put it, the fixation with downsizing has become the new 'corporate anorexia'."[69]

Surveys conducted by the American Management Association in 1994 highlight the superficial and shotgun character of most corporate "downsizing" efforts.[70] Only a third of corporations reported that their downsizing efforts had actually resulted in productivity gains; fully 30 percent reported that productivity had declined. A vast majority of companies surveyed reported that their restructuring efforts had placed a high priority on changing corporate culture, but less than a quarter reported that these results were "very successful." Far from generating uniform improvements in performance, one of the surveys concluded, "the surest after-effect of downsizing is a negative impact on employee morale"; 83 percent of corporations which had downsized between 1989 and 1991 reported that "employee morale had declined in 1994."[71]

In their panic, in their herding behavior, corporations have been swinging their machetes wildly. More often than not, Cameron concludes, downsizing occurs by brute force. "That's like throwing a hand grenade into a crowded room—you don't know which 25 percent you are going to kill."[72] Many more production employees than managers and supervisors have been hit by the grenades.

AND SO we end the chapter where we began. Corporate bureaucracies have grown to massive size. Walter Wriston jokes that half of those bureaucratic employees may be redundant; "[figuring out] which half is the difficult problem."

The media have reported widely that corporate downsizing has begun to attack this problem of overweight. But the share of managers in total employment has been increasing since the reports of downsizing began, not decreasing. And corporate downsizers haven't known "which 25 percent [they] are going to kill."

The same basic questions echo through the entire discussion: Why do we spend $1.3 trillion to cover the costs of the bureaucratic burden? Isn't this too big a price to pay?

Chapter 3

THE STICK STRATEGY

Over the past four years, the Caterpillar corporation, the world's largest manufacturer of earth-moving equipment, has been involved in one of the harshest labor-management conflicts in recent U.S. history. Faced with top-level management determined to bust its union, Cat workers, represented by the United Automobile Workers (UAW), have twice gone out on strike in the 1990s. The second strike ended just as this book was going to press, an epic struggle over the future role, if any, for unions at Caterpillar, and by proxy, at thousands of other U.S. corporations as well.[1]

Much of the conflict dates from the arrival in 1990 of Donald V. Fites as Caterpillar's CEO. Fites was known inside and outside the company as an executive with little patience for the labor union as an institution, which in his critical view "blocks communication channels" and "adds a layer of inefficiency." "Cat has always been a self-appointed, ideologically driven, anti-union corporation," a UAW official notes, "and Fites is proud of that tradition."[2] Under Fites' stern leadership, Caterpillar broke the workers' 1991 strike by threatening to replace all the striking workers permanently once the conflict was over, an announcement tantamount to a declaration of war in the ebb-and-flow of U.S. labor-management relations. And from the beginning of the current strike Caterpillar has been determined, according to *Los Angeles Times* reporter Barry Bearak, "to do what no major manufacturer had ever done before: to run its plants at full-speed with its biggest union out on the street. Once and for all, the UAW would be taught who was indispensable and who was not." "What it is," Fites says, "is not so much a battle about economics as it is a battle about who's going to run the company."[3]

Much talk in the business and popular press these days focuses on a new era of cooperation in U.S. corporations, echoing with buzzwords like "high-performance workplaces" and "total quality management." But corporate commitment to cooperative relations appears to be paper-thin. Caterpillar has become the symbol of hard-nosed, hard-ball, union-busting, conflictual management in the United States. And in March 1995, Donald Fites won a poll of 3,300 American chief executives, earning the designation by *Financial World* magazine as its CEO of the year. The symbolism was clear, the message amplified: U.S. executives were rooting for Cat. In the cover story reporting Fites' award, he was described admiringly as one who runs his company "with gusto and a steady, tight hand on the wheel. Clearly, he's not one to back away from a good game of chicken."[4]

THE "WAGE SQUEEZE" has become familiar to many observers. The "bureaucratic burden" is less familiar but certainly echoes resonantly for some. However widely recognized, nonetheless, these two crucial features of the U.S. economy are always discussed and analyzed separately, as distinct and discrete phenomena.

But the wage squeeze and the bureaucratic burden in the United States are integrally connected; each contributes directly to the other. They comprise two essential components of a system of production and management in the United States that builds on conflict and hierarchy, insecurity and coercion. "The United States has the highest amount of conflict between Business and Labor of any democratic nation," concludes MIT labor expert Thomas Kochan. "The bitterness and lack of trust for each other's basic legitimacy is a national disgrace."[5] This conflictual system of production and management not only suffocates the people who work in it but also tears at the fabric of our communities and hobbles our economy's performance.

In short, "fat" and "mean" go together like the proverbial horse and carriage. In our economy, it would appear, you can't have one without the other. The international data certainly feed such a suspicion, since the United States, as the figures in the preceding chapters illustrate, has recently featured *both* the slowest real wage growth *and* the top-heaviest corporate bureaucracies among the leading advanced economies.

But I want to demonstrate real functional interdependency, not merely statistical association. Low and falling wages and bloated management are both integral features of a system of labor management. They feed each other. This entails an argument about what we in the social sciences leadenly describe as "mutual determination." Neither piece of the puzzle has priority over the other; they foster and reinforce each other, deepening their interdependence, strengthening their respective places as part of the foundation of the U.S. economy.

This chapter traces the mutual interaction between the wage squeeze and corporate bloat. It makes a case *both* that stagnant wages beget legions of managers and supervisors *and* that top-heavy corporate bureaucracies dramatically dampen production-worker earnings. It begins by showing how stagnant wages promote bloated management.

Addicted to the Stick

After devastating losses in the 1980–81 recession, Ford Motor Company began to experiment with an employee involvement program to try to improve productivity.[6] The experiment returned substantial and apparently surprising dividends. Reviewing the experiment with UAW leaders, Philip Caldwell, Ford CEO, marveled that the Ford workers had so many ideas to contribute to production management. Donald Ephlin, a vice-president of the autoworkers union, replied: "I don't know what the hell's so surprising about that. They've got more invested in the company than you have."[7] Donald Petersen, president of Ford at the time of the innovations, eventually understood Ephlin's message. "I came to see that the easiest people to motivate to perform better were the hourly [assembly-line] workers," Petersen later said in an interview. "They understood that their jobs were at stake."[8]

Caldwell's skepticism is typical of corporate executives in the United States and Ford's commitment to its employee involvement program is not. Caterpillar is carrying the torch for U.S. corporations, not Ford.

Across the advanced capitalist economies, at a broad level of generalization, two quite distinct types of labor-management systems reflect sharply contrasting approaches to managing production workers and encouraging productive job performance. One approach features relatively cooperative labor-management relations, including a fair degree of employment security, positive wage incentives, often with substantial employee involvement and also often with strong unions. The other builds upon much more conflictual labor-management relations, including relatively little employment security, reliance on the threat of job dismissal as a goad to workers, minimal wage incentives, sometimes weak unions.

The former system relies on the carrot, the latter on the stick. As is commonly recognized, Germany, Sweden, and Japan provide examples of the former kind of approach, even though among their labor-management systems there are also important differences.[9] And, as many have pointed out in recent years, the United States tends more and more to represent the archetype of the latter system, also exemplified by Canada and the United Kingdom.[10]

There is, of course, tremendous variety in the way individual corporations manage their labor relations in the United States. While it is true that labor union strength has been declining and the traditional collective bargaining system along with it, as Thomas A. Kochan, Harry C. Katz, and Robert B. McKersie note in their important book on *The Transformation of American Industrial Relations*, "there is considerable diversity in the patterns of adaptation and the practices that result as the parties move away from this system."[11] But when we contrast the majority of U.S. corporations with their counterparts in Germany, Japan, or Sweden, the differences are much more striking than the similarities. And one of the principal differences is that a huge proportion of

U.S. corporations rely on what I am calling the Stick Strategy in managing their labor relations. And it is in the conflictual kinds of systems featured by most U.S. corporations—those depending primarily on the stick—that the link running from stagnant wages to bloated bureaucracies takes hold.

Let us begin the argument by simply taking note of the phenomenon of falling real wages. As traced in Chapter 1, real hourly spendable earnings for production and nonsupervisory employees, the most complete measure of production workers' hourly take-home pay, reached their postwar peak in the United States in 1972 and have since declined by more than 10 percent. The explanation for this pattern of declining real wages is complicated and there are many competing explanations of its sources, which I shall review in detail in Chapters 7 and 8. But for the purposes of discussion in this chapter, let me simply hypothesize that *one* of the principal sources of the trend toward falling real wages for production and nonsupervisory workers since the mid-1970s has been an increasingly aggressive corporate approach to bargaining with unions and with individual employees.

During the boom years of the 1950s and 1960s, many corporations and most labor unions understood that they would jointly share in the economy's prosperity. As one feature of that compact, real wages steadily rose. Since the mid-1970s, many U.S. corporations have abandoned that understanding.[12] They have demanded union givebacks on both wages and benefits. They have tossed away the presumption that, over time, their employees are entitled to wage or benefit increases. They have grown more and more hostile to arrangements guaranteeing employment security, turning increasingly to temporary and contingent workers. When they hire replacements, they are inclined to insist on two-tier, or even multi-tier, wage systems, steadily ratcheting down the earnings that workers with given skill levels could reasonably expect on the job.

Referring to the choices facing workers in the age of the Caterpillar conflict, Robert Townshend, a 22–year-old worker in Illinois, remarks:[13]

> These guys on strike walked into good-paying union jobs right out of high school; well, those days are long gone. Try getting a job now. People are paid $6.50 an hour to do what they do at Cat for $18.
>
> Union people are always arguing about job security. Well, who *is* secure today? Just because you work for a corporation doesn't mean you're immune from insecurity. That's life in the '90s.

Robert B. Reich, Secretary of Labor in the Clinton administration, generalizes Townshend's observations, arguing that business has breached an "unwritten social contract":[14]

> The most important part of the contract is that if the worker is diligent and reliable, and if the company is making money, that worker keeps his or her

job. The second principle is enjoying rising wages and benefits as a company's profits improve. This social contract is no longer with us.

Let us take as given, in short, that U.S. corporations are embarked on the "slow-wage-growth path." And let us also note, as a kind of corollary, that job security seems to be eroding in the United States along with the falling wages. Why does this portrait imply anything about bloated U.S. corporate bureaucracies? What does it have to do with the way that American corporations structure their managerial ranks?

In cooperative systems of labor management, one of the principal carrots extended to workers is the promise of steady increases in real earnings and the assurance (implicit if not formally-bargained) that the dividends from rapid productivity growth will be shared between owners and workers.[15] These wage incentives reinforce other dimensions of the cooperative approach such as strong employment security. And when those incentives are in place, workers seem to be able to coordinate many of their own activities in production, relieving their corporate owners of the need for intensive and continuous monitoring and supervision. Because they earn a substantial share of firm profits and because their employment security would be threatened only in the event of firm failure, workers and their unions understand the need to work productively, taking substantial responsibility for spurring themselves and even for bringing along their mates who may not work so diligently.

British economist David Soskice, one of the foremost students of these contrasting labor-management systems, emphasizes the mutual understanding upon which this cooperative system rests: "The basic form of this agreement is that the unions underwrite the flexibility of the system . . . ; and that in return they are given a position within the system that enables them to ensure that that flexibility is not abused."[16] Only with and because of that understanding can the corporations' need for hierarchical authority be relaxed. In these kinds of systems, Soskice continues, unions "act as a guarantor of work-force cooperation. . . . The national unions are able to act in this way in part because, in the last resort, they can exert sanctions on workgroups and union officials at company level. . . . [T]here is a complex balancing act which produces work-force co-operation and co-operative management worker relations."[17]

With a coercive approach, by contrast, a much more fundamental conflict between owners and workers is likely to persist over workers' labor effort. Corporations are naturally interested in their employees' working as hard as possible. In the absence of strong wage benefits and employment security, however, what provides the worker with the incentive to work anywhere nearly as intensively as the corporation would prefer? Indeed, why should he or she work very hard at all? Workers may occasionally feel a sense of firm loyalty or may be moved, as in World War II, by patriotic fervor. Over the long haul, however, such inducements don't pay the bills. Reflecting on this basic conflict, a vice-president of public relations at General Motors concludes: "We are not yet a classless society. . . . [F]undamentally the mission of [workers'] elected representatives is to get the most compensation for the least amount of labor. Our responsibility to our stockholders is to get the most production for the least amount of compensation."[18]

The solution to such motivational problems in the absence of strong wage incentives and well-established job security, in general, is a combination of intensive supervision of employees and the threat of job dismissal.[19] If the worker can't be trusted to work diligently when left to him- or herself, the firm needs to watch the worker closely, monitoring nearly every move, alert to those unwanted moments of shirking, evading, and lollygagging that undermine firm performance. And if the worker is caught shirking, the firm needs to be able credibly to threaten dismissal or other comparably serious penalties such as reduction of promotion opportunities.

And so, in the absence of the carrot, conflictual systems are likely to display legions of stick-wielders as one of their central features, armies of supervisors and managers saddled with the principal direct or indirect responsibility for ensuring that production and nonsupervisory workers don't shirk on the job. European sociologist Gösta Esping-Andersen argues that this is one of the most important differences between American and European labor relations: In the United States, he concludes, "industrial relations tend to be combative, and American unions cannot, as in 'neo-corporatist' settings, be counted on to police the rank and file. Thus, the American firm is obliged to exercise control with the aid of armies of supervisory staff."[20]

Can't trust your workers when left to their own devices? Peer over their shoulders. Watch behind their backs. Record their movements. Monitor them. Supervise them. Boss them. Above all else, don't leave them alone. As one recent study observed, "American companies tend, fundamentally, to mistrust workers, whether they are salaried employees or blue-collar workers. There is a pervading attitude that, 'if you give them an inch, they'll take a mile,' because they don't really want to work."[21] A welder in Ford's South Chicago plant recalled in a 1990s interview the atmosphere on the plant floor before Ford launched its employee involvement program: "Ten years ago, the supervisors did a lot of screaming. They were always hollering at the top of their lungs, instead of talking to us like we're human beings. We really had no input at all." A workmate echoed the recollection: "It was 'Do it and shut up!'"[22]

This reliance on managerial control in U.S. corporations took deep root during the 1940s and 1950s. They faced a challenge from the unions, and they chose to respond with the Stick.

When the union movement first spread like a brushfire after the mid-1930s, many workers and unions focused on trying to forge greater control on the job, greater leverage over their job security and work effort. Yale labor historian David Montgomery writes:[23]

> The power which unionizing workers won on the job at this time was far more significant to them and to their employers than whatever wage gains they won. Shop stewards and committee men and women, backed up (often physically) by the employees in the departments they represented, translated the inextinguishable small-group resistance of workers into open defiance and conscious alternatives to the directives of the management. Union contracts, where they were won, undermined company favoritism, obliged firms to deal with the workers' elected delegates, and secured workers against arbitrary dismissal, thus strengthening their sense of collectivity and bolstering their courage in confronting management.

In principle U.S. corporations could have moved at that time in more cooperative directions. But instead they fought back, concerned that their basic control over production was being undermined. After World War II, General Motors President Charles E. Wilson warned a Senate committee that "our American system" was being threatened by a movement "imported from east of the Rhine." Unless we move to confine and turn back this movement, Wilson urged, "the border area of collective bargaining will be a constant battleground . . . as the unions continuously attempt to press the boundary farther and farther into the area of managerial functions."[24] Corporations regained the upper hand. Among their central victories were contractual "management rights" clauses that ceded them unilateral power over all issues not explicitly covered by the terms of the collective bargaining contract, and production organization and relations were the principal examples studiously ignored in the contracts. General Motors was the pacesetter in its struggles with the United Auto Workers. Labor historian David Brody summarizes GM's approach:[25]

> The company would not bargain on matters designated as within the sphere of management. It opposed any form of labor-management cooperation that gave the union a place, however minor or advisory, on management's side of the line. It policed the agreement like a hawk. On handling grievances, the labor-relations vice president remarked in 1949, "we have been making every reasonable effort to settle picayune cases . . . but have conceded no ground whatsoever on fundamental principle matters which would have the tendency of watering down management's responsibility to manage the business." On matters of discipline, above all, the company enforced its authority rigorously.

A choice had been made, a choice to consolidate and deepen a system of top-down corporate control. With that choice, as we saw in Chapter 2, the bureaucratic burden grew rapidly during the 1950s as the structure of managerial authority built upon these initial foundations. "On matters of discipline, above all," U.S. corporations were prepared to enforce their control.

As it turned out, for a time, they were able to hold the Stick at least partly in reserve. The extraordinary and to some degree unexpected prosperity of the postwar boom enabled corporations to reward many workers for their acceptance of managerial prerogatives, for their pulling back from the frontal challenges of the thirties and forties. Reaping the dividends of rapid growth through the mid-1960s, corporations were able to provide many workers, mostly unionized, a *quid* for the *quo* of restored managerial prerogatives. Steady increases in real wages, improving employment security, improving working conditions—all formed part of what Labor Secretary Reich calls the "unwritten social contract" prevailing during that period, what my collaborators and I call the "limited capital-labor accord."[26] Because the basic premises of labor management during this period relied on top-down control while some workers garnered rewards that the Stick Strategy does not always or even often bestow, I call this the period of the Little Stick, as in speak softly and carry a little stick.

The period of the Big Stick began in the early 1970s. Economic conditions no longer permitted corporations to hold the Stick in reserve. With profits falling, an economic environment emerged in which, *in the context of production relations existing in the United States*, intensive supervision became both increasingly necessary and potentially more and more fruitful.

Increasingly intensive supervision grew more and more *necessary* after the early 1970s because, far from sharing productivity dividends with employees as a way of spurring their effort, corporations on balance have been driving down wages and taking away other employee benefits and protections as well. In contrast to the postwar boom, when healthy corporate profits and rapid productivity growth helped make rising real wages possible, the onset of the wage squeeze eliminated that luxury. Corporations were faced with clear alternatives: Either they could revamp their managerial structures entirely, abandoning the structure of top-down control established after World War II, in order to forge the kind of cooperation and gain- and pain-sharing that might have smoothed the transition to an era of lower and falling profits; or they could deepen their reliance on top-down control and make up for the loss of worker incentives that falling wages imposed with an intensification of supervisory control. They chose the Big Stick.

Some simple trends illustrate the point about the disappearance of the carrot, the erosion of worker incentives: During the long postwar boom, when "the unwritten social contract" was still in place, productivity growth and production-worker real wage growth moved in tandem. Their average rates of growth were similar and their annual movements jogged up and down together, with a positive year-to-year correlation between them of 50 percent. During the 1980s, by contrast, productivity growth increased at an average annual rate of 1.2 percent a year while production real wages declined at a rate of 0.6 a year—dramatic evidence that none of the productivity dividend, however much reduced since the boom years, was being shared with workers. Meanwhile, the correlation between their annual movements had fallen to less than half its boom level, suggesting a much looser (and statistically insignificant) relationship between the growth in what workers were producing and in what they were taking home.[27]

Reich concludes: "As the economy grows, people who work the machines and clean the offices and provide the basic goods and services are supposed to share in the gains, but that hasn't been happening."[28] Workers may be driven by the fear that if they don't produce, they won't be able to move ahead. But on the job, day in and day out, if they don't have a clear, direct, and demonstrable stake in how well the firm performs, why should they push themselves, unless someone's watching and keeping score?

The strategy of intensive supervision has also become increasingly *fruitful*, as well, because the threat of dismissal has become increasingly credible in the United States. Since the mid-1970s and especially in an era of "downsizing," production workers up and down the ranks have understandably grown more and more fearful about their job security. In Spring 1995 a colleague of mine was conducting some workshops about the economy with production workers in a variety of manufacturing industries. Roughly 100 workers took part in the workshops. At one point, the workers were asked to raise their hands if they felt "secure about their jobs over the next five years." Twenty years ago, we think that fifty or sixty workers would have responded affirmatively. In Spring 1995 in these workshops, not a single participant raised his or her hand.

Their fears are not without some cause. Displacement rates—the percentage of workers with three or more years of tenure who have permanently lost their jobs—were no higher in the recession of 1991–92 than in the downturn of 1981–82. But displacements had become a much more general threat; they were now "less concentrated," a recent BLS study concludes, "in manufacturing and blue-collar jobs and more broadly distributed across industries and occupations."[29] It was much harder to believe than before that one's job was an island insulated from the waves of boom and bust.

Longitudinal data, based on surveys that follow the same workers from year to year, show how much employees' job security eroded during the 1980s. According to some important research recently conducted by Stephen J. Rose, chief economist of the National Commission for Employment Policy, those with "strong" employee job tenure, defined as those who changed employers only once during a ten year period, declined from 67 percent of workers in the 1970s to only 52 percent in the 1980s.[30] Relying on the same surveys, Peter Gottschalk and Robert Moffitt also find "an increase from the 1970s to the 1980s in the proportion of respondents reporting a change in main-job employer."[31]

And those who experienced greater insecurity paid the price. During the 1980s, according to Rose's study, those who were still able to maintain "strong" job stability watched their real annual earnings increase by nearly a third. By sharp contrast, those who experienced "weak" employer stability watched their earnings drop by an eighth.[32] Rose's findings, in the view of Anthony Carnevale, director of the National Commission for Employment Policy, "validate the popular view that job security is on the wane and that the price of embracing change is high. . . . The growing incongruity between measures of our overall positive economic performance and the declining economic security of individual workers suggests profound structural changes in the way our economy is producing and distributing the growing largesse."[33]

Since the mid-1970s, in short, wages have been falling, creating the need for supervision. And job security has to some degree been eroding, reinforcing the credibility of punishment if supervisors catch their workers slacking off. And thus we have the foundation of a basic argument that U.S. corporations need supervisory troops out on their posts, keeping their firms safe from the malingerers and laggards of the world. Not to mobilize those battalions would pose risks for the bottom line.

Let me be clear about what I have and have not argued up to this point. In an economy tending to rely on top-down systems of labor relations, such as were created in the United States after World War II, falling wages create strong pressures for an intensification of managerial supervision. *Given a wage squeeze*, the Stick becomes even more necessary than before.

But were there other sources of the rising bureaucratic burden in the United States, especially after the early 1970s, which had nothing to do with the wage squeeze? And how do I reconcile this link from falling wages to intensifying supervision if the bureaucratic burden *also* grew rapidly during the 1950s when real wages were rising?

Chapter 8 more formally considers alternative explanations of the size and growth of the bureaucratic burden both in the United States and across countries. It argues that an analysis that takes heed of the nature of labor-management relations does a fairly good job of explaining when and where the bureaucratic burden becomes heavy. This same kind of analysis, based on an understanding of the logic of top-down systems of labor-management control, can help explain the growth of the proportion of supervisory employees in the United States during both the Little Stick and the Big Stick periods. When and where the Stick Strategy applies, the argument goes, we can make sense out of the kinds of managerial structures that emerge. Where the Stick is wielded, supervision is essential.

For at least some readers of this book, these arguments may seem a bit alien and improbable. Many book readers tend to come from occupations where job performance is not directly monitored, where pride in your work or control over your product provide strong motivation on the job and a supervisor does not loom in the background. The closest many of us get to the intensively supervised work situations described here may be those messages we get at the beginning of some phone transactions: "Please be advised that in order to protect the quality of our product, this conversation may be monitored or recorded."

Millions of workers in less advantaged situations, however, experience intensive supervision nearly every day in every way. In outreach educational work with rank-and-file workers during the mid-1970s, some colleagues and I learned striking lessons when we encouraged our workshop participants to describe the social geography of their workplace. Who worked where? How were the work stations aligned? Where was the supervisor's station? We asked them to draw maps on butcher paper taped to the walls.

Time and time again, two patterns crystallized. First, the workers always knew who their informal work group leaders or shop stewards were and recognized that a lot of their social transactions flowed through that leader's work station. Second, and especially striking, it was almost uniformly the case that the company had placed the informal work group leader's or steward's work station as close as possible to the supervisor's. That way, with the work group's social life flowing through that node, the supervisor could vigilantly observe what was happening on the shop floor, catching subtle signs of group efforts to "work to speed" or slow down their pace. The workers knew where their supervisors were located. And they knew they were watching.

Indeed, this experience of direct supervisory observation seems to be fairly widespread among U.S. workers. In the Class Structure Surveys organized by Wisconsin sociologist Erik Olin Wright, to which I first referred in the previous chapter, we have some direct evidence of the shadows cast by the monitoring system. Among those private nonfarm workers who do *not* have supervisory or managerial responsibility, 94 percent report that it is "very easy" or "fairly easy" for their supervisors to check on their work.[34]

How frequently? Among those same workers, 40.2 percent report that their work is checked "more than once a day" or "at least once a day" while another 32.6 percent report that it is checked "several times a week" or "about once a week." (As evidence that this intensity of monitoring is not simply a function of all organizational bureaucracies, among nonmanagerial and nonsupervisory workers in *government* agencies, less than half as many workers report monitoring on a daily or more-than-daily basis.)

Supervision, in short, seems to be a prevailing experience for most workers in the United States. But to this point the logical argument has touched only on the strong probability that U.S. corporations would need legions of *front-line* supervisors, those with immediate responsibility for monitoring and goading workers. It doesn't yet address the need for layers and layers of supervisors and managers rising above that immediate front-line.

Once again, the basic logic of the argument is fairly simple: When supervisory systems are put in place, they acquire a hierarchical imperative all their own. Where authority is exercised from the top down, as I argued in the previous chapter, you need managers and supervisors to check on the supervisors. How can the top levels be confident that the supervisors won't conspire with the workers to slow the pace of work? Who is to guarantee that the front-line foremen and supervisors will stay on the workers' case?

This problem of keeping tabs on the supervisors, indeed, helps explain the emergence of bureaucratic management in U.S. corporations in the early part of the twentieth century. Under the earlier systems of management, foremen had held virtually unlimited authority to hire, fire, and promote workers. While this helped promote discipline, it also sometimes led to much too cozy a relationship between the foremen and their troops. The foreman became increasingly likely, as one observer noted in 1916, "to hire the friends of the employees of his department on the basis of friendship rather than fitness" and to "sell jobs" or "hold his favorites in soft assignments."[35]

Suspicion of that kind of relationship continued through the 1940s and early 1950s, when the top-down structures of managerial control took firm root in the United States. As a result, in systems of what Richard Edwards has termed "bureaucratic control" in U.S. corporations, supervisors and managers are themselves subjected to monitoring and supervision.[36] There are rules they must follow. And if they don't follow those rules, their promotion and pay may suffer. In these systems, Edwards notes that "those who were formally charged with the responsibility of evaluating—foremen, supervisors, and managers—were themselves subjected to bureaucratic control. . . . Sanctions were still applied by the foremen and supervisors, of course, but their application was subject to review by . . . higher levels of supervision. . . ."[37]

This supervision of the supervisors shows up in the data from the Class Structure Surveys. Among employees with supervisory or managerial authority, few are free from their bosses peering over their shoulder: Roughly 23 percent report that their work is checked "more than once a day" or "about once a day" while close to 40 percent report monitoring "several times a week" or "about once a week." Only 15 percent respond that their work is "never" checked." If you rely on top-down hierarchies, you have to check up on everyone, not just production and nonsupervisory employees on the shop and office floor.

Once these systems of supervision up and down the ladder have been established, finally, there are strong tendencies for them to become increasingly centralized, with power flowing from the top to the bottom but little trickling up from the line. In order to maintain their leverage over subordinates, those at the top find they need to hold the reins tightly and keep their information close to the chest. Military analogies are pervasive when these kinds of hierarchical systems of corporate control are evaluated. Don Petersen, president of Ford in the 1980s, described the company's structure before they moved toward greater employee involvement: "Ford had a very top-down management system, with orders from on high, like an Army command system."[38] In his classic study of the logic of bureaucracies, French sociologist Michel Crozier writes:[39]

> the power to make decisions and to interpret and complete the rules, as well as the power to change the rules or to institute new ones, will tend to grow farther and farther away from the field where those rules will be carried out. If the pressure for impersonality is strong, such a tendency toward centralization cannot be resisted. . . . The price the organization has to pay for it is still greater rigidity. People who make decisions cannot have direct firsthand knowledge of the problems they are called upon to solve. On the other hand, the field officers who know these problems can never have the power necessary to adjust, to experiment, and to innovate.

AND SO we have the basic argument that where wage growth and job security do not provide clear motivation for employees, conflictual systems arise featuring top-heavy bureaucratic structures. Some comparative international data appear to confirm this basic linkage between conflictual labor-management systems and top-heavy corporations.

In one recent study, for example, I explore evidence of this connection across the advanced economies.[40] Echoing many other studies, first of all, I find clear indication of differences in the character of labor-management relations. Compared to most other economies, for example, the United States provides far less employment security—with no statutory provisions for mandatory advance notification of plant shutdowns or mandatory severance pay in cases of plant closures—and features one of the lowest proportions of unionized workers and very decentralized bargaining relationships.

Because many of the characteristics of economy-wide labor-management systems tend to vary together—if a system features one kind of employment insecurity, it will be likely to feature another—it is possible to construct composite indices approximately measuring where labor-management systems fall along the spectrum ranging from conflictual to cooperative. One such indicator I have constructed, based on the quantitative technique of factor analysis, ranks the advanced economies on a standardized cooperation index varying around zero.[41] Not surprisingly, given our customary expectations, Sweden has the highest positive score on the index, suggesting the *most* cooperative labor-management relations, while the United States has the lowest negative score, indicating the *least* cooperative relations.

Taking advantage of this simple measure of the cooperative character of labor-management systems, finally, I find a close relationship between an economy's score on this cooperation index and its Bureaucratic Burden, relying on the measure introduced in the previous chapter, the percentage of non-farm employees working in managerial and administrative occupations. Figure 3.1 illustrates this connection for the same twelve advanced countries whose real wage growth and bureaucratic burdens we have already examined in the previous chapters. Referring back to the earlier discussion on countries thought to exemplify the cooperative and conflictual approaches to labor relations, respectively, I have labeled on the graph the points for the three cooperative archetypes—Germany, Japan and Sweden—and the three conflictual representatives—the United States, Canada, and the United Kingdom.

The bottom axis of the figure displays the cooperation index, ranging from -3.18 for the U.S. to +1.85 for Sweden. The vertical axis measures the Bureaucratic Burden, exactly the same measure we explored in Chapter 2, for 1980. (I use 1980 here because the data on which the cooperation index is based also come from around the early 1980s.) As the plots seem to indicate, the *more* cooperative the labor-management system (toward the right of the

FIGURE 3.1
More Cooperation, Fewer Bosses?
Percent administrative-managerial employment and cooperation index

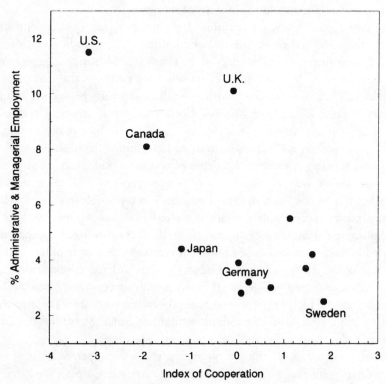

Sources: See text and notes.

horizontal axis), the *lighter* is the bureaucratic burden (toward the bottom of the vertical axis).[42] As the pattern in the graph suggests, indeed, the correlation between the two variables is -0.72 (statistically significant at 1%), indicative of an inverse association between cooperation and bureaucracies. More cooperation, fewer bosses.[43]

Pushing for More at the Top

In the late 1970s a group of twenty-one experts on corporate management were convened to discuss the problems U.S. corporations were facing in the marketplace. They were asked a variety of questions about the orientations and priorities of business leadership. At one point they were asked about management's relative emphasis on company profits or managerial control. When presented with the statement, "In many cases control and power are more important to managers than profits or productivity," all of these experts agreed or agreed strongly.[44] In the view of this group of experts, at least, managers paid more attention to their own bottom lines than to the company's.

This common observation about U.S. corporations holds the key to the second linkage necessary for the core argument of this chapter. I have just traced the connection running from the "slow-wage-growth strategy" to top-heavy corporate bureaucracies. What about the connection running in the opposite direction? Why would top-heavy corporations tend to create downward pressure on production-workers' earnings?

Here, too, the argument is fairly direct. Once top-down bureaucratic hierarchies are in place, they tend to acquire an expansionary and costly dynamic all of their own, which in turn pushes down production workers' earnings. This dynamic has two important dimensions, one involving the *size* of the bureaucratic apparatus and the other involving managerial and supervisory *salaries*.

Let us first consider the number of managerial and supervisory employees. On the basis of the discussion in the preceding section, we might suppose that corporations would hire only as many managers and supervisors as were absolutely necessary to accomplish their warranted tasks of management and supervision. The criteria of profitability and productivity would be their guide. If at the margin an additional manager did not contribute more to the firm's revenues than it cost to hire him or her, there would be no additional hire.

But firm profitability is not the only guide to corporate decisions. Another crucial factor comes into play: the power and prestige of individual managers in the corporate hierarchy. In large bureaucratic organizations, an executive's rank and individual performance are not the only determinants of salary and promotion. Another clear correlate of executive power, prestige and success is the number of his or her subordinates. The larger the number of employees working under an individual executive, especially in direct staff positions, the greater his or her clout. It becomes a kind of numbers game. In their important study of U.S. corporate bureaucracies, Mark Green and John F. Berry conclude that "top executives often act on the belief that, in American business, bigger is better." Because the path to success is so competitive and insecure, the structures of corporate power often provoke managers "to find safety in numbers and surround themselves with supportive staffers."[45] And not everyone can continue climbing up the corporate ladder; there are only so many places at the top. "One way to reduce turnover or postpone disappointment," Robert M. Tomasko observes, "is to add extra rungs to the ladder."[46]

The drive for better information at the top also fuels this expansionary dynamic. When decisions are made close to the bottom of the hierarchy, those making decisions already have most of the information they need. But when decisions are concentrated at the top, high-level managers must acquire what they don't already possess. Their appetite for information adds additional layers. MIT economist Lester Thurow writes:[47]

> [W]ith the onset of the new information technologies, ordinary bosses could implement what extraordinary bosses had always preached. Bosses could do a lot more bossing, just as doctors could do a lot more doctoring.
>
> To do so, however, one had to build up enormous information bureaucracies. Information could be gotten, but only at the cost of adding a lot of white-collar workers to the system. . . .
>
> To the boss, more information seems like a free good. He orders it from subordinates, and the cost of acquiring it appears on the budgets of his subordinates. Subordinates in turn can neither refuse to provide the requested information nor know if the information is valuable enough to justify the costs of its acquisition. . . . Essentially, both bosses and subordinates are imprisoned in standard operating procedures that create an institutional set of blinders.

Some of these characteristics of hierarchical corporate bureaucracies became evident in the 1930s and 1940s, as those bureaucracies first took shape. By the 1950s and 1960s, economists were finally beginning to take their internal logic seriously. Among many economists who have explored that logic, Oliver E. Williamson of the University of California–Berkeley was one of the first to pick up on this dynamic, writing in the 1960s:[48]

> staff is a source of job *security*, prestige, and flexibility as well. . . . That staffs have a tendency, sometimes legitimate and certainly natural, to grow has been widely observed. What may appear originally as a legitimate expansion, however, can, in the absence of binding constraints, easily lead to a general condition of excessive staff through the firm.

In this respect, corporate culture recalls some of the logic of the feudal political economy in Western Europe in the Middle Ages. In that culture, where there was no clear market test of the power of an individual feudal lord, one of the most important determinants of a lord's power and prestige was the size of his manorial retinue. The more bailiffs and wardens and servants and clerks working under his lordship, the more power he could claim over his serfs and the more prestige he could garner with neighboring lords. The preeminent French medieval historian Georges Duby summarizes this dynamic:[49]

> In a society still primitive, and at a time when food supplies were limited, the "man of power" showed himself first of all as the man who could always eat as much as he wished. He was also open handed, the man who provided others with food, and the yardstick of his prestige was the number of men whom he fed, and the size of his "household". Around the great lay and religious leaders congregated vast retinues of relatives, friends, people receiving patronage . . . , [and] guests welcomed with liberality who would spread tales of the greatness of a house. . . . This way of life assumed housekeeping on a gigantic scale. . . . The springs of wealth had to be inexhaustible. It was the privilege of the noble at all times to avoid any appearance of shortage.

Similarly, in U.S. corporate culture as it crystallized during the 1950s and 1960s, with bureaucracies so large and market power so strong that the pressures of competition were not so manifest, executives could enhance their power and prestige by, as it were, expanding their retinues. Feudal baronies prospered and grew in the European countryside in the eleventh–thirteenth centuries. And the equivalent of feudal baronies prospered and grew in U.S. corporations in the postwar period. Reflecting on this baronial culture in the early 1980s, an officer of Chemical Bank concluded: "The way you got ahead was getting more people under you than your rival had, which created more bureaucracy, of course."[50]

This dynamic creates a pressure for managerial ranks to expand even to greater size than might otherwise be justified by the criteria of profitability.[51] When General Motors undertook in the mid-1980s a painful review of its poor market performance, for example, one central conclusion seemed inescapable: "Too many people [were] assigned to the same programs."[52] As one management consultant reported in the early 1980s about his firm's analyses of U.S. corporate bureaucracies, "We normally find thirty percent to forty percent waste."[53] Management guru Peter F. Drucker observes wryly, "A certain amount of fat may be needed; but few [American] businesses suffer from too little fat."[54] In his review for the American Management Association of the problem in the mid-1980s, Robert M. Tomasko concluded: "Very few companies . . . set out to create organizational structures with an overabundance of staff people or layers of management. But, as these examples [in his study] have illustrated, bureaucratic bloat seems more common than not."[55]

The second dimension of the expansionary dynamic involves managerial salaries. All else being equal, of course, managers would rather be paid more than less and would prefer that their salaries grow as rapidly as possible. Many top managers have sufficient autonomy to reward themselves with handsome salary increases from year to year. And if raises for their middle-level managers don't follow, substantial incentive problems will.

As a result of strong upward pressures on managerial salaries, a trickle-down effect is likely to dribble through the ranks, with increases in lower-level salaries necessary in order to maintain incentives and to encourage teamwork. Fueled by this kind of dynamic, Tomasko observes, "the drive for greater compensation will continue to inflate the management bulge, making it very difficult for a company to be streamlined."[56] In other words, the effort to lift some boats will contribute to a rising tide.

Consider the factors affecting managerial salaries. It is certainly true, on the one hand, that those in the managerial hierarchy expect good performance to lead to pay increases. According to the 1991 Class Structure Survey, among managers and supervisors in the nonfarm private sector more than four-fifths report their view that it is "probably true" or "definitely true" that "if people in a job like yours do good work, they'd be pretty sure to get a pay raise."

But patronage also matters. As one management authority concludes about bureaucratic tendencies in U.S. corporations, "Advancement is slow and based upon seniority, personal loyalty and loyalty to the corporate form of culture."[57] Among the same group of managerial and supervisory employees in the Class Structure Survey, more than half think it is "probably" or "definitely" true that "a sure way to get a raise in a job like yours is to have close personal connections to people who are important. . . . " This proportion is roughly as high, to put it in perspective, as those who view job seniority as a ticket to a jump in pay.

So we can add a dynamic toward increasing managerial salaries to the previous imperative toward expanding managerial ranks. If we multiply salaries times employment, we arrive at the total amount of compensation paid to managers and supervisors. If both components of that product are likely to expand, then total managerial compensation is likely to expand by the force of simple arithmetic . . . whether or not the corporate bottom line would justify such growth.

But won't the stockholders, represented by the board of directors, step in to curb bureaucratic excess? Won't the forces of competition help keep this managerial gluttony in check?

No and yes.

No, in part, because managers have considerable autonomy from owners and market pressures within large corporations. The debate is rich and ever growing about *how much* authority management retains in comparison with stockholders and the board of directors.[58] But many agree that managers have considerable power within the corporation and that the bottom line is not the only factor affecting managerial decisions. Contrasting the prevailing economic model of firm profit maximization with the newer "behavioral" model of managerial control, Oliver E. Williamson notes:[59]

> [The traditional model] requires that managers choose to operate the firm in a stewardship sense of attending to the stockholders' best interest by maximizing profits. The behavioral model proposes that managers operate the firm in the only fashion consistent with the assumption of self-interest seeking—in their *own* best interests. . . . And the greater the degree of managerial autonomy, the more likely are these expansionary dynamics to take firm root.

Some studies have confirmed, indeed, that the proportion of administrative personnel in corporations, what I am calling the bureaucratic burden, tends to be higher when the separation between management and owners is relatively wider.[60] Others have found some evidence that the more successful the firm and therefore the more likely that owners will relax in the vigilance of their guardianship, the greater the likelihood of relative managerial autonomy.[61]

And *yes*, to some degree, it will be true that the guardians of profitability will seek to protect corporate profits from erosion by an excessive and constantly soaring tab for managerial compensation. Stockholders and directors and creditors will not sit still and watch profits suffer for long. Or outside predators will sense a prime opportunity for profitable cost-cutting and make a move to acquire an obviously top-heavy corporation. Where current owners have considerable clout or outside buyers acquire leverage, they will presumably use that clout to force managers to toe the line. It would appear, indeed, that many of the mergers and buyouts so prevalent during the 1980s served at least partly to reassert owner interests and curb managerial prerogatives. Based on his careful review of this process, Michael Useem concludes:[62]

> Mindful of the [threat], incumbent managements moved during the mid- to late 1980s to improve stockholder returns by paring the work force and cutting other costs. Corporate acquisitions and leveraged buyouts brought new management teams to the fore where others had seemingly fallen short. The resulting restructuring reached a large proportion of the nation's major companies, and the opening of the market for corporate control brought a significant fraction of companies more directly under the immediate oversight of ownership interests.

Richard E. Caves and Matthew B. Krepps also find at least suggestive evidence that the waves of outside mergers and buyouts in the mid-1980s were associated with at least marginal reductions in the proportion of nonproduction employees in manufacturing.[63]

But this doesn't necessarily mean that the expansionary dynamic will be kept completely in check. Stockholders and directors and creditors care about profits. If room for expanding managerial compensation can be created by cutting into other costs in the corporate ledgers, then both the managers and the owners can scratch where they itch.

During the long postwar boom, when large American corporations successfully roamed the globe in search of markets and profits, there was plenty of room for expansion across the board. Corporate output and productivity increased rapidly enough to allow substantial increases in all of the major items on the balance sheet—production compensation, supervisory compensation, interest, profits, and, financed by profits, dividends, and investment. Where the demands of major claimants outstripped the rate of growth of output and productivity, the rising costs were typically passed on to consumers through price increases. Leonard Woodcock, president of the United Auto Workers late in this period, was once asked if the union's wage demands were excessive. He replied patiently that the Big Three auto companies had a formula for determining the price of their autos and that wages were simply factored into this formula. In effect, he insisted, as one management observer reflects on the story, "such costs were not excessive if they could be passed on to the public, and they were."[64]

However, since the 1960s corporations have faced tougher choices. As productivity growth has slowed, corporate budgets have less easily afforded such expansionary costs. And with intensifying global competition, it has become much more dangerous than before to try to pass these costs on to the consumer through higher prices.

A zero-sum game has ensued. As a result, the continuing growth of managerial and supervisory compensation depended on other sources—interest or dividends or investment or production compensation. They couldn't all expand at once; the continually rising costs couldn't be passed along.

Interest and dividends were sacrosanct. Because internally generated profits were declining from the mid-1960s, corporations were forced to search for funds for expansion from sources outside the firm, through equity or credit markets. In order to raise money effectively in the form of equity, they needed to ensure an established record of steady dividend flows. And in order to be able to reassure potential lenders in credit markets, firms had to be able to guarantee interest payments. And so, dividends and interest payments were protected against incursions either from declining profits or expanding managerial compensation. Between 1973 and 1989 (two business cycle peaks), for example, dividends as a share of gross domestic product (GDP) in the nonfinancial corporate business (NFCB) rose from 2.8 to 3.5 percent and corporate interest payments increased from 3.0 to 5.0 percent.[65]

If managerial compensation was to continue to find room for expansion, therefore, two remaining targets remained vulnerable: investment and production-worker compensation. Both targets got blasted.

Net fixed nonresidential investment—spending on machines and factories and offices which make the economy more productive in the longer run—declined from 4.4 percent of GDP in 1973 to only half that much, 2.2 percent, in 1989.[66] Investment declined over this period for a number of reasons: slower growth in demand, for example, and record-high interest rates in the 1980s. One additional and crucial reason was declining profits, the nonfinancial corporate before-tax profit rate fell from its postwar peak of 15.0 percent in 1966 to 10.4 percent in 1973 and further to 8.7 percent in 1989.[67]

And one of the important reasons for declining profits, especially after the early 1970s, appears to have been the continuing push for expanding managerial compensation. Business observers in the 1980s came increasingly to talk about the shortsightedness of corporate leaders—their short time horizons, their concern for the quarterly bottom line, their neglect of the long-term future of their enterprises. But something else was going on besides a change in psychology in the corporate boardrooms. Among many other pressures, the push for ever-increasing managerial compensation was operating at full throttle. As long as dividends and interest payments were protected, boards of directors didn't seem to mind so much that funds left over for investment were shrinking.

The damage on profits was important. But the real hit fell on compensation for production workers. In an era or economy featuring broader and stronger unions, workers presumably could have resisted this squeeze from steadily expanding bureaucratic compensation. But since the early 1970s, workers have been pushed increasingly on the defensive. The decline in union representation accelerated. Workers faced their increasingly aggressive employers more and more on their own. With the threat of unemployment becoming ever more immediate, could they be expected to have stood firm and to have resisted the management offensive?

And so there has been a massive income shift, within the total category of wage-and-salary employee compensation, from production and nonsupervisory earnings to nonproduction and supervisory salaries. Figure 3.2 illustrates this redistribution. For each of the business cycle peaks since the early 1970s and for 1993, the most recent year for which data were available at the time of writing, it graphs private nonfarm employee compensation as a share of national income—the total height of the bars—and shows as well the portions going to production and supervisory employees within that sector—the light and dark portions of the bars respectively.[68]

In 1973, 40.1 percent of total national income went to private nonfarm production workers while the rest of total employee compensation, 16.2 percent of national income, was paid to supervisory employees. By the end of the period top-level employees had immensely increased their share, from 16.2 percent to 24.1 percent of national income. And this growth came

FIGURE 3.2
A Shift in Compensation
Compensation of production and supervisory employees as shares of national income, United States, 1973–93

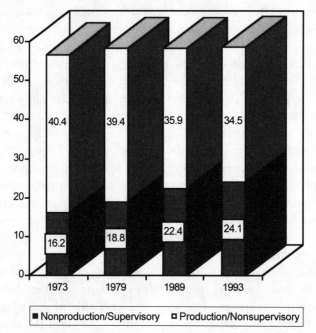

Sources: See text and notes.

almost entirely at the expense of production workers. Since total employee compensation as a share of national income scarcely budged, moving from 56.6 percent in 1973 to 58.6 percent in 1993, it was workers on the shop and office floor who bore the brunt of the continuing upward march of supervisory compensation. Dividends and interest payments survived the push. Production worker earnings did not.

Many different kinds of enterprises make up these trends in compensation. Do the same tendencies show up if we confine ourselves to a more uniform set of establishments? Consider data for manufacturing. There, too, compensation shifted greatly from production to nonproduction employees. Between 1973 and 1992, the nonproduction share of total compensation increased by eleven percentage points. Not surprisingly, the biggest portion of the shift—nearly seven percentage points—took place during the 1980s.[69]

This income shift is one of the best kept secrets of the U.S. economy. Many economists are fond of pointing to the stability of factor income shares—the relative proportions of income going to workers' earnings and to profits. They note that total employee compensation and profits have remained fairly constant as a share of total national income—shifting by only one or two percentage points over the postwar period. This stability shows up in the total height of the bars in Figure 3.2, which stay within the range between 56.6 and 58.6 percent. "It is remarkable how constant labor's share has been over the last 150 years," remarks Harvard economist Lawrence Katz. "This is one of the strongest regularities of advanced economies."[70] But in their complacency about the "stability" of income shares, economists have tended to overlook by far the most important distributional shift on the factor income side in the entire history of the postwar economy.

We can put this distributional shift in perspective. How big a shift does it represent? With what can we compare it? In the two decades from 1973 to 1993, total transfer payments from the Social Security system, about which such continuing alarms have been sounded, increased their share of national income by 3.3 percentage points. With escalating borrowing and soaring interest rates fattening the coffers of the financial sector, total interest payments as a percent of national income increased by 2.5 percentage points between 1973 and 1993. The defense buildup during the 1980s, another source of widespread alarm, resulted in a shift of 1.1 percentage points between 1979 and 1989. All of these trends, the focus of considerable attention and public debate, seem to pale when set beside the compensation shift to employees at the top. Over the same twenty years, as the figure shows, nonproduction and supervisory compensation as a percentage of national income *increased by almost eight percentage points*, from 16.2 to 24.1 percent—almost two and a half times the Social Security shift, more than three times that for interest payments, more than seven times the reallocation resulting from the defense buildup. Where is the attention and public debate over that massive transfer? And where is the proper concern about the impact of the push for more at the top on the persistent squeeze of production-workers' wages?

This is not to argue that the push for greater compensation among nonproduction and supervisory employees is the only or even necessarily the most important source of the wage squeeze. Nor that managers and supervisors are the only kinds of employees enjoying the stream of compensation in the "nonproduction and supervisory" category. For our purposes in this chapter, I intend much more simply to suggest that the internal dynamics of top-heavy bureaucracies in U.S. corporations have tended to contribute toward downward pressure on production-worker compensation. Without that pressure from the top, one could infer, the impact of the wage squeeze might not have been so severe.

Horse and Carriage

Thus we get the basic argument that stagnant wages contribute to the creation and reproduction of top-heavy corporate bureaucracies *and* that top-heavy corporate bureaucracies contribute to strong downward pressure on wages.

These are simple but strong hypotheses. It is not at all easy to test them, since there are many influences on wage growth and many influences on bureaucratic staffing requirements. But I ought to be able to show evidence that the two characteristics are at least associated with each other. The next task is to demonstrate the connection between stagnant wages and bloated corporations, to find evidence in one or another domain that there is an inverse relationship between the two: Where the Stick Strategy prevails, the bureaucratic burden should be relatively high and real wage growth relatively stagnant. Where a more cooperative approach to labor management holds sway, the bureaucratic burden should be substantially lower and real wage growth considerably more rapid.

It's not easy to find evidence of this relationship within the United States because the Stick Strategy is so pervasive among firms and across industries. Data on individual firms are difficult to come by. If we look in the aggregate across industries, most industries share a common sociopolitical environment and most firms within those industries manifest a common dedication to discipline by the Stick. There is not yet enough variation in the institutional setting in the United States to make the search for a broad spectrum ranging from cooperative to conflictual conditions very meaningful.

A test across the advanced countries seems more important. Once we turn to the comparative international terrain, as already noted, we find dramatic differences among the developed economies in the character of their labor-management relations. Some appear to rely on the stick and some depend on the carrot. With such a wider range of circumstances, do we find that stagnant wage growth is associated with top-heavier corporate bureaucracies?

Figure 3.3 presents some basic data exploring that relationship. It covers the twelve countries for which we have the best comparative data on wage growth, the same twelve countries reviewed in Chapter 1. The horizontal axis presents the same data as in Figure 1.2, the average annual real wage change for production workers in manufacturing between 1973 and 1989. (A more limited analysis of real wage change for the narrower interval between 1979 and 1989 yields a similar picture.) The vertical axis represents the same measure of the bureaucratic burden first encountered in Chapter 2, the percentage of total nonfarm employment working in administrative and managerial occupations in 1980. (I use 1980 here, rather than 1989 as in Figure 2.1, in order to provide a measure for the level of managerial burden that lies *in the middle* of the time period being examined.) As in Figure 3.1, I have labeled here the six countries that many take as representatives of the conflictual and cooperative approaches.

Except for the single striking case of the United Kingdom, there is a fairly strong negative association, as hypothesized, between the bureaucratic burden and real wage growth. As anticipated, the United States stands out for its swollen bureaucratic burden *and* for its virtually flat real wage growth. If the

FIGURE 3.3

Corporate Bureaucracies and Real Wage Growth

Percent managerial and administrative employment, 1980; percent change, production-worker real wage, manufacturing, 1973–89

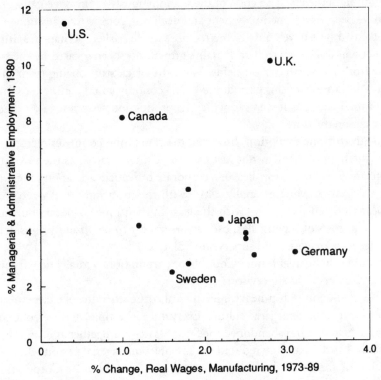

Sources: See text and notes.

United Kingdom is removed momentarily on the grounds that it seems to be such an outlier, the simple correlation coefficient between the two variables is –0.78 (statistically significant at 1%). (Even with the United Kingdom included, the simple correlation is –0.50—still statistically significant at 1%.)

It may make the most sense, further, to think of the countries as falling into two groupings—rather than falling on a continuum. One group, including Germany, Japan, and Sweden and six other countries, clusters in the lower right corner of the graph. (The one country in this group with relatively slower real wage growth is Denmark; many economists view Denmark's system of labor-management as a kind of hybrid case, with a relatively unsuccessful mix of cooperative and conflictual features that result in relatively higher inflation and unemployment than in most of the more cooperative examples.) The United States and Canada, two of the three more adversarial economies represented here, lie in the upper left. Only the United Kingdom departs substantially from this pattern.

Why is the United Kingdom so anomalous? Consider the following observations: although the United Kingdom does feature sharply conflictual labor relations, as befitting its high relative bureaucratic burden, many of its unions have remained fairly strong and have been able to sustain rapid real wage growth nonetheless. The costs of these anomalously rapid wage gains appear to have been rising unemployment and declining competitive advantage. The chickens might have come home to roost much earlier, perhaps resulting in slower real wage growth, had Britain's growth not been greased by the steady flow from its North Sea oil fields. With the black stuff oozing from the sea throughout most of this period, the U.K. economy could continue to live beyond the means, as it were, to which its production system would otherwise have condemned it.[71]

With this one exception, however, the remaining countries seem to support the hypothesis. It is not just that the United States has the slowest real wage growth and the top-heaviest corporate bureaucracies among these leading economies. More generally, those with the most rapid real wage growth appear to be able to get by with the least burdensome corporate bureaucracies. The costs of buying all those carrots appear to be offset by considerable savings in managerial and supervisory salaries.

Could it happen at home? Could U.S. corporations actually do without all those managers and supervisors?

The addiction to top-heavy, hierarchical corporate bureaucracies runs deep and wide in U.S. managerial culture. Every once in a while, however, one comes across a firm that has abandoned the Stick Strategy altogether and, as one of its rewards, has dramatically reduced the size of its managerial personnel.

One of the more dramatic such examples is the Nucor Corporation, a major manufacturer of steel and other metal products. This is no corner grocery, no fledgling cabinet-makers cooperative. In 1994 Nucor ranked 379 on the Fortune 500 list of the largest U.S. industrial corporations. Its 1994 sales were a hair under $3 billion, its assets just over $2 billion, and its profits $227 million—up 83.5 percent from the previous year.[72]

Nucor rose to prominence as a steel-maker in the 1980s.[73] From the beginning its top management showed a maverick streak. They distrusted corporate bureaucracies. F. Kenneth Iverson, Nucor's CEO, sought to distance himself from what he felt were the inertial, brain-dead managers encamped in the headquarters of his Big Steel rivals. "These monstrous bureaucracies are unwieldy to say the least," Iverson says. "Don't get me wrong in my criticisms of Big Steel. My argument is with all of corporate America."[74]

From the beginning, Nucor sought to keep its managerial bureaucracy as small as it possibly could. As it grew to Fortune 500 size, Iverson refused to expand their ranks or even to move out of the small, cramped, rented office space in which they had begun, the company biographer reports, "because he was afraid of self-congratulation and because he didn't want any more managers at the company. He literally slammed the door on management." And so, the managerial structure at Nucor looks leaner, sparer, more skeletal than in perhaps any other major U.S. corporation.

How do they do it? By the logic of the argument in this chapter, they have had no choice but to use the carrot with their employees. At the least, the employees needed strong wage incentives and some kind of assurance of employment security to feel motivated to manage themselves. Richard Preston describes some of the basic conditions of employment at Nucor:

> The Nucor workers earned pay that was double or triple the average laborer's pay in the small towns where Nucor built its mills. Nucor gave its employees their bonuses every week, so that they did not have to wait around for the end of the year to see what kind of spare change the management might chuck in their direction, after the management had decided upon its own bonuses. Iverson gave the Nucor production workers a steady ten percent of the Nucor Corporation's pretax profits every year for their retirement plans.

There were no contractual guarantees of job security, but practice amounted to the same thing. "[Iverson] did not lay anybody off, although he never promised not to lay people off," Preston writes. "Iverson had managed to get through twenty-five years in the steel business without a layoff. Except once, when a Nucor general manager laid off forty Nucor workers. Iverson ordered the manager to rehire the workers, and soon afterward he fired the manager. The message was not lost on the company's managers. There has not been a layoff since then."

The result of these carrots has been effective employee self-management, even though they don't glorify it with any such fashionable term. Production employees, skilled and semi-skilled alike, work in teams of about thirty employees. They guide themselves and police themselves. They work hard. "The pressure to keep up production comes from the rules," Preston concludes, "and the rules are enforced by the production team itself." The managerial philosophy seems clear. As one project manager explains, "I understand that at the [other Big Steel companies], the engineers and operational people are terribly frustrated. They don't get a role in decisions. They are merely *given* a project. The board of directors and a few high-ranking managers of the company make all the decisions, and then those decisions are thrust on the operational people." Summarizing his view of the role of management at Nucor, Iverson explains: "When there's a deep-seated conflict between management and labor, it's because of autocratic management practices," he argues. "A manager says to himself, 'I'm going to make the guy do it.' Not 'I'm going to help him do his job.' You can't *make* a person do something."

Nucor is not necessarily a model for all U.S. companies to follow. For one thing, its employees are not unionized and the management is strongly anti-union; Iverson and other executives believe that unions are not sufficiently flexible to tolerate the Nucor style of management. The example of the United Auto Workers collaboration with Toyota and GM at their experimental NUMMI plant in Fremont, California, among numerous examples, would seem to indicate they're wrong.[75] Experience with unions in many European countries also seems to cast doubt on the company's prejudices. Unions could conceivably support the Nucor style, not oppose it.

Another U.S. corporate example illustrates this possibility of union-management synergy. Magma Copper, headquartered in Tucson, Arizona, is not as large as Nucor, but it's not a Mom and Pop store either.[76] In 1994 its sales totaled $890 million, its profits $87 million. It employed roughly 5,000 workers.[77]

In the mid-1980s Magma was a wreck. The company's relations with its workers and unions teemed with conflict. It carried a huge debt resulting from its spinoff from the previous parent company. Its unit mining costs were among the highest in the industry. And, reeling from low copper prices, Magma was showing bright red on the bottom line.

As with Nucor, the chief executive played a key role in its transformation. J. Burgess Winter assumed the helm of Magma in August 1988. Facing a clear crisis in the company's future, he decided in 1989 to explore whether the company could forge a completely different kind of relationship with its unions, one in which the workers and unions assumed a real partnership with management and effectively joint responsibility for the success of the company. Many other copper companies had been trying to get rid of their unions. "I didn't see the need to do that," Miller reported in an interview. "If you can work within the framework of a union, you can accomplish a hell of a lot. There's a structure there for communications."[78] After three years of careful, sometimes halting, always delicate discussions consuming an estimated 300,000 man-hours, and after the company invested $3 million in the process, Magma and its unions, led by the Steelworkers, signed in 1991 what *Fortune* called a "revolutionary labor agreement."[79] The contract was to last for fifteen years, with no-strike guarantees for at least seven. It formally created joint labor-management "work-redesign" teams to explore ways of improving productivity and joint "problem-solving" teams to deal with contract disputes, with the parties agreeing to submit contract disputes on economic issues to binding arbitration. As William H. Miller reports in *Industry Week*, "labor experts suggest the contract may be the first to provide for both teams *and* arbitration."[80]

The contract, though obviously important, came more as a culmination than as an initiation of the transformational process at Magma. Workers and management had already participated in intensive efforts to change work relations, improve productivity, and transform a culture of conflict into a reality of cooperation.

In one of the major projects, a 150-member labor-management team worked for months to design new methods for mining ore from a new site, aiming to turn a questionable venture into a viable operation. "The company had spent more than $150 million trying to come up with new technology to develop the [new site]," Miller reports, "but had abandoned the project."[81] Within a year, by deploying new ways of organizing production and reorganizing job categories, the team had succeeded in designing an operation that then achieved productivity roughly two-thirds higher than the previous best returns at the firm's principal underground mine.

By 1995, at the time of writing, Magma has become a proselyte of participatory and cooperative methods of labor management. And it has the record to justify its zeal. Over the seven years of the firm's effort to reconstruct its ways of doing business, CEO Winter reported in 1995, "productivity has increased by 86%, production costs have decreased by a dramatic forty cents per pound, production has increased by 70%, safety has improved to award-winning levels, absenteeism and grievances have gone down dramatically, and our stock price has increased by over 400%."[82] In 1994, though its revenues ranked only 20th within the top firms in the metals sector, its rate of return on revenues ranked 2nd.[83]

As with Nucor, the carrot could only work if the workers were provided clear and manifest incentives and protections. In exchange for the union accepting limited wage increases, the company contractually agreed to grant the workers 40 percent of all money saved as a result of productivity improvements; in 1993, the agreement earned the workers an average annual bonus of $4,700.[84] As with Nucor, there are no explicit contractual guarantees of job security, but both management and labor have understood that job redesign and production reorganization must build upon the existing workforce rather than shrinking or replacing it. Without the productivity improvements, the largest mine was targeted to close within a couple of years. It now thrives.

And with the carrots in place, indeed, Magma has been able to pare its supervisory battalions. The company has reduced its organizational structure from eight levels of managerial and supervisory hierarchy to only four. "Thanks to improved labor relations," the *Wall Street Journal* reports, "Magma has eliminated bosses from many shifts and crews. . . . The elimination of some supervisors [has] lowered management costs."[85]

CEO Winter believes that the Magma experience frontally challenges many of what he calls the "myths" that guide prevailing corporate practice in the United States:

• "It is perhaps one of the most basic of management myths that *management must lead*. . . . [But] one of the advantages of having the [joint labor-management strategic planning group] develop the organization's strategic goals is that the people who are actually responsible for the accomplishment of declared goals have invented them, own them, and are aligned with them."

• "[Our previous] management held to the truth that the only way *to deal with unions was with force* because we had not invented any other way of being with each other. . . . But we have discovered that this too is a myth. . . . In case after case, it is the unions and workers who have contributed, in full partnership with management, to the many breakthroughs in productivity."

• "It is a well accepted tenet of management that the *hierarchy of authority* is an essential element in an organization's formula for success. . . . We have found some structure is necessary, but much less than the traditional. Rigid hierarchies are the corporate cholesterol of organizations. . . .We increasingly rely on the use of teams and we frequently bypass protocol to get the job done quicker and better." [86]

Union leaders at Magma appear to share Winter's enthusiasm. "I was one who thought the union had laid down with the enemy," comments Manuel Medina, president of the Steelworkers local. "But it's [been] like the Berlin Wall coming down."[87] "We've already tapped vast resources," reports Don Shelton, now union coordinator of the Joint Union-Management Cooperation Committee. "But we can go far beyond what's in our heads now. . . . How can other companies and other unions miss this kind of boat?"[88]

Nucor and Magma are important examples, not because they should be held out as *the* models of corporate transformation, but much more simply because they so dramatically illustrate the opposite of the typical U.S. corporate experience. The wage squeeze and the bureaucratic burden go together in most U.S. corporations. At Nucor and Magma, like the horse and carriage, strong employee incentives and reduced corporate management go together. You don't have to live in another country, or work for a Japanese employer based in the United States to escape the Stick Strategy on the job.

What About the "High-Performance Workplace"?

The argument that the Stick Strategy dominates production practices in the United States runs counter to a widespread popular perception that U.S. corporations are transforming themselves, creating a softer, fuzzier workplace providing much greater employee involvement and stronger worker incentives. Within the new innovative corporation, one celebrant trumpeted in the mid-1980s, "a wave of 'participative leadership' is rising to enlist the commitment of a new breed of employees who seek self-fulfillment."[89] *Business Week*, often the forecaster of which way the corporate winds are blowing, announced in a 1994 Special Report:[90]

> Mobility. Empowerment. Teams. Cross-training. Virtual offices. Telecommuting. Reengineering. Restructuring. Delayering. Outsourcing. Contingency. If the buzzwords don't sound familiar, they should: They are changing your life.

The last decade, perhaps more than any other time since the advent of mass production, has witnessed a profound redefinition of the way we work. . . . The new compact between company and worker dismisses paternalism and embraces self-reliance.

The world of work is definitely changing. Some changes, in some companies, seem promising. But there are two problems with the prevailing celebration: The extent of adoption of truly "high performance workplaces" is narrower and more superficial than often advertised; we have not yet witnessed a "revolution" in U.S. labor relations. And, at the very same time that some employers are abandoning the Stick Strategy, at least as many, probably more, are adopting, consolidating, and deepening it.

The source of the celebration is apparent. Many corporations in the United States have been at least experimenting with one or another innovation bearing such banners as "high-performance practices," "employee involvement," "employee participation," or "flexible work organizations." Recent surveys indicate how widely these experiments have spread. In one major survey of Fortune 1000 companies, the proportion of firms with at least one employee-involvement practice had reached 85 percent in 1990, although the programs in these firms usually affected no more than about a fifth of employees and often less.[91] In an important, randomly-selected 1992 survey of all private-sector employers with fifty or more employees, MIT economist Paul Osterman found that somewhat more than a third of employers in his sample had adopted at least two innovative practices affecting at least 50 percent of their principal production-worker employees; this is one of the highest proportions yet recorded.[92] Isn't this enough to signal some kind of movement?

Adopting an innovative practice is not the same thing as transforming the workplace. Experimenting with a few workers is not the same as engaging all of them. Even in Osterman's survey, the threshold of at least two innovative practices does not by itself signal a revolution. Nor do his results indicate that any more than the "core" group of employees is affected. In their careful and comprehensive review of such surveys, Eileen Appelbaum and Rosemary Batt conclude: "Summing up these diverse surveys is difficult, but it seems reasonable to conclude that between one-quarter and one-third of U.S. firms have made significant changes in how workers are managed and about one-third of large firms have serious quality programs in place or have experienced significant gains from their quality programs."[93] At most, however, since many of those programs touch only a portion of employees, it would appear that only as many as about 10 to 15 percent of all employees have actually been affected by these programs.

Furthermore, merely tinkering with the Stick Strategy leaves untouched some of the major premises. Few of the company programs flow from coherent strategies to transform substantially the way they do business. In a detailed review of the recent literature on such programs, economist Susan Parks emphasizes that "the types of practices discussed here are often applied piecemeal or are misapplied and are just as easily discarded when they fail to produce results."[94] Thomas A. Kochan, Harry C. Katz, and Robert B. McKersie agree: "Recent evidence shows that there has been widespread *experimentation* with a variety of participatory techniques and substantial changes in work rules. The data also show, however, that the extent of work restructuring is often limited and piecemeal."[95] Visit these experimental programs, the *Economist* observes, "and you often find that the changes are marginal, introduced out of faddishness rather than conviction."[96] "We consider these to be marginal changes," Appelbaum and Batt add, "because they do not change the work system or power structure in a fundamental way."[97]

And when the experiments are token or piecemeal, they're as likely as not to fail to achieve their objectives. One interesting study looked at the effects of General Motors' early efforts to implement Quality of Work Life (QWL) programs in a number of its plants. The programs barely scratched the surface. They included "quality circles," informal meetings among workers, union officials, and managers, and "other forms of enhanced communication between labor and management." GM hoped the programs would improve product quality and labor efficiency. The study found that differences across the plants in the basic quality of labor relations, such as rates of grievances and disciplinary actions, had substantial effects on plant performance. But it also found that, by itself, "hourly workers' involvement in programs addressing quality of working life has no impact on economic performance." The underlying quality of the labor relations shaped the results. The authors further observe: "the plants with comparatively good industrial relations performance tend to develop relatively more extensive QWL involvement, and not vice versa."[98] Change the basic structure of labor relations if you want results, this and other studies seem to suggest; don't futz around with glorified versions of a suggestion box.

Even the most coherent approaches often leave the core of the Stick Strategy unaffected. One common approach, the model that probably receives greatest notice in the business press, encourages worker productivity but retains top-down control of the process. This model, which Appelbaum and Batt dub "lean production," emphasizes the use of managerial initiatives and is symbolized by the criteria used for awarding the annual and influential Malcolm Baldridge Award for innovative corporate initiatives. Judged by these criteria, Appelbaum and Batt conclude, many corporations are pursuing "high-performance workplaces" that seek "improvements in performance by combining total quality marketing and production processes with a more traditional hierarchical organization and with employment policies such as the careful selection of new employees, training, and performance evaluation. . . ."[99] Without a strong com-

mitment to wage growth, and with "a more traditional hierarchical organization" still in place, the model features "fat and mean" with a smiling, friendlier
workplace manner and more efficient managerial practice.

Many firms, indeed, hope to have their cake and eat it too. They announce
programs to encourage higher employee productivity but often fail to support
other programs that provide strong worker rewards or cut substantially into
managerial power or perquisites. There is a long history in the United States
of this kind of one-sided experimentation. Appelbaum and Batt conclude
from their systematic canvass of both survey and case-study evidence:[100]

> Earlier rounds of work restructuring in the 1930s and 1950s were largely ideo-
> logical: work reform was viewed as a tactical tool for improving workers' atti-
> tudes and job satisfaction. The emphasis was on motivation, and workers
> rarely had the discretion or authority to alter the production process or to have
> a say in how the gains were to be distributed. The link between job satisfac-
> tion and productivity proved to be fuzzy at best. Workplace innovations were
> discretionary actions initiated by management to pacify workers and could be
> cut back in times of crisis to reduce costs.
>
> Much of what is happening in U.S. firms today still fits that description. In
> the name of trendy theories—from total quality management and process
> reengineering to skill-based pay, quality improvement teams, and worker
> empowerment—many companies are trying to motivate employees while
> downsizing their work forces and driving down wages and benefits.

Even *Business Week* worries about the asymmetry. "We increasingly demand
that our workers take on responsibility and risk, yet their pay is falling. Will
$8-an-hour machinists do high-performance work? 'The real answer is, we
don't know yet,' says MIT's Osterman. 'But you can't expect workers to keep
contributing their ideas when they don't get rewarded for them.'"[101]

There are many sources of corporate resistance to major workplace transformation. But it seems clear that at least one important barrier stands tall: Hardly
surprisingly, large layers of corporate management enjoy their current positions, power, and emoluments and would like to keep them. The record of
managerial resistance to participatory innovations reaches back to the 1970s.
Often pushed by top-level executives to change their ways, middle-level supervisors and managers cry out, "what about me, what about me?" In one influential study of supervisory resistance, Janice A. Klein of Simmons College
found that supervisors strongly resist new participative programs because of
"concerns shared by most supervisors, regardless of their age, background, or
leadership style"—obvious concerns such as job security, job definition, and
intrinsic, habituated resistance to less hierarchical styles of management.[102]
After their review of close to 200 case studies, Appelbaum and Batt conclude
that "sharing power, authority, responsibility, and decision making is un-
charted territory for most U.S. managers, and many are reluctant to cede

power to workers on and off the shop floor."[103] Again reviewing widespread evidence, Kochan, Katz, and McKersie write: "The problem is that management is often unwilling to, or unaware of the need to, make complementary changes in managerial practices and production methods, and without such changes in management practice, changes in work practices or labor-management relations have yielded limited payoffs."[104]

Transformed labor relations would probably help revive both corporations and our economy. "If unions were to disappear," warns the head of Ford Motor's cooperative labor programs, "the country would be in serious trouble."[105] The problem, *Business Week* declares, is that "most employers couldn't agree less."[106] Many, probably most U.S. corporations continue to go about their business, wielding their sticks, clubbing their workers when necessary, pushing down their wages and eviscerating their security and benefits. So much emphasis has been placed on "high-performance" innovators that we've learned much more about them in recent years than about those who carry on as before. Wages have been falling. Job security has been eroding. Companies haul out the tanks to avoid and even to break their unions. Firms have been relying more and more on contingent and temporary workers, relieving themselves of the obligation to pay benefits. We'll look in detail in the next three chapters at some of the consequences of this continued predominance of the Stick Strategy in the U.S. economy. For the moment, we must pause with a simple observation. Some firms are seeking to reward and involve their workers. Many more firms appear to fatten the bottom line by cheapening their workers' labor power. "Management often avoids participatory workplace restructuring," Kochan, Katz, and McKersie note, "because an alternative low-wage option is readily available."[107] "Not all firms in all American industries are pursuing a low-road strategy," labor economist Bennett Harrison reports. "But the evidence that a large number *are* doing so seems so compelling that we should worry about the future prospects for a restoration of the historic American economic pattern of growth at high wages with declining inequality."[108] *The Economist* peels away the public relations:[109]

> Even while they talk about creating high-quality jobs, many businessmen are revamping mass production, cutting labour costs, contracting-out, increasing flexibility by using part-time workers and using computers to "customise" products.
>
> Indeed, many of the trendiest workplaces are old-fashioned factories in disguise. . . . The high-performance workplace may sound good in academic seminars. To many managers, struggling to control costs and beat the competition, flexible mass production may sound even better.

Many celebrants of the "high-performance" revolution are wearing blinders.

Part II

PAYING THE PRICE

Chapter 4

LIVES AND LIVELIHOODS

S hould we care about the Stick? Aren't wages high enough in the United States to cushion the effects of the wage squeeze? We may be saddled with bloated corporate management, but hasn't the economy been growing in the 1990s anyway? Maybe the Stick Strategy works . . . and we simply have to focus more on its pluses than minuses.

In fact, we in the United States pay an exorbitant price for the kind of production system our corporations pursue and maintain:

• The toll begins with the millions of workers and their households who have experienced the wage squeeze most directly: They suffer the indignity of earning less and less for their work, watch their expectations of rising living standards vanish with the harsh winds, work longer and harder hours merely to afford basic necessities, and feel the mounting stress of falling wages and longer hours not only at work but also at home.

• The costs are also high for thousands of communities around the country that bear the indirect costs of declining working and living standards. Businesses in affected communities suffer from declining demand. Tax bases shrink, eroding essential public services for those directly feeling the wage squeeze *and* for those who have somehow managed to escape its bite directly. The affluent minority which has managed to prosper in the 1980s and 1990s shrinks back into its protected suburbs and gated communities, huddling together in the hopes that they can avoid the wider distress. Cities and counties become more and more sharply divided into the reserves of the haves and of the have-nots.

• The price mounts higher still because the aggregate economy itself suffers from U.S. corporate reliance on the Stick Strategy—imposing costs on all of us whether or not we think we've evaded the blows of the Stick. By almost every conceivable measure, advanced economies which rely on more cooperative systems of labor management have outperformed the U.S. economy for

97

at least the past twenty years. We in the United States bear the burden of the Stick Strategy like weights around our ankles. The U.S. economy sputters along the "low road" to economic growth and prosperity, and we all lose as a result.

• The count continues. The aggregate costs are not only economic but also social and political. The conflictual character of our production system spills over into conflicts in the broader society, helping erode whatever sense of community and cooperation we may once have shared. Those who have been feeling the vise most directly lash out at Others, like blacks and immigrants, whom they angrily hold responsible for their plights. Anger and frustration boil over in the political arena as well, contributing to cynicism, declining citizen participation, volatile rejection of political leadership and even of the efficacy of government itself. "Insecure workers could turn into a xenophobic populist force," Rosabeth Moss Kanter warns the corporate community; "focus groups [with corporate employees] report more anger at government and big business, more protectionist attitudes and less involvement in their communities."[1]

Many read of falling wages and spreading job insecurity and figure that it's somebody else's problem. No such luck. The Wage Squeeze, the Bureaucratic Burden, and the Stick Strategy have become inescapable forces in the United States over the past decades. We all pay the price and we all suffer the consequences. We are unlikely to confront these problems directly unless and until we fully tally their costs. This and the following two chapters provide a partial accounting of at least some of those costs. This chapter begins with the direct impact on the lives and livelihoods of working Americans experiencing the squeeze itself.

Making Ends Meet

Both Paul and Jane Lambert had worked full-time in the Cleveland area throughout the 1980s. When Paul lost one of his jobs (after a plant shutdown), he refused to take unemployment and cobbled together two part-time jobs instead. Their combined income, even with both working the equivalent of full time, fell slightly below $25,000 (in 1994 dollars). With three kids, they could barely make ends meet. They hadn't gone out to eat, they reported, "within living memory, not to a McDonald's or anywhere else."[2]

Interviewed in 1990, the Lamberts were beginning to worry that they might never escape the constant pressure to make every penny count. Paul Lambert spoke bluntly about their situation:[3]

You know, I was talking to a friend of mine the other day. We want to make a decent living. We've been eating it. For a long time—for many years—we've been on the other end of the stick. We've been beat into a corner. How do you get to where we can do what we need to do to survive? I've got other friends like this. They're crazed because they can't make it.

The Lamberts are typical, not exceptional. The vast majority of U.S. households can barely make ends meet. Historically we've advertised the United States as the "land of plenty." To billions abroad, that's how it looks. But given our vast wealth and productive potential, we can hardly boast about the struggle so many Americans endure in just getting by. The core problem, purely and simply, is that the average U.S. worker's wage doesn't put much on the table. As a result, further, the typical working household is working too many hours for too little return.

Some simple arithmetic illustrates the problem for a prototypical household. In 1994 the average production and nonsupervisory worker's hourly wage in the nonfarm private sector was $11.13.[4] Assume that one member of our hypothetical household was lucky enough to be able to work full time year-round at that wage. Assume a second household member worked half-time year-round also at the average wage. The combined total household income for 1994 would thus have been $30,037.[5]

Let's also assume the household includes two kids. How far did their wages carry the family?

The tax collector took some off the top. At average tax rates for this kind of family, that left an estimated $24,961.[6]

Housing is a fixed expense. Assuming typical patterns of housing expenditures—at the rate of about a third of before-tax income—our hypothetical working family spent $10,182 on their housing costs (including all utilities, repairs, and miscellaneous operating costs).[7] A little more than half of this amount went directly for rent or, if they were owners, for home amortization and interest payments. At $468 a month, they managed adequate but hardly luxuriant quarters—maybe enough to afford a separate bedroom for each child, but not too much more.

What did they do with the remaining $14,779? They spent about $3,300 on food at home, which came to roughly $2.28 per person per day; that didn't cover too many fancy cuts of beef. They also spent $1,952 on health care, $3,394 on transportation, and $1,862 on clothing. Were they riding high on the hog? After paying for school lunches and lunches at work, they were probably able to afford about two dinners out for the whole family at McDonald's each month. Assuming they drank only beer at home (no fancy imported brews), they could buy close to three six-packs of Bud every two weeks.

This spending pattern left $4,776 for all "other expenditures," including "life insurance, entertainment, personal care, reading, education, tobacco and smoking supplies, cash contributions, and miscellaneous expenditures." Let's hope they weren't movie lovers and that their kids weren't in college.

And perish the thought that they were hoping to save for a rainy day. Given their income and the typical expenditure patterns for that kind of household unit, they actually spent roughly $2,400 more than they earned, borrowing the extra or running up credit card debt.[8]

This is not an example aimed to illustrate extremes of poverty; it illustrates living standards for a family with *two* workers earning the *average* wage for private nonfarm production and nonsupervisory employees.

How far-fetched is this hypothetical example? In 1993 the median before-tax income of families in the bottom 80 percent of the income distribution, not including households with single individuals, was $24,730.[9] And, according to the Survey of Consumer Expenditures in 1991, on average among all consumer units the bottom 80 percent of the income distribution were net borrowers, spending almost $2,000 more per year (in 1994 dollars) than they earned in before-tax income. So our hypothetical example is indeed close to the mark.[10]

I have begun this chapter by stressing the situation of the *average* worker in part because discussions of the wage problem often tend to concentrate on poverty at the bottom tail of the income distribution or the stunning increase in inequality between the top and the bottom.

The former focus is reasonable, since the story about poverty in the United States is shocking. Poverty rates in the United States have risen more or less steadily since the inception of Reaganomics in the early 1980s. In 1993, the official "poverty" standard came to $14,763 for a family of four.[11] By 1993, 15.1 percent of the U.S. population lived below the official "poverty line"—a total of 39.3 million Americans—up from 11.7 percent in 1979. Among children 18 and under, 22.7 percent lived in "poverty."[12] Poverty rates among children in the United States, by standardized definitions, are more than twice those in Germany and more than three times those in Sweden.[13]

Many accept, moreover, that the official "poverty" standard is far too low, that households need considerably more than that threshold in order to be able to afford a minimally and nutritionally adequate standard of living.[14] Polling results consistently show that for the "minimum income necessary to live in their communities" respondents estimate that families need something like 150 to 160 percent of the official poverty standard.[15] At income levels up to 150 percent of the poverty line, indeed, a majority of polling respondents in the mid-1980s reported that they were unable to afford food, clothing, or medical care at some point during the year.[16]

The focus on inequality is also understandable. As is now widely recognized, the inequality of the distribution of income and wealth in the United States has soared since the beginning of the 1980s. From the mid-1960s through the late 1970s, for example, the shares of the top 5 percent and the bottom fifth of the household income distribution had remained roughly constant. Between 1978 and 1993, by contrast, the ratio of the income share of the top 5 percent to the bottom 20 percent increased by more than a fifth.[17] And almost all of the increase at the top was concentrated in the top 1 percent of households.[18] The inequality of the distribution of wealth rose even more dramatically. Over just six years from 1983 to 1989, the two years for which we have the most recent detailed surveys on wealth distribution, the wealth share of the top one percent of households climbed by fully 15 percent, to a total share of almost 40 percent.[19] This increase in wealth inequality, Edward N. Wolff notes, "is almost unprecedented", rivaled only by the Roaring Twenties. The distribution of wealth in the United States now appears to be the most unequal among the advanced countries. A recent study commissioned by the Organization for Economic Cooperation and Development (OECD), for example, reports that the gap between the rich and the poor was wider in the United States in the mid-1980s than in any of the other fifteen developed economies covered in the study.[20] Wolff observes:[21]

> [Early in the 20th century,] America appeared to be the land of opportunity, whereas Europe was a place where an entrenched upper class controlled the bulk of wealth. By the late 1980s, the situation appears to have completely reversed, with much higher concentration of wealth in the United States than in Europe. Europe now appears the land of equality.

Conservative commentators like Michael Novak are fond of deriding liberal concern about inequality. The wealthy have earned their fortunes, they often aver, and the poor have probably earned their misfortunes. "Besides," Novak asks, "why even suggest that it's wrong for 'the top 1%' (or even the 'top 20%') to invest successfully, so that their wealth keeps growing? . . . Our current system encourages the wealthy to keep investing. That's socially useful."[22]

But focus on either the poor or on the gap between the rich and the poor tends to miss the central point, because it tends to emphasize the extremes of the income distribution, the "atypical" experience. I place so much emphasis in this book on the wage squeeze, rather than on poverty or rising inequality, because meager livelihoods are a *typical* condition, an *average* circumstance in the United States, not an extreme condition. You don't need to earn especially low wages in the United States to face spare cupboards. The average hourly wage will serve you just fine.

And this begins to help explain why it might be the case that the *decline* in real wages over the past twenty years has had some of the severe consequences I trace in this and the following chapter. Millions of American households work and live on the edge. There is no cushion. Even a small decline in wages, at the margin, can hurt severely and force considerable sacrifices.

In 1972, the average (nonfarm private production and nonsupervisory) before-tax wage was $13.11 in 1994 dollars. By 1994, it had declined to $11.13. Take it from the average worker every hour, forty hours every week, and that's enough to reduce the median working family's annual before-tax income by more than $4,200 a year. If there were already a big cushion, a considerable margin, such a loss in earning power might be easily absorbed. But there wasn't before and there certainly isn't now. The wage squeeze has pinched where it hurts most, hitting basic family necessities. In a March 1995 Marist Institute poll, one in three reported that they had trouble meeting their monthly housing expenses during the past year. Overall, more than half said that they "always" or "sometimes" worry whether they'll be able to "meet your family's expenses and bills."[23]

It would be more than a little surprising if the wage squeeze had not had major repercussions on people's lives. "It's not surprising that young men form the most conservative and anti-elitist segment of the population," NYU sociologist Richard Sennett observes: "they are in that crucible time of life when realities—from McJobs and the necessity of living with one's parent in one's twenties to the prospect of three-job marriages—all dim hopes for self-determination."[24] Americans used to look forward to rising living standards. "People are satisfied today if they can keep their incomes and living standards from declining," reports Richard T. Curtin, director of consumer surveys at the University of Michigan. Florence Skelly, vice chairman of the Yankelovich polling outfit, agrees: "Happiness is being able to cut it with less."[25]

Working More . . .

The first and most obvious repercussion has affected working time. Workers and their households have struggled to stay afloat—and to preserve their prevailing standards of living—by logging more hours per year as a way of trying to compensate for the decline in their hourly earnings. "It kind of stinks, the two of us having so many jobs," laments the wife in a four-job couple. "You argue about money and about hours. . . . We go different ways too much."[26]

A first, purely statistical hint of this phenomenon comes when we look at the relationship between workers' wages and family incomes. While workers' hourly wages have fallen for more than twenty years, real median annual family incomes have remained more or less flat. In 1973, median family income was $36,893 in 1993 dollars. In the most recent data available at the time of writing, real median family income in 1993 was $36,959. Twenty years passed and family median incomes rose by $66, a whopping increase of exactly 0.2 percent.[27] Arithmetically, the only way for real median annual income to have stayed roughly constant, while hourly wages were falling in real terms, was for average hours worked per family per year to have increased.

Harvard economist Juliet B. Schor has helped dramatize this important trend.[28] She provides a fairly precise chronicle of the different ways in which the push toward longer hours has taken hold. Some of these paths have primarily involved households themselves "choosing" additional work, while some have resulted from corporate compulsion. Either way, people in the United States have been working more.

Often at least one member has begun "moonlighting." Sometimes this happens when people who have lost a well-paid job work at two or more jobs as a way of making up the difference. Sometimes people work an extra turn when they lose working hours at their main job, forced to work part-time involuntarily. And some choose to moonlight simply because it becomes impossible to maintain expected family living standards when inflation, taxes, and direct wage cuts erode real hourly take-home pay.

Our most direct source of evidence about moonlighting comes from surveys by the Bureau of Labor Statistics that explicitly ask household members if they are holding more than one job. In May 1995, 8.0 million workers (sixteen years and over) held more than one job, amounting to 6.4 percent of all employed. A substantial majority of these moonlighters—nearly three-fifths—worked *full time* at their primary job, slapping the extra gig on top of an already full working schedule.[29] (If anything, these official survey data probably undercount the number of moonlighters. Schor speculates: "The real numbers are higher, perhaps twice as high—as tax evasion, illegal activities, and employer disapproval of second jobs make people reluctant to speak honestly."[30])

During the 1970s the frequency of moonlighting remained roughly constant. But as the wage squeeze accelerated during the 1980s, so did moonlighting. In 1979, only 4.9 percent of all employees held at least one extra job. By 1989, that had increased to 6.2 percent. And the bulk of those 1989 moonlighters were clearly taking on the extra work for strictly economic reasons.[31] In May 1989, more than a third were doing extra turns in order "to meet regular household expenses" while another quarter were doing it to "pay off debts" or "save for the future."[32] Had the 1979 rate applied in 1995, roughly two million fewer workers would have been moonlighting.

A second source of additional working time, primarily among workers in manufacturing, has come from overtime work. Overtime hours are highly cyclical, so it is important to look at comparable points in the business cycle. In 1994, the average civilian unemployment rate was 6.1 percent while overtime hours per week in manufacturing averaged 4.7. In 1978, the unemployment rate was also 6.1 percent, but average overtime hours were only 3.6. Controlling for the cycle, weekly overtime hours had increased by almost a third over those sixteen years.[33]

This trend has been driven from both sides of the labor market. Many firms have tended to rely increasingly on overtime in large part because, when demand for their products has been high, they have wanted to avoid new hires in order to save on the benefit costs, especially health insurance, which each additional new employee imposes. Sometimes given the choice to work the extra hours and sometimes not, workers have typically leaned toward the extra working time at least partly to compensate for declining wages or job insecurity. As one auto worker noted in an interview, "You have to work the hours, because a few months later they'll lay you off for a model changeover and you'll need the extra money when you're out of work. It never rains but it pours—either there's more than you can stand, or there isn't enough."[34] For many U.S. workers, the likelihood of more than they can stand has been increasing.

Some workers, indeed, are forced to work extra hours and don't even get paid for it. This is a violation of the Fair Labor Standards Act, of course, and so the practice, however widespread, is hidden; we have absolutely no idea how prevalent it might be. In one recent case, however, 183 current and former employees of the Food Lion grocery chain filed a class-action suit charging that the company pressured them to work extra hours—"off the clock," as it's called—without any extra compensation.[35] They were impelled, they claimed, because the company set unrealistic productivity goals and dealt harshly with employees who did not meet their targets. One employee reported, "My supervisor would always say, 'Do what you have to do to get the job done, but don't let me catch you working off the clock.' I took that to mean: 'Work off the clock, but don't get caught.'"[36] In 1993 Food Lion settled the suit with the Labor Department, agreeing to pay $16.2 million in back wages for an estimated 30,000 to 40,000 employees. The *Wall Street Journal* reported this as "the largest settlement ever by a private employer over wage and hour violations."[37]

A third apparent source of work pressure has come from a modest erosion in paid time off—vacation time, holidays, and sick pay. Lawrence Mishel and Jared Bernstein have compiled a series on the number of paid days off for workers in the nonfarm business sector. Paid time off increased steadily from the mid-1960s through the late-1970s, rising from 15.1 days per year in 1966 to 19.8 days in 1977. *But then, as the wage squeeze deepened, this trend was reversed.* From 1977 to 1989, Mishel and Bernstein report, annual days off with pay dropped from 19.8 to 16.1.[38] Almost back to the 1960s.

This reversal apparently reflects two kinds of sources. Some firms have actually cut back on paid time off for their employees as part of a drive toward cost-cutting. And, probably more important, as firms have tended to move increasingly toward temporary, contract, and contingent employees, the number of workers who themselves have decent time-off packages has declined. Europeans are astonished at how little vacation most American workers enjoy, and the astonishment grows.[39]

Finally, and undoubtedly most important, more members of households have joined the labor force during the era of the wage squeeze. Most notable is the continuing increase in the labor force participation rates of married women. In 1973, 42 percent of all married women (with spouse present) were members of the labor force. (This was already a substantial increase from twenty years earlier.) By 1994, that figure had increased to just over 60 percent.[40]

The combined effects of these different sources has been substantial. We have two alternative measures of the trends.

Schor provides a direct estimate from individual data in the annual Current Population Surveys. Controlling for the business cycle, she found that average annual hours of paid employment for labor force participants rose through each business cycle peak from 1969 to 1973, from 1973 to 1979 and then again from 1979 to 1987, the most recent year for which she was able to perform the calculations. Over the whole period the increase was sizable: in 1969, annual hours of paid employment averaged 1,786 hours per labor force participant. By 1987, average annual hours had risen to 1,949, an increase of nine percent—the equivalent of an extra 13.6 hours a month.[41] Mishel and Bernstein provide a similar kind of calculation through the early 1990s. By their measure, average annual hours were staying at their new higher levels at least through 1992.[42]

More simply, we can estimate average annual hours worked *per capita* rather than *per worker*. This measure reflects the total amount of labor that U.S. households committed to the economy in order to support themselves *and* their dependents. Average hours per capita declined fairly steadily from the late 1940s until the early 1960s, as workers and households were able to take advantage of rising wage and salary income *and despite* the steady increases in married women's labor force participation rates during the boom years. The trend reversed itself, with average hours beginning to rise, in the mid-1960s when real earnings growth began to slow. Average annual hours per capita have increased most rapidly since the mid-1970s as households have tried to stave off the squeeze of declining real hourly earnings. Between 1966, when working hours had dropped close to their postwar low, and 1989, another business cycle peak, average annual working hours per capita climbed from 682 to 785, an increase of 15 percent.[43] Hours worked declined during the 1990–91 recession, of course, but by 1994 they had recovered to 774, almost back to their level at the previous cycle peak and still considerably above their levels in the earlier peaks of 1966, 1973, and 1979.

This substantial increase in working hours may seem a bit of a stretch for many readers because it seems to conflict with a widespread impression about working-time, a perception that millions of workers have been voluntarily shifting toward part-time schedules in the search for greater flexibility and more time at home. It is certainly true that there has been an increase in the percentage of workers on part-time jobs. In 1979, for example, 17.6 percent of the employed worked part-time. By 1993, that percentage had increased to 18.8 percent.[44]

But most of the increase in part-time work has not been freely chosen. As employers have cut back on hours in some kinds of jobs and turned increasingly toward temporary and contingent employees, millions of workers have been pushed out of full-time work against their wills. Most studies show that after controlling for cyclical factors virtually all of the increase in part-time employment since the 1970s has come through increased *involuntary* part-time work, not through more widespread voluntary part-time schedules.[45]

When we look at working hours, of course, we are only looking at part of the working day. We also need to keep track of housework as well. Indeed, if it turned out that the amount of housework that Americans were clocking at home was *declining* by more than the increased paid hours in the labor market, then the picture might seem less somber.

This has not been the case. We can again turn to Schor for estimates of trends in the number of hours of work at home.[46] Among labor force participants, household work did not decline between 1969 and 1987, leaving the substantial increase in paid hours of work intact and imposing. Among all adults, including those not in the labor force, household work did decline somewhat overall, but not enough to compensate for the increase in hours worked. On average across the entire adult population, Schor estimates that total hours worked per year at both paid and household work increased by forty-seven hours between 1969 and 1987, *the equivalent of almost exactly one extra week of labor at all tasks combined.* This rise, remember, *reverses* a long and steady downward movement in annual hours worked for decades leading up to the 1960s.

The pattern, not surprisingly, was very different for men and for women. Among all adults, men worked somewhat less per year at paid work as male labor force participation rates declined (primarily through later labor market entry and earlier retirement) and somewhat more at home (an apparent consequence of shifts in relative paid working time among men and women and some increased commitment by men to sharing the housework). By contrast, women dramatically increased their total annual hours in the labor market and reduced household work along the way. On balance, nonetheless, average total annual hours increased for both adult men and adult women.

One further consequence of the wage squeeze is that, with long working hours and pinched finances, fewer households are using paid child care. It is true that part of this trend can be attributed to more fathers contributing to child care, partly because they've been losing their jobs and partly because some are sharing more of the housework. But the underlying move toward less paid child care, according to a detailed *Washington Post* report, has been "due mostly to economics and tight family budgets." One dramatic consequence, apparently, is a substantial increase in latchkey kids, now perhaps as many as 5 million.[47]

Opinion polls confirm that Americans feel the time squeeze acutely. In a comprehensive nationally representative poll conducted by the Families and Work Institute in 1992, 80 percent said they "agree" or "strongly agree" that "my job requires working very hard" and 43 percent that "I have excessive amounts of work."[48] According to the Harris Poll, for example, respondents' estimates of their total available leisure time fell from a median of 26 hours a week in 1973 to slightly under 17 in 1988.[49] According to the Gallup Poll, similarly, those satisfied with the amount of leisure time they enjoy dropped from 76 percent in 1963 to 67 percent in 1993.[50] The poll results are based on subjective self-reporting and must be taken with several grains of salt. But it would appear that more and more Americans have become aware of the acute pressure that longer hours have placed on their lives. As one writer and organizer who works on this issue in the Boston area concludes, "Too many of us are too busy, trying to squeeze more into each day while having less to show for it. Although our growing time crunch is often portrayed as a personal dilemma, it is in fact a major social problem that has reached crisis proportions over the past twenty years."[51]

But is the time squeeze caused by the wage squeeze? Can we chalk up the trend toward more hours as a consequence of the Stick Strategy and the falling real wages it has helped impose?

The time squeeze has many sources, of course, and it would be foolish to try to reduce them to a single, ultimate cause. But the wage squeeze has played a critical role in pushing workers and their households toward working more.

The simplest, *prima facie* case comes from looking at the relationship between average annual hours and real hourly take-home pay over the period of the wage squeeze. Average annual hours per capita, as we have already seen, began to increase in the mid-1960s. Real spendable hourly earnings began to decline after the early 1970s. How closely were these two trends related?

Figure 4.1 plots average annual hours per capita against real spendable hourly earnings (in 1994 dollars) for the years from 1973 through 1994—the period over which the wage squeeze has occurred. Each point represents a year, showing the combination of working hours and hourly take-home pay prevailing in that year. At the beginning of the period, in 1973, average annual hours were close to their lowest level and wages were close to their highest. By the end of the period in 1994, in contrast, wages were close to their lowest level in the period (only 1993 featured lower real take-home pay) and annual hours were now relatively high (not quite at the 1989 peak but recovering from the 1990–91 recession).

The points trace a distinctly negative relationship, as the regression line illustrates. The simple correlation between the two variables for this twenty-two-year period is –0.70 (statistically significant at 1%). At the level of simple statistical association, it seems fairly clear that relatively longer annual hours went together with relatively lower real spendable hourly earnings. Earn less, work more.

But statistical association does not mean causation. It simply means that the two variables moved together. In which direction might causation run?

FIGURE 4.1

Earning Less, Working More

Average annual hours per capita and real spendable hourly earnings, 1973–94

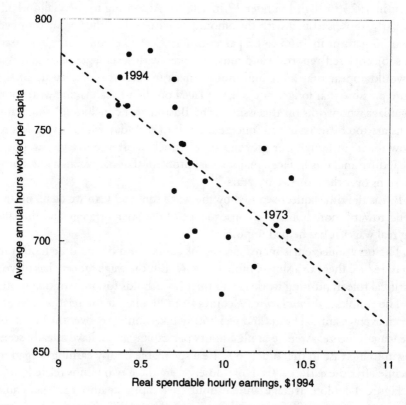

Sources: National Income & Product Accounts, Economic Report of President.

I have already sketched a proximate case that causation runs from falling wages to longer hours. Could it run in the opposite direction? One chain is certainly possible: it could be that the supply of workers increased over the period, for example because married women were joining the labor force for independent reasons, and that this rising labor supply was creating slack labor markets and, as a consequence, downward competitive pressure on wages. For a while, this may have been the case, since unemployment rates climbed from the late 1960s through the late 1970s. During the 1980s, however, the strong negative association continued even while labor demand was growing rapidly and unemployment rates were drifting downward. By the mid-1990s, unemployment rates were back down to their levels of the early 1970s, suggesting that labor markets were roughly as tight in the two periods. But real spendable hourly earnings were at their peak in the early 1970s and at their nadir in the mid-1990s. It seems unlikely, as a result, that the decline in wages was being driven by independent or exogenous trends in labor supply resulting in increasingly slack labor market conditions.

So how likely is it that falling real wages actually do explain a substantial portion of the lengthening working year? Here we need to move beyond statistical association to examine the specific links in the causal chain that such an argument would imply.

Movements in annual hours per capita are a product of forces on both the demand-side and supply-side of the labor market, shaped by the actions of both firms and workers and their households. In order to consider more fully the plausibility of the argument that falling wages have contributed substantially to longer hours we need to look at both sides of the labor market.

From firms' perspectives, it is certainly credible that falling wages may have encouraged employers to use relatively more labor in production. Most economists have long thought that there is a negative relationship between wages and labor demand: as wages fall, if other factors are equal, firms are likely to substitute labor for capital and expand the total hours of employee time that they hire on the market. It becomes relatively cheaper to hire workers than to buy machines.[52]

But this tells us only that firms are likely to want to hire relatively more hours of labor, at given levels of total demand, if product wages fall. It says nothing about how they will distribute those hours among their employees, about what happens to total employment and thus to hours *per worker*. It might be, for example, that as firms substituted toward labor they would simply hire additional employees but not change the number of hours they expected each employee to work. Here, other factors are likely to come into play: rising benefit costs may impel firms to make heavier use of overtime among their current employees, for example, or to rely increasingly on part-time or temporary or contingent workers among whom they can evade benefits obligations. So we cannot say directly that firms are necessarily likely, when other things are equal, to push their employees to work longer hours just because wages have been falling. But there is nothing pointing in the opposite direction, either. Labor demand, in short, probably has relatively little impact on the connection between falling wages and rising annual hours.

Which takes us to the other side of the labor market, to labor supply. The argument that falling wages has prompted people to seek longer hours, additional jobs, or to enter the labor force would imply that workers' labor supply has what economists call a "backward-bending" or negative slope. As wages rise, labor supply would fall. And *vice versa*. This is not the way the labor supply curve is most commonly drawn in the textbooks, but it is considered to be theoretically possible. Is it a plausible relationship over the past twenty-five years?

The principal evidence about labor supply comes from analyses of labor force participation rates, the decision on whether or not to look for work.

Almost all economists agree that we need to consider male and female labor supply separately since men and women have historically borne such different relationships to the labor market. The current consensus appears to be that among men there is little relationship between the wage and hours of labor supply one way or the other; so many men have historically participated in the labor force that there seems to be little room for an either positive or negative relationship between labor force participation rates and wages.[53]

With women, however, wages appear to matter. Here, there are two wage effects. Women's decisions to enter the labor force do appear to be affected by the average wages that they themselves are earning. And they also appear to be influenced by men's wages, presumably the wages of other men in their households who work. The problem with the former effect is that the estimates are all over the map and do not appear to be very reliable; they are very sensitive to data sets, time periods, and methods of estimation. By contrast, the male wage-effect seems fairly clear and strong: as male wages go down, female labor supply goes up.[54]

And this, indeed, appears to be one of the main forces, if not *the* primary force, driving the relationship between wage and hours over the past twenty-plus years. As we saw in Chapter 1, it is primarily male wages that have been declining in real terms; female wages on average have withstood the wage squeeze at least during the 1980s and early 1990s. And, as we saw earlier in this chapter, rising female labor force participation rates have been one of the principal contributing components of the increase in average annual hours. Not only have more women entered the labor force; those already working have been taking on more work. Reporter Peter T. Kilborn concludes in a recent review of these trends:[55]

> Women who once went to work to buy the extras for their families are paying for more and more of the basics, piling job upon job as their husbands' earnings fall. . . . For the most part, it is the wives and mothers among this huge population of lower-paid women whose husbands' wages have fallen the most and who are becoming the new bulwarks of the family economy. These women take full-time jobs and then go to school to qualify for better ones. Others combine two or more jobs.

One husband Kilborn interviewed, after recounting his own job problems and his wife's contributions to their livelihood, pointed to his wife and concluded sparely: "That's the reason we're making it."[56]

. . . And Enjoying It Less

Of course in theory there might be another explanation for Americans' working more: It could be that people have been choosing to work more because they have been enjoying their jobs more, not because they have been earning less.

That's a logical possibility. But trends in the organization of work over the past twenty years hardly make this likely. Since the mid-1970s the working experience for the vast majority of workers has grown increasingly distasteful.

This should come as no surprise. I have already argued that U.S. corporations have increasingly come to rely on the Stick Strategy since the mid-1970s. And the Stick Strategy is hardly designed with an eye to maximizing employees' delight on the job. As one engineer visiting a GM plant described the prevailing atmosphere, "Workers were held accountable through a system of intimidation: Do your job and your supervisor won't yell at you."[57] If firms refuse to trust their workers or to provide them with positive work incentives, they shouldn't expect their employees to respond with nothing but love and devotion. Club a worker with the stick and she or he is probably not going to kiss you on the cheek in response.

Within the general structures promoted by the Stick Strategy, further, it seems especially likely that those who experience the *most intensive* supervision will display the *lowest levels of job satisfaction*. The less you're left on your own, the more your boss or supervisor watches over your shoulder, . . . the less you're likely to get a charge out of your work.

We find some interesting proximate confirmation of these expectations in the Class Structure Survey (to which I've already made such extensive reference in Chapters 2 and 3), which includes questions about workers' job satisfaction. (I turn to the Class Structure Survey for this kind of evidence, rather than many other surveys that include information about job satisfaction, because it contains such useful and explicit information about people's positions within and experience with the supervisory hierarchy.)

But first a warning: In looking at job satisfaction, we have to remember a common finding. Workers typically report that they're satisfied with their jobs—apparently because admitting otherwise would seem so embarrassing. The common pattern, as a result, is that average *levels* of job satisfaction in polls of workers are almost always relatively high, perhaps higher than we might suppose given subjective impressions of the frequency with which many employees seem to grumble about life on the job. If we can learn anything at all about the determinants of job satisfaction, consequently, we need to concentrate on *differences* in reported job satisfaction across different groups of workers and over time rather than on absolute levels of satisfaction.

Even with these cautions in mind, we can find in the Class Structure Survey data two striking patterns. First, not surprisingly, it would appear that those who are bossed enjoy their jobs less than those who do the bossing. Remember from Chapter 2 that among private nonfarm employees in the 1991 Class Structure Survey, 36 percent work at jobs with managerial and supervisory responsibility. Among that group 75 percent report high levels of job satisfaction.[58] Among the 64 percent who are themselves supervised, only 64 percent report high levels of job satisfaction—a dramatically lower percentage as these kinds of polling results on job satisfaction go.

Perhaps more interesting, it would also appear that respondents' job satisfaction bears a direct negative relationship to the frequency with which their supervisors check on their work. The more intensively workers are monitored, the less they appear to enjoy their jobs. Looking just at those in *non*managerial and *non*supervisory jobs, for example, we find that 73 percent of those whose supervisors check on their work "never" or "less than once a week" express high levels of satisfaction with their jobs. Among those who are monitored "about once a week" or "several times a week," 68 percent report high levels of satisfaction. Among those whose supervisors watch them "about once a day" or "more than once a day," finally, only 59 percent report similar levels of contentment.[59] Being targeted on at least a daily basis appears to leave a relatively more acidic taste in most employees' mouths. The 1992 national survey of the Families and Work Institute finds similar patterns. "Workers with more job autonomy and control of their work schedules," they report, "are less burned out by their work, are more satisfied with their jobs, and take more initiative at work."[60]

If U.S. firms have become increasingly dependent on the Stick Strategy since the mid-1970s, then, and if it seems so unlikely to provide rewarding working experiences for those at the bottom of the hierarchy, we ought to find fairly clear evidence that workers have become increasingly dissatisfied with their jobs over the past twenty years. And indeed we do.

Observers began to notice evidence of this trend from its beginning. Sensing something in the winds, the U.S. Department of Labor commissioned three early surveys on the quality of workers' experiences on the job—in 1969, 1973, and 1977. Because the surveys were consistently structured and administered, it was possible to trace the trends across that first phase of the shift in corporate practices. Having changed relatively little from 1969 to 1973, workers' reported job satisfaction declined dramatically between 1973 and 1977, precisely when, as I argued in Chapter 2, many corporations shifted into their Big Stick phase. The principal author of the study comparing the surveys, Michigan sociologist Graham Staines, concluded: "The sky has finally fallen. Workers in virtually all occupations and demographic categories evidenced appreciable and unmistakable manifestations of rising discontent."[61] A similar pattern appeared in the continuing surveys of job satisfaction conducted by the Opinion Research Center. The percentage of workers surveyed who expressed job satisfaction—who reported they like their job "very much" or "a good deal"—remained fairly level, at about 70 percent, over the business cycle peaks of 1948, 1966, and 1973. But from 1973 to 1979, this measure of job satisfaction plummeted from 68 percent to 59 percent.[62]

The decline in job satisfaction continued into the 1980s. Surveying workers not only on the general issue of their job satisfaction but also on more specific aspects of their working experiences, such as managerial responsiveness to employee problems and fairness in the application of company rules and procedures, the Opinion Research Corporation found substantial declines from the 1970s into the early 1980s.[63] By the late 1980s, the business press was sending out stern warning signals to U.S. corporations.

In 1989, for example, *Fortune* magazine featured a prominent cover story about "The Trust Gap." "Relations between employer and employed are not good, and at an especially dicey moment," the story apprised. "Just when top management wants everyone to begin swaying to a faster, more productive beat, employees are loath to dance." In just five years according to one survey, for example, the percentage of employees agreeing that "the company treats you with respect and consideration" had declined from about 40 percent in 1983 to about 30 percent in 1988. Citing another survey, *Fortune* noted the surprising result that workers expressed greater concern over such work quality issues as "increased recognition of employee contributions" than over job security. Apparently reflecting the top-heaviness of U.S. corporations and the extensive supervision of middle-level managers and supervisors, the Hay Group found in a broad 1988 survey that "the attitudes of middle managers and professionals toward the workplace are becoming more like those of hourly workers, historically the most disaffected group." The wage squeeze was also leaving more and more employees aghast at soaring top-level salaries; one management expert is quoted, "The gap is widening beyond what the guy at the bottom can even understand." "No one contends," the *Fortune* story concluded, "that relations between top management and everybody else are as acrid these days as, say, during the Pullman strike [in 1894]. . . . Today's grievances are less salty, more subtle. But they smoke and gutter all the same—some with a peculiar brilliance." [64]

In the early and mid-1990s, of course, the business press has grown aglitter with another story, the spread of the "high-performance workplace." For all that glitter, however, as I argued in Chapter 3, management reliance on the Stick Strategy has continued to dominate actual practice on the shop and office floor. Commitment to and serious development of substantially more participatory, less hierarchical labor-management relations has been both narrow and shallow, more smoke than substance. And, not surprisingly, the erosion in employee satisfaction, the spread of broad-based worker discontent, has continued. In one survey that asked questions consistently over a twenty-year period, for example, those describing themselves as "extremely satisfied" with their jobs declined from 47 percent in 1973 to only 27 percent in 1994.[65] The Gallup polling organization has asked over many years whether its respondents find their time on the job or their time not on the job the most enjoyable; those favoring on-the-job time declined from 38 percent in 1955 to only 22 percent in 1993.[66] Even in the short span since the late 1980s, employee satisfaction has been falling along several critical dimensions. Between 1989 and 1993, for example, the percent of employees "satisfied" with their job security declined from 87 percent to 79 percent, hardly a surprising result, given the concern about "downsizing," and those "satisfied" with the amount of on-the-job stress to which they're exposed dropped from 76 to 60 percent.[67]

Mounting strain on the job has not escaped the notice of corporate leaders and managers. Former *New York Times* reporter Hedrick Smith wonders how long the strain can continue to simmer before boiling over. "In the mid-term elections of November 1994, public anger over economic insecurity exploded—at government politicians, rather than at corporate America and its managers. Yet even some corporate leaders and business magazines have commented that the social compact between employer and employee has been stretched to the breaking point in America. . . ."[68] A middle-level manager reflects on these strains in his daily life on the job:[69]

> This year, I had to downsize my area by 25%. Nothing has changed in terms of the workload. It's very emotionally draining. I find myself not wanting to go in to work, because I'm going to have to push people to do more, and I look at their eyes and they're sinking into the back of their heads. [People] numbing. But they're not going to complain, because they don't want to be the next 25%.

That fear seems to have spread pervasively. "As the ruthless combination of corporate power and conservative politics increases its dominance over American life," *New York Times* columnist Bob Herbert writes, "legions of faithful and mostly middle-class American employees are tormented by the fear that they will be the next to walk the employment plank."[70]

Chapter 5

VALUES AND JOBS

Conservative pundits and politicians love to point the finger, finding one or another symbolic scapegoat to blame for a wide variety of social problems. Their targets shift constantly: Teen pregnancy. Lazy workers. Ungrateful immigrants. Violent movies and ugly rap lyrics. Welfare chiselers. Gangsta teens at loose on the streets. Racial quotas.

Lying behind all these social problems, they further insist, are corroding social values. "New social maladies have emerged," Ben J. Wattenberg argues. "At best the situation is unhappy; at worst, perhaps combustible. I have come to the conclusion that the values issues are no longer merely *co-equal* with economic concerns. *The values issues are now the most important.*"[1] It's not just that the "values" issues resonate with the electorate, Wattenberg insists; it's that they have substantially shaped the economic problems about which liberals have been wringing their hands. "The values issues and social issues are important in their own right," he continues, "but they also have an enormous impact on the economy."[2]

I would argue instead that the wage squeeze and the Stick Strategy underlying it account for as much or more of some of the most notorious economic and social problems in the United States as any other single factor. Name the problem—the "family breakdown," "welfare dependency," "teen pregnancy"—and, I would argue, we can find falling real wages or job insecurity lurking in the background as a primary contributing cause of that problem. The U.S. corporate production system, and the kinds of jobs it provides or fails to provide, holds the key to understanding much of what we currently debate in the policy arena. In seeking to understand the stresses and strains on Americans' lives and communities, rather than spending so much time blaming deviants or moral pestilents we should focus much more clearly on the character of employment in the United States.

Conservatives have shifted the discussion almost entirely toward cultural factors, blaming people and their values for many of their own problems. We need to redress the balance and bring the quality of people's jobs back into the discussion. Values matter, of course. But jobs matter at least as much, if not more.

This chapter seeks to develop the basis for that argument. It is a strong claim. These kinds of economic and social problems are indeed complex; much more original research would be necessary in order to assess the relative importance of falling wages in contributing to their evolution. And in many cases the contributions of falling wages to social disfunctions are indirect, operating through several links of the causal chain.

"Family Values"

Conservatives and the Christian right love to rail against the decline of the "traditional family" and to wail about the erosion of "family values." They're inclined to blame a rending of our moral fabric. If only more of us would read William Bennett's *Book of Virtues* aloud to each other, they seem to suggest, we might be able to pull our lives and our families from the quicksand of moral decay. Former vice-president Dan Quayle, in his combative speech before the Republican National Convention in 1992, minced no words:[3]

> Like so many Americans, for me, family comes first. When family values are undermined, our country suffers. All too often, parents struggle to instill character in their sons and daughters, only to see their values belittled and their beliefs mocked by those who look down on America. Americans try to raise their children to understand right and wrong, only to be told that every so-called "lifestyle alternative" is morally equivalent. That is wrong.

The right-wing sermonizers, with their screeds about the corrosion of our moral values, have distracted the rest of us from appreciating the effect of the changing nature of job opportunities in the United States. There are some real and serious problems with family life in the United States. But all families, whether "traditional" or single parented, would be better off if they could build on a more adequate and secure economic footing. The more clearly we understand some of the roots of family problems in the evolution of the Stick Strategy over the past twenty-five years, the better the chance we will have to address and perhaps even to moderate them, however the family, in its many forms, continues to evolve.

There are a number of different dimensions to developments in families in the United States. Each of these dimensions needs to be stated and characterized carefully, since what appear to be problems for some may be blessings for others.

The "Breakup" of the Family

First, and obviously, there have been major changes in the structure of house-holds themselves. In a phrase, the "traditional family" has been withering. In 1960, roughly three-quarters of households were "family households" headed by a married couple; by 1993, the share of married-couple families had dropped to only 55 percent of total households. Single-person households in-creased as a percentage of total households from only 7.2 percent in 1960 to 29.3 percent in 1993. The percentage of all households headed by females rose from 18.2 in 1960 to 29.0 in 1993. As a result of these and many other developments, such as the growing tendency for the elderly to split off from the rest of their families and to live by themselves, average household size has dropped dramatically, falling from 3.3 people per household in 1960 to only 2.6 in 1993.[4]

To the political right this represents the "breakup" of the family. But are these developments actually a problem, a turn for the worse?

For the prototypical, traditional, patriarchal male household head, the ero-sion of the traditional family appears to be a serious problem indeed.[5] In the good old days, according to a mixture of history and myth, many men ruled their families as kings of the roost, bringing home the bacon and being served drink and slippers as reward.[6] For many men, changes in their family relation-ships have involved wrenching emotional dislocations. That would have been hard enough. But to the extent that many men over the past four decades have been increasingly likely to experience divorce, live on their own, lose their "homemakers," assume housekeeping and childcare responsibilities, and work out relatively more complicated relationships with their kids, institu-tional changes in the family have been difficult indeed.

The story is somewhat more ambiguous for women. On the one hand, many women have enjoyed their increased independence from traditional family relations. For those who found such relationships oppressive or de-meaning, many have found it easier to get out of difficult situations through divorce or separation, and many others have had less trouble resisting pressure to get into potentially difficult marriages in the first place. On the other hand, many of the women who have become heads of households, particularly those with children, have become increasingly exposed to poverty and economic in-security and have had notable difficulty trying to provide adequate care for their children. It's difficult, probably impossible, to weigh these opportunities and costs and judge whether on balance recent changes in the family have had positive or negative consequences for women. The crucial point, in the end, is that for many women "family breakdown" has spelled relief.

Even for kids, finally, it's not obvious that the "breakup" of the traditional family has been an unalloyed disaster—even though children's interests are often the expressed rationale for many conservative lamentations about the disappearing "family." On the one hand, it may certainly be the case that many children with divorced or separated parents have trouble adjusting to new distances, separations, and negotiated visiting rights, and that they would "prefer" to live with their two parents together. On the other hand, it's not clear that in the traditional family kids were better off when sparring, mistrustful parents stayed together "just for the sake of the kids" and sustained homes that felt more like war zones than nurturing havens. Nor is it clear in the modern context that children living in homes with both parents fare better in their lives than those living outside of such traditional relationships.

Recent research has tended to find, for example, that "parental conflict has a greater impact on the social and psychological adjustment of children than divorce";[7] that "much of the effect of divorce on children can be predicted by conditions that existed well before the separation occurred";[8] and that adjustment problems among kids differ far more substantially across families of different background characteristics, such as their income and exposure to poverty, than they do between intact and divorced parental couples.[9] In general, it would appear that preexisting problems in families cause much more trouble for kids than the actual outcomes of separation and divorce. "At least as much attention needs to be paid," one research report concludes, "to the processes that occur in troubled, intact families as to the trauma that children suffer after their parents separate."[10]

So changes in the structure of families have involved both problems and opportunities. What, besides decaying moral values, bra-burning feminists and Murphy Brown, might have contributed to these changing structures?

It is commonplace to observe that economic stress corrodes marriages. As one *U.S. News & World Report* special study concluded about the 1990–91 recession, "financial uncertainty is driving couples apart. . . ."[11] In order to apprehend the economic dynamics over a longer period, it makes most sense to trace out the connection from the perspective of women, at least in part because they have continued to assume primary responsibility for the children.

One reason we think that many women stayed within relatively dominating, often oppressive married relationships was that economically they had little choice. Typically full-time "homemakers," they depended on their husbands for support of their children and themselves. As employment opportunities for women have expanded, however, and more recently as the gap has narrowed between male wages in the vise of the wage squeeze and female earnings somewhat better cushioned from its consequences, it would make sense if, at least at the margin, growing numbers of women would choose to escape from difficult marriages or to avoid marriage altogether. Their rising relative economic fortunes would make such a move toward relative independence possible. "Greater access to paychecks . . . ," a *U.S. News & World Report* survey concludes, "has enabled many women to leave unhappy marriages."[12]

University of Vermont economist Elaine McCrate has provided us with some important and provocative support for this supposition.[13] She analyzes the dramatic decline in the percentage of women who are married and not separated. In order to assess the importance of women's relative economic opportunities inside and outside of marriage, she develops an Index of Women's Economic Independence. This index captures the relationship between the standard of living that a woman and her children could expect to enjoy if the woman headed the household independently and the standard of living they could expect if they lived within a traditional married-couple family (even if the wife also worked). The ratio is driven by the changes in the relative proportions of men and women who work and their relative earnings. Not surprisingly, this Index of Women's Independence has risen substantially over the past thirty years.

McCrate then explores econometrically the relative importance of this measure of women's economic independence in contributing to the rise in nonmarriage among adult women. She finds strong evidence that the growth of women's economic independence was positively associated with the decline in the percentage of women married and not separated, even after controlling for other factors that might also have contributed.[14] If other things are equal, when women have been able to function better on their own, more of them appear to have broken or avoided the marital bonds.

Although McCrate's analysis is highly exploratory, it seems to resonate with life around us. Many women indeed appear to prefer life after their escape from traditional married-couple relationships, even if they have children. In one early-1990s survey, for example, 40 percent of divorced mothers thought their financial condition was better a year after the divorce than before, and another 20 percent reported it just about the same. Only 8 percent reported their overall situation for taking care of their children as worse than before. And nearly three-fifths said they had more leisure time, while only 21 percent reported less.[15]

One of the principal causes of the "breakup" of the traditional family, in short, would appear to be the relative decline in male earnings. For those women who have found the patriarchy of *pater et familias* confining, to say the least, men have had less and less to offer women economically to keep them in bad marriages. McCrate writes, "recognition of men's power as an incentive for women to leave marriages explains much of the growth of nonmarriage under conditions of rising personal economic independence of women. . . ."[16] Women (and many men) have had numerous reasons for wanting out of the old-style family relationship, but the rise in women's relative economic independence has certainly helped grease the skids.[17]

What should be done? From many vantage points, of course, the "breakup" of the traditional family, to the extent that it has often involved cruel and dominating relationships, should be encouraged . . . if that would mean that men and women, in more freely choosing to live together and potentially to raise children, could share relatively more equal, reciprocal lives together than was typically the case in the past. If this could happen, how might economic factors help *encourage* men and women to remain together?

Many men and many conservatives would hope for an explicit reversal of the economic trends that have contributed to corrosion of the old-style married-couple families. Protagonists of patriarchy would prefer to constrict job opportunities for women if greater employment opportunity and improving gender earnings equality have helped pave the way for women to move out of traditional marriage. Such motives help explain the strong recent backlash against affirmative action for women and the continuing harping about women who "abandon" their families by going to work. The inveterate Rush Limbaugh, always on the case, applauds those women who have "decided to give up their outside jobs altogether so that they could stay home and raise their kids." He hastens to add:[18]

> I am gratified to see this trend occurring, not because I have any problem with women in the workplace. I simply believe that children are better raised, and that the family unit is more sound, when a mother stays home with her children during their formative years. More and more women are making that choice, and it is driving the feminists nuts.

For those of us who support increasing gender equality, by contrast, we must assume that traditional married-couple relationships will shrink as a percentage of total households until and unless many men become more likely and more willing to relinquish some of their traditional dominance in the home, to share more equally in the tasks of the household as women are sharing more equally in the responsibilities of paid employment, and to abandon their pretentious demand that they remain *primus inter pares*. It has happened. Many men have made that move. In her study of men making choices about family life in a world of seachange, New York University sociologist Kathleen Gerson finds a significant number of middle- and working-class men, perhaps a third in her sample, who have been turning toward greater family involvement. "Rare is the man who has taken on equal responsibility for domestic life," she reports, "but a growing group of men are turning toward family involvement with an enthusiasm hardly seen before."[19] Nostalgia cannot recreate the families of yore. Growing equality at the workplace and growing commitment to shared work and lives at home can begin to place family lives and values on a much stronger, more enduring, and more resilient foundation.[20]

Trouble at Home

We've looked at the shift in the structure of households. But there is also good reason to examine what's going on inside them. A variety of critical stresses and strains have been rending American families, nuclear and otherwise. And changes on the job front have played a major role.

One of the most important problems, of course, has been domestic violence, primarily directed against both women and children. Much of this abuse was never reported and therefore hidden in the past, so it is nearly impossible to project whether and how sharply domestic violence has increased over the past thirty years. But we are becoming acutely aware of how widespread it is in U.S. households today.

For women, the home can often feel like Bosnia. New surveys by the Bureau of Justice Statistics help shine a brighter light on domestic violence. They suggest that something like one million women a year are victims of violence at the hands of an intimate—by a husband, ex-husband, boyfriend or ex-boyfriend. Compared to men, "women were about six times more likely to experience violence committed by an intimate."[21] A study by the Commonwealth Fund in 1993 suggests higher numbers, finding that seven percent of American women either married or living with a man were physically abused by their partner. If accurate, the survey would suggest close to four million women suffering domestic violence in that year alone.[22]

Violence against children is also widespread. In one Gallup survey, for example, 26 percent of American teenagers reported having been hit or physically harmed by an adult at home.[23] Commenting on the results, George H. Gallup Jr. reported, ". . . many of our young people are at great risk in places where they in all expectation should feel the safest. . . . If this were a disease, we would be searching frantically for a solution."[24]

Domestic violence, however acute, is in some ways the tip of the iceberg. Many in families feel acute stress; some resort to violence. We have no way of cataloguing fully the dimensions of family strain in the United States. But it certainly makes sense to assume that the problem is widespread, at least in part because of the incidence of violence and abuse it tends to breed.

And this is where the problems at work come home to roost. It is difficult to argue that those most prone to domestic violence are those who experience the most acute pressures on the job. But it is not at all difficult to find evidence that those experiencing relatively greater stress in their home and family circumstances are likely, other things equal, to be experiencing pressures at work.

The linkages begin in the interplay between general economic pressures and individual job experiences. We have long known that higher unemployment rates tend to result in a wide variety of significant individual health problems, including stress.[25] But we have only recently begun to appreciate how macroeconomic problems can result in stress on the job, which itself can spill over into relationships at home. As cost pressures and productivity problems push firms toward job restructuring, workers feel the strain. Recent research by Rudy Fenwick and Mark Tausig of the University of Akron suggests, for example, that "macroeconomic changes also affect individual stress because they lead to changes in routine, day-to-day job structures that represent increased and continued exposure to stressful conditions."[26] Their research seems acutely relevant for workers' experiences over the past twenty-five years as reliance on the Stick Strategy has deepened: ". . . even if individuals are not laid off or subject to negative financial events, their well-being is affected by changes in day-to-day exposure to stressful conditions because their job structures become more stressful."[27]

The next link comes from the differential impact of those general economic pressures on workers with different kinds of jobs. Particularly through the contributions of social psychologist Melvin L. Kohn and his colleagues, we have appreciated for some years now that the quality of the working experience has enormous impact on the kinds of personalities and orientations individuals develop as well as on the personal problems they tend to display. It is only a slight oversimplification to observe that the more autonomous and self-directed the work, the less alienated and troubled the workers.[28]

The final link in the chain comes when workers carry their problems home from the job. Not everyone can blow it off in a bar after work. Job stress is highly likely to result in individual stress within the home environment. Among mothers, for example, stress levels increase with lower incomes and longer hours. One relatively recent study of close to 1,000 mothers concludes that "mothers with more children, who work longer hours and receive lower incomes, and who are married to husbands with lower incomes, were likely to have more stress."[29] Another study of women with children found that women who were dissatisfied with their work situation, whether at home or on the job, were twice as likely to display identifiable symptoms of real depression than those who were satisfied.[30]

But it's not work *per se* that induces stress, either for women or for men. Among women, it appears that paid employment in decent circumstances generally improves mental well-being: one study finds, for example, that mothers who earn enough to improve family income, who are employed because of couple preference, and who receive help with housework and child care show less depression and anxiety than women who are homemakers.[31] But for both men and women, if work hours get too long, stress and depression follow not far behind. For women in particular, getting out of the house seems to reduce depression; it is only when the combined total of paid-work and housework hours gets too high that the relationship reverses itself and longer hours increase depression.[32]

Further, problems on the job appear to have a greater impact on problems at home than *vice versa*. In a 1992 survey conducted by the Families and Work Institute, for example, respondents rated job-to-home problem spillover as being more than three times more severe than spillover in the reverse direction. "While this finding is not surprising, it is disturbing," the survey report suggests. "It appears that family members and friends must endure the stresses and problems that arise from work as well as from personal/ family life."[33]

And so, we have every reason to think that the wage squeeze and other components of the Stick Strategy have exacerbated trouble at home over the past twenty years. Incomes have fallen. Hours have increased. Job satisfaction has declined. Demands on the job, at least for many workers, have risen. It would be foolish to speculate about whether individuals on average are more or less stressed out today than they were in the early 1970s. But it seems reasonable to conclude that people's experiences at work haven't helped. The conservatives' plaints about moral decay seem somewhat beside the point. As Ellen Galinsky, James T. Bond, and Dana E. Friedman of the Families and Work Institute conclude, "work-family solutions will be most effective if they focus on the nature of jobs [and] relationships at work. . . ."[34]

Teen Pregnancy

Many Democrats, including President Clinton, have joined the conservative clamor over teen pregnancies and births to unwed mothers. The rhetorical flourishes of right-wing analysts like Charles Murray, who wrote in 1993 that "illegitimacy is the single most important social problem of our time—more important than crime, drugs, poverty, illiteracy, welfare, or homelessness because it drives everything else," are certainly extreme.[35] But many across the political spectrum seem to agree that unwed teen mothers are a scourge spreading virulently across our moral landscape. Ben J. Wattenberg, in language which apparently so appealed to President Clinton that he called the columnist late at night to express sympathy with the arguments, goes to town on this one:[36]

> Thus, the stark illegitimacy rate touches, and helps shape, every problem discussed in this book. The missing father of the house does not insist that his son stay off the streets in the evening. That contributes to criminality and drug use. It also leads to diminished educational standards: A boy on the street is not doing his homework. If he is black or Hispanic that same undereducated boy later becomes a walking argument for the need for quota hiring. It leads to loose sexual standards, which, starting the cycle afresh, leads to more out-of-wedlock children. It does not seem to be an accident that the erosion of the inner cities in America coincided with the stunning rise in out-of-wedlock birth.

Sometimes it's difficult to figure out what all the fuss is about. Births to teenage mothers have not increased even in absolute numbers over the past twenty years and birth rates for teenage women have dropped by roughly an eighth. In 1970, one out of six mothers was a teenager; in 1990, only one out of eight mothers was a teenager. Births to unmarried mothers have increased, rising from 11 percent of all births in 1970 to 28 percent in 1990. But this is not primarily a phenomenon among teenage mothers; more important, it appears to reflect an increasing willingness by women of many ages (and often their mates as well) to have children even if they are not married. The percent of unmarried births accounted for by teen mothers has actually dropped sharply, falling from 50 percent in 1970 to only 31 percent in 1990.[37]

Nor, finally, is this primarily or even increasingly a problem among African American teens, as the rhetoric and symbolic language of public discourse would sometimes seem to suggest. Although it is true that the rate of unmarried births is higher among African American women than among white women, a majority of unmarried births are to white mothers. The majority of teen mothers are also white. And the percentage of unmarried births accounted for by African American mothers has dropped considerably, falling from 54 percent in 1970 to 41 percent in 1990.[38]

Nonetheless, to some, unwed teen mothers are a "problem" to be treated separately and ostracized severely. If so, once again, they would do well to pay much more attention to the roots of teen pregnancy in the deteriorating economic conditions facing many teens, both male and female, over the past twenty-five years.

The conventional wisdom on the economic dimensions of teen pregnancies has been simple and clear. Teen mothers make bad choices, morally, instrumentally, (or both), and condemn themselves and their kids to a much greater likelihood of poverty and economic hardship than if they had waited to bear children. In the words of the *Wall Street Journal*, "generations of [teenage] women have lost opportunities for education and work because of their own out-of-wedlock children."[39]

It is true that teenage mothers tend to experience lower adult earnings than other women. But it is possible that the causation runs in the opposite direction from that presupposed by the conventional wisdom. Instead of bad choices inducing teen pregnancy that then causes lower adult earnings, it may be that realistic expectations of lower adult earnings induce some women to bear children relatively early, because the economic opportunity costs of doing so are likely to be fairly low in the first place.

Can we distinguish between these two possible chains of determination? Once again, we can turn for illumination to Elaine McCrate. She has published several articles in which she formally considers these alternative possibilities involving the connection between teen pregnancy and lower adult earnings.[40] Some of her conclusions are striking.

In one direction, controlling for other factors, she finds that teen motherhood has virtually no effect on adult earnings—confounding conventional wisdom. She does find evidence that teen mothers complete fewer years of schooling, but she also finds that for black teen women, in particular, staying in school longer adds relatively little to their future earnings in any case. In the other direction, she finds strong evidence that expected adult earnings have a dramatic (inverse) effect on teen motherhood: the lower the earnings that teen women expect to earn as adults (if other things are equal), the greater the likelihood that they will not postpone motherhood.

Complementary research by University of Michigan social scientists Greg J. Duncan and Saul D. Hoffman supports McCrate's findings. They also find that higher expected adult earnings dramatically reduce the likelihood that a teen will become an unmarried mother. Furthermore, they observe that, once they have controlled for family background, relatively higher available AFDC benefits (in the teen's state) do *not* have a statistically significant effect on the likelihood of out-of-wedlock births.[41]

The implications of this research stand the conventional wisdom on its head. McCrate comments:[42]

> In the contemporary debate on the causes of poverty, particularly among the black poor, the results weigh in heavily on the side of economic and structural determinants, rather than individual or cultural factors. . . . The analysis supports the proposition that policies promoting higher wages for women with otherwise poor employment prospects are likely to reduce their early childbearing. . . . Poor women simply need the same options which more privileged women already take for granted.

"Phyllis Schlafly remarked," McCrate concludes, "that 'most women would rather cuddle a baby than a typewriter.' It is even more true that most women would rather cuddle a baby than a toilet brush in a hotel, or dirty dishes in a hospital food service operation, or nothing at all in an unemployment line."[43]

Welfare "Dependency"

The last refrain in the recent family-values chorale sings a dirge about welfare "dependency." Welfare ruins families, conservatives and "new Democrats" lament. Families will be stronger—and our economy more productive—if we can push parasites off the dole.

As with concerns about teen pregnancy, once again, this dirge builds upon the culture-of-poverty argument. Moms with kids on welfare "choose" welfare instead of employment because they aren't stalwart enough to appreciate the independence that employment provides. Many liberals say that poverty rates are abysmally high in the United States compared to other advanced economies, and that we need some kind of strong welfare program to help raise people out of abject poverty. But it's misleading to compare poverty rates in the United States with those in Europe, conservatives reply, because our poor are different, lazier, more shiftless. "Liberals always say, 'Gee, if we could only do it as well as the Europeans,'" Douglas Besharov, a resident scholar at the right-wing American Enterprise Institute retorts. "But the problem is we don't have the same kind of poor people. Our problem is with poor people who don't work."[44]

Is that the problem? It is true, as Christopher Jencks and Kathryn Edin write, that many Americans, perhaps a majority, "see 'dependence' as an inherently pathological condition. We badly want to live in a society where all people can 'stand on their own two feet.'"[45] The problem is that the kinds of jobs afforded by firms pursuing the Stick Strategy often make "standing on their own two feet" close to impossible for many now on the welfare rolls. One need not sift through all the arguments and counter-arguments about the current welfare system and alternative reforms to show the devastating effects that the current range of available job opportunities has on the character and frequency of welfare "dependency."

Most important for this argument is simply that most welfare mothers participate in the labor market at least intermittently, moving in and out of welfare, in and out of jobs. For example, a study by economists at the Institute for Women's Policy Research (IWPR) found a substantial majority of AFDC recipients participated in the labor force over a two-year period: 43 percent of mothers on welfare had worked at least 300 hours of paid work, while another 30 percent spent a significant portion of time looking for work. Over the two-year period, the mothers in the sample spent 77 percent of their time on welfare and 23 percent off the rolls. During the period they were on the rolls, they spent more than 30 percent of their total time working or looking for work. This was almost twice as much time as they spent doing "nothing," neither work nor school nor tending their children, but somehow, in the popular image, "depending on the dole."[46]

In testifying before Congress, Roberta Spalter-Roth, a co-author and research director of the IWPR, reported that the "findings show that most welfare recipients are not pathologically dependent on AFDC. The stereotypes of women who sit around all day watching TV, having children whom they fail to care for, and drawing welfare checks paid by hard-working Americans are greatly exaggerated."[47] Only one quarter of AFDC recipients is totally dependent on AFDC income, the study shows; the remaining three-quarters package AFDC together with some combination of income from paid work, earnings and benefits of other family members, and other resources.

But if they're so interested in working, the conservative critics will ask, why don't welfare mothers leave the rolls and depend entirely on income from paid employment?

The answer seems fairly clear: Many women with children either earn such low wages or work at such bad jobs (or both) that even if they worked full-time they could not come close to supporting their families at or above the poverty level, even as it is measured by the meager official standard, without the additional support they receive from welfare.

Consider the economics of women supporting themselves and their children. Laura Lein and Kathryn Edin have interviewed poor single mothers in the Boston, Chicago, San Antonio, and Charleston, S.C. metropolitan areas and have begun to put together a detailed portrait of their income and expenditure patterns.

A typical welfare mother with two children in Chicago in the early 1990s had an income from AFDC and food stamps alone of only $7,356 in 1993 dollars, considerably below the poverty line for a family of three. Mindful of the possibilities for "packaging," however, Lein and Edin found that the typical AFDC mother was able to lift her family a bit above the poverty level through paid work (with the earnings mostly unreported to welfare), some support from the absent father, and additional support from relatives and boyfriends.

Would she have been better off if she had worked full time, year round at the minimum wage of $4.25? Assuming that the minimum-wage job did not provide health coverage, her fate depended entirely on the availability of child care: if she is able to find free child care for her kids, perhaps from a grandmother, then she can improve her standard of living by 20 percent. But, under the more likely eventuality in the United States that she cannot find free child care and has to pay the going market rates, her standard of living (remember that under this scenario she's off the welfare rolls) would decline by 20 percent.[48]

Working full time, year round at $6 an hour doesn't change the picture at all: Hourly earnings increase, but food stamp benefits and the earned income tax credit decline. Worse still, with the somewhat higher earnings from paid work, she loses eligibility for Medicaid benefits for her children (because her paid earnings lift her family above the poverty line). As a result, the basic economics remain almost exactly the same: If free child care is available, a roughly 20-percent improvement in standard of living by leaving the rolls; no free child care, roughly 20-percent decline.

These numbers would be less devastating, obviously, if we had different systems providing health insurance and child care in the United States. But we don't. Health care reform has fallen flat on its face. Substantial expansion of publicly subsidized child care isn't even on the drawing table, and yet the examples just reviewed underscore how absolutely critical the availability of free or subsidized child care has become in a woman's decision to stay on or move off welfare. With our current job market, where welfare mothers' primary jobs when they worked paid an average of $4.88 an hour (in 1994 dollars),[49] our prized "self-sufficiency" simply won't allow a woman with a couple of children to escape from poverty. As the IWPR study concludes, "*packaging* AFDC with paid employment is necessary because neither the available employment *nor* AFDC alone provides enough income to raise families above poverty."[50] In 1993, 29 percent of working women earned less than $6 an hour.[51] At those prevailing wage rates, supporting children as a single working mother is as easy as sleeping on a bed of nails.

We've been looking at simple arithmetic. The problem of welfare and work is compounded by the *quality* of jobs available to many women in the labor market. At the low-end of the job ladder, most jobs that are available provide few if any benefits and little or no job security. They typically feature intrusive and often capricious supervision, with workers frequently victims of their bosses' arbitrary and usually unmitigated authority. It is difficult enough to maintain steady employment at these kinds of "secondary" jobs, as many of us call them, even without the additional burden of raising children by oneself. Add the problems of juggling insecure jobs and unsympathetic bosses together with child care dilemmas, health emergencies, and housing crises . . . and "combining single parenthood with a job . . .," Christopher Jencks and Kathryn Edin conclude, "will sometimes be unworkable."[52] The case of Roslyn Hale, a welfare mother who's moved in and out of paid employment, illustrates the problem: According to a *New York Times* reporter's summary of her job history, "she . . . got a checkout job at a convenience store. But it required her to work the overnight shift, where drunks from a nearby bar taunted her and one threatened her at knife point. She left and found work at another convenience store, where she felt safer. But business took a downturn, and Ms. Hale was laid off." The cycle repeats itself. "I have worked," the mother reports, "gotten on aid, worked, gotten off aid. . . ."[53]

We get an especially acute glimpse into the complexity of these problems from Jason DeParle's 1994 profile of Mary Ann Moore, a Chicago mother of four children, who has also moved on and off the welfare rolls for years.[54] DeParle summarizes:

> At 33, Mary Ann Moore is a walking catalogue of the problems that can arise after a welfare recipient finds work. She has landed and lost at least 11 jobs in the past five years and gone through perhaps twice that many since receiving her first welfare check at 19. She has driven trucks and peddled nuts, fried eggs and bathed invalids. She has cruised the aisles of a mail-order warehouse on roller skates, pulling merchandise from shelves that stretched to the sky. She has strapped a revolver onto her 6-foot frame to guard the high-rises at Cabrini-Green, where she was raised.

Moore's problems in holding many of these jobs have rarely involved inadequate skills or tepid motivation; they have often involved problems with tensions and petty exercises of authority on the job. On her current job helping manage the kitchen at a shelter, on which she had been faring relatively well at the time of the article, for example, there was a ban on incoming phone calls. "I got kids," Moore exclaims. "How you gonna tell me I can't get no calls? I can't work no place my kids can't call me." Management finally relented, which helped Moore stay on the job, but the receptionist still claimed the authority not to patch calls through. Only after Moore banned the receptionist from using the coffee pot were they able to reach an accommodation. Finally, Moore can receive calls. [55]

As DeParle notes, the dignity that women on welfare potentially derive from going to work is elusive. If we want to help promote dignity and financial self-sufficiency for these women, we in the United States need to move beyond our reliance on a Stick Strategy that has etched neediness indelibly into the lives of scores of millions of American workers.

The "Underclass"

One further issue exposes us to the classic debate about the relative importance of the "culture of poverty" and the world of work. It is said that we have a new "underclass" in the United States[56]—a new generation of Americans outside the mainstream, mostly male, mostly black, many of them teens, mostly in core inner city neighborhoods, a new breed whose tough lives have developed even tougher attitudes, . . . hardened, callous, violent, impervious to conventional social standards. As the story goes, nothing can reach the members of this new underclass, these boys in the 'hood. If they survive their teens, they will be destitute or living on a different kind of dole, in their prison cells.

As conservative ideology has lengthened its shadow across public discourse in the 1980s and 1990s, more and more people have attributed the spread of the underclass to the incorrigibility and intractability of its members, their misoriented callousness, their preoccupation with violence and immediate gratification, their moral stance—in short, to a more vicious cycle of the "culture of poverty" than we've known before. You want to fix the problems, fix the values. Conservative theorist Richard Neuhaus focuses clearly on this dimension. "Of course not all who are 'socially incompetent' are in the underclass, not by a long shot. But many of them are. The underclass is the most concentrated population of those who cannot or will not cope when it comes to family responsibility, education, work, and living within the criminal law."[57] A number of African American intellectuals have recently echoed these calls for individual accountability in African American communities. Conservative writer Shelby Steele argues, for example, that "there will be no end to despair and no lasting solution to any of our problems until we rely on individual effort within the American mainstream, rather than collective action against the mainstream, as our means of advancement."[58]

But as with the other issues reviewed in this chapter, these public presuppositions have tended to overlook the role of deteriorating job opportunities almost altogether. For many young African American men in the United States, job prospects are slim. Wages when they work are spare. Job security

"What do you wanta' be if you grow up?"

is a will o' the wisp. Nowhere does the specter of the Stick Strategy cast a gloomier pall than over the lives of the "underclass."

The issues are complex, the evidence thorny, and the debates of interpretation rancorous. I want to make a point about a simple connection, not to resolve all the arguments. Here as elsewhere, people have been paying the price of the Stick Strategy. Perhaps nowhere else has the price been as high as among the young men of the inner city.

Before we can even consider this argument, however, we need to be careful in how we define the "underclass." When we look for definitions, we often find crude stereotypes. The stereotypes are easy to fashion but hard to fit to a more complex reality: The term "underclass," Jencks writes, often "conjures up a chronically jobless high school dropout who has had two or three children out of wedlock, has very little money to support them, and probably has either a criminal record or a history of welfare dependence."[59] But relatively few people fit this kind of stereotype even closely, much less perfectly.

Or, we tend to find criss-crossing, overlapping denotations, focusing in varying combinations on poverty, joblessness, race, neighborhood, criminal activity, and moral attitudes. For some clarity, we can turn to one of the most common and influential definitions: University of Chicago sociologist William Julius Wilson defines the "underclass" as a group "outside the mainstream of the American occupational system" or, more expansively, as those "who lack training and skills and either experience long-term unemployment or are not members of the labor force . . . and families that experience long-term spells of poverty and/or welfare dependency."[60] Because I have already discussed some of the dimensions associated with the family side of this definition, such as teen pregnancy and welfare dependency, I shall concentrate in this section on men.

In order to focus our inquiry, Jencks usefully suggests that in looking at men we concentrate especially on the "jobless poor," those of working age who are unemployed or outside the labor force *and* who live in poor families, while nonetheless understanding that there could be many other possible filters for our inquiry. This allows us to distinguish between those men who are poor despite working steadily and those whose poverty is associated with the absence of employment. It also allows us to distinguish between those "jobless" men who, for whatever reasons—independent income, family support—evade poverty and those who endure it.

Using this working definition, Jencks finds that the incidence of the jobless poor was higher among adult men for both whites and African Americans in the 1970s and 1980s than in the 1960s, but did not show any clear and obvious tendency to rise from the 1970s to the 1980s. Confirming popular perceptions, the frequency of the jobless poor was considerably higher for African Americans than for whites, reaching 3.5 times the white rate in 1986 in the noninstitutional population.[61]

Perhaps the most striking pattern over time, and certainly one that contributes to the popular perceptions, is that the relative disadvantages of African American men have intensified considerably since the 1970s. As we saw in Chapter 1, hourly earnings have declined more sharply for African American men than for white men. And relative rates of joblessness have deteriorated among black men as well.[62]

Why has the "underclass" grown and its problems intensified? And, in particular, since so much of the recent discussion focuses on the racial dimension, why has the plight of younger African American men grown more acute? Many tend to assume that these different aspects of the "underclass" phenomenon can be most usefully attributed to the characteristics of the "underclass" themselves. They have become relatively less skilled, less intelligent, or less committed. They may effectively be held accountable for their own conditions, a classic instance of "blaming the victim." If they behaved differently, or acquired more advantageous characteristics, they could lift themselves out of the "underclass." (One major exception to such promises of melioration, of course, involves the resurgent focus on the relatively lower IQ scores of African Americans. If disadvantages for African Americans are substantially due to lower intelligence, and that relatively lower average intelligence is genetically determined, then the victims can be blamed but can't be helped.[63])

But, perhaps surprisingly, since these impressions are so widespread, we find relatively little evidence to confirm this simple kind of explanation. There has not been any increase in the numbers of men who have dropped out of school before high-school completion, and, in particular, dropout rates among African Americans have been declining fairly substantially since the 1960s.[64] Nor does it appear, despite all the publicity about falling SAT scores and virtual illiteracy among inner-city youth, that there has been a general decline in cognitive skills among those coming out of school. The SAT evidence is somewhat misleading, to begin with, because only students who want to go to college take the test. A much more comprehensive standard is the National Assessment of Educational Progress (NAEP), administered since 1970 to all high school students. By this evidence, average cognitive skills have been improving or holding steady. And, especially striking given the popular stereotypes, average cognitive achievement among African American high school students has increased fairly steadily since the 1970s.[65]

This evidence is insufficient, however. It is not enough to show that average levels of cognitive skills have been improving or that the percentage above a certain basic level has been growing. Since the skill requirements of making it in our advanced, complex society grow ever more daunting, it may be more relevant to look at trends in the relative *equality* of educational and cognitive achievements. Are the relatively less skilled, even if their levels of achievement have been improving, falling farther and farther behind?

Apparently not. Educational attainment has grown more equal by race over the past twenty years. Perhaps more important, standard measures of reading and writing skills have also grown relatively more equal by race over the past twenty years.[66] In one systematic analysis, John Bound and Richard B. Freeman conclude that interracial differences in educational attainment explain little or none of the deterioration of African American men's labor market position since 1973. Nor do they find evidence that a widening of the gap in skills not picked up at school can help explain that deterioration; "we find little support for the hypothesis that deteriorated labor market skills of young blacks due to, say, poor schooling, worsened family background resources, or increased drug use, explains their declining economic position."[67]

If not skill factors, what does help explain the deteriorating economic position of younger African American men, the exemplary bearers of the "underclass" banner? Resisting prevailing temptations to put forward single-factor or unicausal explanations, Bound and Freeman identify a host of important factors, including shifts in industry demand, the declining minimum wage, reduced vigor in affirmative action enforcement, and eroding union strength.

Among these factors, as a number of other analysts have made clear, the stark and sharp decline in decent job opportunities, especially in the bottom half of the earnings distribution, has had especially strong impact. In the Midwest, for example, Bound and Freeman find that a major role is played by the "huge drop in the proportion of young black workers in manufacturing"[68]— jobs that in the Midwest had been relatively high paying and had contributed to the gradual improvement in the economic fortunes of African American men in the 1960s and early 1970s. Jencks thinks that the decline in decent jobs may help explain some of the very particular patterns that have helped shaped popular impressions of the "underclass"—intermittent work habits among many younger African American men, with many older African American men eventually dropping out of the labor force altogether. He hypothesizes:[69]

- "Good" jobs (that is, steady jobs that paid enough to support a family) became scarcer after 1970.
- Firms increasingly reserved these jobs for the college educated and for men with good work histories.
- Young men without higher education therefore found it harder to get good jobs. They responded by postponing marriage and by taking poorly paid, short-term jobs.
- The substitution of short-term jobs for steady jobs drove up the percentage of young men who were idle in a typical week but had little effect on the percentage who were idle for long periods.
- As young men get older, they become increasingly reluctant to take poorly paid short-term jobs. Some find steady jobs. Others drop out of the labor market entirely.

But even with this scenario, which places such paramount emphasis on declining job opportunities, many might nonetheless fault African American men for "giving up" too quickly or easily, for not hanging in there and working steadily like everyone else. Haven't they become incorrigible?

Two factors seem especially important in responding to this concern.

First, on average younger African American men have not become "incorrigible," at least not yet, at least not as far as we can tell from the evidence. When job opportunities improve in areas—location, industry, occupation—for which younger African American men can reasonably qualify, their employment rates, work records, and earnings all tend to improve dramatically. Complementary studies by Richard B. Freeman and by MIT economist Paul Osterman found, for example, that young black male economic fortunes improved dramatically in the mid- to late-1980s where acute labor shortages developed in central-city areas and where low-end earnings were bid up as a result. Comparing across metropolitan areas, for example, Freeman found:[70]

Local labor market shortages greatly improve the employment opportunities of disadvantaged young men, substantially raising the percentage employed and reducing their unemployment rate. . . . Labor market shortages also significantly increase the hourly earnings of disadvantaged youths, particularly blacks. In the 1980s the increase for young men in tight labor markets was large enough to offset the deterioration in the real and relative earnings of the less skilled that marked these years.

Osterman conducted some special labor market surveys in Boston in the 1980s, where the "Massachusetts Miracle" was helping drive employment and spread prosperity even into the inner city. And welfare benefits remained among the nation's most generous during this period (before the current Republican governor William Weld began his scorched-earth program). "If the neoconservatives are right [about the intractability of the underclass]," as Osterman frames the problem, "generosity should have inhibited the response of poor people to the economic opportunities afforded by long-term growth. If the liberals are right, the combination of full employment and active social policy should have paid off in a reduction of poverty rates."[71] As far as the data would allow reasonably firm conclusions, Osterman reports that the "liberals" win this face-off. "Full employment does in fact deliver many of the benefits its advocates have promised. Poverty rates fell substantially in Boston, and it is very clear that the poor did respond to economic opportunity when it was offered." Indeed, his findings held especially firmly for African Americans. "Blacks have benefited a good deal from full employment in Boston," he writes; "thus, given opportunity, they evidently responded in 'acceptable' ways."[72]

Second, it is not even all that obvious that young African Americans "behave" all that differently from whites. Their opportunities differ, clearly, but it is not clear that they respond to those opportunities differently than whites do or would.

To consider this possibility, we need to distinguish carefully between "joblessness" and, among other conditions, "shiftlessness." The jobless are either unemployed or out of the labor force. The "shiftless"—to try to pin a precise definition on the tail of a normatively loaded term—are those who are not only "jobless" but evidently don't want to work, either because they are independently wealthy and choose not to or, as University of Chicago sociologists Marta Tienda and Haya Stier write, "because they are lazy and prefer other forms of support, even if the support is grossly inadequate to maintain a decent life-style."[73] Are a large proportion of the "jobless" in inner-city neighborhoods truly "shiftless"?

According to some special surveys undertaken for the Chicago inner city, Tienda and Stier think not. In general, most inner-city adults work and most of those who do not work nonetheless appear committed to working if they can find suitable opportunities. Something like five or six percent of inner-city adults might reasonably conform to their definition of "shiftlessness"—being not only jobless but also showing virtually no interest in working even though they would be capable of it. The percentages are higher among African American men who were not parents than for others, but this is a relatively small group. "Most of the evidence," Tienda and Stier conclude, "showed that willingness to work was the norm in Chicago's inner city."[74]

One key to assessing behavior in this context involves what economists call the "reservation wage"—the wage in available work below which potential workers may decide that it's simply not worth the effort, that it makes sense to try to find some other way of surviving. To listen to the conservatives, it would sometimes appear that workers ought to be willing to work at any wage, that the dignity of employment should be enough no matter how dirt-cheap the wage level. But both standard economic theory and survey results suggest that *everyone* will have some "reservation wage," a self-defined mini-mum wage below which they won't accept a job.

If the underclass were truly incorrigible, then we ought to find that their reservation wages were relatively or "unrealistically" high, that they were un-willing to work at wage levels that more "reasonable" or ambitious workers would be willing to accept. There is much that we don't know on this issue. And we need to be careful in reaching conclusions in any case, since what people may say is their "reservation wage" may not be very reliable. But it does not appear, in general, that African American men are holding them-selves out of the labor market simply or primarily because their wage stand-ards are too high. In the Chicago inner-city survey, for example, Tienda and Stier found that "black men appeared most willing and white men least will-ing to accept low-paying jobs"—the average wage rate expected by those who had worked and wanted a job was $5.50 an hour for black men, $6.20 for Mexican and Puerto Rican men, and $10.20 for white men.[75] It is a measure of how low our wage standards have sunk in the more than two decades of the wage squeeze that $5.50 an hour may strike some readers as "unreasonably" high a standard. But if there are other ways of surviving at a roughly compar-able living standard, should everyone always prefer working at a chump's job for chump's change? How many meals can the "dignity" of paid employment actually provide?

Crime and the Garrison State

Surely, though, there are many members of the "underclass" who carry it too far. It's one thing to choose not to work. It's quite another to choose to rob, sell drugs, shoot and kill. Haven't I glossed over the criminal element of the underclass? Isn't the life of crime one of the main income alternatives to paid employment, especially for younger black men? No manner of problems in the labor market can condone—as a *Washington Post* headline I remember from the 1960s labeled them—"hopheads and hoodlums."

Yes, there is too much street crime. And yes, the scourge of random shooting that has come to plague some inner-city neighborhoods is tragic and intolerable. But no amount of moral outrage should divert our attention from two important economic stories about "crime in the streets." Both are speculative, because there is still so much we don't know in this area. Both need to be addressed nonetheless. One involves the relationship between criminal activity and job opportunities. The other involves the reasons for the mad-cap rush in the United States to lock everyone up and throw away the key—the growth of our own home-grown American version of the garrison state.

Jobs and Crime

Despite years of investigation and mountains of studies, the social science literature on the economic determinants of crime remains murky. It is certainly possible, given the available evidence, that crime increases when unemployment, inequality, or poverty (or some combination of these factors) rise. But these effects are not so well established and robust that we can take these general connections as gospel.[76] For any conclusion we might want to reach, further qualifications inevitably seem necessary.

Does neighborhood disadvantage condition higher crime rates, for example? Yes and no. General measures of the relative income and occupational status of neighborhood residents do not seem to be associated with variations in neighborhood crime rates. But more specific measures of the degree of a neighborhood's absolute deprivation—poverty rates, lack of resources—do seem positively associated with crime.[77]

For purposes of the discussion in this chapter, however, the questions posed in this literature have often been too general and too global. The more specific question that is relevant here is whether the deepening reliance on the Stick Strategy in the United States over the past twenty years has contributed significantly to the character and incidence of crime on the streets? With the question posed in this way, it begins to look as if the connection between jobs and crime resembles the connection between jobs and welfare in several important ways.

During the 1980s and early 1990s, despite all the hyperbole and legitimate fears, most crime did not appear to increase; it may even have decreased. Standard measures of reported crime, which keep tabs on "offenses known to the police," show that the rate of property crime fell from 1979 to 1993—from 5,017 reported crimes per 100,000 population in 1979 to 4,737 in 1993. The general category of violent crime shows an increase, but this was essentially confined to only two subcomponents, forcible rape and aggravated assault. The incidence of robbery—a property crime classified definitionally as violent—did not increase from the early 1980s through the early 1990s.[78] In addition, the measure that many criminologists consider a more accurate barometer of crimes and attempted crimes, "victimization rates" reported by crime targets in what are called "victimization" surveys, showed a decline: The total victimization rate of crimes against persons in 1980 was 116 per 1,000 people, while the rate in 1992 was 93 per 1,000. The victimization rate of total crimes against persons in 1992, indeed, was the lowest since the surveys were initiated in 1973.[79]

At a purely superficial level, this would appear to suggest a very weak linkage between jobs and street crime. With real wages falling and job insecurity rising during the 1980s, we might have expected property crime rates to have increased. Instead, they declined slightly. The *prima facie* evidence does not seem to point toward a big impact of the Stick Strategy on crime.

But the recent leveling off of street crime rates is only part of the story on the crime front over the past fifteen years. Perhaps the most important development—and one which certainly captured the popular imagination—was the apparent spread of illicit drug activity, especially in many inner cities. and the rise of crack, a dangerously concentrated form of cocaine. Although it is not so obvious that the actual incidence of drug use increased, drug arrest rates soared and the "war on drugs" pushed the problem to the top of the headlines.[80]

It is here that some of the economic connections to crime seem clearest. For many if not most of the actual participants in the drug trade, the distribution and sale of drugs is clearly seen at least in part as a means of economic survival. Indeed, it is with the drug trade that we might expect to find the clearest interactions between work and crime, since the economic returns to other kinds of property crimes are often so minuscule for perpetrators on the street, as opposed to those on Wall Street.[81]

A recent case study by Robert MacCoun and Peter Reuter of Washington, D.C. of arrestees for drug offenses provides some useful clues:[82] Most "drug offenders" both work at a variety of legitimate jobs *and* deal. Of those in their sample, 60 percent work at least five days a week at paid employment. Their imputed earnings per hour on their drug "jobs" was high, estimated at around $30, but it would apparently have been much lower if they concentrated on drug-dealing full-time (since there are only a few prime times during the week when the drug trade flourishes). "Among dealers who are caught by the criminal justice system," MacCoun and Reuter write, "drug selling is indeed a much more profitable activity than that same population's legitimate occupations, both on an hourly basis and in total monthly earnings."[83] Despite these substantially higher (imputed) hourly rates, however, the life of drug crime remained a part-time gig. "Though more lucrative than their legitimate employment, drug dealing still did not launch this population on a path to high incomes. . . . The finding that most persons charged with drug selling are currently employed is somewhat perplexing. If drug selling is so profitable, why maintain a legitimate job as well—particularly one with a relatively modest wage?" MacCoun and Reuter suggest a number of possible explanations. Dealers may be diversifying their risks. They may find straight work and dealing complementary, especially if they can cultivate potential drug customers on the job. Perhaps most suggestive, they speculate that "perhaps a more useful way of viewing the relationship of drug dealing and legitimate work is to see that the former provides an underground form of 'moonlighting' for poorly educated urban males—an opportunity for a few hours of more highly paid work to supplement their primary jobs."[84]

In this respect, the "criminal activities" of drug dealing among inner-city men begin to resemble the "dependency activities" of inner-city women, a comparison which seems to have escaped most analysts studying either drug crime or welfare. As we have already seen, many women try to make up for the inadequate wages of either welfare or low-wage jobs through "packaging," through trying to find ways of combining a number of different sources of income in as complementary a fashion as possible. Similarly, many younger men appear to try to "package" straight jobs with a life of crime in order to make up for the inadequacy and insecurity of either kind of income-earning activity by itself. Among younger adults, Mercer L. Sullivan observes in his study of youth crime and employment in the inner city, "occasional crime for economic gain overlapped with early employment."[85]

These interactions between straight time and crime time are sometimes subtle. In an interesting longitudinal analysis of young men's economic activities over nearly a decade, for example, economists Ann Dryden Witte and Helen Tauchen find that the time constraints on combining straight and illegal activities appear to have a greater influence on crime than do income opportunities alone.[86] The more time that young men spend at work or school (if everything else is held constant), the lower will be their probability of arrest; they apparently have less time to commit crimes and less time to get caught (or perhaps simply better alibis if suspected). But more conventional measures of income-earning opportunities appear to have less effect: all else equal, for example, those with a high school degree are just as likely to be arrested as those who have dropped out. It isn't so much how much you'll earn at a straight job, it would appear, as a natural and quite conventional effort to spread one's risks and cover one's bets that appears to influence life along the criminal path.

If the connections running from job and income to crime are subtle and complicated, however, the return linkage from criminal history to economic opportunities is stark and inescapable. Those with past involvement in the criminal justice system pay a heavy price. John Bound and Richard B. Freeman report a "striking adverse effect of past incarceration on employment."[87] The effects are big, too. The soaring increase in incarceration rates during the 1980s, especially among African American men, has apparently had a dramatic influence on employment rates, again especially among African American men. So many African American men are in prison or bearing the imprint of the criminal justice system like scarlet letters on their chests that their rate of joblessness, which is, as we have already seen, a signal barometer of the "underclass", has been destined to soar.[88]

What seems crucial, then, in considering the connection between jobs and crime, in the end, is not so much why so many people commit crimes as why we condemn so many caught in the web of our criminal justice system to years if not lives behind bars. This may be the front-page story about crime and jobs in the United States over the past twenty years.

Prisons and the Garrison State

I assume that most readers are familiar with the basic facts: Since the late 1970s, incarceration rates have soared without precedent in the United States. Our prison and jail populations have grown nearly beyond bounds. We've been building new prisons as if we're determined to compensate for the end of the Cold War. We are becoming, it would appear, something akin to a Garrison State. Mike Davis writes about the phenomenon in the state of California:[89]

> California has the third-largest penal system in the world, following China and the United States as a whole. . . . An emergent "prison-industrial complex" increasingly rivals agribusiness as the dominant force in the life of rural California and competes with land developers as the chief seducer of legislators in Sacramento. It has become a monster that threatens to overpower and devour its creators, and its uncontrollable growth ought to rattle a national consciousness now complacent at the thought of a permanent prison class.

In 1979, there were 301,470 inmates in federal and state prisons and another 158,394 in local jails. By 1992, those numbers had grown to 851,205 in prisons and 441,781 in jails.[90] The prison incarceration rate per 100,000 resident population had climbed from 133 in 1979 to 330 in 1992. When we add in the total number of people on either probation or parole, the criminal justice system in 1992 had 4.8 million people in its grasp, accounting for 2.5 percent of the entire adult population—including, among adults, 4.4 percent of all males, 1.7 percent of all whites, and fully 8.3 percent of all blacks.[91]

It wasn't cheap extending the grasp of the system. In 1991, total government expenditures on the criminal justice system—including police, courts, and corrections—totalled $75 billion. These outlays represented an increase in total system expenditures of 166 percent in real terms over those in 1979, during a period of increasingly tight state and local budgets. Total criminal justice system employment could have filled a fairly large city: In 1990 employees in police, courts, and corrections had swelled to 1.7 million, up by 40 percent over their levels in 1979.

These are not small numbers. Criminal justice system employment in 1990 amounted to just under 10 percent of all government employment at all levels. Criminal justice system expenditures in 1991 were one-fourth the level of all state and local government expenditures on education, for example, and close to three-fifths the level of all state and local spending on public welfare.[92]

Where were we putting all these people? By 1991, the number of federal and state prisons in the United States had mushroomed to 1,315. According to the best available estimates, at least 400 of these prisons opened their gates for the first time during the 1980s. In 1991, construction of yet another 218 federal and state prisons was planned to the tune of a minimum projected capital cost of $3.2 billion.[93]

And when we didn't feel secure enough from all this public spending on our own safety, we turned to the private sector. In 1979, 282,000 workers were employed as private guards. By 1994 those numbers had ballooned to 717,000, an increase of 250 percent, bringing private protection employment to more than 40 percent the level of public employment in the criminal justice business.[94] If we project recent trends into the twenty-first century, lawyer Adam Walinsky writes, "most of the new [security] officers will be privately paid, available for the protection not of the citizenry as a whole . . . but of the commercial and residential enclaves that can afford them."[95]

And the growth is expected to continue. In the Labor Department's projections of the fastest growing occupations through 2005, "guards" are on the list of the occupations with the most rapid expected absolute increase in employment levels and "correction officers" make the list for those with the highest expected rates of growth.[96]

Most Americans simply shrug their shoulders at these numbers. We've been carefully taught that we must spend all this money to keep our streets safe, that we have no other alternatives in the war on crime.

But as soon as we compare ourselves with other countries, we are even more notable on the incarceration front than we are in conflictual labor relations. In 1992–93, according to the best comparable data available, the U.S. incarceration rate per 100,000 population was 519. The next highest rate among the leading advanced countries was Canada at 116, barely one-fifth as high. The only countries in our ballpark were Russia, at 558, and South Africa, at 368.[97]

You would think, if we listened to the public justifications for our addiction to incarceration, that our crime rates must be correspondingly higher than those in the other leading advanced countries. But the differences in crime rates are nowhere nearly as large. Looking at victimization surveys, measuring citizens' reports of criminal victimization and therefore avoiding some of the biases potentially inherent in reported arrests, property crimes and robbery rates in the United States are not even the highest among the advanced countries, and are certainly not five times as high. For property crimes, for example, victimization rates in 1992 in Australia, Canada, the Netherlands, and New Zealand were all higher than in the United States. And yet, the average of the incarceration rate for those four countries was 98 (per 100,000 resident population), only 17 percent the rate in the United States.[98]

Why are we so determined to put people behind bars? This is an interesting puzzle about which we're just beginning to develop hypotheses. There are many explanations, including factors as diverse as bureaucratic imperatives, symbolic politics, racism, and plain public fears.[99] Cynicism and resignation clearly matter. As Wendy Kaminer observes, "The drive to imprison more people for longer periods of time seems unstoppable, fueled not just by fury and fear but by a sense of resignation. It is as if all we can do is warehouse people until they die or are too old and decrepit to threaten anyone on the outside again."[100]

For the purposes of the discussion here, two important possible explanations stand out.

First, and obviously, the U.S. criminal justice system, and perhaps large portions of the citizenry as well, believes that many African Americans simply belong behind bars. African American men, a spare 6 percent of the total population, now account for more than half the total prison population, and the proportions continue to grow.[101] In 1990, of all African American men between the ages of twenty and twenty-nine, one in every four was either in prison or on probation or parole.[102] Just five years later, in 1995, the proportion had climbed to one in three.[103] "What is even scarier," Princeton political scientist John J. DiIulio Jr., comments, "is these data don't look at what is just around the corner." DiIulio projects, based on recent developments, that the proportion may even rise to one in two within a few more years.[104] "If current trends continue," Queens College sociologist Andrew Hacker warns, "a period of imprisonment will be a typical experience for almost all Americans born black and male."[105]

Does the structure of jobs in the United States matter, following the theme of this chapter? Again the issues are complicated, as the discussion of the previous section should indicate. But it is difficult to avoid some simple suppositions. Andrew Hacker is bold enough to state them starkly:[106]

> Black men who engage in crime are twelve times more likely than white men to commit the kinds of offenses that land perpetrators in prison. The explanation is simple. Among all races and classes, including the very rich, there are some people who have what might be called larcenous proclivities. Those who are white and wear white collars are better able to arrange thefts that are difficult to detect. Even blue-collar workers can steal from loading docks and construction sites with a fair degree of impunity. But if you are black and poor or unemployed and drawn toward unlawful taking, you haven't many options other than holding up small shops or preying on pedestrians. Moreover, you

are more likely to get caught, since the police devote most of their energy to looking for people like you.

At issue here is more than a lack of decent jobs and steady pay. We have created a large stratum whose members have concluded that they are scorned by the larger society, which wants them locked far away and out of sight.

The second possible explanation is much more speculative. But as I've continued to compare the character and impact of labor-management systems across countries, I've been unable to escape the mounting suspicion that those countries with the top-heaviest systems of labor control are also those who lock up the highest proportion of their populations. Why should the number of managers and supervisors at work be connected with the number of people behind bars?

However speculative, however far-fetched, the statistical association is manifest. We can take the same measure of the bureaucratic burden we first encountered in Chapter 2 and compare it with the incarceration rates introduced above. Among the leading advanced countries, there are eleven for which we can compare the two characteristics. (This adds a couple of countries to the list that we've studied in earlier chapters in order to fill out the number of observations.) Excluding the United States, since its incarceration rate is so extreme, the simple correlation between the percent of nonfarm employment in administrative and managerial occupations in 1989 and the incarceration rate per 100,000 population in 1992–93 is 0.73 (statistically significant at 1%). (Including the U.S. in the sample lowers the correlation somewhat, since the United States lives in a world by itself on the prison front, but the correlation remains high at 0.44, still statistically significant at 5%.) Countries with top-heavy corporate bureaucracies tend to lock a lot of people behind bars. Indeed, looking more closely at the numbers, the countries cluster tightly in two groups. There are the countries that seem most clearly to feature conflictual labor relations, to rely on the Stick Strategy—in this sample, in addition to the United States, Canada, the United Kingdom and Australia. And there are those that build their labor relations upon substantially more cooperative foundations—in this sample of eleven countries including Belgium, Denmark, Finland, Germany, Japan, the Netherlands, and Sweden. In the former group, the average incarceration rate, excluding the United States in 1992–93, was 100—and would have been 205 if the U.S. had been added to the four. In the latter group, the average was 62.[107]

The most striking pattern in the data is how closely clustered are the two groups of countries. Repeating how speculatively I advance this connection, I venture Figure 5.1, again excluding the United States because its incarceration rate puts it off the scale. On the horizontal axis lie the countries' incarceration rates. On the vertical axis is our familiar measure of the bureaucratic burden. The two groupings are tight. There appear to be two kinds of countries.

FIGURE 5.1

Bureaucracies and Prisons

Percent administrative and managerial employment, incarceration rates, 10 advanced countries (excluding U.S.)

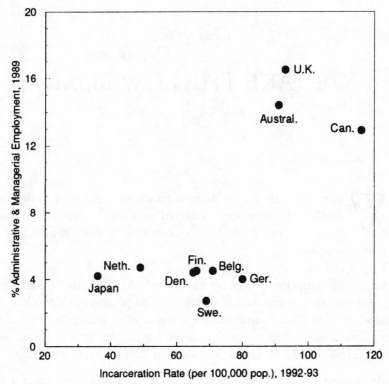

What could tie together those two groups of countries? There are a number of possible explanations. But I cannot shake the suspicion that habits of control bred in one social domain spill over to other areas of social life. Accustomed to controlling their employees from the top down, the countries with relatively more conflictual labor relations systems also seem to be addicted to locking up their offenders. Subordinates are supposed to follow orders. The culture may extend not only to the workplace but also to the criminal justice system. The shadows of the Stick Strategy may cast their darkness over much more of our society than we have even begun to imagine. When we finish toting up the costs of our reliance on the Stick in the United States, should we include the human and financial costs of our jails and prisons and cops and guards? I've begun to suspect that we should.

Chapter 6

WE TAKE THE LOW ROAD

Whrough cooperation hen international competition hit the U.S. full force in the early 1980s," *Business Week* observed in a 1992 cover story, "most manufacturers slashed labor costs by extracting concessions or shipping jobs overseas."

General Electric was one of those companies. Its electric motors division was facing stiff competition from both lower-waged rivals in the United States and from overseas operations. Like many U.S. corporations, GE took to the offensive. It demanded substantial wage concessions and closed two of its plants. Cowed, its workers accepted an eleven percent pay cut and relinquished scheduled raises of $1.30 an hour. The *Business Week* account continued:[1]

> What looked like a sweet deal then, GE now sees as a blunder. True, the pay cuts saved $25 million a year. And the plant closings eliminated 1,000 jobs. But both company and union officials say worker morale sank like a stone. "Productivity went to hell," says [GE's industrial relations vice-president]. . . .

Many who compare the advanced economies refer to two distinctive strategies for economic management. The "high road" seeks to build economic growth and prosperity through cooperation and strong worker rewards, including relatively rapid real wage growth. The "low road" relies on conflict and insecurity, control and harsh worker punishments, and often features relatively stagnant or even declining real wage growth. Both are coherent strategies, both can conceivably work.

Most U.S. corporations have been traveling the "low road" with accelerating speed over the past twenty years. We saw in the previous two chapters how high a price individual workers and their families have been paying. But we have all been paying another price, perhaps equally severe. A reasonable argument can be made that the "low road" strategy is much bumpier than the "high road" as a macroeconomic path toward rapid and stable economic

144

growth. Millions of Americans have borne the costs of the Stick Strategy in their lives and livelihoods. All of us have shouldered the burden of the severe macroeconomic costs that it imposes. The low road is a plausible route for corporations to travel. But the U.S. economy as a whole could apparently do better—probably much, much better.

Readers may resist this preview of arguments to come. Once upon a time, perhaps in the 1970s and 1980s, the United States was lagging behind some of its major competitors. But this is the 1990s. Many think that the U.S. economy has revived while other European economies have begun to suffer from arteriosclerosis. What about the U.S. "jobs miracle"? What about massive unemployment in Europe? We may be traveling the "low road" in the United States, but isn't that now the quicker route to prosperity?

This is a widespread perception, but it's off target. Vast differences exist among the European economies, no less than between the United States and Japan. It turns out, when we look more closely at countries within "Europe," that those economies that have most clearly pursued the "high road" of cooperation, that have most clearly relied on the Carrot rather than the Stick, have continued to feature much lower unemployment rates than in the United States. Other European economies, with less cooperative industrial relations, are the ones that have faltered. Whether the comparison is within Europe or across the Atlantic, the high road remains a relatively smoother thoroughfare.

Productivity Potholes

Rapid productivity growth is critical for the health of a macroeconomy, a judgment with which almost all economists would agree. "Depression, runaway inflation, or civil war can make a country poor," writes Stanford University economist Paul Krugman, "but only productivity growth can make it rich."[2]

Why? Rapid productivity growth creates room for rapid wage growth, reductions in working hours, and more productive investment. It creates the possibility that future generations will be able to enjoy a more comfortable standard of living. It can help substantially to reduce inflationary pressures, and, as a result, to permit looser monetary policy and, potentially, lower interest rates. With lower interest rates, investment may blossom further. And thus, rapid productivity growth in the future can be sustained through labor-enhancing technology. It's a virtuous cycle.

It therefore matters critically what kinds of strategies corporations adopt to improve productivity. The Stick Strategy is one such approach. Another main alternative, which I shall call the Carrot Strategy for the purposes of discussion in this and subsequent chapters, relies on cooperation, wage-growth incentives, job security, and productivity bonuses.[3] Is it possible to compare their relative effects on productivity growth? Which works better as a spur to workers—the fear of the stick or the taste of the carrot?

Common sense might lead us to expect the Carrot Strategy to have substantial advantages. Imagine two workers in the same industry, working in firms with more or less comparable machinery. One works in a firm with massive, top-down management, little job security, stagnant wages, no chance to help participate in organizing or planning production. The other works in a firm with a much less obtrusive bureaucratic structure, substantial job security, rapid wage growth—particularly if and when productivity itself improves—and the opportunity to participate in decisions about the organization of work. It seems likely that the worker tasting the Carrot will make a much more substantial commitment to the progress and future of the enterprise.

But we don't need to rely on our intuitions to pursue this comparison. After twenty years of concern about sluggish productivity growth, a mountain of studies is now available reviewing the effects of worker participation and control on productivity, especially in the United States. The principal message of this literature is unambiguous. Productivity is higher, if all other things are equal, in enterprises that feature relatively greater worker involvement in production, participation in decision-making, and profit-sharing. In a major survey of much of the existing research, for example, David I. Levine and Laura D'Andrea Tyson, then both at the University of California–Berkeley (Tyson more recently chaired the Council of Economic Advisers in the Clinton Administration), conclude: "In most reported cases the introduction of substantive shopfloor participation (job redesign and participative work groups) leads to some combination of an increase in satisfaction, commitment, quality and productivity, and a reduction in turnover and absenteeism, at least in the short run."[4]

These gains cannot be obtained simply by arm-waving and cheerleading, by management declaring to workers that it's turned over a new leaf and will henceforth pay much more attention to their views. Token gestures in the cooperative direction are not enough; real changes in the character of the system are required. As Levine and Tyson further conclude, "the size and strength of the effect [of participation on performance] are contingent on the form and content of participation."[5] Their reviews and others' seem to point to at least four crucial conditions for a successful move toward a more cooperative approach: real sharing of productivity gains with workers; significant employment security (so that workers won't worry that production innovations will result in layoffs); substantial institutional changes to build *group* involvement, not just individual participation (since much of workers' contribution to production depends on group effort and coordination); and protection of the rights of individual employees (so that "whistle-blowers" and "trouble-makers" won't fear for their jobs).[6]

And this seems best to describe the experiences of those relatively few, large U.S. corporations who appear to have transformed their labor relations. Xerox and the Amalgamated Cloth and Textile Workers Union (now merged with garment workers into the combined union called UNITE) have had such success over the past ten years with fully cooperative programs, for example, that Xerox is planning to bring something like 300 jobs back from abroad to a new plant in New York where it expects substantial costs savings, despite relatively higher wages, because of the higher productivity and product quality which cooperation entails.[7] At Scott Paper, similarly, joint management-labor teams give workers more decision-making power inside the company, "a move so successful in reducing costs and boosting quality," *Business Week* reports, "that other paper companies, such as Champion International Corp., are copying it."[8]

A final lesson from many of these studies seems crucial: Productivity gains can't be achieved through piecemeal reforms. The Carrot Strategy has an internal logic, a structural coherence, which cannot be patched together easily. Among other dimensions, it depends heavily on a supportive institutional environment, a set of government policies and regulations that encourage cooperation and discourage excessive use of the stick.

This means that, even though the historical experience with American experiments may seem promising, we cannot place too much emphasis on the literature reviewing participatory experiments in the United States, since all those experiments share a common national institutional environment that, to say the least, does *not* encourage cooperative approaches. Some policies affecting labor-management relations may vary from state to state, such as right-to-work laws, but in general tests of the differences between the Stick approach and the Carrot alternative are insufficient and incomplete within the American context.

This suggests that we should try to learn as much as we can from comparisons across countries featuring different kinds of labor-management systems, however difficult and vexing those comparisons may be. And here, at least at first blush, available evidence seems to suggest strong comparative advantages on the productivity growth front among those economies most clearly featuring a cooperative approach in the organization of production.

We can begin with the simplest possible piece of evidence. Grouping the advanced economies into those featuring cooperative labor-management systems and those displaying conflictual approaches, we can compare average productivity growth rates between the two groups of countries.

A number of different observers have provided us with classification or ranking schemes for dividing countries into these two categories, not all of which perfectly agree.[9] It seems safest to settle on the countries about whose features there seems to be the greatest agreement, and to leave out some intermediate cases with mixed characteristics. Among the dozen advanced countries we've been following since Chapter 1, this would give us, at least for the purposes of preliminary analysis, Japan, Germany, the Netherlands, Norway, and Sweden as representatives of the cooperative approach and the United

States, the United Kingdom, and Canada for the conflictual model. (This treats, for example, France and Italy as intermediate cases, economies displaying notable aspects of both kinds of approaches.)

Looking across the business-cycle peaks from 1973 to 1989, we can compare average annual productivity growth rates for the business sector for these two groups of countries. (I cut the comparison at 1989 in part because in the most recent year for which data were available, 1993, these economies were at very different points of their respective cycles. The last section of the chapter extends the story into the 1990s.) In the five cooperative economies, productivity grew at an average annual rate of 1.9 percent over those sixteen years.[10] In the four conflictual countries, the average productivity growth rate was a much more moderate 1.1 percent, barely more than half as fast.[11]

Some may worry about one aspect of this comparison: Focusing on the business sector includes the service industries, where U.S. productivity growth has historically lagged considerably behind that among its competitors. But even if we look just at manufacturing, the one area where U.S. firms began to experience a bit of a revival during the 1980s, the differences are nearly as pronounced. Among the cooperative countries, average annual pro-

FIGURE 6.1

Productivity Growth in "Cooperative" and "Conflictual" Economies

Average annual % productivity growth, 1973–89, business and manufacturing sectors

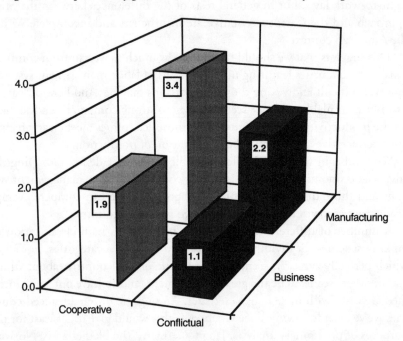

Source: Author's tabulations, OECD and BLS data; see text and notes.

ductivity growth between 1973 and 1989 was 3.4 percent. Among the conflictual economies, it averaged 2.2 percent.[12] Figure 6.1 graphically presents
these comparisons between cooperative and conflictual economies, with the
front row of bars for the business sector and the rear row for manufacturing.

These comparisons are intriguing, but we need to be careful about the inferences we draw from them. The implication in the context of this discussion is that productivity growth rates have been more rapid in the cooperative
economies *because* they feature relatively more cooperative systems of labor
management. But there could obviously be other explanations for productivity growth rates having nothing to do with the character of economies'
labor-management relations. We know that productive investment, which
typically increases the amount of capital that each worker gets to use, normally enhances productivity growth. Perhaps these differences between the
two groups of countries are due to different paces of investment?

There are indeed differences in the rate of increase in capital per worker
across these countries, to which we shall return in the following section. But
even after controlling for these differences, we still find that the impact of
labor relations remains strong.[13]

In one recent study, for example, labor economists Robert Buchele and Jens
Christiansen, of Smith and Mount Holyoke Colleges respectively, study differences in productivity growth rates among the G-7 economies over the period from the early 1960s through the late 1980s.[14] They control for the effect
of the rate of increase in the capital-labor ratio, which of course had a positive
influence on productivity growth rates. Having taken capital intensity into account, they examine the effect of their own measure of the cooperative character of the countries' labor-management systems, which they derive from a
factor analysis of a number of different dimensions of those systems. On their
scale, the three among the G-7 economies with decidedly the lowest scores on
their index of cooperation were the United States, the United Kingdom, and
Canada (in that order, from the least cooperative)—which is consistent with
my categorization of these three countries as conflictual examples in the preliminary tabulations above. They find that the degree of cooperation in an
economy, if other things are equal, has a positive (and statistically significant)
impact on productivity growth. Their study thus leads them to feel comfortable with a starkly simple generalization. After all the quantitative bells and
whistles, they conclude that "co-operation fosters productivity growth. . . ."[15]

We can think about the effect of labor relations on productivity in a
slightly different way. In cooperative systems, productivity-enhancing automation is presumably suspected and resisted less by workers, and perhaps
even jointly planned and implemented by them, because their employment
security tends to reduce their fear of technological layoffs.[16] This would lead
us to expect that a given incremental increase in capital intensity, in the quan-
tity of buildings and machines and equipment with which each employee can

operate, should give a bigger boost to productivity in relatively more cooperative economies than in their adversarial counterparts. With the carrot, there should be a bigger productivity bang for each buck of investment.

And, indeed, this is what we find from a simple comparative analysis of our eight representative economies. I take my measure of capital productivity from econometric rather than algebraic analysis, estimating across the years from the peaks of 1966 to 1989 (the longest peak-to-peak period for which consistent data comparisons could be made) the amount that the productivity growth rate increases over time from each unit increase in the capital-labor ratio.[17] The higher this amount, the more productive the capital investments have been.

Figure 6.2 presents this measure of capital productivity for the five cooperative and three conflictual economies in this comparison. For the cooperative cases, the average impact of a unit increase in the capital-labor ratio was 0.49 percentage points increase in the rate of growth of employee output. For the conflictual representatives, it was only 0.28 percentage points. With the kind of employee insecurity and resistance we would be likely to expect under the

FIGURE 6.2

Bigger Bang for the Investment Buck?

Capital productivity, 1966–89, "cooperative" and "conflictual" economies

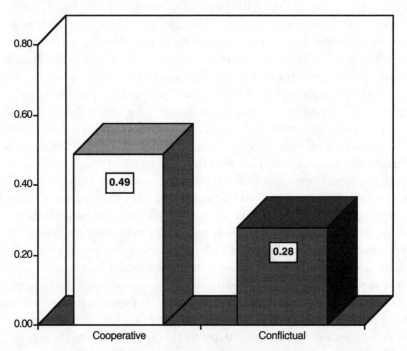

Source: Author's regression estimates based on OECD data. See text and notes.

Stick regime, capital investments appear to generate considerably less additional productivity than they might under a different kind of labor-management system. There could of course be other reasons that this measure of capital productivity is higher in the cooperative economies, but this comparison is at least consistent with the possibility that the nature of labor relations affects the investment harvest.

Other analyses convey, although less precisely, similar impressions. In a review of the available literature written from a North American perspective, Roy J. Adams concludes: "Although there are multiple causes for the relatively poor productivity performance of Canada and the United States during the past three decades, it is becoming increasingly clear that the institutions of industrial relations play a critical role in the achievement of high and increasing productivity. . . . Countries that have been able to integrate labor into socioeconomic decision making and develop cooperative labor management relations are now generally able to outperform us."[18]

These analyses focus on the *direct* impact of labor relations on productivity growth, building on microeconomic views of the efficacy of different ways of organizing life on the shop and office floor. But there may also be another important *indirect* effect of labor-management systems on productivity growth that works through a macroeconomic connection.

This comes from the different effects of "full" or nearly "full" employment on labor relations. With the Stick Strategy, the threat of job dismissal is a crucial component of its disciplinary arsenal; the boss needs to rely on a threat to fire the worker as the ultimate penalty in order to make the supervision-by-stick effective. But when unemployment rates are very low, the effectiveness of that threat of dismissal is softened if not completely cushioned. Why should the worker, who hasn't been given much reason to feel loyal to the firm in the first place, care about the bosses' prodding if the chance of finding another job after termination is very high?

Pursuing the logic of this argument, I would argue that in economies governed by the Stick Strategy there is a kind of macroeconomic tension between "full" employment and rapid productivity growth. With unemployment rates very low, productivity growth may sputter—as the discipline threat attenuates. When unemployment rates drift back up during and after a recession and the immediacy of the discipline threat is reinstated, productivity growth may accelerate. What's good for growth in the short run may be bad for long-term prosperity.

This tension is much less likely to affect the macroeconomy where the Carrot Strategy prevails. There, employment security is one of the conditions that helps seal the cooperative bargain. Relatively low unemployment in the overall economy helps reinforce worker incentives at the level of the shop and office. As the economy approaches "full" employment, productivity growth may glow, not sputter.

Two pieces of evidence attest to this tension between employment and productivity growth incumbent in the Stick-Strategy economies.

University of Michigan economist Thomas E. Weisskopf looks at productivity growth across the leading advanced economies.[19] He finds that unemployment has a reinforcing relationship with productivity growth, other things equal, in a relatively conflictual setting—an effect which is strong for the United States (and weak for the United Kingdom). As anticipated, in other words, there is a tension between *low* unemployment and productivity growth—as unemployment drops, productivity growth slows. But in other countries that serve as models of cooperative labor-management systems, namely Germany and Sweden, he finds evidence suggesting the opposite kind of effect. Controlling for other influences, there is a *negative* relationship between unemployment and productivity growth—as unemployment falls, productivity growth accelerates. Rather than a tension between high employment and rapid productivity growth, Weisskopf finds mutual reinforcement. He concludes:[20]

> The hypothesis that high unemployment will have favorable effects on productivity performance is most likely to be valid where capital-labour relations remain most conflictual and workers least secure. But where private and public institutions afford workers some influence over economic decision-making and a significant degree of security, it is low rather than high unemployment which appears most likely to sustain high levels and rates of growth of productivity.

A second suggestive piece of evidence comes from the Buchele and Christiansen study cited above. In addition to finding a positive association between cooperation and productivity growth, they also find that the effect of labor relations on productivity depends to some degree on the level of unemployment prevailing, that it is contingent upon an interaction between the degree of cooperation and the condition of the macroeconomy. Buchele and Christiansen observe:[21]

> Where labour relations are characterized by conflict and work is motivated by the threat of dismissal and loss of income, low unemployment and measures that make workers more secure undermine labor discipline and productivity growth. Where labour relations are co-operative and workers have a secure stake in their employer's long-run competitive success, low unemployment and improvements in worker rights actually appear to reinforce the positive relationship between co-operation and productivity growth.

These analyses assess the relative importance of labor relations in shaping cross-country differences in productivity *growth rates* over time. It is somewhat more difficult to analyze differences in productivity *levels* across countries at one point in time because that requires choosing a suitable year, establishing the appropriate exchange rate, and sifting through a welter of influences that affect different industries in different ways. One major study has performed such comparisons, nonetheless, for a variety of industries in manufacturing in the United States, Germany, and Japan. Although the authors express surprise at some of their results, they confirm the importance of differences in production organization:[22]

> Somewhat surprisingly, there are very large differences in productivity among plants that look similar and that produce similar products (after accounting for differences in design for manufacturing). These productivity gaps result from the way in which work is organized. . . . [Some industries in Japan stand out.] [The nature of the improvements] not only includes the optimization of time and motion, but also the management structure. For instance, the delegation of responsibilities, such as production worker empowerment and suggestion systems where improvements are directly implemented, played a large role in the way operations in Japan were able to achieve high productivity. . . .
>
> The organization of functions and tasks was seen as a factor affecting relative productivity in all of our case studies. It is particularly important in steel, metalworking, autos, auto parts and consumer electronics. Based on McKinsey benchmarking studies and surveys, it is clear that there are many companies in all three countries that can make large improvements in productivity by improving the organization of their factories.

The Short End of the Stick?

U.S. corporations' reliance on the Stick Strategy has fostered a wage squeeze and rising employment insecurity for millions of workers. And, on the macroeconomic front, it apparently contributes to slower productivity growth than might prevail with a different kind of labor-management system. Why stick with the Stick? Why would so many U.S. corporations rather fight than switch? Even without yet considering other dimensions of the macroeconomy, wouldn't they be better off by moving toward a more cooperative structure for our labor-management relations?

There are a number of different reasons for the persistence and durability of the Stick Strategy in the United States, some of which, such as the vested interest that top management holds in top-heavy managerial structures, have already been discussed. These different factors can be consolidated and clarified by focusing closely on the bottom line.

For this it's essential to draw a crucial distinction between *productivity* and *profitability*. It may be that many establishments would be more productive if they switched from the Stick Strategy to the Carrot. And it may be, as Paul Krugman puts it, that "only productivity growth can make [a country] rich." But the country as a whole does not make the decisions governing our production relations. Corporations make those decisions. And what makes corporations rich, most directly, is what appears on the bottom line—which is profitability, not productivity.

It is true that higher productivity enhances profitability, if all other things are equal. Do more participatory and cooperative work relations therefore necessarily raise profitability? "At first blush," macro economist Alan S. Blinder writes, "the answer seems obvious: if worker productivity goes up and profits are shared, owners of capital must come out ahead." But when we look more closely, the conclusion seems less obvious. "For example," Blinder continues, "suppose workers on profit sharing earn, on average, 10 percent more than workers on straight wages. Then if a firm is to benefit from profit sharing, labor productivity must rise at least 10 percent. If it rises only 5 percent, the firm loses money despite the gain in productivity."[23]

This set of hypotheticals closely matches the cases of many U.S. employers. Those following the low road often pay low wages. It may be that in the U.S. context firms would have higher productivity if they applied the Carrot Strategy but that their profits might not be higher. They might gain considerable increases in output per hour as a result of providing stronger incentives to their workers, but those gains might be balanced or outweighed by the rising compensation costs necessary to help provide those incentives.

We have much less evidence about the effects of worker participation on profits than about its effects on productivity. Some recent studies do point toward positive improvement in corporate financial returns resulting from greater employee involvement, but the results are not conclusive.[24] At least one recent study underscores the amount of short-term investment that workplace transformation requires, sometimes in new equipment but more substantially in the costs of training and reorganization. These results, Mark A. Huselid and Brian E. Becker speculate, may help explain "why firms are often reluctant to embrace such policy changes; there may well be significant short-term costs" even if the long-term payoffs may be substantial.[25]

This uncertainty about payoffs doesn't *necessarily* mean that concern for the bottom line will prevent most U.S. firms committed to the Stick from switching to the Carrot. For one thing, the arithmetic relationship between productivity and wages could be dramatically altered if firms took advantage of greater workplace cooperation by severely trimming their bureaucratic burden. This dynamic seems to have been important in the cases of Nucor and Magma Copper reviewed in Chapter 3. One of the principal reasons the Ford Motor Company rated its experiments with employee involvement very highly, at least in the mid-1980s, was that ". . . corporations can reduce the number of supervisory personnel when hourly employees engage in more self-management."[26] This is why top and middle management resistance to more cooperative labor can prove so decisive. If one of the biggest potential payoffs to the Carrot Strategy is resisted by the very actors who must lead the way, it's no wonder that relatively few firms are bounding onto the high road.

But won't some other firms, with less insecure managers and less timorous owners, step into the breach, grab the golden ring, and begin to compete the sluggish firms out of existence? Most mainstream economists used to think, indeed, that there was only one efficient way to organize activities in a market economy and that, as long as conditions were sufficiently competitive, the most efficient "equilibrium" would always emerge and prevail in the end. Some have shifted their perspectives and now think that there may often be *many* alternative possible outcomes freely chosen by actors in a competitive market economy. It might conceivably be the case that one particular set of choices would produce the most favorable outcomes if everyone could start from scratch. In existing historical situations, however, other perfectly respectable paths may be chosen because they provide reasonably favorable outcomes and because they are closer to the circumstances within which decision makers are making their moves.

And if most firms choose one of those historically conditioned paths, it may be extremely difficult for other firms to buck the tides. Managers get used to top-down control. Workers get used to the cynicism and resignation that the Stick Strategy induces. Some eager beaver firm may believe that the Carrot Strategy offers a chance at the holy grail, but that firm may find it difficult to hire, retrain, and reindoctrinate all the managers and workers it needs for its quest. One set of outcomes might be more advantageous for firms, in short, *if they were able or forced to begin from a different place or in a different environment.* But another set of outcomes may be the best, most profitable, most efficient targets for firms *given where they began and given their resources and surroundings.* In the context of something like the American institutional structure, David I. Levine concludes, "the market system may be biased against participatory workplaces. Despite the potential efficiency of such workplaces, characteristics of product, labor and capital markets can all make participation unprofitable for the individual firm. As a result, the economy can be trapped in an inefficient position"—*given where it began.*[27]

The Stick Strategy is what most U.S. corporations know best and do best. Labor economist Bennett Harrison observes: "The consequence of a generation of managers taking the low road to a restoration of profits is the cultivation of the *habit* of competing mainly on the basis of cheapening labor power, rather than upgrading technology and skills."[28] Many will freely choose to continue down that road because that is how they best apply the resources they command. In the current environment, this may be their best option. To move toward another, conceivably more advantageous strategic orientation, corporations may need a hefty kick in the rear.

This helps highlight perhaps the most important reason for the persistence of the Stick Strategy in the United States: Government policies in the United States tend to support corporate reliance on the Stick Strategy rather than to counter it. The real value of the minimum wage has dropped substantially since the late 1970s, tempting firms with the easy recourse of paying dirt wages. Few restrictions apply to firm layoff or shutdown decisions, tempting firms to avoid strong employee guarantees of job security, to move more and more to "contingent" employment relations. The playing field is tilted against workers moving to organize trade unions, tempting firms to follow their nose to the bottom line and to continue to oppose unionization aggressively. More tepid policy support for maintaining low unemployment rates in the United States than in the more cooperative economies makes it riskier for firms to build long-term employment relations with their workers, an essential condition for reliance on the carrot.[29]

Firms face few pressures to adopt a cooperative approach and many temptations to avoid it. In a word, as Bennett Harrison concludes about the United States, "managers try to beat out the competition by cheapening labor costs."[30] There's almost nothing to stop them. Eileen Appelbaum and Rosemary Batt conclude: "the institutional framework in the United States makes fundamental reorganization of the work system in American companies more difficult than it needs to be and provides perverse inducements to firms to compete on the basis of low wages rather than high skills."[31] Lester Thurow offers one example of how decisive this external environment has been over the past decades:[32]

> With falling real wage rates and very low minimum wages relative to average wages . . . , it just did not pay employers to invest in new labor-enhancing service-sector technologies in the United States. People were cheaper than machines. Abroad, minimum wages were much higher relative to average wages . . . , and real wages were continuing to rise. Machines were cheaper than people.

Some tend to blame corporations' reluctance to transform their production systems on their preoccupation with a quick buck, as if their psychological problems could be cured by group therapy sessions. But their reluctance doesn't involve executives' attitudes or psyches so much as it stems from the structural environment within which corporate planning and decisions are made. Thomas A. Kochan, Harry C. Katz, and Robert B. McKersie write:[33]

> Some writers have posited that American management possesses a particularly strong ideological attraction to the "low road." We are not convinced that American management's fundamental desires are so different from those of managers in other countries. Rather, there are fewer incentives to pursue participation [and cooperation] in the United States, and the "low road" is much more available here than in some countries. We believe the element of feasibility, not desirability or innate ideology, explains managerial actions.

One example that underscores their argument involves Japanese corporations setting up operations in the United States. If attitude were everything, then

Japanese firms would apparently prefer the kinds of cooperative production relations that dominate their operations at home. But environment matters too. As a result, we find growing numbers of Japanese firms setting up "low-road" plants, especially in Southern California.[34] Kochan, Katz, and McKersie observe that "much of this industrial migration is motivated by efforts to escape high labor costs . . . to take advantage of low wages in the United States. . . . [I]t is helpful in understanding an ominous trend underway in North American industrial development."[35]

Nonetheless, if a company for whatever reasons chooses to swim against the current, it has a high chance of success. There are a number of notable examples: Motorola, Xerox, Corning. . . . It can be done.[36] And the formula for success is not all that mysterious. A Japanese company official commented to U.S. management guru W. Edwards Deming about his company's experiences in applying standard Japanese-style labor relations—much more cooperative than U.S.-style approaches—to production operations on U.S. soil: "One Japanese plant manager who turned an unproductive U.S. factory into a profitable venture in less than three months told me: 'It is simple. You treat American workers as human beings with ordinary human needs and values. They react like human beings.' Once the superficial, adversarial relationship between managers and workers is eliminated, they are more likely to pull together during difficult times and to defend their common interest in the firm's health."[37]

It can be done, but it probably won't be until and unless we dramatically alter the institutional environment in which most U.S. corporations operate.

The Investment Imperative

Although productivity growth is the key to the future prosperity of the economy, it isn't the whole story. One of the principal determinants of productivity growth over the long haul is the pace of productive investment. The more machines, factories, and offices with which workers are equipped, the more productive they will become. So, investment is also crucial for our future lives and livelihoods.

Perhaps macroeconomic evaluation of the relative advantages of the Stick and Carrot Strategies may change once investment is taken into account. Could it be that, although the Stick Strategy appears to score badly on the criterion of productivity growth, it may score much better when we look at capital accumulation?

Once again, simple international comparisons are instructive. We can look at investment performance across the advanced countries and compare its relative buoyancy in our representative cooperative and conflictual economies. Do those countries pursuing relatively more cooperative approaches to labor relations outperform conflictual economies as dramatically in investment performance as they do in productivity growth? Or do the relatively more conflictual representatives recover some of their lost ground?

Two different measures of investment performance are relevant. The first, more common in international comparisons, measures the share of gross domestic product devoted to gross fixed nonresidential investment, the kinds of investment that add to an economy's productive potential over the long run. The more an economy commits of its total resources to these kinds of investments, the greater will be its long-run growth potential.

By this first measure, the relatively more conflictual economies fare badly. Over the 1973–89 period, gross fixed nonresidential investment as a percentage of GDP averaged 10.8 percent in the economies featuring relatively more adversarial labor relations (the United States, the United Kingdom, and Canada).[38] In the relatively more cooperative economies, by contrast, the investment share was a much more robust 14.2 percent. (Even if we take Japan— with its unusually high investment share of 15.3 percent—out of the sample of cooperative economies, their advantages in investment performance remain; the remaining four average a healthy 13.9 percent, still almost 30 percent higher than for the conflictual economies.)

A second measure more precisely translates this investment performance into magnitudes that are crucial for longer-term productivity performance. Productivity growth depends to a considerable degree on the rate of growth of capital intensity, the ratio of productive capital to worker hours or employment. To evaluate performance along this dimension most precisely, we need to be able to look at differences in the average annual rate of change of the capital-labor ratio across our two types of economies. Rankings by this measure will closely follow rankings by the investment share, of course, since both are driven by the amount of investment taking place. But they will not necessarily be identical, because since the capital-intensity measure is affected by movements in employment while the investment share is affected by variations in gross domestic product, and the relationship between employment growth and GDP growth varies substantially across our sample.

Still, the conclusions we draw from this comparison are essentially the same as for the analysis of investment shares. In this case, the average annual rate of growth of the capital-labor ratio over 1973–89 was 2.2 percent for the conflictual economies and 3.3 percent for the cooperative ones.[39] (Again, taking Japan with its unusually robust investment performance out of the comparison does not eliminate the cooperative group's advantage. Now, the average annual growth in capital intensity is 2.8 percent for the cooperative representatives, still a full one-quarter higher than the rate for the conflictual economies.)

Figure 6.3 shows both comparisons for investment performance, with the average investment shares in the back row and the average rate of growth of the capital-labor ratio in the front.

FIGURE 6.3

Investment Performance in "Cooperative" and "Conflictual" Economies

1973–89: Average % growth, fixed capital per employee; and ratio, fixed investment/GDP

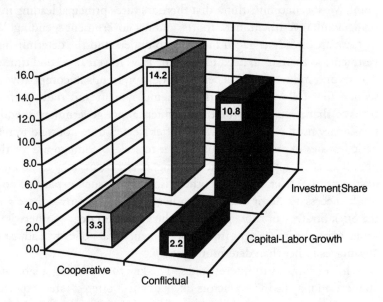

Source: Author's tabulations, OECD data; see text and notes.

Why should investment performance differ so dramatically between these two kinds of economies? And do those differences actually have anything to do with the nature of their labor-management systems?

These questions are best explored in two different ways. The first and more common angle of approach considers the factors that affect investment at the *aggregate* level of the economy. This involves primarily *macroeconomic* considerations.

Many different models of aggregate investment are used within the economics profession to explain movements in investment.[40] But there does seem to be general agreement that across all the different models three main factors *may* affect macro movements in investment. Expanding *aggregate demand* can help spur firms to make investments because they expect to be able to sell more widgets. Relatively lower *interest rates* may also stimulate investment because firms pay less to finance additional plant and equipment. Higher firm *profits,* finally, are also likely to boost accumulation either because corporations will have larger cash reserves to pay for their new offices and machines or because firms anticipate that they will earn a higher rate of return on their investments (or both). All three of these factors can operate simultaneously as stimuli to investment; they are not mutually exclusive determinants.[41] So we need to sift through each of these three influences to assess the connection running from labor-management systems to accumulation.

The aggregate demand effect does not require detailed discussion at this point. Most economists think that there are three principal leading influences on demand: investment, net exports, and net government spending. With the first, we are already engaged in trying to understand the determinants of investment, so there is no need to examine it, as it were, a second time around. The second influence will depend centrally on trends in competitiveness; the section that follows, on inflation, unemployment and trade performance, turns to that issue. With the third influence, net government spending, expansionary fiscal policy in the world after Keynes does not tend to reflect the basic features of an economy but rather to seek to compensate for their failures. If an economy is otherwise faltering, governments may try to push down on the fiscal accelerator. If it's otherwise healthy, such expansive policy will not be necessary. So, if one or the other kind of economy—those guided by the Stick Strategy or those guided by the Carrot Strategy—otherwise has advantages on the investment front, government fiscal policy will adjust to those advantages rather than determining them.

Which brings us to interest rates. The key to unlocking a labor-relations connection may lie in two factors likely to affect interest rates: expected inflation, and movements in a nation's trade position. The next section will look at both and whether one or the other kind of labor-relations strategy might affect either prices or competitiveness or both.

We're left with the question of profits. Here we encounter most clearly the critical characteristic differences between the "low road" and the "high road." The key to ample profitability over time is that productivity growth needs to be at least as rapid as wage growth. If wage growth gets out of control, retained earnings may be squeezed. As a result, the funds for financing may be constrained and investment may not seem either attractive or financially feasible.

Along the low road, by definition, wage growth will stagnate. The problem, as we've now seen, is that productivity growth is also likely to lag—to "go to hell," as in the case of the GE electric motors division. The critical issue is how low each of them falls. The intrinsic risk of the Stick Strategy is that, for all the pressures resulting from production-place discipline and labor-market competition, wage growth may not stay low enough. Or that as wage growth falls, the erosion of worker incentives may push productivity growth lower still.

Along the high road, by contrast, wage growth will necessarily remain relatively rapid in order to sustain worker incentives and to reinforce the spirit of cooperation. And apparently, productivity is likely to grow rapidly at least partly as a result. But will wage growth begin to outrun productivity growth, putting profits in a vise and dampening investment?

It is unlikely that we could resolve these questions in the abstract, on the basis of *a priori* reasoning. The recent literature suggests that there are two kinds of economies in which a manageable relationship between productivity and wage growth is likeliest—those that are well coordinated, as those featuring the Carrot Strategy are often likely to be, and those that are most vigorously competitive, as the Stick economies have typically evolved. Those in between, with mixed systems featuring some cooperation and some conflict, some coordination and some disconnected decentralized bargaining, run the biggest risks of wages raging out of control.[42]

Partial concrete evidence suggests that the cooperative economies enjoy a slight advantage on this front. Again looking at the period between 1973 and 1989, we can compare the difference between the productivity growth rate and the rate of change of real wages between our groups of relatively conflictual and cooperative economies.[43] If this difference is positive, profits have been protected from excessive wage growth. If the difference is negative, wages have been squeezing into the firm's surplus that might otherwise be available for investment. Over this period, the five cooperative economies enjoyed a decent positive productivity dividend: the rate of productivity growth was 0.4 percentage points higher than the rate of real wage growth. The three conflictual economies fared less well: Over those same sixteen years, real wage growth actually exceeded productivity growth, resulting in a net deficit of –0.3 percentage points.

Considering the dynamics of profitability and investment, in short, provides little reason to alter our conclusions about the advantages of cooperative economies. Traveling the high road, they are able to achieve relatively higher rates of *both* productivity growth *and* real wage growth. Traveling the high road, further, they seem to be able to manage the balance between productivity and wages in such a way that corporate profits are protected to help finance investment.

One more difference between the two kinds of systems may affect investment performance. It comes from the logic of firm decisions about their factors of production. Where wage growth is rapid, firms may be pushed to invest in capital equipment simply because labor is becoming more expensive and, in order to make more effective use of those increasingly costly employee resources, it makes more sense to shift production toward more capital-intensive techniques. We can think of this as the "modernization effect." High wages contribute to productivity growth not only by offering workers a carrot but also by forcing employers to modernize or get out of the kitchen. To quote Lester Thurow again about the cooperative experience, "Machines were cheaper than people."[44]

It is difficult to test for this effect very precisely. But partial support for the idea comes from looking among our eight representative economies at the association between real wage growth and growth in the capital-labor ratio. If the modernization effect operates, we would expect a fairly strong positive relationship between the two variables: in economies with relatively more rapid wage growth, we should find among other effects that firms are pushed to modernize and increase their capital intensity, expanding their plant and equipment *in relation to* the labor they employ.

This is indeed what we find. Among our eight economies during the 1973–89 period, there is a strong positive correlation between real wage growth and the rate of growth of the capital-labor ratio of 0.59 (statistically significant at 1%). In the more cooperative economies, firms apparently prefer modernizing to getting out of the kitchen. But in a conflictual economy such as the United States, low-productivity jobs continue to exist partly because the huge reservoirs of low-wage workers encourage firms to continue cooking with backward techniques.[45] "Low-road companies try to squeeze the last ounce out of older capital equipment," Bennett Harrison observes, "rather than steadily retooling and upgrading their technical capabilities."[46] Another reason why investment performance in the low-road economies appears to suffer.

Inflation, Unemployment, and Trade Performance

Three dimensions of macroeconomic performance dominate much of the media discussion about our economy: inflation, unemployment, and competitiveness.

Here, perhaps, the low-road economies might finally have their day in the sun and the high-road economies run aground. If there is rapid wage growth, as we expect from relatively more cooperative systems, will they experience more wage-push inflation? And if there is more rapid productivity growth, as we have also seen is typical in the high-road systems, won't jobs be eliminated and the displaced swell the ranks of the unemployed? If wage growth remains slow, won't the conflictual economies be better situated to compete with low-wage newly industrializing countries?

On the inflation front, one standard measure is the rate of change of the price index for total economic output—the price deflator for gross domestic product (GDP). In our three adversarial examples, over the 1973–89 period the average annual rate of inflation by this indicator was 8.0 percent. In the five cooperative economies, it was 5.8 percent, more than one-quarter slower.[47] Both groups of countries experienced the same oil price shocks (in 1973 and 1979) during this period, so both were exposed to some of the same inflationary influences from the outside. And yet, the high-road economies managed to cushion those shocks more effectively. The bars in the rear row of Figure 6.4 show the results of this comparison.

Lower inflation in the face of more rapid wage growth cries out for explanation. Like all of the other macroeconomic dimensions reviewed in this

chapter, inflation has many sources. But the key to the puzzle of slower inflation along the high road comes from a simple but resonant maxim: "Inflation
results when too much money chases too few goods." The cooperative
economies' advantage during this period came because there were not "too
few goods." Over time, there tend to be too few goods when productivity
grows relatively more slowly, especially in relationship to wage growth and
output growth. If productivity is slow relative to wage growth, workers will
be tossing all their earnings after "not enough goods." If it's slow relative to
output growth, then total demand will be chasing "not enough goods." In the
cooperative economies, productivity growth was not "too slow." We thus see
once again why productivity growth is so crucial for an economy. If it speeds
up, everything else equal, inflationary pressures will moderate. If it sputters,
inflationary pressures will gain momentum.

But isn't inflation controlled by the central banks? We're used to thinking
in the United States that the Federal Reserve Board manages the rate of inflation with its decisions about interest rates and the money supply. Inflationary
pressures starting to build? In steps the Fed with its feet on the brakes. Inflationary pressures cooling off? The Fed begins to push down, however gently,
on the accelerator.

FIGURE 6.4
Stagflation in "Conflictual" and "Cooperative" Economies
1973–89: Average annual % unemployment; and ave. annual % change, GDP price deflator

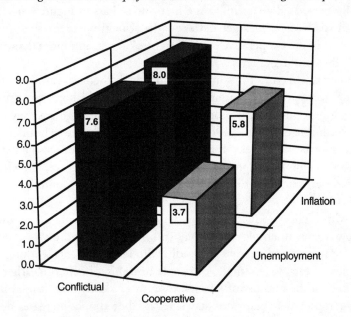

Source: Author's tabulations, OECD data; see text and notes.

But this image suggests that central banks determine changes in the underlying economic environment rather than react to them. If productivity growth rates increase, again holding everything else constant for the moment, there will be less inflationary pressure to which the central bankers will need to respond. They can afford to think about keeping interest rates low when inflationary pressures are low, and those pressures are likely to be lower when productivity growth is higher.

For those who are keeping score, then, it appears that we should mark down another clean strike for the high-road economies. Their inflation rates historically have been lower, it would appear, primarily because their productivity growth rates have been more rapid. And it would appear that their productivity growth rates, to at least some degree, have been higher because of the more cooperative character of their labor relations.

Perhaps the score will finally even out when we consider unemployment. It is commonplace, and even algebraically axiomatic, to expect that rapid productivity growth, holding everything else constant, will mean that firms require less labor to produce the same level of output. This should mean that fewer workers will be hired or some will be laid off and that unemployment will rise.

This may be what we expect. But we do not find that unemployment rates have been relatively higher historically in the cooperative economies, despite their more rapid productivity growth rates and despite all the recent hoopla about high unemployment in Europe. We can compare the average annual rates of civilian unemployment for our two groups of economies for the 1973–89 period. Here again, as the first row of bars in Figure 6.4 indicate, the high-road economies get better marks. Unemployment averaged only 3.7 percent in the cooperative economies but 7.6 percent, more than twice as high, in the conflictual ones.

The key to this result lies in what happens to the total number of hours that employees work per year and the total amount of labor supply provided by the adult population. If productivity growth increases firms may need to hire fewer hours of labor. But if each employee works fewer hours per year, through shorter workweeks, for example, or longer vacations, the reduction in hours can simply be spread around the existing workforce, allowing each worker to stay on the payroll while working fewer hours around the clock and the calendar.

Or, with higher productivity growth rates and potentially slower increases in employment, unemployment may still not rise if, at the same time, the labor supply does not increase so rapidly, with fewer students working during their school years, for example, or people beginning to choose earlier retirement. Even if the number of jobs increases more slowly than it might otherwise, unemployment rates can stay level if labor supply increases no more rapidly than labor demand.

Historically, these possibilities have held the key to economies' reconciling rapid productivity growth with relatively low unemployment. In the cooperative countries, as Juliet B. Schor has pointed out in *The Overworked American*, working hours have continued to decline through most of the postwar period, allowing those economies to achieve a combination of rapid productivity growth and low and relatively stable unemployment.[48] Even in the United States during the postwar boom, when productivity growth was much more rapid than over the more recent decades, unemployment remained relatively low; to a considerable degree this occurred because, as we saw in Chapter 4, hours worked per capita were declining through most of that period rather than increasing.

If hours worked per employee and labor supply hold the key to cushioning the potentially negative effects of rapid productivity growth rates on unemployment, then what holds the key to favorable movements in annual hours worked and in labor supply?

Chapter 4 has already supplied the clues. If wage growth is rapid, workers may be content to work fewer hours per year. Labor supply may also increase less rapidly. The rapid wage growth may allow workers in the cooperative economies to anticipate rising incomes in spite of somewhat fewer hours. And it may permit their choosing and enjoying more leisure time than they would otherwise have chosen.

And this possibility, indeed, seems to contain the kernel of the high-road economies' more favorable showing with unemployment rates. Yes, their productivity growth has been more rapid, creating at least the *potential* of rising unemployment. But with more rapid wage growth along the high road as well, they've worked fewer hours and been able to spread the available work around. In the United States, between 1973 and 1989, average annual hours worked among production workers in manufacturing remained almost exactly flat; with wage growth stagnant, hours worked per year stagnated as well. In the three representative conflictual economies taken together as a group (including the United States), annual hours worked in manufacturing declined by an average of only 2.3 percent over those sixteen years. In the five cooperative economies, in sharp contrast, annual hours declined by an average of 8.5 percent—almost four times more rapidly.[49] Rapid wage growth encouraged the hours reduction, the work was shared, and unemployment did not rise as much as rapid productivity growth might otherwise have warranted.

One final dimension of macro performance commands our attention—international competitiveness. An economy's performance in global markets will affect domestic economic opportunities through its influence on final demand and on prices. And if a central bank needs to raise interest rates in order to protect the value of its domestic currency, investment may suffer and, with it, productivity growth.

Do differences in labor relations matter even for foreign trade perform-ance? Do the cooperative economies retain their advantages over their conflic-tual counterparts on this terrain as well?

Over the long run, one of the most important influences on an economy's trade performance, perhaps the most important, are the relative costs of pro-ducing its goods at home. If Japan-based firms can make television sets rela-tively more inexpensively than U.S.-based firms, there is a strong likelihood that those Japan-based firms will increase their share of world television ex-ports. The value of the dollar might fall, potentially offsetting the cost disad-vantages of the U.S. television manufacturers, but this insulation from their competitive fates is likely to be short-lived.

The relative costs of producing goods on global markets are a function of what are called "relative unit labor costs", the relative amount it costs a firm to produce each widget or television compared with that for widgets and televi-sions in other countries. A country's unit labor costs, in turn, are themselves driven by the relationship between wages and productivity. Suppose a firm's hourly wage costs increase by a dollar and its hourly output by only fifty cents; its unit labor costs will go up. But if the firm's hourly output increases by $1.50 instead, given the dollar increase in wages, unit labor costs will decline.

In short, trade performance is likely to depend heavily on relative move-ments in productivity and wages. And we have already seen what we need to know in order to evaluate the cooperative and conflictual economies along this dimension. Productivity growth has been relatively more rapid in the cooperative countries. Although real wages have also grown relatively more rapidly, the "productivity dividend"—the difference between productivity growth and real wage growth—was positive in the cooperative representatives over the 1973–89 period and negative in the conflictual ones.

It should not surprise us, therefore, that unit labor costs have grown more rapidly in the conflictual than in the cooperative economies. Here, full data for the eight countries do not go back to 1973, so we must confine ourselves to the peak-to-peak comparison for the 1979–89 cycle. Over this decade, unit labor costs (measured in domestic currencies) increased by an average of 6.0 per year within the adversarial group. They increased by an average of only 4.2 percent per year among the cooperative representatives, roughly a third less.[50] Although wages in economies like the United States grew much more slowly than wages in competing economies, sluggish productivity growth more than offset those potential wage advantages.

What About the 1990s?

But what about the 1990s? Hasn't the U.S. economy restored much of its vi-tality, enjoying another steady run of stable growth? And haven't some of the other economies we've looked at here begun to falter?

We can get a sense of the halcyon views many economists hold about the recent U.S. economy from an article by *Los Angeles Times* reporter Jonathan Peterson in early 1994.[51]

> Imagine a utopia of next-to-no inflation, a fantasy land of declining deficits, a dreamscape of rising job prospects and new opportunities.
>
> Sound like an economist's mad ravings? In fact, these visions are now held by various authorities on the U.S. economy who describe underlying conditions—and future prospects—as the healthiest in 30 years. . . . "I see rebirth, revival and renewal," said Allen Sinai, chief economist at Lehman Brothers, Inc., a financial services firm in New York. "The economy is the healthiest I've seen since the early 1960s."

These may sound like fairy tales, Peterson continues, because for most Americans the "renewal" has passed them by. "The rave reviews may sound crazy to the millions of Americans scraping by with low wages or none at all."

Many economists are still buoyant about the economy's performance. And, as we have seen throughout this book, most Americans still wonder when they'll get their turn.

In this respect, not much has changed on this side of the Atlantic. The U.S. economy grew moderately rapidly during the 1980s. Economic growth in the 1990s has been following essentially the same pattern. The growth has not been shared. Inequality continues to rise.

Perhaps most crucially, despite the trumpets occasionally blaring in the business press about economic revitalization, productivity growth has not leapt to a higher and more vibrant level in the United States. Celebrants of the increasingly unregulated economy in the United States are convinced that we've escaped from the doldrums of the 1970s and 1980s. "Thanks to Corporate America's restructuring and high-tech investment," a *Business Week* article concluded in 1994, "the long-term trend of productivity growth is on a path not seen since the 1960s."[52] Unfortunately, despite these attestations, productivity is still stuck on its longer-term trend path of a little more than one percent growth a year.[53] Some complex issues of measurement complicate the evidence, but recent studies leave little room for disagreement about the basic trends. Federal Reserve Board economists Stephen D. Oliner and Daniel E. Sichel summarize these results:[54]

> Has investment in new information technologies and a wave of corporate restructurings led to a productivity revolution in the United States? The answer to this question seems pretty clearly to be "no." Adjusted for the biases associated with measuring real GDP in 1987 dollars, aggregate statistics show essentially no improvement in trend productivity growth in the 1990s from the disappointing pace of the previous two decades. Moreover, such an outcome should not come as a surprise. Despite the rapid growth in business purchases

of computer hardware and software, computers still account for too small a share of business capital to have had a major impact on U.S. productivity. . . . And, although corporate downsizings make for good anecdotes, there is little evidence to support claims that a recent spate of such activity has contributed much to productivity growth for the United States as a whole.

The celebrations of economic revival on this side of the Atlantic, it would appear, are premature.

On the other side of the Atlantic, we need to take a close and careful look. It is certainly true that during the 1990s many European countries have been fighting recession and high unemployment rates. But many have also been recovering from their recession. What requires more careful examination is their somewhat longer-term experience. Perhaps the "high road" is showing signs of age and disrepair?

Comparisons between our groups of "conflictual" and "competitive" economies for the 1990s are complicated by the case of Germany. Since German reunification in 1989, the German central bank has persisted in keeping interest rates unusually high at least in part in order to attract into Germany some of the foreign capital which the government believes is necessary to help finance the modernization and reconstruction of the eastern part of the country, the former East Germany. As a result, the German economy was submerged in a freezing bath of restrictive monetary policy through at least 1994. Even if we rely on data which track developments exclusively in the regions comprising the former West Germany, this policy "shock," as economists would be inclined to call it, shows up as a traumatic recession for the period from 1990 through at least 1994.

If for this reason we momentarily take Germany out of our group of cooperative economies, how does the comparison look for the most recent period? Between 1989 and 1993, the most recent year for which the full set of comparative data were available at the time of manuscript completion, the cooperative economies (minus Germany) appeared to continue to display more impressive performance numbers than the conflictual economies along the principal dimensions we've examined in this chapter, despite the fact that the United States was the first among the group to begin to pull out of the early-1990s recession.[55] Average annual productivity growth in the business sector remained almost 50 percent more rapid in the cooperative than in the conflictual economies. The investment share, one of our measures of investment performance, was roughly one-fifth higher. And the pace of inflation was slower.

But the crucial issue for comparison concerns unemployment. When we pursue these questions, we immediately confront a widespread impression of epidemic unemployment in Europe. English economist Charles R. Bean, writing in 1994, expresses a common perspective:[56]

Prior to the first oil price shock [in 1973] the unemployment rate within the European Community stood at less than three percent of the work force. Thereafter it rose remorselessly, peaking at 11 percent in 1985. Although it fell to a little over eight percent by the end of the decade, it has since increased again and at the time of writing more than one in ten of the labor force are still without jobs.

We also confront a widespread view that these soaring unemployment rates have resulted from "inflexibility" in European labor markets and, indeed, from precisely the rapid real wage growth that has been featured in this book from the beginning. "In much of Europe and Japan," one economic consultant remarks, "neither workers nor managers are comfortable with the flexibility and rapid change needed."[57] Harvard economist Richard B. Freeman captures the prevailing view about the trade-off between jobs and wages: "The evidence that the United States has done better than Europe in employment growth but worse in growth of real wages and productivity suggests that perhaps these are two sides of the same coin. Maybe the United States 'paid' for employment creation through low or declining wages, while Europe 'paid' for high or rising wages with sluggish growth of employment."[58]

This chapter has sought to compare cooperative and conflictual economies, not to compare Europe and the United States. If all European economies traveled the "high road," perhaps recent experience would force us to modify the conclusions drawn in the earlier discussion. But conflictual England is as much a part of Europe as cooperative Sweden or Germany. For the purposes of discussion in this chapter, treating all European economies as if they're the same is like comparing apples and broccoli.

The concern about high unemployment in Europe therefore requires posing a much more specific question in this context: The previous section reported that average unemployment rates over the 1973–89 period were substantially lower in the five representative cooperative economies than in the three conflictual archetypes. Does this comparison look substantially different for shorter, more recent intervals? What about the 1980s? What about the 1990s? Prevailing perceptions might lead us to expect that the cooperative economies' advantages on the unemployment front would erode or even disappear the closer we moved to the present.

This is not the case. Whatever combination of years are examined over the recent past—even if we keep the freezing German economy in the cooperative group—average unemployment rates in the five cooperative economies remain substantially lower than in their adversarial counterparts.[59] During the 1980s, unemployment rates averaged 4.7 percent in the cooperative group and 8.8 percent in the conflictual. During the 1990s, the gap was marginally smaller, with 5.0 percent in the former and 8.6 percent in the latter. Over the full period from 1980 through 1994, the cooperative economies' margin was 4.8 percent to 8.8 percent.[60] Figure 6.5 graphs this comparison.

What reconciles this strong unemployment performance by the cooperative economies with the alarums about massive unemployment throughout Europe? One source of the cooperative group's favorable standing, of course, is that it includes Japan—which is obviously outside Europe and has the lowest average unemployment rates among the eight countries in this continuing comparison. Even with Japan excluded, however, the average for the other four members of the cooperative group for the full 1980–94 period is 5.4 percent, still almost 40 percent below the conflictual average.

More important as an explanation for these apparently anomalous results is that on the unemployment front the cooperative economies clearly outperformed *other* European economies, many of them featuring more conflictual labor relations.[61] In a ranking of unemployment rates from *lowest* to *highest* across 20 OECD economies for 1991, when the European recession was hitting hard, our five cooperative representatives ranked first (best), second, fourth, fifth, and seventh among the twenty countries. Only Portugal and the United States from outside the cooperative group kept them from sweeping the top five positions. Among the larger advanced economies, two

FIGURE 6.5
Unemployment in the 1980s and 1990s
Average annual unemployment rates, 1980–94, "conflictual" and "cooperative" economies

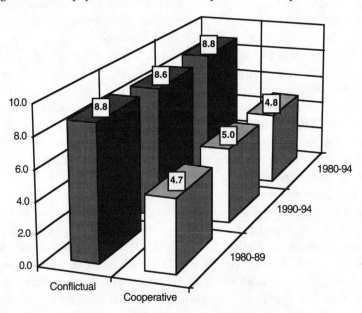

Source: Author's tabulations, OECD data; see text and notes.

groups clustered toward the bottom of the ranking—the other conflictual economies, including Canada and the United Kingdom, and those with mixed labor-management systems, such as France, Italy, and Denmark.[62]

The United States is touted for its "jobs miracle" and its successes on the employment and unemployment front. But Japan, Germany, Norway, and Sweden all have had lower average unemployment rates than the United States, even during the 1990s. Only the Netherlands fared worse, and its average unemployment rate during the 1990–94 period was barely higher than that for the United States. Even facing an increasingly threatening global environment, the cooperative economies have by and large been able to keep a steady course along the high road. Balancing wage growth, productivity growth, labor supply, and unemployment requires coordination and cooperation. Where the institutions for such coordination remain in place and the will for cooperation prevails, a reasonable balance can still be achieved. In situations where the cooperative economies were still "capable of mobilizing such support and self-discipline," Oxford economist Andrew Glyn writes, "full employment and an extension of other egalitarian policies was sustainable."[63]

So the basic story line remains. Even during an era of rising unemployment in many European economies, the high road still looks attractive. The price we pay for traveling the low road remains substantial.

Part III

TRIMMING THE BLOAT, EASING THE SQUEEZE

Chapter 7

SKILLS MISMATCH OR
GLOBALIZATION?

In 1992, Sprint, the third largest U.S. long distance service, acquired a small San Francisco company called La Conexion Familiar (The Family Connection).[1] Sprint coveted La Conexion because the small firm seemed to have a strong niche marketing long-distance phone services to Latinos. Sprint was not disappointed. Only a year after the acquisition, the company reported buoyant business and predicted a tripling of revenues over the next three years.

Then, suddenly in 1994, Sprint announced that it was closing down La Conexion and firing all its workers. (It was apparently no coincidence that the shutdown announcement came only eight days before a union certification election, to vote on whether the workers would join the Communication Workers of America, was scheduled to take place at the plant.) La Conexion's 235 employees, mostly immigrant, women, and Latina, were each handed a cardboard box for their belongings, searched, and told to vacate the premises immediately. The impact of the announcement was devastating. Jon Pattee reports: "Tears and anger spread along with the news [of the shutdown], and one single mother, struggling to put her daughter through school after her husband's death, passed out and had to be hospitalized." Even though the union tried to help employees find jobs, many remained unemployed long after the closing. "People didn't expect to be fired," a former La Conexion employee reports. "Many of them ended up with lots of personal and financial problems. There were couples that separated over the problems the firings caused in their daily lives."

And still, the workers organized to fight the closing. Despite the financial problems they were still facing, a union organizer reports, "they call, they come around, they want to know what's going on with the campaign. They still keep their sense of humor. They want to see justice."

These kinds of stories have echoed more and more resoundingly throughout the U.S. economy over the past fifteen to twenty years. The Stick has clubbed individual workers, individual plants, entire communities. For millions it has shattered the "American Dream." And many have fought back, struggling to cushion the blows.

Lauren Caulder was born in the 1950s. She grew up believing in the "American Dream." She studied hard, worked hard, and expected that she would reap the rewards. She hasn't.[2]

> I'll never have what my parents had. I can't even dream of that. I'm living a lifestyle that's way lower than it was when I was growing up and it's depressing. You know it's a rude awakening when you're out in the world on your own. . . .
>
> I took what was given to me and tried to use it the best way I could. Even if you are a hard worker and you never skipped a beat, you followed all the rules, did everything they told you were supposed to do, it's still horrendous. *They lied to me.* You don't get where you were supposed to wind up. At the end of the road it isn't there. I worked all those years and then I didn't get to candy land. The prize wasn't there, damn it.

What happened to the "candy land"? Why did the American Dream dissolve? How best do we understand the sources of the wage squeeze clouding the lives and livelihoods of scores of millions of Americans? And what should we do about it?

I have argued in previous chapters that both the wage squeeze and the bureaucratic burden reflect the heavy reliance by most U.S. corporations on the Stick Strategy. Firms in the United States travel the "low road." Workers and their immediate families, our communities, and our economy all bear the costs.

This analysis points toward an obvious policy conclusion: Those of us who think the price for working Americans, our communities and our economy is too high should pursue government policies which would help replace the Stick with the Carrot, which would aim to push U.S. corporations on to the "high road" toward economic growth and prosperity. Can we take the "high road"? I argue in the final chapter of this book that we can. I present a simple "five-step" program which could potentially launch a process of transforming labor relations in the United States and, eventually, help transform our economy.

This program for steering toward the "high road" is hardly the standard fare of economic policy debate in the United States. These are not the recommendations we're hearing from the leadership of either political party. Many of those who even acknowledge the devastating consequences of the wage squeeze appear to throw up their hands, shrug their shoulders, and move on to the next policy matter at hand. ("Yes, that's a serious problem, but what we really need to do is get tough on criminals.") Some actually propose solutions to the wage squeeze, often recommending skills training for the unskilled and disadvantaged. Virtually no one proposes to confront some of the basic contours of corporate management and labor relations in the United States.

Why such a disparity in policy approaches? Why are the recommendations outlined in the final chapter so atypical? One of the main reasons is that most economists and public policy analysts incline toward very different explanations of the wage squeeze and of rising inequality in the United States. It would be premature (and unscholarly) to move directly to policy proposals based on the analysis of the earlier chapters of this book without first considering alternative explanations of falling wages. In this chapter I consider prevailing explanations of the wage squeeze, following in Chapter 8 with more direct presentation of the evidence supporting my own preferred explanation.

Most economists and policy analysts have concentrated on two alternative explanations of falling wages and rising inequality:

• One perspective—probably the more prevalent—attributes declining wages and mounting inequality to the changing skill requirements of the economy, creating a "skills mismatch." The labor market has shifted profoundly, according to this view, in the relative demand for and supply of different kinds of skills. Working people in the middle and at the bottom have struck out: firms' need for low-skilled workers has abated while the supply of low-skilled workers has continued to grow. This has created an over-supply of workers at the lower ends of the labor market that has pushed down their wages, especially relative to those of more highly skilled workers. The spread of advanced technology, notably computers, has left unskilled workers behind.

• The other perspective attributes falling wages and rising inequality to globalization. Two effects are considered important. First, as international competition has become more intense, U.S. workers have been more and more exposed to the harsh trade winds of the global labor market, especially those blowing from the developing world. Since American workers earn substantially more than those in the Third World, they have been faced with the unwelcome choice of either granting wage concessions to U.S. corporations or facing wholesale loss of their jobs as employers move to lower-wage pastures. Second, low wages and insecure employment abroad have fueled increasing immigration to the United States, where relatively low-skilled arrivals have crowded low-wage labor markets and depressed earnings both for themselves and for many native workers.

These two perspectives comprise the usual suspects. Despite a much wider variety of *possible* explanations, Syracuse University economist J. David Richardson observes, "'trade' and 'technology' have been isolated for special attention."[3] In this chapter I evaluate these two prevailing views. Although each can make a small contribution to the project of explaining the wage squeeze, especially the argument focusing on the global economy, neither comes close to a complete or adequate account.

The "Skills Mismatch"

The explanation focusing on skills is commonly labeled the "skills mismatch" hypothesis since it highlights an imbalance in the demand for and supply of different kinds of skills. [4] Those who have been experiencing the wage squeeze most acutely suffer, it is said, because their relatively low skills face a "mismatch" with the rising, technologically driven demand for high-skilled employees.

Observers almost all the way across the political spectrum, from conservative through center to liberal, have settled on the "skills mismatch" as the most important explanation of the collapse of earnings for all but the best-paid employees. On the right, John C. Weicher, a senior fellow at the conservative Hudson Institute in Washington, D.C., argues, as reported by a *New York Times* story, that "wages may be falling because many of the workers now entering the labor force are poorly educated and therefore have less value to employers. The declining value of young American workers reflects the decline of the nation's educational system. . . ."[5] Labor Secretary Robert B. Reich, one of the relatively more liberal members of the Clinton Administration's cabinet, echoes many of the same interpretative inclinations: "[There is a] mismatch between the skills Americans have and the skills the economy requires. . . . The long-term crisis in advanced industrial nations reflects in part a shift in relative labor demand against less-educated workers and those doing routine tasks and toward workers with problem-solving skills."[6]

What tends to differ across the political spectrum is not the explanation, which is surprisingly consistent, but the policy conclusions drawn from it, which vary dramatically. Conservatives tend to accept fatalistically the consequences of the skills mismatch as a natural evolutionary product of a competitive labor market. [7] If it's broke, conservatives further aver, the market will fix it. Reflecting on interviews with those on the right about the problem of falling wages in spite of rising productivity, Keith Bradsher of the *New York Times* reports: "Conservative economists question whether the new pattern will persist. People will tend to leave companies that consistently pay them less than the value of their work, they contend, so companies will have to increase pay as their workers produce more."[8]

Among centrists and liberals, by contrast, the policy implication of the skills mismatch view is that the government should help lower-skilled workers overcome their labor-market handicaps through public investments in education and training. In the final report of the Brookings Institution's Center on Economic Progress and Employment, for example, Martin Neil Baily, Gary Burtless, and Robert E. Litan focus clearly on this policy solution to the problem:[9]

> One reason the wages of less skilled workers have stagnated or tumbled in recent years is that they find themselves in excess supply in a labor market that no longer rewards brawn without skill. The most effective way of reducing

earnings inequality is to increase the relative skills of those now at the bottom of the wage and skill distribution. Many of our proposals are therefore aimed at giving special help to workers who have not gone to college.

The central facts that frame the skills interpretation are fairly elementary. Since the early 1980s, real earnings of those with the most education have increased while real earnings of nearly everyone else have declined. Or, to compress those two trends into a single encompassing tendency, the ratio of better-educated workers' earnings to worse-educated workers' has risen substantially.[10]

Table 7.1 provides one example of the kinds of changes in earnings that inform these conclusions. It shows the total percentage change in real hourly earnings for adult workers over the years from 1979 to 1993, estimated separately for men and women with different levels of educational attainment. As

TABLE 7.1

Rising Earnings Gaps by Education

Percentage change in average real hourly earnings, workers aged 25–64

	1979–89	1989–93
Men		
High school dropouts	−17.3%	−8.9
High school graduates	−12.8	−6.5
Some college education	−6.0	−7.2
College graduates	3.3	−0.8
4 years of college	−1.2	−1.1
5 or more years of college	9.1	3.1
Women		
High school dropouts	−7.9	−1.7
High school graduates	−1.5	−1.3
Some college education	7.8	−3.6
College graduates	13.3	3.2
4 years of college	11.8	4.4
5 or more years of college	15.5	5.7

Sources and Notes: Tabulations from *Current Population Survey* from unpublished tables provided by research staff at the Bureau of Labor Statistics. Figures in table are total percentage changes in average hourly wages for workers aged 25–64, excluding the self-employed, deflated by CPI-U-X1 price deflator.

the table shows fairly clearly, those with the least education fared worst while those with the most fared best. Among men, only those with more than a college education enjoyed actual increases in their real hourly earnings for both the 1979–89 and 1989–93 periods. Among women, those with at least some education beyond high school avoided the wage squeeze during the 1980s while only those with a college degree (or more) escaped it in the early 1990s. And since the vast majority of the workforce in the United States does not possess the precious college sheepskin—in 1993 barely more than one-fifth of private nonfarm workers had at least a college degree[11]—the table confirms what Chapter 1 has already shown, that the vast majority of the workforce has been enduring real wage declines.

These figures establish merely that workers with different levels of education fared better or worse on the earnings front. They do not demonstrate that those different earnings trajectories *resulted from a skills "mismatch."* Rising earnings differentials by skill level occurred primarily during the 1980s. The first and in some ways most important kind of evidence advanced to support the skills mismatch view compares what happened with the supply of skills and the demand for skills in the 1980s *when compared with previous decades.*

Shifts in supply by themselves don't help very much, especially in explaining the falling absolute and relative wages of those with less than a college education. In the 1980s, compared to previous decades, the supply of lower-skilled workers, unlike the supply of better-educated workers, did not increase especially rapidly. These movements in relative supply would usually lead us to expect that the earnings of less skilled workers would actually have *risen* during the 1980s compared to those of more skilled workers. But the opposite occurred. "Far from helping explain the 1980s fall in the relative earnings of the less skilled," McKinley L. Blackburn, David E. Bloom, and Richard B. Freeman write in an oft-cited study, "the changes in supply make an explanation more difficult."[12]

Thus the burden of interpretation shifts primarily to trends in the demand for labor.[13] "By the mid-1980s," as research on these issues developed, Sheldon Danziger and Peter Gottschalk note, "researchers began to abandon supply-side explanations and to evaluate demand-side factors. This shift was partially prompted by the inability of supply-side explanations to explain the rising inequality."[14] Researchers looked for a shift in employment *away* from low-skilled industries and occupations *toward* high-skilled industries and occupations. But the evidence that these kinds of shifts occurred from one industry to another is not persuasive. A common finding, as Kevin M. Murphy and Finis Welch report, is that "the changes in average wages are changes that occur *within* industries; they are not simply artifacts of shifts in the industrial distribution of employment."[15]

For most mainstream proponents of the skills mismatch view, only one plausible suspect remains in the lineup. If relative supply shifts don't cut it as an explanation of falling real wages, and if shifts in demand across industry don't do much either, the explanation for rising skills differentials and falling wages among the lower-skilled must result from a shift in demand among *kinds of jobs* within industries. And to most who've pursued this line of investigation, that spells *technological change* that has increased the premium earned by higher-skilled workers. If you've joined the battalions of the computer literates, and especially of the computer sophisticates, you've earned your rewards. If you still can't tell the difference between a floppy disk and a frisbee, you've paid the price.

A problem in advancing this interpretation is that it's extremely difficult to measure such technological changes as increasing computerization in a way that facilitates analysis of its role in explaining earnings. "While the technology argument is plausible," Danziger and Gottschalk stress, "it can only be tested indirectly since direct measures of technology are not readily available."[16] Nonetheless, the conclusions remain strong. In one of the most influential studies supporting this view, John Bound and George Johnson argue that the "major cause [of relative wage changes in the 1980s] was a shift in the skill structure of labor demand brought about by biased technological change", technological change, that is, which biased firms toward skilled employees and away from their unskilled counterparts.[17]

With this and a few other studies completing the linkages, we arrive at the core of a strikingly pervasive interpretation of the wage squeeze, that real wages have fallen for large categories of labor because they have become technologically obsolete.[18] Bound and Johnson affirm the conventional wisdom in concluding that changes in production "in favor of workers with relatively high intellectual as opposed to manual ability—a process that accelerated during the 1980s because of computers—is responsible . . . for most of the wage phenomena that have been observed."[19]

The first problem with the "skills-mismatch" story stems from the methods by which the argument is constructed. As many have admitted, it is difficult directly to observe the technological phenomena that play such a central role in the explanation. The argument proceeds by a process of elimination: other supply and demand factors do not seem to have played a prominent role, so technology—especially the flood of computerization—must be our culprit. In the statistics involved, what happens is that after controlling for other factors, none of which seem especially important, what is left over is called a "residual." This is the portion of the increase in inequality or the decline in wages that has not yet been accounted for statistically. Then, inferences about what's driving trends in those "residuals" are made, in this case, by associating them with technological change: "Within our accounting framework," Eli Berman,

John Bound, and Zvi Griliches write, for example, "we attribute the residual to production-labor-saving technological change."[20]

But this kind of reasoning is very indirect. It is entirely possible that something else besides technology is accounting for those "residuals." Among the economists who most favor the skills-mismatch view, virtually no other possible explanations are explored. So the evidence for the role of technology, in the end, is established almost entirely circumstantially.

Some of the proponents of this hypothesis are at least candid about these methodological problems. Kevin Murphy and Finis Welch comment that "explanations for whatever has generated the increase [in earnings inequality] should be sought at the industry level. (The term 'technological change' comes to mind, but it only underscores our ignorance.)"[21] Bound and Johnson, two of the most influential supporters of the technology interpretation, admit in similar fashion: "The obvious problem with this view is that the evidence in favor of it is largely circumstantial; it is very difficult to claim to have found a 'smoking gun' in what is essentially an argument involving residuals."[22] But it's the only suspect they are willing to consider. "At the risk of arguing tautologically," they continue, "the source of this shift *has to be* technology."[23]

This methodological problem with the explanation places the burden of proof on skeptics to find some alternative explanation(s) that fit the evidence even better. I pursue that possibility in the next chapter by arguing the evidence in favor of an analysis based on the perspective advanced in this book. In the meantime, there are some substantive problems with the skills-mismatch argument *even on its own terms.*

The first is a simple but nontrivial problem with the timing of the trends to which the argument refers. Most of the proponents of the skills-mismatch explanation focus on broad changes from the 1960s and 1970s to the 1980s, noting big changes in the latter decade as a whole. They note that the employment shares and earnings of low-skilled workers declined during the 1980s while various indices of computerization increased. If we pry open that decade and break it down into shorter intervals, however, some anomalies appear.

The most important changes in employment shares for low-skilled workers occurred during the recession of 1980–82, when the proportion of lower-skilled workers in manufacturing (and to some degree in the services) fell; after 1982, low-skilled workers' shares of employment remained relatively constant.[24] Similarly, the biggest collapse in the real hourly earnings of the bottom half of the wage distribution had occurred by 1984.[25] By contrast, the acceleration in computerization occurred only once the decade is well underway, beginning in 1983–84.[26] But if computerization is supposed to have shifted demand away from low-skilled workers, why did the acceleration of computerization occur *only after* most of the decline in low-skilled workers' shares had already taken place? Were businesses so shrewd and prescient that they *anticipated* the coming trends in computerization and began dumping their lower-skilled workers, as it were, before the deluge? The technology explanation would be more plausible if the timing had occurred the other way around, with accelerating investment in computers coming first and the ostensibly resulting shift in low-skilled employment and decline in low-skilled wages taking place gradually *after* those investments had been made and the computers were put into operation.

A similar problem in timing involves the argument that computerization drove the relative increase in the earnings of college graduates. Computerization accelerated beginning in the mid-1980s, as already noted. But the real earnings of male college graduates actually began to fall in absolute terms after 1987.[27] (See the data in Table 7.1 for the footprints of this decline for the 1989–93 period.) Since 1989, Lawrence Mishel and Jared Bernstein note, "college-educated workers have not been gaining in absolute terms and have made little if any gains in relative terms."[28] As shown in Chapter 1, this has been especially true for men. But the supply of male college graduates has not suddenly spurted, creating a glut of university sheepskins.[29] And the pace of technological change has if anything accelerated into the 1990s. Is it so obvious that we can attribute the relatively rising earnings of college graduates during the 1980s as a whole to the influence of technological change when trends toward the end of the decade appear to confound the logic underlying such inferences?

A more substantial problem occurs when we examine the available evidence about the relationship between technology and the demands for different groups of workers. One of the problems with much of the skills-mismatch literature is that it tends to equate the *educational levels attained* by workers in various jobs with the *skill requirements* of those jobs. But we have learned from a generation of studies what most of us have already grasped intuitively—that people learn a variety of things in school, many of them bearing little relation to what they eventually do on the job; and that jobs require many different kinds of competencies, only some of them directly related to what their occupants have learned in school.[30] Data that directly measure the kinds and levels of skills that different jobs require, as well as case studies that have examined the specific effects of different kinds of technical change on the skill requirements in various types of work both cast doubt on the "skills-mismatch" argument.

We can begin with data for the whole economy on the skills that different jobs demand—cognitive, interactive, or motor skills, for example. The *Dictionary of Occupational Titles* assesses thousands of individual jobs.[31] In the aggregate, it does appear that "cognitive" requirements—the need for reasoning ability and specific knowledge on the job—and "interactive" capacities—the ability in particular to coordinate and manage people—have both grown steadily over at least the past thirty years. But, strikingly, it does not appear that there was an acceleration in the pace of these skill demands during the

1980s. Through 1985, David R. Howell and Edward N. Wolff find that the pace of skills upgrading actually slowed with each succeeding period from the 1960s, with the rise from 1980 to 1985 being considerably slower than for either 1960–70 or 1970–80.[32] And Susan Wieler discovered that there was on balance no increase in the inequality of the distribution of skill requirements during the 1980s, even among the most technologically advanced manufacturing industries.[33]

Perhaps looking more closely at trends in particular kinds of jobs and industries can turn up better support for the technology story.

In manufacturing, skills requirements of many blue-collar jobs did rise during the 1980s.[34] But inequality in the distribution of skill requirements among these production jobs does not seem to have increased.[35] Nor did employment shift substantially away from jobs with relatively lower skill requirements to those with higher or growing demands—at least after the beginning of the 1980s. Perhaps most important, the oft-cited example of widespread computerization in manufacturing actually appears to have had relatively little impact on job requirements. In an important study, Jeffrey H. Keefe finds, contrary to expectations, that the diffusion of numerically-controlled machine tools "has had no significant impact on overall machine shop skill levels."[36]

It is not even clear that skill demands have been rising in office occupations. In some jobs affected by automation, skill requirements have increased—systems analysts, for example. In others, by contrast, skill demands appear to have declined substantially—for typists, office equipment, and telephone operators, among others.[37] But even in those sectors where computerization has seemed most prevalent, employment does not appear to have shifted away from relatively lower-skilled jobs. In banking and insurance, for example, computers were installed quickly and pervasively, but most firms have tended to report relatively little change in their staffing patterns.[38]

There is another problem with the usefulness of the argument for nonmanufacturing. Through the 1980s and early 1990s, productivity growth in the nonmanufacturing sector was tepid, essentially flat.[39] The technology argument, intended to apply to jobs both inside and outside manufacturing, would suggest that rapid technological change should have contributed to rapid productivity growth in both sectors. But, as Steven J. Davis and Robert H. Topel observe, the "meager growth in labor productivity [in nonmanufacturing] does not fit comfortably with an explanation for relative wage developments that postulates an important role for skill-biased technical change. We are left with a conundrum: If skill-biased technical change has been so important, why has labor productivity growth [in nonmanufacturing] been so slow?"[40]

There is one final link in the skills-mismatch argument—in some ways the most important—which we must also examine more closely. This step contends that *earnings have shown a relative increase* in those occupations filled by better-educated workers *because* those jobs require greater skills *and because* demand in those jobs has been growing more rapidly. This implies a direct and solid connection between the skill demands of a job and the earnings paid to its occupants. A firm's willingness to hire a worker, the logic goes, will be directly associated with the additional value that worker will bring to the firm, his or her "marginal productivity." Produce more and you earn more.

The skills-earnings association is sometimes assumed axiomatically, based on a particular kind of reasoning that dominates neoclassical economics. This connection between skills and earnings would have to exist, so the story goes, because if a firm didn't tie a worker's earnings to his or her productivity, some other firm would. And in a competitive world, the firm that more reverentially honored the connection would win out in the competitive struggle in the market place. Not to tie wages to productivity would be irrational. And in a perfectly or highly competitive economy, the reasoning concludes, no profit-maximizing employer can afford to be irrational. And thus we often find purely axiomatic assertions: Robert Topel of the University of Chicago writes, for example, that "I will define relative marketable 'skills' in terms of a person's position in the overall distribution of wages."[41] Equation by assumption, in short, but not by direct test or evidence.

The evidence, in fact, supports at most a weak association between skill requirements on the job and pay. In their detailed studies of the actual skill requirements of jobs, rather than simply the educational levels of their workers, Howell and Wolff find that the correlation between skill demands of jobs and the average hourly wages of those jobs is quite low for nonsupervisory workers, although substantially higher for supervisory employees.[42] This result, they conclude, "is consistent with the findings of many recent studies that worker skills cannot adequately account for the structure of earnings, particularly for production workers."[43] Also relying on direct measures of job skill requirements and looking at changes over time, Susan Wieler found that between 1982 and 1990 changes in the actual skill composition of jobs across industries had no significant statistical association with changes in industry earnings levels.[44] Just because skill requirements went up or down, apparently, had relatively little to do with whether or not earnings went up or down.

A second source of skepticism about the skills-earnings connection arises when we try to look more closely at trends in skills and earnings at different layers of the occupational hierarchy. The association between direct measures of technology and earnings does appear to have some force when we look exclusively at employees in the highest skilled categories, such as professionals. When we turn to other groups, however, the association collapses. When Steven G. Allen looked at changes in research and development (R&D) spending as an indicator of technological change, he found an association between R&D spending and workers' earnings in manufacturing, but virtually none in the rest of the economy. And, more strikingly, he found that "rising R&D activity is associated with higher wages for college graduates, but is *completely unrelated to wages of other educational groups.*"[45] Jeffrey H. Keefe looks at one of the most specific and apparently obvious cases of technological change: the spread of numerically-controlled (NC) machine tools. Have wages increased where NC techniques have most widely penetrated? Keefe finds that controlling for other factors, machine shop wages bear no significant statistical relationship to the proportion of operators using NC machines in those shops. The size of the shop matters, the union representing its workers has an effect, the presence of a formal skills training program carries weight . . . but the diffusion of NC techniques appears to be entirely independent of workers' earnings.[46]

Where employment has increased most rapidly, one would expect to find wages rising in response to rising demand. Not so. In the service sector, the 1980s witnessed the rapid growth of many specific industries and occupations featuring relatively high and rising skills levels; wages in those industries, however, remained low and stagnant. And in moderately skilled occupations in manufacturing where employment increased most rapidly during the 1980s, wages were scratching rock bottom. Within manufacturing, David R. Howell concludes, "goods industries with high-wage low-skill workforces appear to have restructured in the 1980s by radically lowering wages and gradually raising skill requirements."[47] In a companion study of changes in the composition and quality of employment, Maury B. Gittelman and Howell write:[48]

> Our results, in contrast [to the technology story], suggest that this last decade was characterized less by an unusually strong and persistent decline in the demand for workers in low-skill jobs than by sharp declines in the employment and relative earnings . . . in the *middle* of the job quality structure, particularly between 1979 and 1983.

Lawrence Mishel and Jared Bernstein provide one of the most detailed available studies of the potential impact of technological change—and more specifically computerization—on wages and inequality.[49] "Any explanation of the greater within-industry employment and wage shifts that occurred in the 1980s," they conclude, "must incorporate many more factors beyond automation, computerization, and R&D activity, especially for explaining growing wage inequality at the bottom of the wage distribution."[50]

But does the technology story even explain the rise in relative earnings for the most highly-skilled workers? Who are these workers who earned such handsome returns for their college and postgraduate degrees? They may not be the computer whizzes and "symbolic analysts" on whom the mismatch proponents concentrate.

The detailed occupational data in the BLS household surveys for 1983–93—the period when the pace of computerization accelerated, are revealing. Among workers in the private nonfarm sector, real hourly wages between 1983 and 1993 fell or stagnated for such obvious technologically-related candidates as "computer operators" and "engineering technicians," while the most rapid increases in real earnings at the high end of the scale occurred for doctors, lawyers, and judges. Average real wages for computer operators increased by only 3.8 percent over those ten years while those for engineering technicians fell by 1.3 percent, for example; by contrast, real earnings for the doctor-dominated category of "health diagnosing professionals" rose by 31.2 percent and for lawyers and judges by 29.7 percent. These doctors, lawyers, and judges are hardly the pioneering men and women of the computer age, blazing trails of computer-age sophistication, whose technological skills are said to be in the greatest demand.

In the end, then, the evidence in favor of the "skills-mismatch" explanation of declining wages is far from conclusive. In their comprehensive and judicious survey of the recent literature on increasing income inequality, Frank Levy and Richard Murnane conclude: "As a *positive* proposition, evidence of an accelerating skills mismatch is weak."[51] Have we found a modern version of the story about the emperor with no clothes?

Globalization

Look at the numbers for the United States: In 1966, imports accounted for only 5.5 percent of gross domestic product. By 1994, they had climbed to 14.4 percent of GDP. In 1973, U.S. exports and imports of goods were almost exactly in balance. More than two decades later in 1994, the U.S. merchandise trade deficit had soared to $166 billion.[52] U.S. corporations were swimming in the global ocean, to be sure, but they were barely keeping their heads above water.

In addition to the "skills-mismatch" hypothesis, the other predominant explanation of the wage squeeze refers to this increasing exposure and vulnerability in the United States to the pressures of the global economy. According to this alternative view, two principal and interconnected international threats have contributed substantially to falling wages: Global competition, especially from the developing countries where wages remain at mere fractions of their U.S. levels, has been an irresistible undertow dragging down American workers' earnings. And the continuing flow of new immigrants to the United States, many of them from low-wage countries, many unskilled, is said to have been undercutting the competitive position of American workers in their domestic labor markets.

Compared with the technology argument, the focus on globalization does not spread quite as pervasively across the political and ideological spectrum. Many of those who focus particularly on the trade and immigration threats tend to come from left-of-center, liberals and progressives especially concerned about the impact of these forces on the jobs and wages of unskilled workers, often observers with the greatest involvement in or connections to the union movement. Vernon M. Briggs Jr., a liberal economist at Cornell

University who has long studied the relatively poor and disadvantaged in U.S. labor markets, writes:[53]

> The contemporary era began in the mid-1960s. It has been marked by the resumption of mass immigration and a sustained effort to reduce tariff rates and coverages. Putting aside the many platitudes associated with immigration and free trade, the fact is that the nation has now entered into uncharted waters. So far, if the standard for judgment is the impact on the American worker, the signs are not encouraging.

Trade and Wages

The trade-and-wages argument focuses primarily on global competition from the developing countries. Now that capital and technology are so mobile and footloose, Third World workers can be made more productive nearly overnight. And with their wages remaining at a quantum level below developed-country workers', it's virtually inevitable, according to this view, that goods produced in at least some of the developing countries will be far less expensive than competing goods produced in the advanced world. Heaven help the advanced-country workers in those exposed sectors.[54]

What do the basic numbers reveal? The manufacturing sector, most obviously and directly exposed to import competition, has experienced a substantial employment contraction since the beginning of the 1980s, the period in which import competition became most intense. Between 1979 and 1994, despite the much touted surge in employment in the U.S. economy during the 1980s and 1990s, total manufacturing employment fell from 21 million to 18 million, an absolute decline of 14 percent. And the share of manufacturing employment in total private nonfarm employment declined dramatically from 28.5 percent in 1979 to only 19.1 percent in 1994.[55] Employment in several key manufacturing industries was hit especially hard: between 1979 and 1993 jobs in electronics dropped by nearly 600,000, in basic steel by 570,000, and in the combination of textiles and apparel by 520,000.[56] Where industry employment was tightly clustered geographically, as in steel communities in the rustbelt such as Pittsburgh and Youngstown, Ohio, the impact has been devastating. A garment worker in Pennsylvania's Lehigh Valley, long a center for that industry, comments: "I love my work. It's been good to me and it's been a good job for the kids. But I told all my children to try to stay out of the factories. It's not going to be there through their lifetimes."[57]

Hammered by these job losses, the trade perspective continues, production-workers still employed in many of these impacted industries necessarily felt the vise on their own earnings as well. According to the argument, when demand drops, if other things are equal, wages are sure to follow. We can look at movements in the real hourly wages of production workers in specific industries over the 1979–93 period to get some sense of where, according to this argument, workers felt the damage most severely. Real hourly wages declined from 1979 to 1993, for example, by 11.0 percent in basic steel, by 8.3 percent in textiles, and by 15.0 percent in apparel. Compare this to a sector like chemicals where U.S. industry continued to retain some of its international advantage: real hourly earnings in chemicals rose from 1979 to 1993 by 17.1 percent.[58]

But, as with the basic facts to which the skills-mismatch argument refers, this evidence is mostly circumstantial. These numbers and examples merely suggest that jobs have disappeared and wages have ebbed in manufacturing more generally and in a number of specific industries more particularly. They in no way yet establish that these job and wage losses have transpired *because of* intensifying import competition. But many think that this linkage is immediate and powerful. *Business Week* concludes in a cover story on "The Global Economy": "The increase in trade bears much of the blame for an unprecedented surge in income inequality between the most- and least-educated halves of the U.S. work force."[59]

Perhaps the most comprehensive presentation of the trade-and-wages argument has come in a recent book by English economist Adrian Wood, *North-South Trade, Employment and Inequality*.[60] Its clarity and precision make it easy to trace through the essential logic of the argument.[61]

We begin with the huge increase in the export of manufactures from the South to the North over the past 30 to 40 years. (Throughout this discussion, South is defined as the "developing countries and territories" while the North is defined as "developed market economies.") "The South's exports of manufactures to the North, which were negligible in the 1950s," Wood writes, "had risen to about $250 billion by 1990, involving growth of about 15 per cent per year in real terms."[62]

The first and essential point, Wood stresses, is that most of these increasing exports have been based on comparative advantages among the developing countries in manufacturing industries relying heavily on *unskilled* labor. Trade theory used to emphasize that different endowments of capital and labor determined trade patterns. Increasingly in a world where capital is relatively more mobile than labor, Wood argues, differences in the supplies of different kinds of labor matter most. "The most fundamental question is why this trade exists at all—what is the source of the economic gains from exchange of manufactures between North and South?" Wood asks. "The answer is that the North has a relatively large supply of skilled labour, while the South has a relatively large supply of unskilled labour."[63] As other trade barriers have eroded, as transport and telecommunications costs have declined substantially, for example, skill differences have both mattered more in affecting trade and have become an increasingly powerful magnet for trade specialization.

This growing trade has had a central and enduring consequence on the composition of trade and therefore on the composition of manufacturing industries in both the North and the South. These twists in the composition of trade and manufacturing output, Wood concludes, have had the kind of impact that standard labor market theory would lead one to expect. In the North, in particular, the declining demand for unskilled relative to skilled workers has contributed substantially to widening the gap between better- and worse-paid workers.

Like the technology perspective reviewed in the previous section, the trade- and-wages argument largely relies at this step on inferential evidence. Wood argues that we can plausibly attribute at least a substantial part of widening differentials by skill level in the North to the skill-twisting effects of expanded North-South trade. He considers other possible explanations of rising earn- ings inequality, as well as patterns of mounting unemployment in many de- veloped countries, and concludes that the North-South trade argument is the most promising.

These conclusions resonate widely with the experiences of many workers and unions in manufacturing. Although I feel much closer intellectually and politically to the proponents of the trade view than to its critics, many of the critics are closer to the mark on some of the basic evidence. Globalization has been notable and its consequences important. But the trade-and-wages con- nection provides a substantially incomplete explanation of the collapse of wages in the U.S. We need to look beyond the trade factor if we want to understand the wage squeeze more fully and effectively.[64]

A first concern arises from noting the potentially limited scope of the trade-and-wages explanation. The emphasis on imports highlights increasing competition among goods that are traded in the international economy and are therefore vulnerable to the threat from low-wage developing economies. These goods are what economists call "tradeables," such as cars and comput- ers, and are distinguished from those "nontradeables" like haircuts and heart bypass operations that tend not to be involved in or exposed to competition from abroad. (Yes, some of the rich and famous may fly to Paris for haircuts from their favorite stylists, but these are the rare exceptions.)

Most of the tradeables are manufactured goods, and it is in manufacturing where the greatest impact of deepening import competition is thought to have landed. But if import competition were the primary or even exclusive explanation of the wage squeeze, we would expect wage decline to have been much more severe in manufacturing than in other nontradeable sectors and perhaps to find that earnings elsewhere had escaped the wage squeeze al- together. This we do not find. The wage squeeze has been widespread, not at all limited to manufacturing. Nor has wage decline in manufacturing been the sharpest across all sectors.

Table 7.2 provides a glimpse of this limitation of the import-competition argument. It tracks the levels and rates of change of production-worker real hourly earnings by major industry sector in the United States over the period

TABLE 7.2

The Wage Squeeze by Sector

Real earnings ($1994), production and nonsupervisory employees, 1–digit industries, 1979–94

	1979	1994	% Change
Mining	$17.00	14.89	–12.4%
Construction	18.57	14.72	–20.7
Manufacturing	13.42	12.06	–10.1
Transportation, public utilities	16.34	13.86	–15.2
Wholesale trade	12.80	12.05	–5.8
Retail trade	9.07	7.49	–17.4
Finance, insurance, real estate	10.55	11.83	12.1
Services	10.73	11.05	2.9
Total private nonfarm	**12.34**	**11.13**	**–9.8**

Sources: Hourly wages by sector from *Employment & Earnings,* June 1995, Table B-2. Deflated by CPI-U-X1, from *Economic Report of the President, 1995,* Table B-61.

of the intensification of import competition, from 1979 to 1994.[65] (The wages are adjusted by the consumer price index in order to examine the trends through workers' lenses.) As the table shows, real hourly earnings fell in manufacturing by 10.1 percent over this period. Despite the impact of import competition, this decline in manufacturing was roughly equivalent to the average for all private nonfarm sectors, which dropped by 9.8 percent. And manufacturing was hardly the only sector that experienced wage decline: five of the other seven sectors also suffered real wage deterioration, with only two escaping the vise. Nor, finally, did wages in manufacturing fall most severely: real hourly earnings declined more rapidly in mining, construction, transportation and public utilities, and retail trade—none of them sectors that are heavily exposed to competition from goods and services imported from abroad.

This picture does not negate the severity of the wage squeeze experienced by manufacturing workers. But even if low-wage import competition substantially explains the decline of wages in manufacturing, an issue to which we shall turn presently, it is unlikely to account for much of the wage decline elsewhere in the economy. And even if we take manufacturing out of the picture, the wage squeeze was the typical experience for production workers in the U.S. economy. Manufacturing workers accounted for only one-sixth of total private nonfarm production-worker employment in 1994. At the least, we would apparently need some other kind of explanation for the wage squeeze affecting, on average, the remaining 65 million production workers in the private nonfarm economy.

Of course the trade impact on wages could have spread beyond manufacturing for either or both of two reasons. First, it could be that the influx of workers from manufacturing into other sectors "crowded" those other sectors, as economists sometimes put it, creating an excess supply of workers for other kinds of jobs and generating downward pressure on wages elsewhere. "As these people were laid off or suffered wage cuts," *Business Week* writes, "they created a glut of job candidates that helped hold down pay among the 64 million workers, across a wide spectrum of industries, who never went beyond high school."[66] And it could be that at least some goods and services in other sectors have also become increasingly exposed to international competition, spreading the pain outside of manufacturing. Both of these possibilities serve to remind us that, in order to assess the trade-and-wages connection fully, we must consider its overall impact on the entire economy and not just on manufacturing. I shall turn to these aggregate effects below.

But even when we limit ourselves just to the manufacturing sector itself, we need to be careful about how we frame the argument. First, it is essential to distinguish between import competition due to lower wages abroad and import competition exacerbated by a rising value of the dollar. When the dollar's value is relatively high compared to the currencies of other competing economies, we can buy many more foreign goods and services with a bundle of bucks than when its value is relatively low. When the dollar rises, therefore, imports tend to surge and exports tend to lag.

This is exactly what happened in the early to mid-1980s. After the Federal Reserve jacked up interest rates in 1979 in order to shock inflation and strengthen the dollar, the value of the dollar soared in international exchange markets. In 1979, the multilateral trade-weighted value of the U.S. dollar, which takes into account the proportion of our trade conducted with the full range of our competitors, was at an index level of 88. By 1985, as Americans who traveled abroad in the mid-1980s nostalgically remember, the trade-weighted value of the dollar had soared to an index level of 143, an increase of 62 percent. It was much less expensive for Americans to buy imports than before. And it was precisely during that period that manufacturing employment took the sharpest hit. As the trade deficit in manufactured goods sky-rocketed from only $3 billion in 1979 to $138 billion in 1986, total manufacturing employment declined from 21 million to 18.9 million. After the mid-1980s, trends reversed: By the business cycle peak in 1989, the dollar-value index had dropped to 99, the trade deficit in goods had fallen back down to $106 billion and, indeed, manufacturing employment had recovered slightly to 19.4 million before declining again as a result of the 1990–91 recession and some of the "downsizing" that has persisted during the recovery.[67]

I make this point not to argue that fluctuations in the value of the dollar are the *only* factor affecting the movements in imports and exports and their effect on domestic manufacturing employment, but rather much more simply to remind us that fluctuations in the dollar's value have a huge impact on trade performance and that we should keep track of those movements in assessing the reasons for the influence of the global economy on our domestic performance. It was during the early to mid-1980s that many observers began to sound the alarms about intensifying import competition. But at that time it might have made as much sense to point the finger at the Fed's insistence on keeping real interest rates at record-high levels than at the low wages earned by workers in the developing world.

Another important caution about the trade-and-wages connection in manufacturing involves the sources of imports coming into the United States. The public alarms about global competition often appear to treat all import competition in manufacturing as if it's originating from relatively lower-wage countries such as Mexico, South Korea, and China. But the bulk of our trade deficit in merchandise exports and imports, which consists almost entirely of manufactured goods, occurs with other advanced countries where manufacturing wages are now substantially *higher* than in the United States, not lower.

Take 1994, for example. It was a bad year for the merchandise trade deficit in the United States; the continuing economic recovery, which like all recoveries tended to raise imports more than exports, had been accompanied by an increase in the merchandise trade deficit to $166 billion, a record high for the post–World-War-II era. Of that deficit, close to three-fifths originated from our trade with other advanced countries. There, we ran the biggest imbalances with Japan, accounting for two-fifths of the total deficit, and Western Europe. But in both areas, as Chapter 1 showed, hourly wages in manufacturing were higher than ours: in Japan, 25 percent higher; and in Western Europe, roughly 14 percent higher. Apparently, economies where workers earn higher wages can flatten us in international competition at least as effectively as those with lower waged workers. And as Chapter 6 suggested, if we want to understand the trade advantages that many other advanced countries have enjoyed, we should pay more attention to the sluggish pace of our productivity growth than to the levels of our workers' wages. When we talk about the impact of intensifying import competition, in short, we should be careful to distinguish between impacts from lower wage competition and those from "higher road" competition.

But these are only cautions. What kind of direct evidence do we find that, indeed, lower employment and wages in at least the manufacturing sector in the United States stems from rising import competition from the developing world?

We can look first at employment impacts. In a study relatively sympathetic to the trade argument, for example, Harvard economists Jeffrey D. Sachs and

Howard J. Shatz estimate that production-worker employment in manufacturing dropped by 6.2 percent between 1978 and 1990 as a result of our growing trade deficits with low-wage developing countries, accounting for a loss of roughly 880,000 production-worker jobs in manufacturing.[68] These job losses were certainly severe, but they account for only two-fifths of the total decline in production-worker employment in manufacturing and come to less than one percent of total private nonfarm employment in 1990. Given the wage squeeze affecting workers throughout the private nonfarm economy, these job losses cannot account for much of the overall wage decline pinching U.S. workers. Unless, of course, there were dramatic spillover effects from trade-induced losses in manufacturing to wage dynamics in other sectors.

Which then brings us to estimates of the direct impact of intensifying trade competition on earnings themselves. One conclusion from the studies of the "skills mismatch" previously reviewed should dampen our expectations about the effects of trade on earnings. If increased import competition were to have had a major impact on wage movements, that impact would be likely to occur primarily as a result of changes in patterns of demand *across industries*. Those industries most vulnerable to import competition would suffer relative to those that were better insulated. As noted above, however, most studies find that shifts in industry demand provide very little help in explaining rising earnings inequality; most of the action has occurred within industries, whether exposed to global winds or not, and not across industries.

Armed with such cautions, several studies have tried to look directly at the effect of mounting foreign competition on workers' wages. They involve different methodologies, but they are similar in finding relatively small overall impact. In one of the most careful and widely cited studies, for example, George J. Borjas, Richard B. Freeman, and Lawrence F. Katz estimate that between 1980 and 1988 increased U.S. trade accounted for only about one-tenth of the increase in the inequality between college-graduates' earnings and high-school graduates' wages and a little more than 15 percent of the increasing gap between dropouts' earnings and those among workers with a high school degree or better.[69] And in this study the translation from changes in relative supplies of workers with different skill levels to changes in their relative earnings relies on an estimate in which *no behavioral influence on relative earnings other than the change in relative labor supplies, such as the possible effects of the decline in unionization, is considered.*[70] Had other factors been taken into account, it is quite possible that even this 10–15 percent estimate would have been lower.[71]

On balance, there seems to be little consensus about the size of the trade impact. Most agree that increasing global competition has had some effect on the wage squeeze, especially among workers in manufacturing. Some studies find virtually no impact, but others infer at least modest influence. Those who are most dubious about the trade explanation, for whatever reasons, tend to emphasize the former studies, naturally, while those most inclined to weight it highly tend to concentrate on the latter. Reviewing these sometimes conflicting interpretations, Gary Burtless writes that "caution strikes me as prudent." "Before accepting the conclusion that fluctuations in merchandise trade or durable goods imports could explain a large move in wage inequality," he continues, "most analysts would need to be persuaded that the number of workers affected by trade is large enough to make a big difference in the overall distribution."[72] For this and a number of other reasons, Richard Freeman, in a recent survey of the debate about globalization, concludes that "we lack compelling evidence that trade underlies the problems of the less skilled."[73]

One final dimension to the trade argument must be considered. Many believe not only that import competition from developing countries has jolted the advanced countries but also that transnational corporations (TNCs) have taken advantage of their increased size, leverage, and mobility to transfer many operations they might otherwise maintain in the advanced world to lower-wage sites in the Third World. Many "imports" then show up not as directly imported goods but as *intra*-firm intermediate purchases, with outsourced products "purchased" by the parent corporation and finished at domestic plants.

As with other dimensions of the trade argument, there is both kernel and chaff in these views. There is no question that many multinational corporations at least nominally based in the United States have moved some of their plants abroad. But some of the concern seems misplaced, especially when we try to explain the wage squeeze itself. The overall share of U.S. manufacturing trade that is TNC based, first of all, actually *dropped* from the late 1970s through the early 1990s, rather than increasing dramatically as anticipated. In 1977, for example, TNCs accounted for 20.5 percent of all U.S. trade, while the portion in 1990 was only 18.4 percent.[74] Employment controlled by TNCs also declined. Direct manufacturing employment of TNCs in the United States fell by 14 percent from 1977 to 1989, as might be expected on the assumption that they were shifting operations abroad, but employment in TNC majority-owned manufacturing affiliates abroad *also* dropped by 14 percent over the same period.[75] Further, contrary to many expectations, most TNC manufacturing employment in majority-owned affiliates abroad is located in the advanced countries rather than in the developing world. In 1989, for example, two-thirds of jobs in majority-owned affiliates were located in developed countries and only one-third in the developing world.[76]

It is true that TNC trade and employment involving the *developing* world has been increasing, as the multinational story would expect. But the numbers involved are very small. The increase in manufacturing employment in TNC majority-owned foreign affiliates in the developing countries between 1977 and 1989 came to only 60,000, from 1.02 million to 1.08 million. More striking still, only 4,000 of this growth involved production workers;

almost all of the increase in developing-country jobs in majority-owned TNC foreign affiliates involved nonproduction workers.[77] This kind of TNC expansion of production abroad, by itself, is unlikely to have had much impact on wages one way or the other.

On balance, then, the trade-and-wages argument provides at best a partial explanation of the wage squeeze and probably not a major one. Increased international competition has occurred and it has had some important effects. But we should be careful not to exaggerate its importance.[78]

One problem with adopting such a skeptical position, in the context of prevailing debates, is that skepticism about the trade argument is regarded, by some, at least, as tantamount to support for the technology explanation. So little attention has been paid to alternative explanations that these two views are often regarded as the only games in town. I do not believe, for reasons sketched both here and in the next chapter, that either explanation holds much promise. The rules of the game should be changed to admit other contestants.

A second problem with adopting skepticism about the evidence on the trade-and-wages connection is that it has become equated with a free-trader's stance on foreign trade policy. Much of this association results from the vigorous arguments that economists Paul Krugman and Robert Lawrence have made on both fronts.[79] They argue that the trade-and-wages connection is weak and they also argue that *because* of that weak connection we should be extremely cautious about proposals for government intervention to shape our trading relations with the rest of the globe.

Some of their skepticism about the relative importance of globalization for the wage squeeze at home seems appropriate; indeed, as I stress in Chapter 6, the problems associated with the "low road" strategy pursued by most U.S. corporations deserve much more of our attention than the global threat as such. Nonetheless, I disagree sharply with the policy recommendations Krugman and Lawrence derive at least partly from their skepticism about the evidence. They vigorously endorse free trade policy. "The logic of the case," Richard B. Freeman writes, "does not dictate such."[80] One can favor "managed trade" policy, endorsing active government efforts to structure our international economic relations, while at the same time viewing the trade-and-wages connection as being relatively weak. An immediate concern about the impact of import competition on jobs and wages is not the only reason to favor "managed trade." Robert Kuttner articulates a more general rationale:[81]

> We need to acknowledge that laissez-faire is a false idol, for both domestic and global political economy. . . . [It] does matter if American workers have access to high-productivity jobs, and it matters whether enterprises that provide those jobs are located in the United States . . . This may strike some purists as distastefully mercantilist, but until the millennium of global government

comes or until all nations have roughly the same labor and social standards, it is a necessary accommodation to the reality of political economy. . . . One pursues such policies [of managed trade] not because one dislikes foreigners but because the invisible hand does not produce equitable outcomes and the visible hand remains a national one.

Krugman has himself written, "precisely which goods [a] country exports cannot be determined from its resources alone. That final determination rests in the realm of chance and history."[82] Indeed, governments should seek to influence the "chance and history" on which our future economic well-being will partly depend.

Immigration and Wages

The second strand of concern about the foreign threat focuses on immigration to the United States. Many believe that the expanding flow of unskilled immigrants to the United States since the 1960s has flooded low-wage labor markets, adding to the supply of unskilled workers and helping drive down wages for lower-skilled workers whether indigenous or foreign-born. Although few economists have paid close attention to these possible effects, some believe that they are crucial. When push comes to shove, some available evidence suggests, *New York Times* economics columnist Peter Passell writes, "that in one place or another, more unskilled immigrants mean lower wages and fewer low-end jobs for those already here."[83]

Perhaps most important, the immigration-and-wages connection apparently resonates widely with the public, helping fuel the recent anti-immigrant backlash. In the voting in California in November 1994 for Proposition 187, which aimed to curb immigrants' rights and access to public services, many of the supporters appear to have come from communities suffering economic hardship. Blacks in particular voted more numerously in favor of the resolution than one might have expected from their long-standing support for public aid to the poor. While Hispanics heavily opposed the proposition and non-Hispanic whites favored it by a margin of two to one, black voters were evenly split.[84]

These kinds of fears seem to have spread widely throughout the country. One recent Gallup Poll asked participants, "Do you think immigrants mostly *help* the economy by providing low cost labor, or mostly *hurt* the economy by driving wages down for many Americans?" Almost two-thirds responded that immigration hurts, including almost three-quarters of blacks.[85]

The policy implications of this concern are fairly clear. Especially if immigrants are driving down the wages of low-skilled native workers or taking jobs away from them, immigration policy should seek to curb the inflow of low-skilled immigrants. Following through on the logic of these views, 76 percent in the same Gallup poll thought that immigration should be either stopped or reduced "until the economy improves."[86] Vernon Briggs draws the conclusions quite starkly: "the nation's legal immigration system must be amended to prohibit the admission into the United States of unskilled adult workers as immigrants or nonimmigrants, regardless of the admission category. . . . [We need an immigration system] that admits people primarily on the basis of the human capital endowments they bring (and that the U.S. labor market seeks)."[87]

According to the immigration-and-wages argument, an accelerating inflow of immigrants has probably affected wages in the domestic labor market through two complementary channels.

• If the skills of arriving immigrants are lower on average than those of native workers, the average skill level of the entire active labor force will decline. If there is a direct relationship between wages and skills, then it will follow that the average wages of the employed population will also decline—simply because average skills have declined.

• If there has been a diminishing demand for unskilled workers, then the arrival of additional low-skilled workers will "crowd" low-wage labor markets and will be likely to drive down the wages of native workers in those low-wage labor markets as a kind of spillover effect.

We can review the evidence supporting these suppositions much more briefly than in the previous sections since economists have paid far less attention to the immigration connection than to either technology or trade (even though the immigration threat is formally part of the global argument) and there are many fewer studies of its effects.

There is no question that the flows of immigrants have themselves increased substantially over the past couple of decades. During the 1950s, 252,000 legal immigrants entered the United States on average each year. By the 1970s, the average annual flow had reached 449,000. In the 1980s, the incoming tide had grown further still, to nearly 600,000 a year (not counting the huge numbers of formerly illegal aliens who were granted amnesty by the 1986 Immigration and Reform Control Act).[88] During the early 1990s, the upsurge has apparently continued, with average annual flows in 1990–94 soaring to roughly 900,000. By 1994, the percentage of Americans who were foreign-born had reached 8.7 percent, the highest level since World War II.[89]

More important for the immigration-and-wages argument, immigrants entering the country more recently appear to have become relatively more unskilled *in relationship to the native labor force*. In 1970, for example, 48.2 percent of the immigrant population were high school dropouts compared with 39.6 of the native population. By 1990, the high-school dropout share among immigrants had dropped somewhat, to 36.9 percent, while the percentage of dropouts among natives had plunged to only 14.8 percent. In 1970, in other words, immigrants were less than ten percent more likely to have dropped out of high school; by 1990 their dropout rate was two and a half times as high.[90]

Several who have attempted to study the impact of recent immigration on workers' wages have relied heavily on these facts about immigrants' skill levels. They estimate how much of an impact the immigrant inflow has had on the distribution of skills among the employed. And then, relying on standard assumptions about the close relationship between skills and earnings, they further estimate how much effect those immigrant-caused differences in skill differentials are likely to have had on earnings differentials.

In the most influential of these studies, George J. Borjas, Richard B. Freeman, and Lawrence Katz get mixed results on the immigration-and-wages linkage.[91] When they study the rise in the ratio of the earnings of college graduates to high school graduates during the period from 1980 to 1988, they find that the surge in immigrant workers did not contribute at all to rising earnings differentials; based on their evidence, they conclude that "immigration flows . . . are unlikely to have had much effect on the college/high school earnings ratio." By contrast, when they turn to the increasing differential between the earnings of those with a high school degree or beyond and those who didn't finish high school, they find evidence that immigration had a far more substantial impact. They conclude that the effects of immigration on the relative supply of high school dropouts did indeed account for a substantial portion of the relative decline in dropouts' earnings—roughly 25 percent of that relative deterioration—and therefore "adversely affected the relative earnings of American high school dropouts."[92] As the authors note, their results suggest a much larger effect of immigration on dropouts' relative earnings than estimated by other studies in the literature.

Should we accept these results as confirmation of the immigration-and-wages relationship? Once again, I am skeptical, in this case primarily because of the problem of the relationship between skills and earnings.

Like several others, the Borjas, Freeman, and Katz analysis relies centrally on the presumption of a strong linkage between skills and workers' earnings. As already briefly noted in the discussion on trade, the essentially axiomatic assumption that earnings bear a close relationship to skill levels enters their analysis at two different points.

• In a first step, workers of different skill levels are combined into aggregate skill groups by assuming that their "efficiency" in production is strictly proportional to their wages; this amounts to the proposition that their productivity is a direct function of their earnings, which assumes what ought to be tested.

• In a second step, once these different aggregate skill groups are formed, the translation from labor-supply effects to earnings effects is mediated by a simple estimation of the association between skills and earnings without allowing any other factor (except a linear time trend) to affect earnings, again effectively assuming what ought to be tested.

But what if the relationship between skills and earnings is much looser than these axiomatic calisthenics allow? I return to the study by Howell and Wolff, among several, which I cited in the discussion of the "skills mismatch." They find that the relationship between skills and earnings is quite low, especially for nonsupervisory workers. They conclude (as quoted above) that their results are "consistent with the findings of many recent studies that worker skills cannot adequately account for the structure of earnings, particularly for production workers."[93] The evidence on the effect of immigration on earnings builds on the assumption that earnings are relatively lower if and when workers' measured skill levels are lower. But if other factors explain a substantial portion of the variation in earnings, then this presumption may produce misleading findings. Howell and Wolff, among others, find that the presumption is least useful for production workers. And it is only among the least-skilled workers, high school dropouts, that Borjas, Freeman, and Katz identify a substantial immigration effect. These are precisely the workers among whom their crucial assumptions appear to be least useful.

In general, there are not yet enough studies of the effects of immigration to feel very confident about their results. As with the evidence about the trade connection, prudence seems warranted. Many studies find little or no impact, while a few suggest a more substantial influence. A survey of the recent literature concludes: "Despite the popular belief that immigrants have a large adverse impact on the wages and employment opportunities of the native-born population, the literature on this question does not provide much support for this conclusion. . . . [E]mpirical estimates in a variety of settings and using a variety of approaches have shown that the effect of immigration on the labor market outcomes of natives is small."[94] "While immigrants may well obtain some jobs sought by or already held by native workers," Gregory DeFreitas concludes, "they generate a roughly comparable volume of new jobs" through their productive contributions to the economy and the extra purchasing power they provide.[95] For all of the plausibility of the immigration-and-wages connection, a more adequate explanation lies elsewhere.

Veil the Corporations, Blame the Victims

What seems most important, as we consider alternative explanations, is to consider alternative angles from which to view the evidence. If we rely primarily on the assumption that earnings are tightly connected to skills, then we may conceivably find that changes in the demand for and supply of unskilled workers have affected wage and inequality trends. If we allow for other possibilities, as I shall try to do in Chapter 8, we may find that the wages of less-skilled workers have fallen for other reasons than their relatively declining skill levels.

The bulk of the literature on the wage squeeze and rising inequality won't help us much with such exploration of additional explanations. In most of the debates over sources of the wage squeeze, the range of alternative perspectives is severely constrained. Technology and trade, with a nod toward immigration—those are the candidates. For those who participate most actively in this debate, my strong skepticism about both the "skills mismatch" and globalization must seem like nihilism. What else is there?

The Market Works

Why is the range of debate about the wage squeeze so narrow, especially if the explanations considered in that debate are as unpersuasive as I've argued here? The first reason builds on the remarkably resilient conviction among most mainstream economists that our economy essentially resembles the world portrayed by traditional economic theories of market competition.

This conviction figures heavily in both the skills-mismatch and the globalization perspectives. In this respect, rather than competing, the two views complement each other. According to the skills-mismatch perspective, unskilled workers have suffered because demand has shifted away from jobs requiring relatively few skills. According to the analysis emphasizing trade, increased import competition from the developing world is one of the principal reasons that this demand shift away from unskilled jobs has occurred. Central to the immigration-and-wages connection is the extra bulge in the supply of low-skilled workers resulting from recent immigration flows, just when the job picture for such lower-skilled arrivals has grown least promising. In all three cases, the analyses emphasize the importance of balance or imbalance in the labor market between the demand for and supply of workers of varying skill levels. And in all three cases, proponents are inclined to presuppose a strong, almost self-evident connection between wages and skills.

These analytic orientations make the most sense if you believe that the world closely resembles the competitive models of traditional economic theory. In such models, it's virtually axiomatic, as I noted in the section on skills, that the demand for a worker's services should vary closely with his or her skills. If an employer ignored that rule for hiring and promoting employees, some other employer would grab the most productive of the available workers and use the productivity advantages to charge relatively lower prices and steal away the competitor's customers. This is economic behavior as the "scissors" diagrams of supply and demand in elementary texts present it. In a competitive labor market, the wage for any category of workers must settle at whatever level balances the supply of and demand for workers in that category. If there were too *few* workers bidding for jobs in that market, then there would be "excess demand" and employers would bid up wages in competition for the best available workers. If there was an "excess supply"—too *many* workers competing for those jobs—then workers would bid down wages as each tried to land a job by offering employers their services for a lower wage.

Throughout the elaboration of this traditional model, the employer remains hidden behind a veil, a passive participant in the process affecting wages. In the traditional analysis the employer makes hiring decisions by taking the prevailing wage as *given,* one which he or she cannot directly influence. The wage is determined in the market. The employer has no discretion about the level of wages it makes sense to pay. Firms sit back and watch, responding to market signals, minding their own bottom lines.

But if the world doesn't behave according to this competitive model, other factors might help explain the wage squeeze. And once we look, we find that more and more economists, both inside and outside the mainstream, have begun to move beyond the traditional model. Those outside the mainstream, especially in the older "institutionalist" tradition, have long believed that the traditional neoclassical approach is misdirected.[96] But growing numbers of economists of quite mainstream orientation are now finding themselves increasingly uncomfortable with the traditional view that employers do not actively seek to influence the wages they pay.[97] Spreading evidence, especially about the dynamics of relatively low-wage labor markets, Princeton economists David Card and Alan B. Krueger write, appears to be more consistent "with the view that firms have some control over wage setting than with the extreme view embodied in the standard model that they take the 'market wage' as given."[98] The time has apparently come to lift the veil on corporations and to examine directly their preferences, strategies, and actions about wages.

Inculpating the Unskilled, Domestic and Foreign

Before finally turning to a different kind of story about the wage squeeze, however, I want to note one other reason that I think helps explain the narrow range of prevailing explanations for the wage squeeze.

The dominant ideology in the United States is highly individualistic. We are inclined to hold people responsible for their fates, to blame individuals for their misfortunes. Columbia University anthropologist Katherine S. Newman heard the reverberating echoes of this moral stance wherever she turned in her recent study of people enduring *Declining Fortunes:*[99]

> American culture is based in large part on an underlying social Darwinism that sees justice in the rule of the survival of the fittest. We believe that those who are well equipped to compete will reap material rewards and that, conversely, those who cannot "cut the mustard" will (and should) suffer deprivation.

Traditional economic analysis reinforces these inclinations. It views the economy as the aggregation of the activities of individuals making decisions on a virtually featureless plain. These individual actors make the best decisions they can, given the resources and information at their command. Institutions are hidden, structural forces obscured. In a world resembling the traditional competitive model, the composite outcome of those individual decisions is the best we can attain, its "optimality" ensured by the competitive discipline of the marketplace.

Viewed through these lenses, individuals place their bets, through their rational decisions, and must take their winnings . . . or losses as they come. We act, and we must assume responsibility for those actions. Avoiding that responsibility, trying to fix the blame somewhere else, would violate the basic principles of accountability in a competitive market economy.

When it comes to the labor market, oddly and ironically, the fact that corporations are institutions, and that their owners are hidden under the veil, means that they're rarely considered when economists think about accountability in these terms. The spotlight shines on individual workers. If their earnings are too low, it's because their skills are too low. And if their skills are too low, they have no one to blame but themselves. They should have made the effort to acquire more skills.

- This orientation applies to the *skills-mismatch* view, which obviously suggests, as I put it at the beginning of the book, that when the going gets tough, the tough get trained.
- It also figures, somewhat less obviously, in the *trade-and-wages* connection. The source of the wage squeeze domestically, according to that argument, is import competition. The problem: too many unskilled workers abroad. The solution: either impose restrictions on imports, which the free traders rule out altogether, or find ways to train the unskilled abroad—pretty difficult for a garment worker in the Lehigh Valley to organize—or accept the consequences.
- And it's perhaps most evident in the case of the *immigration-and-wages* explanation. Excess supply in low-skilled labor markets? Low-skilled immigrants have glutted those markets. Solution: Either keep the immigrants out, which rubs up against both our long-standing traditions of welcoming immigrants—the Statue of Liberty still extends its lighted beacon—and strong neoclassical prejudice against restricting the mobility of either capital or labor. Or, once again, accept the consequences.

While corporate actions remain veiled, in short, we blame the victims.

Chapter 8

WIELDING THE STICK

In the mid-1970s the U.S. economy was in trouble. Profits had dropped precipitously since their peak in the mid-1960s. Productivity growth was lagging. The Nixon Administration's decisions in 1973 to abandon the Bretton Woods system—ending the era of fixed exchange rates pegged to the U.S. dollar—and to institute wage and price controls seemed to signal that important institutional restructuring was underway.

The Conference Board, a major consulting organization for large U.S. corporations, convened a series of eight meetings beginning in September 1974 for about 350 CEOs of American corporations.[1] The meetings were intended to help top business brass step back and reflect on the spreading economic trouble.

A consensus emerged fairly quickly. The easy days of the long postwar boom were coming to a close. The participants' workers had been getting complacent, perhaps even a little lazy. The shock of the recession would undoubtedly help. It would help restore, as one executive put it, "the healthy respect for economic values that the Depression did." Our workers, another added, "don't seem to understand that their success is directly linked to the success of management. They have little or no appreciation of the fact that their jobs, their prospects of an improved standard of living in the future, their chance of advancement are all tied to the success of the business enterprises in which they participate."[2]

The executives also wondered whether the government had become "too" democratic, had begun to overlook the central role that corporations and profits play in a capitalist economy. One executive warned that "dolts have taken over the power structure and the capacity of the nation in the U.S."[3] *New York Times* economics reporter Leonard Silk and political scientist David Vogel, in their reportage on the conferences, summarized the prevailing mood: "A number of executives spoke vaguely of the need for 'war-time discipline', and 'a more controlled society'."[4]

As chronicled briefly in Chapters 2 and 3, U.S. corporations began during this period to deepen their reliance on the Stick Strategy. Their stance toward labor became increasingly confrontational. And they accepted at least tacitly the necessity of occasional sharp recessions to bring about "a healthy respect for economic values." The press largely ignored this shift in corporate strategy. Not so many workers and their union leaders. In 1978 Douglas Fraser, then president of the United Automobile Workers (UAW), wrote in a scathing broadside widely circulated throughout the labor movement:[5]

> The leaders of industry, commerce and finance in the United States have broken and discarded the fragile, unwritten compact previously existing during a past period of growth and progress. . . . [That compact] survived in part because of an unspoken foundation: that when things got bad enough for a segment of society, the business elite 'gave' a little bit—enabling government or interest groups to better conditions somewhat for that segment. . . .
>
> But today, I am convinced there has been a shift on the part of the business community toward confrontation, rather than cooperation. . . . I believe leaders of the business community, with few exceptions, have chosen to wage a one-sided class war on this country. . . .

THE PREVIOUS CHAPTER argued that neither the "skills-mismatch" nor the "globalization" perspectives does a very good job of explaining the wage squeeze since the early 1970s in the United States. And it concluded by suggesting that economists and policy analysts have failed to look beyond those explanations in part because traditional economic theory tends to veil the actions of corporations and because we in the United States have a nasty habit of "blaming the victims."

This chapter explores an alternative perspective—the "low-road hypothesis"—that illuminates the sources of the wage squeeze much better than the consensus views. It proposes that since the early to mid-1970s, deepening and extending their reliance on the Stick Strategy, more and more U.S. corporations have taken the "low road" to economic growth and profitability, seeking to compete by lowering labor costs, and that their choice of this route explains a substantial portion of the wage squeeze as well as the persistence of corporate bloat.

The hypothesis involves two steps. First, corporations have moved aggressively against unions, pushed nonunion employees harder, and lobbied vigorously for government policies that would smooth their travels on the low road. Second, this push over the last twenty years—the "management offensive"—has enabled corporations to promote fundamental institutional changes in both labor relations and the broader political environment that affects the interaction between corporations and workers. These changes have driven both the wage squeeze and the intensification of managerial supervision.

This general approach to explaining the wage squeeze and corporate bloat may seem conspiratorial to some, gratuitously anticorporate to others. But the argument builds carefully on readily available data. What is somewhat novel about the argument is not its individual pieces, many of which are well known, but its general thrust: It lifts the veil on corporate strategies and actions in the United States.

Explaining the Wage Squeeze

The "low-road" hypothesis hardly explains all of the decline in real wages for the vast majority of U.S. workers. And the "skills-mismatch" and "globalization" views do not represent entirely insignificant factors. But institutional changes promoted by the management offensive have constituted a fundamental source of the wage squeeze, probably *the* most important. Addressing the declining fortunes of working Americans requires focusing on corporate strategies and actions much more directly and intensely than is common in public policy debates.

The Management Offensive

The late 1960s and early 1970s provide the backdrop for the story. Corporations were beginning to feel a pinch. The after-tax rate of profit in the non-financial corporate business (NFCB) sector plunged from 9.6 percent—near the postwar high—at the cycle peak of 1966 to 6.4 percent at the peak of 1973, a decline of exactly a third.[6] Corporate profitability declined primarily because of a drop in the profits firms were making on each unit of output, a measure that many economists call the "profit share."

In principle, in a simple accounting (rather than explanatory) sense, the profit share can drop either because of rising hourly wages or declining productivity (or both). In this case, in the business cycle from 1966 to 1973, a slowdown in the rate of productivity growth was the principal culprit.[7] Friction was developing on the shop and office floor. Workers' labor effort was flagging, absenteeism was on the rise. The *Wall Street Journal* reported in 1970:[8]

> Observers of the labor-management scene . . . almost unanimously assert that the present situation is the worst within memory. . . . Morale in many operations is sagging badly, intentional work slowdowns are cropping up more frequently and absenteeism is soaring. . . . Men such as Mr. Burke at Otis [Elevator] contend the problem [of declining worker productivity] is so widespread it's their major headache at the moment.

Under such circumstances, at least in principle, U.S. corporations could have tried to revive profitability by taking either the high road or the low road. Moving on to the high road would have required providing workers the carrot of improving real wages and renewed job security as well as addressing the productivity slowdown directly by involving workers more fully and cooperatively in production. The logic of individual firms' choosing the low road, *a priori*, would have been that they could reinvigorate the profit share by driving down hourly wages and could perhaps improve workers' effort by re-establishing "healthy respect for economic values," by restoring the credibility of at least the threat of worker dismissal.

Beginning in the late 1960s and early 1970s, most U.S. corporations chose the low road. A full explanation for this choice is elusive, but two factors surely played an important role. U.S. labor relations were already organized along top-down principles, relying on intensive managerial supervision; it was apparently easier to bring the Stick more fully into play than to transform the basic structures of labor-management institutions. And the broader environment affecting labor relations in the United States—with its tolerance for decentralized bargaining, substantial obstacles to labor organizing, limited statutory provision for worker benefits and rights—neither encouraged firms to choose the high road nor removed the temptations of life along the lower one.

Whatever the full explanation, corporations chose the low road with gusto.[9] The management offensive, understandably, involved different strategies in union and non-union firms. Whether or not corporations would succeed in achieving their more aggressive aims was bound to be influenced by many factors, such as the depth of the recession of 1974–75. But there can be little doubt that corporations *resolved* to gain substantial ground with both unionized and non-unionized employees.

Many firms went directly after their unions, aiming to tame them or maim them.[10] They brought in sophisticated management consultants, sometimes known as the "new Pinkertons," to help them design their anti-union drives. They pushed for decertification of many unions. They fired union leaders and organizers. They threatened to relocate their plants unless the unions and their members "behaved." The strategy rolled out of the parking lot beginning in the late 1960s and had shifted into high gear by the late 1970s. An index of the number of decertification petitions per union member, according to one count, was almost three times as high in the late 1970s and early 1980s as it had been in the 1960s . And workers' complaints against corporations for "unfair labor practices" soared, also trebling over the same period.[11] Michael L. Wachter and William H. Carter conclude:[12]

> The sharp upward trend in unfair labor practice allegations beginning in the late 1960s and early 1970s provides solid empirical support for the hypothesis that management opposition to unions has increased significantly since the late

1960s. . . . Although it has been claimed by some that management opposition to unions toughened with the Reagan-appointed National Labor Relations Board, the evidence does not support the point. In [our] data, the big uptick in unfair labor practices begins during the late 1970s, not the early 1980s.

One management consultant firm, advertising its services to an apparently sympathetic corporate audience, was unusually blunt in broadcasting its methods. A late-1970s blurb promoting its manual promised: "We will show you how to screw your employees (before they screw you)—how to keep them smiling on low pay—how to maneuver them into low-pay jobs they are afraid to walk away from—how to hire and fire so you always make money."[13]

Non-unionized firms, following the lead of some corporations who had evaded unionization since the 1930s, developed what was euphemistically called the "human resource management" approach.[14] They focused on the individual employee, sometimes providing wage and promotional incentives, sometimes shadowing the worker closely with intensive supervision. They watched the union sector assiduously, monitoring gains that unions were earning for their workers and anticipating what non-unionized employees might need to avoid being tempted to organize. And they did whatever it took to keep unions out of their plants and offices.[15] The nonunion strategy, Thomas A. Kochan, Harry C. Katz, and Robert B. McKersie conclude, reflected "a changing environment, deep-seated managerial values opposed to unions, and increased opportunities and incentives to avoid unions resulting from changing competitive and cost conditions."[16]

Perhaps the most important point about both union and nonunion firms was that they were aware of the shift in their strategies, that they were self-conscious about their plans and actions, especially with respect to wage policy. Conference Board surveys of firms in 1978 and 1983 revealed a substantial shift in corporate approaches both to unions and to wage-setting.[17] On the union front, the surveys revealed a significant increase in the proportion of firms committed to avoiding unions, especially among mid-sized firms. In 1983, the results showed, "These companies are more inclined now to emphasize union avoidance and, possibly, to achieve union decertification as well." On the wage front, the Conference Board found increasing preoccupation with the bottom line. In 1978, the two factors that most frequently influenced firm wage objectives were "industry patterns" and "local labor market conditions and wage rates"—factors outside the firm, influences that reflected firm sensitivity to custom and inherited practice. In 1983, the top two factors were now "productivity or labor trends in this company" and "profits." Interpreting the results, Audrey Freedman concluded: "corporations have switched their wage-setting policies from imitation of other companies' wage increases toward internal criteria. Under growing competitive pressures, companies now base wage changes on labor costs per unit of output, and on expected profits."[18]

Did this shift in strategies reflect the kinds of production-relations imperatives outlined in Chapter 3? Was it related to the logic of the Stick Strategy? Again we find some useful evidence in the Conference Board surveys. It turns out that the corporate actors who were pushing hardest for these changes were not the traditional industrial relations specialists who had overseen union bargaining. Rather, top executives and line managers directly responsible for production took the lead.[19] In particular, analyzing the survey data, one study found strong evidence that "the power of line managers is increasing more in those firms that give a high priority to union avoidance. This finding is consistent with the notion that it is the line managers more than the industrial relations or human resource management professionals who serve as the driving force in union-avoidance efforts."[20] The survey data also revealed a dramatic upsurge in corporate concern about increasing management prerogatives and winning back management rights[21]—a front on which many firms apparently felt they had lost ground since their successes immediately after World War II.

Not surprisingly, the intensifying effort to drive down labor costs worked most effectively in the nonunion sector. From 1976 through the 1980–82 recession, according to data available only beginning in 1976, hourly earnings in the nonunion sector were no longer keeping pace with inflation. Real wages for nonunion workers declined at an average annual rate of –0.5 percent. Despite the spurt of inflation after 1973, the growth of nominal earnings in the nonunion sector did not accelerate.[22]

It was not so easy to curb the wages of unionized workers. Most labor contracts contained "cost-of-living adjustment" (COLA) clauses that at least partly pegged members' wages to inflation. As a result, wage growth among unionized workers was much more rapid than among nonunion employees, and the gap between the earnings of the two groups of workers grew substantially.[23] By a number of different measures, the earnings advantages, or "premium," enjoyed by union workers continued to rise through the 1970s and into the early 1980s. Many corporations had succeeded in getting rid of their unions, avoiding the problem of wage drift in that way, but those that still faced unions at the bargaining table needed a tighter leash.

As a result, the anti-union offensive intensified further in the 1980s. Decertification elections and unfair labor practice complaints continued to grow. Threats of relocation and deployment of the "new Pinkertons" spread. Industrial relations expert Daniel J.B. Mitchell concluded in 1985:[24]

> Management, cheered by what is perceived as a shift in the balance of power, has changed its bargaining goals. Managers in the 1980s are more concerned with the economic fortunes of their enterprises and less concerned with industry wage patterns than they were in the 1970s. They are also more willing to demand givebacks from unions and less willing to make accommodating trade-offs.

A new ingredient had been added. In the mid- to late 1970s, business began intense political lobbying to gain support for its new strategies.[25] One of the first signs that even those corporations who had earlier cooperated with unions now meant business arrived with the decisive defeat of the Labor Law Reform Act of 1978. Organized labor intended the legislation as a marginal reform in rules governing union organizing and elections. Small firms' opposition had been anticipated. But to the astonishment of the entire organized-labor leadership, big business, led by its new lobbying arm, the Business Roundtable, refused any compromise, lobbied Congress intensively, and helped deliver labor a stunning setback. "What was particularly significant," David Vogel concluded, "was the decision of the Business Roundtable to oppose the legislation as well."[26] In his broadside circulated within the labor movement, UAW president Douglas Fraser charged: "The fight waged by the business community against the Labor Law Reform Bill stands as the most vicious, unfair attack upon the labor movement in more than 30 years. . . . Where industry once yearned for subservient unions, it now wants no unions at all."[27]

With the arrival of a conservative in the White House in 1981, the corporate campaign against labor gained a powerful ally. Following President Reagan's dramatic victory in the air traffic controllers' strike and more conservative appointees to the leadership and staff of the National Labor Relations Board (NLRB), the shifting policy winds brought a new, much more frigid atmosphere to labor relations. Thomas Ferguson and Joel Rogers compile some data on NLRB decisions that usefully document the drop in the temperature. In 1975–76, an average of 84 percent of unfair labor practice complaints against corporations were sustained in whole or substantial part, favoring the union side of the complaint. By 1984–85, that average had dropped to 52 percent. In 1975–76, similarly, 65 percent of "representation" cases, involving complaints about corporate actions in union organizing and elections, were decided in favor of the union position. By 1984–85, that percentage had declined to 35 percent.[28]

The early 1980s, reflecting this shift in the policy climate, witnessed an epidemic of union bargaining concessions to employers, often involving actual reductions and givebacks in wages and benefits in the first year of the contract, an unprecedented phenomenon in the postwar era.[29] Beginning in 1982 and 83, *wage growth among unionized workers actually fell below the pace of wage growth among nonunion employees,* a dramatic effect of the wage concessions and bargaining moderation. Unionized workers' wage premiums—the earnings advantages they enjoyed over nonunion members—peaked in 1983 and declined substantially through the rest of the decade. With the cooler climate in the 1980s, a shift in union "wage norms"—an indicator of the trend rate of growth in wages among unionized workers—produced a deceleration in union members' wage growth of 3.6 percentage points. [30]

By the end of the 1980s, then, the management offensive was succeeding on all fronts. Corporations had regained the upper hand. Workers were on the defensive. A new, harsher era in labor relations had dawned. By the mid-1990s, management was marching triumphantly. Profit rates had risen substantially for the first time since the long decline in profitability began in the mid-1960s—up as much as a quarter over their late-1980s levels.[31] Surveying the scene in its 1995 cover story on "The Wage Squeeze," *Business Week* concluded that "U.S. companies now dominate the labor market to an unprecedented degree."[32]

This review has been discursive. Is it possible to be more precise in exploring evidence about the "low road hypothesis"? What sorts of institutional changes resulted from the management offensive? And how did those changes influence the wage squeeze? Some of the effects of corporate intimidation and mounting power have not left a very visible trail. But we can trace others fairly directly along three important fronts—the collapse of the real value of the minimum wage, the decline in union scope and power, and the emergence of the "disposable" worker.

The Falling Wage Floor

The first and one of the most obvious potential sources of the wage squeeze has not resulted from corporations themselves slashing wages and wielding the stick against their workers but rather from a dramatic change in the institutional and political environment in which corporations operate. One of the major consequences of the stronger anti-union climate in Washington in the 1980s came with a major shift in political priorities about the federal minimum wage.

The real value of the minimum wage has dropped precipitously since the late 1970s, resulting in a constantly falling floor for wages. As the floor fell in real terms, many firms were tempted and able to pay some of their workers a wage that was also declining in real terms.

How big a decline in the real value of the minimum wage has occurred?

The lower line of Figure 8.1 plots the real value of the federal minimum wage rate measured in 1994 dollars.[33] Thus, the final solid circle for 1994 rests at a value of $4.25, the 1994 statutory minimum wage rate. The history of the federal effort to place a floor below wages is clearly traced by the dots. It's easiest to divide that history into three fairly distinct phases.

During the postwar boom real wages rose fairly rapidly. The federal government, still shadowed by the memories of poverty during the Great Depression, sought to ensure that the rising tide would truly lift all boats, even those carrying the lowest-waged workers. The statutory level of the federal minimum wage was raised five times between 1950 and 1968. As a result, the nominal value of the minimum wage more than doubled between the late

FIGURE 8.1

The Minimum Wage and the Wage Squeeze

Real minimum wage, real average spendable hourly earnings ($1994)

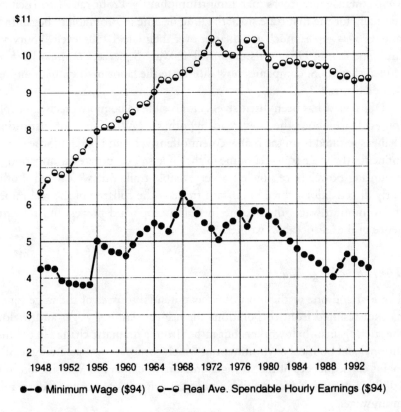

Source: Minimum Wage, see text, notes; Spendable Earnings, see Fig. 1.1.

forties and the late sixties, resulting in a nearly 50 percent increase in its real value between 1948 and the postwar peak in 1968.

The second phase began with the onset of rapid inflation and the stagnation of real wages after the late 1960s. Although the statutory value of the minimum wage was increased another eight times between 1968 and 1979—nearly every year—two factors contributed to a stagnation in its real value through the end of the 1970s. First, simple political inertia made it difficult for legislators to keep pace with the accelerating clip of inflation. Second, corporations began to take the political offensive after the early 1970s, constantly warning about rising labor costs and the squeeze on profits, intensifying Congressional lobbying on behalf of business needs and interests.[34] As a result, the real value of the minimum wage dropped between 1968 and 1979, as Figure 8.1 suggests, falling by eight percent. The minimum wage also declined as a percentage of the average production-worker's wage in manufacturing by ten full percentage points, from 53 percent to only 43 percent.[35]

Then the real value of the minimum wage began a truly devastating slide. Congress sought to adjust for the huge jolt in inflation in 1979–80, increasing the statutory level from $2.90 in 1979 to $3.35 in 1981. But at that point, with Reaganauts controlling the White House and corporate lobbyists intimidating the Hill, the statutory level froze. The minimum wage was $3.35 in 1981 and it stayed there for seven more years. As the graph shows, its real value plummeted, falling (in 1994 dollars) from $5.81 in 1979 to only $4.00 in 1989, declining over those ten years by almost a third. Even though the average manufacturing wage was also declining in the 1980s, the minimum wage fell farther and farther behind, now dropping from 43 percent of the average production-workers' wage in manufacturing in 1979 to only 32 percent in 1989.

Even President Bush and a reluctant Congress could not ignore the damage any longer: Finally, after eight years of total neglect, the statutory minimum wage was increased in two steps from $3.35 in 1989 to the present $4.25 in 1991. But there it has remained frozen again, at least as of the time of this writing. Although a little of the collapse was repaired in 1989–91, the decline continued again through 1994. In 1994, at a level of $4.25, the minimum wage reached only 35 percent of the average manufacturing wage. It was still a third lower in real terms than its postwar peak in 1968. Perhaps most dramatically, as the graph also shows, *the real value of the minimum wage was almost exactly equal in 1994 to its level at the beginning of the postwar boom in 1948, growing by exactly eight-tenths of one penny over that 45-year period.*

Earning $4.25 an hour is not the way to get rich. Working full-time year-round at those wages in 1994 garnered only $7,735 for the whole year; the Earned Income Tax Credit eased the strain by only a hair or two. As *New York Times* columnist Bob Herbert wrote recently about a New York City employee working full-time at the minimum wage. "Ms. Forbes's net pay for one week is $148.75, which is quite sufficient in this town if one lives on a stoop, eats nothing but cat food and never gets sick. If you are a person who likes to live indoors, wear clean clothes, eat a decent meal every now and then, and once in a blue moon take in a movie . . . ," forget it.[36]

Ordinary common sense might suggest that this collapse in the real value of the minimum wage has contributed substantially to the overall wage squeeze. In order to test that simple intuition graphically, I have added to Figure 8.1 the by-now-familiar series for real average spendable hourly earnings first introduced in Chapter 1. This measure (the upper line in the graph) tracks the real hourly take-home pay (in 1994 dollars) of the average production worker in the private nonfarm sector. Visually, the two series appear to move closely together—first, rapid growth, next stagnation, and finally absolute decline. The postwar peak of real take-home pay came in 1972, that of the real minimum wage slightly earlier in 1968. The final collapse in both series occurred after cyclical peaks in 1978. In neither case has the economic recovery from the 1990–91 recession made much difference.

Simple statistics confirm the visual impressions from the figure. For the entire postwar period, the simple correlation between real average spendable hourly earnings and the real minimum wage was 0.63 (statistically significant at 1%). Even if we confine ourselves just to the period after which both had reached their postwar peaks, the correlation for 1973 through 1994 is higher still, at 0.81. Such simple correlations, as many of us have learned in elementary statistics, are often meaningless: when the association of just two variables is being explored, other possible influences on either or both are being ignored. But such correlations nonetheless sometimes provide one of the first hints that the association might actually be revealing. And since common sense affirms what the correlation coefficients reveal—that the collapse of the real minimum wage *might* have contributed to the wage squeeze—it seems like an hypothesis that we ought to explore further.

But virtually none of the literature on either falling wages or rising inequality even pauses to consider the possibility. We saw in Chapter 7 that most analysts and observers attribute these trends to either technology or trade, not to the declining minimum wage. There appear to be two main substantive reasons for this neglect of the potential impact of the minimum wage; one of these reasons is partly ideological. Neither is convincing.

First, explicitly, many believe that the minimum wage actually affects very few workers and, consequently, that its collapse could not have played a major role in trends affecting the vast majority of U.S. workers. Harvard labor economists Richard B. Freeman and Lawrence F. Katz, who are much more sympathetic to the possible role of institutional forces than most of their professional peers, conclude definitively about the United States in a comparative survey of rising inequality: "the fall in the real value of the minimum wage did not greatly affect the distribution of wages, because the U.S. minimum has always been set so low that it determines the pay of only a small minority of workers."[37]

By 1993, according to my own tabulations from the BLS household surveys, something like 5.3 million workers were earning at or below the statutory minimum wage of $4.25.[38] Four percent of workers, even if it totals more than five million individuals, doesn't seem like a very large constituency to most politicians or even to most economists. As a *Newsweek* article at the beginning of the 1989 debate over increasing the minimum wage put it, "*only* 3.4 percent of the American work force [the percentage at that time] now hold jobs that pay the minimum wage or less."[39]

This impression is misplaced. There are two problems with the ways this notion of minor impact is commonly shaped and reinforced.

One involves the usual ways of calculating the impact of the minimum wage. The conventional estimates look at the number of people earning at or below the minimum wage *at only one point in time*. But when the real value of the minimum wage falls, the workers affected are not only those earning at or below the minimum wage level at the end of its decline. Those earning in between where the real minimum wage *used to be* and where it is at the end of the dip are also affected. Since it used to be illegal to pay them such a low wage, in real terms, and it is now legal, their currently low earnings have been made possible, as it were, by the drop.

We should thus look at those earning in the full *range* over which the real value of the minimum wage has declined. Lawrence Mishel and Jared Bernstein, economists at the Economic Policy Institute in Washington, D.C., provide one such set of comparisons. They estimate that in 1991 there were 5.6 million workers—paid by the hour or by other kinds of rates—earning at or below the minimum wage, amounting to 5.7 percent of the total workforce. They also estimate that the number of workers with wages at or below the real value of the 1979 statutory minimum wage, from which the 1991 minimum had fallen by about a fifth in real terms, totaled 16.6 million workers, accounting for 16.8 percent of the 1991 workforce.[40]

A second source of underestimation comes from the *spillover* effects of lowering or increasing the minimum wage. If the minimum wage increases, for example, the increase is likely to place upward pressure on the wages of those earning not only above the old minimum wage but also above the new level. As the floor on wages rises, employers may be pressured to pay more to their employees, even if they're not directly affected by the statutory increase, simply to ensure that they're able to continue hiring and employing the quality of worker they prefer. Economists who consider this effect don't think that the spillover travels very far up the wage distribution, but they estimate that it is a significant effect nonetheless. In their recent study of the minimum wage, for example, Princeton labor economists David Card and Alan B. Krueger report: "We find that the minimum wage has a 'ripple effect' in many firms, leading to pay increases for workers who initially were earning slightly more than the new minimum wage." In studying the increase of the federal minimum wage from $3.35 in 1989 to $4.25 in 1991, they found "some support for the existence of spillover effects up to $4.50 per hour, but little evidence of spillovers beyond $4.50."[41]

Both of these effects are likely to matter. After we take into account those earning in the full range over which the real value of the minimum wage has fallen and when we also anticipate the possibility of a "ripple effect" creating downward pressure on wages of those earning above the old minimum wage level, our view of the impact of the collapsing wage floor broadens dramatically. By my own estimates, the precipitous drop in the real value of the minimum wage from 1979 through 1993 was likely to have affected 23.5 percent of private nonfarm wage-and-salary employees—18.9 percent earning in the range over which the real value of the minimum wage fell and another 4.6 percent potentially impacted by the "ripple effect."[42] This amounted to almost 21 million employees. (The focus here is on private nonfarm workers.) Surely that is a compass whose potential effects we ought carefully to consider. Entirely ignoring the collapse of the wage floor as a possible source of the wage squeeze, as if it hadn't happened, seems worse than benign neglect.

The common failure to consider the collapse of the minimum wage as an explanation for the wage squeeze may also arise from the view of many who think that minimum wage earners are mostly kids picking up spare change after school. Card and Krueger note this view in their recent book: "A widely held stereotype is that minimum-wage earners are teenagers from middle-class families who work after school for discretionary income."[43] Why should we worry about whether or not middle-class kids have been losing ground in their race to acquire the latest Nike hightops or the most recent Boyz II Men or Hootie and the Blowfish CDs?

This impression is both inaccurate and insidious. One problem is that it reflects real misinformation about who earns at or below the minimum wage and in the range affected by its decline. Table 8.1 shows, for private nonfarm wage-and-salary employees, the composition of those earning at or below the minimum wage in 1993 as well as those earning at or below the real value of the 1979 minimum wage—the group potentially affected by the decline in the real minimum wage since the late 1970s.[44] Among those earning at or below the 1979 minimum wage in 1993 dollars, as the table shows, 78.7 percent were adults and only 21.3 percent teens. Perhaps more important in understanding the real source of neglect of minimum wage workers, more than three-fifths affected by the decline were women. While a majority of those earning the minimum wage worked part-time, as the stereotypes would have it, a full 42 percent of those at or below the 1991 minimum and almost half of those at or below the real 1979 minimum were working full-time.

Other tabulations provided by Card and Krueger as well as Mishel and Bernstein further confound some of the conventional wisdom.[45] Fully 36 percent of those affected by the increase in the minimum wage from 1989 to 1991, Card and Krueger estimate, were the sole wage earner in their households, suggesting that the "pin-money" stereotype is far too restrictive. Mishel and Bernstein report, further, that in 1989 roughly 45 percent of workers earning below the 1989 minimum wage of $3.35 lived in families whose incomes fell below the official poverty standard, indicating that movements in the minimum wage affect more than just the middle-class.

The prevailing impression is not only misplaced but treacherous. The substantial majority of those earning at or affected by the decline in the minimum wage are women. Many observers, mostly men, are in the habit of

TABLE 8.1

Who's Affected by the Minimum Wage

Composition of those with earnings at or below minimum wage, 1993, or affected by the de-
cline in real value of the minimum wage, 1979–93

	At or Below 1993 Min. Wage	At or Below Real 1979 Min. Wage
Gender		
Male	41.2%	38.9%
Female	58.8	61.1
Age		
Teenagers	24.9	21.3
Adults	75.1	78.7
Hours		
Full time	41.7	48.7
Part time	58.3	51.3

Source: Author's tabulations from 1993 CPS household surveys.

treating women's earnings as "pin money." But as we have already seen, especially in Chapter 4, female earnings have become more and more essential
over the past twenty years, often because women workers are heading households and struggling to support not only themselves but their kids, often because their husbands' earnings have been buffeted by the wage squeeze and
the wives' incomes have become more and more crucial in sustaining the
family. In a 1995 survey, the Families and Work Institute found that 29 percent of working women reported they earned "all" or "more than half" of
their household's income while another 26 percent estimated they earned
"about half." Only 44 percent responded that they earned "less than half."[46]
To treat those affected by the decline in the minimum wage as if their earnings don't matter constitutes a real slap in the face of the millions of women
in the United States who are struggling to contribute economically on the
most meager of earnings in the most dismal of jobs. As *New York Times*
columnist Bob Herbert writes, the falling wage floor hasn't been "so great for
the warm bodies themselves [predominantly women], who must struggle to
survive on below-poverty wages."[47]

So, if we are ready to acknowledge that the declining minimum wage has potential impact on the collapse of real wages in the United States, how great is that impact?

We have access to three careful efforts to study this question and, fortunately, the three closely agree.

In one, Card and Krueger use the real-life experiment of the increase in the minimum wage from 1989 to 1991 to study the changes in the income distribution across states. Some states, such as Mississippi, contained a very high proportion of workers earning at or below the minimum wage. Others, such as New Jersey, had already legislated their own minimum wage standards, exceeding the federal levels. So, if the increase in the minimum wage was going to have a substantial impact on workers, it was much more likely to have an effect in states like Mississippi than in those like New Jersey. Working from this basic framework, Card and Krueger were able to estimate how much of an impact on income inequality the 1989–91 hike appears to have had. They conclude that it significantly reduced the gap between the top and bottom of the income distribution. Making clear that they consider their conclusions based on state data to be only approximations, they conclude that "the 1990 and 1991 minimum-wage hikes rolled back some 30 percent of the previous decade's accumulated increase in wage dispersion."[48] If a 62–cent *increase* in the real value of the minimum wage could have this kind of *positive* effect on income equality in 1989–91, it stands to reason that the $1.56 *drop* in the real minimum wage in 1979–94 was likely to have had a substantial *negative* effect.

Another study looks directly at the impact of the minimum wage decline on individual earnings during the 1980s. John DiNardo of the University of California at Irvine and Nicole M. Fortin and Thomas Lemieux of the Université de Montréal deploy some innovative techniques for looking at the effects of institutional changes like the falling real minimum wage and declining unionization on the shape of the income distribution.[49] Their study provides one of the first opportunities to assess the impact of the falling real minimum wage on the increase in inequality during the 1980s *alongside* some of the other factors, such as changes in the demand for skills, that have previously dominated the literature.

DiNardo, Fortin, and Lemieux confirm what Figure 8.1 merely suggested. They find that for the period from 1979 to 1988 the decline in the real value of the minimum wage accounted for roughly a *quarter* to a *third* of the increase in income inequality for both men and women, with the results varying depending on which measure of income inequality they analyzed. Not surprisingly, their results indicate that the impact of the falling minimum wage was greatest on the lower parts of the income distribution but explained essentially nothing, for example, of the widening gap between the top 10 percent and the middle of the income distribution. They also report that, in general, the decline in the minimum wage hit women more than men—presumably because, as we have already seen in Table 8.1, a higher proportion of women had earnings during this period within the range affected by the decline—and had an especially severe impact on younger workers.[50]

In a similar though less inclusive effort, Mishel and Bernstein assess the impact of the drop in the real value of the minimum wage during the 1980s on the decline in the returns to education for those at lower levels of the skill distribution. Whereas most analysts presume that these declining returns to schooling reflected technological obsolescence, Mishel and Bernstein show that it is plausible to attribute a significant proportion of them to the collapse in the real minimum wage.[51] They note the close correspondence between their findings and those of DiNardo, Fortin, and Lemieux and observe that these results "indicate that the failure to increase the minimum wage during the 1980s was a major, if not *the* major, factor in the widening of the wage structure at the bottom . . . , especially for women."[52]

Unions on the Run

By the late 1970s many labor leaders, including Douglas Fraser, whose letter was quoted at the beginning of the chapter, believed that most corporations in the United States had rejected the "fragile, unwritten compact" between business and labor prevailing since the early 1950s and had, in effect, "chosen to wage a one-sided class war." By the 1980s, organized labor was suffering obvious and widespread defeats. The "new Pinkertons" who had helped secure the rout could scarcely control their glee. "Unions are on their way out," management consultant Richard I. Lyles trumpeted in a mid-1980s interview. "Twenty-first century historians will look back on this time right now—let's say from about 1982 to the mid-1990s—and they will call it the Management Revolution."[53]

The wage squeeze is also a product of the accelerating decline in the reach and power of U.S. labor unions. This possible influence has received somewhat more attention in the literature on declining wages and rising inequality than the falling wage floor, but it still doesn't rate parity with technology or trade explanations. Declining unionism ought to be taken much more seriously as a factor in the mounting pressure on workers' earnings. The late fifties and sixties provided a premonition of erosion, the seventies a clear early warning signal, and the eighties and early nineties a seven-alarm klaxon.

The accelerating decline of union representation and power is likely to have contributed to the wage squeeze in three important ways.

First, and most simply, fewer workers enjoyed the benefits of union representation and protection. Since it is well-established that, all other factors equal, unionized workers earn higher wages than nonunionized employees, declining rates of union representation would be likely to result in lower wages, on average, for all workers. Fewer and fewer workers would be able to enjoy the union wage "premium."[54]

The decline of what economists often call "union density" has been dramatic.[55] Union representation reached its postwar peak in 1954 at the time of the merger of the AFL-CIO. Union members then accounted for roughly 35 percent of total nonfarm employment. From 1954 through the early 1970s, union density declined slowly, falling to 26 percent of nonfarm employment by 1973. The onset of the management offensive against labor in the early to mid-1970s brought accelerated decline. Union representation fell to 22 percent in 1979 and even more precipitously during the 1980s and early 1990s, to only 14 percent of nonfarm employment in 1994. Figure 8.2 graphically records this accelerating decline in union density.

More important still for this book's focus on workers in the corporate sector, unionization rates among private-sector workers have dropped even lower

FIGURE 8.2

Declining Unionization

Union members as percent of nonfarm employment, 1948–94

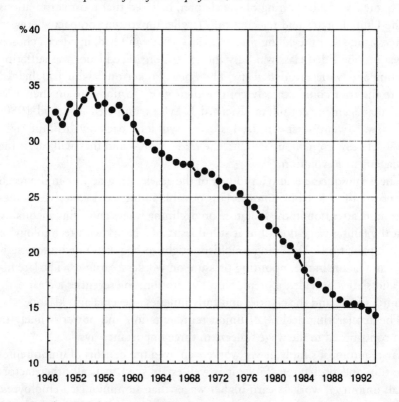

Source: Based on BLS data; see text and notes.

than these general averages indicate. By the early 1990s, they had fallen to less than half their levels in the early 1970s, declining to barely more than 11 percent in 1992.[56] The full measure of the erosion of unionism among private employers was being disguised by the rise of unionization rates in the public sector, now more than three times higher than in the private sector.

Over the past twenty years almost all of the erosion of union density has been accounted for by declining rates among men whose earnings, we have already seen, were pinched by the wage squeeze much more sharply than those of female workers. While the percentage of union members among women employees remained virtually constant from the early 1970s, the unionization rate among men fell by more than 50 percent.[57]

A second reason at least in principle that the decline in union reach and power has probably contributed to the wage squeeze is the mounting defensiveness of unions and their members. As the seventies turned to the eighties, reinforced by rising unemployment and an increasingly pro-business political environment, corporations insisted with growing impunity on wage concessions, benefit givebacks, and a variety of other rollbacks in union workers' contractual perquisites.[58] By 1987, according to Labor Department data, nearly three-quarters of all major contracts provided for at least some worker concessions, and the proportion of concessionary contracts in manufacturing was even higher.[59] These givebacks meant that the "union wage premium" was itself shrinking, as unions on the run found it more and more difficult to command the kinds of bargaining payoffs they had enjoyed in earlier, more hospitable climates. As the section on the "management offensive" showed, the decline began after the recession of 1980–82.

A third kind of impact on the wage squeeze is more indirect but undoubtedly important nonetheless. As with the minimum wage, union contracts have always had a "spillover" effect on wages in the nonunion sector. Nonunionized employers have often felt the need to match, at least in part, union wage gains in order to continue to attract the workers they want. Perhaps more crucially, they have also sought to emulate union wage gains in order to help scratch whatever unionizing itches their otherwise less satisfied employees might conceivably develop.

It is easiest to measure the first of these three kinds of effect, the direct effect of declining union density. A number of studies provide some indication of its likely importance and all conclude that it has been significant. Indeed, what may be most remarkable about this string of studies is the consistency and comparability of their estimates.

In one representative study, Richard B. Freeman looks at the effect of declining unionization on rising wage differentials among males by occupation and by educational level.[60] Using a variety of different approaches to estimation and a number of different samples, he finds a uniform pattern. When the variety of estimates are compared and combined, he finds that declining union density accounted for a little more than one-fifth of the increase in earnings inequality among adult males between 1978 and 1988.[61]

A couple of other complementary studies support Freeman's results. Two of the best, one by David Card and the other the same DiNardo-Fortin-Lemieux study cited for its results on the minimum wage, not only support his findings but echo them almost precisely.[62] In reviewing the literature Mishel and Bernstein note these echoes: "Remarkably, all three studies found that lower unionization can account for the same proportion of the higher wage inequality— 21 percent—even though they employ radically different methodologies."[63]

The first hints of the second kind of effect—of increasing defensiveness of unions—come from the record of union bargaining results. In the early to mid-1980s, as we have seen, corporations secured substantial concessions and givebacks—something that had been virtually unknown before the 1970s. The severity of the givebacks, according to Mitchell's estimates, was greatest in 1983 and 1984.[64] As a result, after rising union wage advantages during the 1970s and early 1980s, the wage advantage of being a union member itself began to decline. Wachter and Carter find that the wage differential between union and nonunion (nonexecutive) workers began to decline after the early 1980s, falling by almost a fifth between 1983 and 1988. In my own estimations, for those in the bottom 80 percent of the wage distribution among private nonfarm wage-and-salary employees—the group that Chapter 1 showed had most directly experienced the wage squeeze—the union wage differential also declined by about a fifth, controlling for other factors influencing hourly earnings, falling from $1.87 an hour (in 1993 dollars) in 1983 to only $1.47 in 1993.[65]

With regard to the third kind of effect it is difficult to come up with meaningful quantitative estimates of the reduced wage pressure on nonunion employers resulting from the "spillover" of mounting union defensiveness. Richard B. Freeman and Lawrence Katz conclude about their own analyses: "If, as many labor relations analysts believe, lower unionization rates reduce the pressure on nonunion employers to pay high wages and provide benefits, this calculation underestimates the full contribution of falling unionization to the rise in inequality."[66]

Unions have been on the run since the early 1970s. Real wages have been falling over the same period. There appears to be more than a merely coincident relationship between these two trends. Based on his study, David Card concludes: "In light of the inability of other observable factors to explain the rise in wage inequality over the 1970s and 1980s [as evidenced by the review of prevailing explanations in the previous chapter of this book] . . . the role of changing unionization is notable. . . . "[67] Even *Business Week* concedes the importance of the effect in their own review of "The Wage Squeeze": "Also holding down wages is the decline of a robust, unionized workforce that used to prod tightfisted employers into sharing more of the spoils."[68] Richard Freeman stresses the significant impact of declining union power on rising inequality but cautions about placing too high a weight on its role. "Overall," he writes, "declining unionization was a supporting player in the story of the increase in inequality, not the main character: Rosencrantz or Guildenstern, not Hamlet."[69] His quantitative estimates are persuasive, his theatrical ratings are not. Along with Card, and based on my own evaluation of the other candidates for top billing in the previous chapter, I would move the effects of deunionization to stage center: maybe not Hamlet, but at least Lady MacBeth.

The Disposable Worker

We hear a great deal these days about a new age of "flexibility" at work. Some employees are working out of home offices. Others have moved to more flexible working hours. Others are combining family and work roles in innovative ways.

But we also hear more and more about a dark side to "flexibility" shadowing the work lives of millions of Americans, the emergence of the "disposable" worker.[70] As U.S. corporations have been traveling the "low road," especially since the early 1980s, growing numbers of workers have faced their employers without any protection against dismissal, without benefits, without rights, without even a modicum of job security. Anthony Carnevale, recently head of the National Commission for Employment Policy, reflected on these trends in a 1992 interview: "Every employer talks about having a flexible work force. But for many employees flexibility is just a euphemism for getting fired or for having a job with no benefits."[71] Writing in *Time*, Lance Morrow signals the trend as the beginning of a new era:[72]

> America has entered the age of the contingent or temporary worker, of the consultant and subcontractor, of the just-in-time work force—fluid, flexible, disposable. . . . [T]he human costs are enormous. Some profound betrayal of the American dynamic itself (work hard, obey the rules, succeed) runs through this process like a computer virus.

In a companion piece, Janice Castro further describes the harshness of the new employment relation:[73]

> Almost overnight, companies are shedding a system of mutual obligations and expectations built up since the Great Depression, a tradition of labor that said performance was rewarded, loyalty was valued and workers were a vital part of the enterprises they served. In this chilly new world of global competition, they are often viewed merely as expenses. Long-term commitments of all kinds are anathema to the modern corporation. For the growing ranks of contingent workers, that means no more pensions, health insurance or paid vacations. No more promises or promotions or costly training programs. . . . As

the underpinnings of mutual commitment crumble, time-honored notions of fairness are cast aside for millions of workers.

It is difficult to assess the effects of this movement toward disposable employment on the wage squeeze because data on categories like "contingent" workers don't go back far enough. But it seems quite likely that when we add the categories of contingent employment together, they now constitute a significant feature of the economic landscape.

We can begin with the growth in *involuntary part-time work*. Between 1973 and 1993, the rate of voluntary part-time work remained almost exactly constant, varying between 13 and 14 percent of nonagricultural employment. By contrast, the rate of involuntary part-time employment, also referred to as those working part-time for "economic reasons," increased by more than three-quarters—from 3.1 percent in 1973 to 5.5 percent in 1993.[74] The wage penalty for being pushed into part-time work is substantial. According to my own estimates for 1993 for private nonfarm wage-and-salary employees in the bottom 80 percent of the wage distribution, those working part-time for economic reasons, controlling for other factors affecting hourly wages, earned almost a quarter less than full-time workers with comparable characteristics.[75]

A second group often counted as part of the trend toward disposable employment includes *temporary employees*, usually defined for the purposes of measurement as those who work for temporary-help agencies. In 1993, roughly 1.7 million worked as temps, dispatched from agencies like Kelly Services and Manpower, Inc.[76] The latter, with 560,000 workers, is now the world's largest temporary-service agency. Employment in this industry is booming, providing, as a 1993 feature in *Time* put it, "the hands and the brainpower that other companies are no longer willing to call their own."[77] Consistent data on temps go back only as far as 1982, but almost all of the increase in temporary employment appears to have occurred since then. Between 1982 and 1993, temporary-help industry employment increased from 0.5 percent of total employment to 1.5 percent. Contrary to some popular impressions, temps are by no means almost exclusively women; in 1993, 43 percent were men.[78]

Other dimensions of the phenomenon receive much less attention. Still widespread and perhaps even growing, for example, is the use of day-labor pools, which most Americans recognize more from the movies than from real life. Long common in agriculture, these day-labor pools now provide workers for a much wider range of industries. A study by the Southern Regional Council found that average take-home pay among these day laborers fell considerably below the minimum wage, and benefits, of course, were only a pipe-dream. An African American running one of these pools was willing to be unusually candid about their character: "To be honest, temporary service ain't nothing but a tossover from slavery. It's flesh peddling. They modify it and dress it up some. But it's slavery."[79]

The more general and in some accounts much more dramatic development has involved the spreading employment of "contingent" workers. Because this phenomenon is so new, and there is no consensus about its definition, estimates of contingent employment range all over the map.

One common definition includes virtually anyone who does not enjoy full-time wage-and-salary employment. An influential study in the late-1980s by Richard S. Belous defined the contingent workforce as including the self-employed, part-time workers, temps, and business services workers.[80] Combining all these different groups, and being careful to avoid double-counting—for example, many temps are also part-time workers—Belous estimated that in 1987 at least 29 million workers in the United States were "contingent" workers—amounting to roughly a quarter of total employment.[81] This kind of categorization has informed more recent estimates suggesting something like a third of total employment in contingent work. "Already," Janice Castro wrote in 1993, "one in every three U.S. workers has joined these shadow brigades carrying out America's business. Their ranks are growing so quickly that they are expected to outnumber permanent full-time workers by the end of this decade."[82]

However reasonable this kind of definition may seem to many, it is not useful here for the purposes of evaluating the "low-road" hypothesis. I am trying to investigate the potential influence of the growth of contingent employment on the wage squeeze among private, nonfarm, wage-and-farm workers. In that context, several of the components of this widespread definition are not pertinent. It makes no sense to include the self-employed, for example, since they are not part of the wage-and-salary work force. Nor does it make sense to count those among part-time employees who work part-time *voluntarily*, since we can reasonably assume, by definition, that most voluntary part-timers have not been *pushed* by their bosses into that situation. Still, many have relied on something like this inclusive definition in part because no other data source based on another definition has been available.

Fortunately, a BLS special survey designed to explore the magnitude of "contingent" employment has just appeared, our first opportunity to probe the dimensions of this essentially new phenomenon.[83] The survey, conducted in February 1995, studies both "contingent" workers and others with "non-traditional" working arrangements such as day laborers.

Although the study provides three different definitions of contingent employment, all of them build on the basic idea that someone has a "contingent" employment relation if they "do not perceive themselves as having an explicit or implicit contract for ongoing employment." Quite reasonably, they draw the boundary on employment horizons at one year, defining those who expect to be with their current employer for *less than twelve months* as those without even an "implicit" contractual commitment for continued service.[84]

We have been focusing throughout on private nonfarm wage-and-salary workers. In February 1995 this grouping included 92.6 million employees.[85] How many of these were faced with "contingent" work or "nontraditional" arrangements?

Making use of detailed published tabulations from the survey, I have arrived at an estimate of the proportion of "disposable workers" among private nonfarm wage-and-salary workers in February 1995. Table 8.2 summarizes these data.

• It begins with the core group of "contingent" workers—private nonfarm employees who expected their job to last for less than a year.[86] This group amounted to almost five million workers, or 5.4 of total private nonfarm wage-and-salary employment.

• I then add an estimate of *involuntary* part-time employees who have *not* already been included in the first group of "contingent" workers.[87] This adds to the category of "disposable" employment those employees who are working part-time involuntarily *even if* they think that situation might last for more than a year. By definition, this remaining group wishes that they could work full time.

• Finally, I estimate the number of workers in three "alternative" employment arrangements who are not already counted as contingent workers but who would "prefer" a "traditional" working situation.[88] This includes those working "involuntarily" as independent contractors, on-call workers and day laborers, and temporary-help agency workers who are not already counted in the previous rows.

As Table 8.2 shows, these estimates suggest that roughly a tenth of the private nonfarm wage-and-salary workforce were in "disposable" employment situations in 1995. This tally is not as large as generated by some common definitions of "contingent" workers, especially because those more widespread definitions include the self-employed and voluntary part-timers, but it is large enough to suggest that this relatively new phenomenon is important.

How much has the emergence of "disposable" employment affected the wage squeeze? Available data make it impossible to answer this question with any precision, since these survey data were gathered for the first time in early 1995 and since detailed earnings information from this same survey had not yet been released at the time of writing. Nonetheless, some ballpark approximations are revealing.

Let's first assume that all of these "disposable" workers were paying roughly the same hourly-wage penalty as estimated above for involuntary part-time workers—that all those pushed into these insecure situations, in other words, were roughly as disadvantaged in dealing with their bosses as were those

TABLE 8.2

Counting "Disposable" Workers

Number and percent among private nonfarm wage-and-salary employees, February 1995

	Number (thousands)	Percent
Disposable		
Contingent workers	4,977	5.4%
Part-time, economic reasons	2,434	2.6
Involuntary nontraditional		
Independent contractors	783	0.8
On call & day workers	745	0.8
Temporary-help workers	251	0.3
Total disposable employment	**9,190**	**9.9**
Private nonfarm wage-and salary employment	92,649	100.0

Sources and Notes: Author's estimates based on BLS data. See text and notes.

working part-time for "economic" reasons. And let's also assume that the rate of growth of all these conditions of "disposable" employment had been approximately as rapid as for those employed by temporary-help agencies; both seem to have emerged almost from scratch during the 1980s.

As shown in Chapter 1, between 1979 and 1994 the real (before-tax) hourly earnings of private nonfarm production workers declined by 9.8 percent. With these simplifying assumptions, we can roughly estimate that the growing proportion of "disposable" workers—with these "disposable" workers paying a price for their "contingent" and "nontraditional" situations—could have accounted for approximately *one-fifth* of the total wage decline.[89] This reckoning would put the spread of disposable employment roughly on a par with the decline of unionization as a potential cause of the wage squeeze.

These estimates, however substantial, don't even consider one of the most important penalties paid by those in "disposable" situations, the absence of employer-provided benefits. According to the BLS survey, for example, only one-fifth of "contingent" employees have health coverage provided by their employers, compared with 54 percent of "noncontingent" (or regular) employees.[90]

The emergence of the "disposable" worker is one of the major results of the move by many U.S. corporations onto the low road. The costs for workers are enormous. Many of those who haven't yet experienced this new, more insecure condition can feel the chill spreading through the labor market. "The anxiety level is very high, regardless of the kind of job you hold," Labor Secretary Robert Reich observes about this trend. "Nobody is safe."[91]

The Combined Effects of the Offensive

We do not have enough information to be able to generate precise combined estimates of the effects on the wage squeeze of all three of these institutional changes. In particular, the emergence of the "disposable" employee is too recent. But we have at least partial evidence that allows us to assess the "low-road" hypothesis and the power of this explanation when compared with the prevailing views reviewed in the previous chapter.

The Dinardo-Fortin-Lemieux study cited above provides the clearest suggestions. It affords our first opportunity to explore the effects on rising inequality of the fall in the real minimum wage and union density in comparison to other influences emphasized in the prevailing literature. In this comparative context, the combined effect of these two institutional changes is indeed large. For example, in their analyses of changes in the standard deviation of wages—a common measure of inequality—the authors find that between 1979 and 1988, when inequality soared, changes in the real minimum wage and union density together accounted for 39.1 percent of rising inequality among men and 33.4 percent among women—with changes in the minimum wage, understandably, playing a relatively more important role for women and changes in unionization a larger role for men. The combined influence of these two institutional changes was even higher for men both before and after the main period they study, reaching 60.8 percent of changing inequality in the 1973–79 period and 74.2 percent in 1988–92.[92] The authors conclude that "labor market institutions are at least as important as supply and demand considerations in explaining changes in the U.S. distribution of wages from 1973 to 1992."[93]

Their conclusions are reinforced by a companion study of differences in the trajectory of male earnings inequality between the United States and Canada in the 1980s.[94] During this period inequality climbed in the United States but remained roughly constant in Canada. Relying on similar estimating methods as in the paper for the United States, DiNardo and Lemieux find that "unions and the minimum wage accounted for two-thirds of the differential growth of inequality between the two countries. It is therefore these labor market institutions, as opposed to demand and supply, that seem to explain most of the difference in the evolution of overall wage inequality in the two countries."[95]

These studies, like most of the literature, investigate the determination of individuals' earnings. We get a similar picture if we view the same issues from a much simpler angle of vision, seeking to account for aggregate changes over the postwar period in one of the measures of the wage squeeze that has occupied us throughout this book—the average real (before-tax) wage for private nonfarm production workers.

Constructing a simplified analysis of the wage squeeze requires making use of measures that capture each of the principal hypotheses about its sources. Both R&D expenditures and an index of the pace of technological innovation represent the potential influence of the skills perspective, while a measure of the intensity of import competition tests the foreign-trade explanation. Testing the "low-road" hypothesis involves a minimum of three measures. Two represent institutional changes reviewed here—the real value of the minimum wage and an index of union density. The third tries to capture the effects of the costs of the bureaucratic burden itself—the share of supervisory workers in total employee compensation—which, as argued in Chapter 3, was likely to have contributed downward pressure on production workers' hourly earnings. I also control for two factors that any of the perspectives would also consider important, inflation and unemployment.[96]

This is obviously a simple analysis, intended primarily for illustrative purposes. The results are revealing nonetheless. While all three measures representing the "low-road" hypothesis have statistically significant effects on movements in real earnings, none of the indices representing either the skills or the trade perspectives have a significance influence. Each of the "low-road" variables has roughly comparable explanatory power. Between them they account for almost 40 percent of the stagnation and decline in real wages during the full period of the wage squeeze, from 1973 through 1989, and roughly 90 percent of the relative decline in real earnings from the 1973–79 to the 1979–89 cycle. This simple analysis, like the previous studies of individual earnings, suggests that institutional changes shaped by the management offensive had a crucial influence on the decline in real wages since the early 1970s.

These illustrative results hardly close the case. Rather, they suggest the plausibility of the explanation for the wage squeeze provided in this chapter and the importance of further analysis and research that substantially expands our horizons beyond the narrow range of explanations dominating recent discussions.

Once we pursue those expanded horizons, will the evidence continue to provide strong support for the "low-road" hypothesis? The institutional analysis presented in this chapter has some comparative advantages that can be briefly noted.

One unattended issue involves the sequence of steps involved in the "low-road" hypothesis. A variety of evidence supports the role of three institutional changes—the decline in the real value of the minimum wage, the erosion of trade union strength and bargaining power, and the emergence of the "disposable" worker—in explaining the wage squeeze. But until now the connection between the first and second steps of the hypothesis—that the management offensive beginning in the mid-1970s underlay those deepening institutional changes—has only been supported inferentially. This seems a reasonable conclusion in the case of the falling wage floor, since few deny that the political climate in the 1980s, when the real value of the minimum plummeted, was the period, as my collaborators and I call it, of "business ascendancy."[97] It seems equally plausible in the case of the spread of contingent employment, since most observers attribute this phenomenon primarily to a shift in corporate labor policies and, in any case, I have been careful to define it to *exclude* those who appear to have "chosen" contingent situations, such as the self-employed and voluntary part-time workers. In this case, Phillip Mattera writes, "it is the employer's quest for flexibility that dominates today's contingent labor, not the employee's. Whatever the worker can obtain in limited hours, short-term jobs and work at home is purchased at a scandalously high price."[98]

Of the three developments, declining union power is the trend for which this link in the chain of argument might be most controversial, since there are a number of other factors that are thought to have contributed to declining unionism, particularly including the growing cynicism that many nonunion workers feel about the union movement itself. I briefly review the relative importance of the management offensive in explaining the erosion of union power in the next chapter.

The next set of issues deals with comparative merits. At a relatively superficial level, at least, the "low-road" hypothesis fits the *timing* of the wage squeeze fairly closely. The management offensive picked up speed during and after the 1973–75 recession, when real wages began slowly to decline. By the 1980s, when the decline in workers' earnings accelerated, the management offensive had reached hurricane force. And it was precisely after the late 1970s that four developments all appear to have gained momentum more or less at the same time: the decline in the real minimum wage, falling union density, emerging disposable employment, and the wage squeeze itself.

In this respect, the "low-road" hypothesis seems to synchronize with the basic wage and inequality trends much better than the skills-mismatch explanation, which, as we saw in Chapter 7, has some significant problems with the timing of its alleged effects over the course of the 1980s. It also appears to fit the timing at least as well as the trade explanation, which closely fits the acceleration of wage decline in the early 1980s, when the trade deficit soared, but has somewhat more trouble for the late 1980s, when the wage squeeze continued but the merchandise trade balance improved substantially.

The "low-road" hypothesis also seems to fit better with the *breadth* of the wage squeeze than either of the other two perspectives. While the impact of declining union strength has been felt most severely in manufacturing, both the decline in the real minimum wage and the spread of disposable employ-ment are likely to have had much bigger effects outside the goods sector than within it: Since wages on average are lower in nongoods sectors—especially in retail trade, finance, insurance and real estate, and services—(see Table 7.2 in Chapter 7), the falling wage floor is likely to have had its most important consequences in those sectors outside manufacturing. Similarly, various kinds of contingent employment have also spread more widely in nongoods sectors, especially in services: According to the BLS estimates for the entire workforce, whereas 34.5 percent of noncontingent workers are employed in the service sector, 54.0 percent of contingent employees work there.[99]

By contrast, both the technology and trade explanations extend more awk-wardly to the nongoods industries. In the case of the technology explanation, as the previous chapter argues, it is less obvious in the services than in manufac-turing that automation has actually resulted in skills upgrading; productivity growth has also been flat, suggesting the weakness of the impact of technologi-cal change in those industries. In the case of the trade-and-wages connection, even more clearly, evidence for the impact of increasing import competition outside of manufacturing is weak. On this issue, Richard Freeman remarks that the trade argument "has a bit of the flavor of a tail wagging a dog."[100]

In addition to this fit with the pattern of the wage squeeze across *industries*, the "low-road" explanation also appears to do a better job of explaining the pattern of the wage squeeze across *occupations*. The wage squeeze affected the bottom four-fifths of the earnings distribution. Since the late 1980s, indeed, it has even begun to hit college graduates. How do we account for such a broad occupational impact?

Here, the difference with the trade and immigration explanations is most obvious. The trade and immigration explanations seem most pertinent—as the study by Borjas, Freeman, and Katz reviewed in the previous chapter shows—for high school dropouts. But in 1993 those with less than a high school degree accounted for only 11 percent of private nonfarm wage-and-salary employees between the ages of twenty-five and sixty-four.[101] By con-trast, the decline of the real minimum wage is likely to have affected close to the bottom quarter of the earnings distribution (see my estimates at the be-ginning of this chapter), and eroding union power is likely to have affected both the bottom and the middle (see, for example, the study by Gittelman and Howell cited in the previous chapter).

The spread of contingent employment probably also helps account for the more recent squeeze closer to the top of the distribution. By most accounts, the disposable trend has been accelerating since the mid- to late-1980s, pre-cisely when the decline in the real earnings of even college graduates began. And college graduates are the one educational grouping among whom con-tingent working situations are relatively more common than that group's rep-resentation in the total workforce. (Among the best educated workers, these contingent employees are much more likely to be professionals than managers; whereas the proportion of professionals with contingent jobs is relatively higher than their share of the total workforce, the proportion of managers is substantially lower.)[102]

Much more generally, when we consider overall impact, the explanation reviewed in this chapter seems to do a better job of actually explaining the wage squeeze than the other main candidates. I argued in the previous chapter that it is difficult to observe very strong *direct* evidence supporting either the technology or the trade explanations. Here, we can directly observe changes in the real minimum wage and in union strength instead of needing to rely on inferences about movements in statistical "residuals." And it appears that those institutional changes have each significantly contributed to falling wages, especially for relatively lower-waged workers. (We have no comparable precise and direct estimates for contingent employment, as already noted, since the data measuring that phenomenon are new.)

Proponents of the trade explanation might reply that increasing import competition lies behind these other developments. In particular, they might argue that the intensification of trade pressure in the early 1980s—rather than the management offensive—helps account for the acceleration in the decline in union density during that decade and, in particular, for the erosion of the union wage premium after the early 1980s. While that argument carries some weight for workers in a number of vulnerable manufacturing industries, it is hardly decisive overall. First, the erosion of union strength began to accelerate, as we saw in Figure 8.2, before import competition had become most intense in the early 1980s. Second, union strength declined in a broad range of sectors, not merely in the manufacturing sectors most exposed to import competition. Between 1983 and 1993, for example, relative union density declined substantially in transportation, communications, and hospitals—none of them likely to have suffered mounting pressures from global competition. And within manufacturing, while the union share dropped substantially in those industries such as steel and textiles, in which (as we saw in Chapter 7) real earnings were especially hard hid during the 1980s, it also declined dramatically in industries such as chemicals where U.S. comparative advantage remained relatively strong, as well as in manufacturing industries considered to have relatively little exposure to import competition such as food and tobacco.[103] The management offensive, as far as we can tell, occurred throughout the economy, while the foreign threat had a narrower impact. The decline in unionism also occurred across the board.

Finally, the "low-road" hypothesis is also consistent with much of the comparative evidence we have about trends in earnings and inequality across the advanced countries.

The first striking indication of this possibility comes from data on trends in inequality itself. Among the eleven countries for which Freeman and Katz present trends during the 1980s in inequality between the top and bottom of the male wage distribution, the three countries experiencing the most rapid increases are precisely those three "conflictual" economies studied in Chapter 6—with the United States showing the greatest rise, the United Kingdom second, and Canada third. By contrast, the four "cooperative" economies for which they present data experienced little or no increase in inequality; Germany actually displayed a *decrease* in earnings differentials. (Data were not available for Norway.) The average increase in wage inequality for the three conflictual economies from 1979 to 1990 was 0.19 index points, while the average for the four cooperative economies was less than 0.01 point.[104] (The results for changes in the female wage distribution are comparable.)

More crucially, most cross-country analyses of the *sources* of trends in wages and inequality attribute a substantial role to the kinds of institutional changes reviewed in this chapter. The DiNardo-Lemieux study of the United States and Canada provides one striking example of this kind of evidence. Closely analyzing the relationship between unionism and income inequality, Freeman concludes:[105]

> the increase in industrial earnings inequality is inversely associated with unioni-
> zation. . . . While the [data do] not prove that unionism is responsible for the
> more modest increase in inequality in [countries such as Sweden, Denmark,
> and Belgium] . . . , the fact that the increase in inequality was less where
> unions were strongest clearly supports the main conclusion of this study—that
> declines in unionization contribute to increases in inequality.

A study by Katz, Gary W. Loveman, and David G. Blanchflower provides at least inferential support for the proposition that the collapse of the real minimum wage in the United States contributed to declining real wages at the bottom of the earnings distribution—in comparison with a country like France where the minimum wage remained relatively high and inequality rose much less.[106] Germany, one of our representative cooperative economies, experienced an actual decline in inequality during the 1980s. In analyzing that trend and comparing the German case with the United States, Katharine G. Abraham and Susan N. Houseman also confirm the importance of institutions:[107]

> On the whole, the different development of wage inequality in Germany and
> the United States cannot be readily attributed to the existence of fundamen-
> tally different demand and supply side forces in the two countries. . . . Rather,
> it appears that institutional factors played an important role in mitigating pres-
> sures for greater wage inequality in Germany. German wage-setting institu-
> tions probably have helped limit increases in earnings inequality. Moreover, the
> German education and training system, which many believe provides a better
> match between demand and supply than the U.S. system, likely has lessened
> the downward pressures on wages for less educated, younger workers. [108]

In short, the "low-road" hypothesis seems promising. If we paid more attention to the Stick Strategy and its consequences in the United States, the wage squeeze would seem less mysterious. Lifting the veil on U.S. corporate strategies and actions, it would appear, is imperative.

Explaining the Bureaucratic Burden

Mountains of studies have explored the sources of falling wages and rising inequality in the United States. Virtually none have sought to explain the bureaucratic burden, the flip side of the wage squeeze. We can thus review the evidence on corporate bloat with welcome brevity. My own previous studies are most relevant for the purposes of this discussion.

Let's look first at the patterns of growth of the bureaucratic burden in the United States. What accounts for the alternately rapid and slow growth in the bureaucratic burden in the United States over the postwar period? Figure 2.2 in Chapter 2 showed that during the Little Stick phase the share of supervisory workers increased substantially through the early 1960s before its growth decelerated. With the transition to the Big Stick phase in the early 1970s, the growth of the bureaucratic burden accelerated again through the early 1980s before leveling off. Does my analysis of the logic of the Stick Strategy help explain this go-and-slow pattern? What follows here summarizes a simple analysis accounting for movements in the employment share of nonproduction and supervisory employees over the full postwar period— from the cycle peak of 1951 through the most recent peak in 1989.[109]

Standard economic analysis suggests the potential importance of three factors:

• The rhythm of the business cycle itself will help account for short-term movements in the supervisory employment share; historically, nonproduction employees have been less likely to experience layoffs during recessions than production workers. We would therefore expect that over the business cycle the supervisory share would be relatively higher during recessions than expansions.

• Automation may also result in a higher proportion of nonproduction workers. Although there remains considerable uncertainty over the general bias of technological change, it seems likely that periods of more rapid increases in capital intensity would be associated with a rising supervisory share, simply because the employment-displacing effects of investment appear to have been relatively more likely to hit production workers.

• Controlling for other factors, we would also expect the costs of hiring nonproduction workers to have an impact. If the hourly cost of hiring a manager or supervisor rises, all other factors equal, firms may hesitate to hire as many nonproduction workers as they might otherwise.

These standard considerations ignore the effects of labor relations, treating the corporate hierarchy as if it has nothing to do with the organization and supervision of production. Two factors seem most important in considering the potential influence of the Stick Strategy itself on the bureaucratic burden. First, as noted in Chapter 3, it is relatively likely that the intensity of supervision will increase if and when the rate of change of real wages declines: fewer carrots, more sticks. Second, where the stick rather than the carrot reigns, the potential effectiveness of supervision will also be likely to increase when there is a relative rise in the costs to workers of actually losing their jobs: "If I don't want to lose my current job because of the threat of income loss or unemployment, I may be more mindful when the boss cracks the whip." In our joint work on productivity growth, Weisskopf, Bowles, and I refer to these first and second influences as the "worker motivation" and the "employer control" effects respectively.[110] Incorporating those two potential imperatives for the purposes of this analysis, I consider the effects of both the rate of change of production workers' real spendable hourly earnings and our measure of the "cost of job loss"—an estimate of the costs to workers of job dismissal.

However simplified, this little model of changes in the supervisory employment share works quite well.[111] It explains close to three-quarters of the annual rate of change in the bureaucratic burden. All five of the variables included in the analysis are significantly associated with variations in the supervisory share, including the "worker motivation" and "employer control" proxies. Taking heed of the logic of the Stick Strategy enhances the model's effectiveness; by conventional statistical standards, we're better off if we include those two labor-relations variables in the analysis than if we ignore them.[112]

Most important, what does this analysis tell us about the sources of the go-and-slow pattern of growth in the bureaucratic burden over the postwar period? And are those results consistent with the brief narrative presented in Chapter 2?

• The principal source of the slowdown in the rate of growth from the 1952–66 boom phase to the 1966–73 cycle is the sharp decline in the cost of job loss after the early 1960s, apparently indicating that the effectiveness of hiring additional supervisory employees was diminishing as workers felt relatively more secure about their jobs.[113]

• Both labor relations variables help explain the acceleration from 1966–73 to 1973–79: Real wage growth slowed, dampening worker motivation. And the cost of job loss recovered, enhancing employer control. Taken together, these two Stick Strategy variables account for 93 percent of the more rapid growth in the bureaucratic burden during this phase when, as I argued in Chapter 2, the Big Stick strategy kicked into gear.

• Three of the variables help account for the slowdown in the growth of the bureaucratic burden during the 1980s. Capacity utilization levels increased during the long 1980s expansion, tending to reduce the supervisory share. The continuing investment slowdown reduced the rate of growth of the capital-labor ratio, casting some doubt on this piece of the technology argument about wages, and therefore evidently diminished the rate of displacement of production workers. And the cost of job loss dropped after its recovery during the 1970s, primarily as a result of declining unemployment rates; this drop diminished the sharpness of this standard instrument in the corporations' disciplinary toolkit, and perhaps contributed to their accelerating move toward more contingent employment relations as an alternative disciplinary device. By contrast, the wage squeeze intensified, which would otherwise have contributed to a continuing growth in the bureaucratic burden, not to its leveling off.

Has this simple model left out any other factors that might help explain movements in the supervisory share and, perhaps, undercut the explanatory power of the Stick Strategy effects?

Only one other study in the literature seems relevant. Richard E. Caves and Matthew B. Krepps look at sources of the variation in nonproduction employment in manufacturing.[114] In addition to some of the standard variables, they test for two additional possible influences. They hypothesize that, as I also surmised in Chapter 3, the mergers and acquisitions movement during the 1980s might have curbed managers' appetite for the expansion of their bureaucratic realms. They find virtually no support for this supposition, however, so I have not separately tested for it here. They also hypothesize that the intensification of import competition may have put pressure on managements to trim their ranks, contributing to the "downsizing" wave. In this case, they do find some evidence to support the possibility for the 1980s, when import pressure deepened. Once I control for the labor relations effects, however, I do not find evidence that the addition of a measure of import competition has any significant effects, either for the whole period or separately for the 1980s.[115] Once we take appropriate measure of the dynamics of the Stick Strategy, intensifying global competition does not seem to have an important role to play in the go-and-slow story.

International comparisons also lend support to the "low-road" explanation for top-heavy corporate bureaucracies. Chapter 3 reviewed evidence that there appears to be a fairly close association across economies between relatively more conflictual labor relations and relatively top-heavier managerial structures. Does this relationship hold up when we try to look at other factors potentially affecting cross-country variations in the bureaucratic burden?

Examinations of patterns across sixteen advanced countries suggest that the influence of labor-management systems on the bureaucratic burden remains strong even after trying to take other possible influences into account.[116] Indeed, these analyses suggest that factors involving labor relations are even more important than the simple test in Chapter 3 revealed.

For reasons of data availability, I study the period at the beginning of the 1980s—by which time the Big Stick phase had driven the U.S. bureaucratic burden sharply upward. No matter what other factors are considered, my composite measures of the relatively cooperative character of labor relations (see Chapter 3) retain a strong influence on cross-country differences in the percentage of employment in managerial and administrative employment: the more cooperative a country's labor-management system, the fewer bosses it appears to require. In addition, the cost of job loss—the measure of the extent of employer control that appears to have had such significant effect on the pattern of changes over time in the United States—also has a strong positive influence on the bureaucratic burden across countries: the greater the potential costs to workers of losing their jobs, at least at the margin, the more payoff there appears to be to a top-down supervisory approach to labor management.

Other potentially important influences do not seem to make much difference. One might have thought, for example, that another source of relatively large managerial bureaucracies in the United States would have been the vast global empires controlled by multinational corporations based in the United States—requiring huge headquarters staffing at home. But there is no evidence that the size of a country's economy or its relative involvement in global trade have any effects on its bureaucratic burden—once the effects of labor relations have been taken into account.[117]

Such comparative studies are far too preliminary to provide more than suggestive results. But the cross-country evidence is consistent with that for the United States. Where the Stick Strategy prevails, it would appear, more bosses are needed to wield the stick. And when the Stick Strategy intensifies, as at the beginning of the management offensive, the legions of stick-wielders grow. Like overweight runners in the marathon, U.S. corporations cannot race fast enough to keep up with their "high-road" competitors.

Chapter 9

CAN WE TAKE THE HIGH ROAD?

I n July 1995 *Business Week* ran a cover story on "The Wage Squeeze."[1] Profits were at record-high levels, four years into the expansion, but workers' earnings were stagnating. Should business worry?

To *Business Week*, ever mindful of corporate interests, the "wage squeeze" seemed to pose two threats:

• One problem involved consumer demand. Since working households spend more of their money on consumption than affluent households—which are typically able to put away a little for a rainy day—a squeeze on wages was bound to crimp consumer expenditures as well. "The risk for Corporate America in all this," the article warned, "lies in the prospect of chronically weak demand." "This is the weakest consumption cycle of the postwar period," one Wall Street economist explained, "which is largely a reflection of the wage slowdown."[2]

• More speculatively, the magazine worried about the prospect of mounting anger and, ultimately, class-based political rebellion. The story concluded as follows:[3] "The sight of bulging corporate coffers co-existing with a continuous stagnation in Americans' living standards could become politically untenable. . . . In the past few years, . . . all but the most elite employees have landed in the same leaky boat. If they all come to stress their common fate more than their differences, it could spell trouble for corporations and politicians alike."

Thus we have the World According to Business, a vivid etching of corporate self-interest. For the rest of us, traveling the "low road" raises substantially different concerns. Part II of this book argued that the price of corporate bloat and the wage squeeze is exorbitant. Millions of workers and households have been directly clubbed by the Stick. Millions more of us are feeling the ripple effects in our schools and communities and government institutions.

All of us must endure the bumpy macroeconomic consequences of travels on the low road. These costs are huge.

Some conservatives and business analysts have finally begun to appreciate the magnitude of these costs and the threats they pose. "The emergence of codes of corporate ethics and the emphasis on fashioning a defensible corporate culture," political scientist James Q. Wilson writes, "are not, I think, merely public relations (though they are sometimes just that). They are, at their best, a recognition that people want to believe that they live and work in a reasonably just and decent world."[4] "When people feel like valued assets of their companies," Harvard Business School's Rosabeth Moss Kanter reports, "they express more satisfaction with their lives and more willingness to help others."[5] It is not enough for conservatives and corporations, Wilson continues, to express blind faith in the invisible hand:[6]

> The problem for capitalists is to recognize that, while free markets will ruthlessly eliminate inefficient firms, the moral sentiments of man will only gradually and uncertainly penalize immoral ones. But, while the quick destruction of inefficient corporations threatens only individual firms, the slow anger at immoral ones threatens capitalism—and freedom—itself.

William J. McDonough is president of the Federal Reserve Bank of New York, a pillar of the establishment. But he too is concerned. At a conference he convened in 1994 to consider the wage squeeze and rising inequality, he expressed his fears:[7]

> These dramatic wage developments raise profound issues for the United States, issues of equity and social cohesion, issues that affect the very temperament of the country. We are forced to face the question of whether we will be able to go forward together as a unified society with a confident outlook or as a society of diverse economic groups suspicious of both the future and each other.

Left to their own devices, however, U.S. corporations show little sign of letting up, of heeding the broader social and moral consequences of their addiction to the low road. *Business Week* characterizes their current views: "To ease up now, many executives feel, would be to snatch defeat from the jaws of victory."[8] "There's a very intense determination in executive suites across America," Mobil's vice-president for administration reports, "not to give away hard-fought improvements. It may be a long time before this shakes through and wages rise."[9] The rest of us cannot afford to wait that long.

This chapter suggests some steps we could begin taking immediately to push our economy toward the "high road." It does not provide a comprehensive blueprint to remedy all the problems of the U.S. economy. It does not present a shop-worn wish list of everyone's favorite reforms. Instead, it proposes five specific steps—all practicable, all easily legislated—which could begin to reduce U.S. corporate addiction to the Stick. This five-step program could be enacted quickly, certainly within the first 100 days of a new political regime—if one can suspend disbelief for a moment and imagine such a possibility—which was firmly committed to encouraging the Carrot over the Stick.

Once enacted, however, these recommended reforms would represent only the beginning, not the end of the project. Changing the way corporations do business in America cannot occur overnight. Federal bureaucrats should not and cannot march into corporate executive suites, firing redundant managers right and left, dictating labor relations strategies and production organization. The most we can ask from the government, in our mixed-market political economy, is that it nip and nudge, like a sheep dog, in the hopes of moving the herd in a different direction.

But this prodding can be crucial. Chapter 6 argued that U.S. corporations continue to rely on the Stick Strategy in large part because of the temptations that their surrounding social and political environment provides. It's so easy to pay low wages in the United States that corporate eyes gleam like kids in a carnival when they enter the labor market. A set of policies aiming to substitute the Carrot for the Stick needs to reduce those temptations, to alter the calculus upon which U.S. firms base their decisions. These five proposals could move us in that direction.

A Five-Step Program

This section considers *only* policy reforms whose primary purpose is to affect the organization of production and the structures of labor management in U.S. corporations.

This inclusion principle neglects many economic policy reforms that would make sense in the United States in confronting other problems—such as reducing the political independence of the Federal Reserve Board so that, at the least, monetary and fiscal policies could be better coordinated. More important for the purposes of this book, it also leaves out policy reforms that could significantly moderate corporate reliance on the Stick but whose primary rationale lies elsewhere.

For example, among the most important sources of the emergence of the "disposable" worker have been our archaic and misguided systems of health insurance and payroll taxation. Alone among the advanced countries, we do not provide some form of universal health coverage. This has meant, especially during the era of skyrocketing health care costs, that employers have had a strong incentive to treat their employees as "disposable" in order to avoid incurring the costs of health insurance. Virtually alone among the advanced countries, further, we finance social security out of a special trust fund rather than out of general revenue. Faced with that separate payroll tax, employers have also been tempted to hire relatively fewer employees on regular lines and to rely increasingly on temps for whom they do not incur payroll tax obligations. Pushing for single-payer universal health insurance and for social security financed through general taxation would make sense for many reasons in the United States. Not the least would be a reduced temptation for employers to shortchange their employees through various kinds of "contingent" employment relations.

Raising the Wage Floor

The first and perhaps most important source of the wage squeeze, Chapter 8 argued, has been the dramatic decline in the real value of the minimum wage. The remedy to this problem seems obvious: *increase the minimum wage and ensure that its real value does not fall in the future.*

There are no mysteries about how to take such a step. Congress has long-standing experience with legislating the federal minimum wage, most recently in 1989 for the two-step increase from $3.35 to $4.25 an hour.

How much should it be increased? During the postwar boom the federal minimum wage averaged around 45 to 50 percent of the average production-worker's wage in manufacturing. By 1994, with the average manufacturing wage at $12.06,[10] the minimum wage of $4.25 had dropped to only 35 percent. A reasonable target would be to shoot for restoring the minimum wage to roughly half the manufacturing wage. Since we would expect further growth in the manufacturing wage by the time we could complete these steps, I would recommend *increasing the federal minimum wage to $6.50 (in 1994 dollars) in several steps.* Far from pricing us out of global markets, this would simply serve to bring our mandated minimum wage up to roughly the levels prevailing in many of the "cooperative" economies—slightly above that in Japan, for example, and somewhat below that in the Netherlands—which, as Chapter 6 showed, have been successfully traveling the "high road."[11] Another substantial benefit would come from the particular impact of a rising minimum wage on womens' earnings, contributing substantially to a reduction in gender inequality.

How quickly? In their comprehensive study of the minimum wage, David Card and Alan B. Krueger found that the recent increase of nearly a dollar phased in over two years worked effectively and smoothly.[12] By this standard, one could reasonably propose increasing the federal minimum wage from $4.25 to $6.50 over a four-year period—say, from 1997 to 2000.[13]

Once there, the federal minimum wage should be tied to the consumer price index so that erosions of its real value will not recur. Some economists worry that an indexed minimum wage would put "excessive" pressure on wages above the minimum wage.[14] But that's precisely the point. In order to push U.S. employers toward the high road, I have argued, their labor costs need to rise. They need to begin modernizing or get out of the kitchen.

Most economists quake at such a prospect. A traditional litany among neo-classical economists has been that increasing the minimum wage is counter-productive, that a rising wage floor would have negative employment effects, displacing many lower-skilled workers from their jobs. But the "new economics" of the minimum wage now suggest that this prevailing paranoia, grounded in the traditional textbook model and amplified by lobbyists for small-business interests, was unfounded. Card and Krueger write:[15]

> In the United States, the debate over the minimum wage has shifted from the question of whether minimum-wage increases cause small or large job losses to the question of whether minimum-wage increases cause any loss of jobs at all. . . . The consistent finding of weak or negligible employment effects in both the United States and elsewhere suggests that the problem may lie with the textbook model, rather than with the evidence.

The "new economics" of the minimum wage has been vigorously criticized in some quarters.[16] But, among many reasons for taking it seriously, the conclusions are consistent with the international comparisons reviewed in Chapter 6: cooperative economies featuring high wage standards and rapid real wage growth, also often mandating considerably higher minimum wages than in the United States, have been able to combine rapid real wage growth with relatively low unemployment. Richard B. Freeman writes in his review of Card and Krueger's book: "This book has caused me to revise upward the level of the minimum wage at which I believe income can be redistributed without causing job losses. I predict it will do the same for you."[17] As one of several steps toward the high road, substantially increasing the federal minimum wage holds considerable promise of both easing the wage squeeze for millions of working Americans *and* removing some of the candy from the low-wage candy store.

More Effective Worker Voice

A second critical source of the wage squeeze has been the decline in union reach and power. This points to an equally obvious potential remedy: *legislation to enhance workers' abilities to achieve effective workplace representation.* I propose three specific pieces of such legislative reform. These do not include all the elements of a comprehensive approach to labor law reform, but merely those elements that could contribute most to encouraging the Carrot approach.

The first would seek to reduce the obstacles to unionization for those workers who seek it. Unions get a horrible press in the United States. And for many it has become commonplace to argue that union density has declined because workers don't believe anymore that unions will represent their interests effectively. There is a considerable debate about the relative importance of a number of different potential explanations for declining union density.

How much has been due, for example, to intensifying management opposition? To organized labor's sluggishness and inertia on the organizing front? To a mounting cynicism among workers about the efficacy of unionization?[18] All three factors have been credited with significant influence, with their relative importance perhaps changing over time.

But there is a prior issue, one of simple democracy. Millions of workers who are not now members of unions would prefer union representation and don't have it. In a representative survey in 1994, roughly a third of non-union private-sector workers said they would vote for a union "if an election were held today."[19] Skeptics have called this a glass more than half empty, noting that a substantial majority does *not* desire union representation. But in 1994 the number of "frustrated" union members in the private sector, as they're sometimes called in the literature, came to *30 million workers.*[20] These are not the workers who have decided that unions won't effectively serve their interests. These are not the ones who regard unions as a bunch of pork-choppers. These are the workers who, in an intensely anti-union climate, would nonetheless prefer union representation. Thirty million is a lot of frustrated workers. If we care about democracy, we ought to care about satisfying the preferences of 30 million Americans. This is two-thirds the numbers of voters who elected Bill Clinton as President of the United States in 1992. Their preferences counted. Why shouldn't those of "frustrated" potential union members?

Why are millions of workers unrequited in their preferences for union representation? Many who have studied declining union membership in the United States argue that workers seeking union representation face a tilted playing field.[21] When workers seek to organize, employers hold most of the cards. Workers feel the intimidation: According to the recent report by the federal Commission on the Future of Worker-Management Relations (known as the Dunlop Commission), "79 percent say it is likely that employees who seek union representation will lose their jobs, and 41 percent of nonunion workers say they think they might lose their own jobs if they tried to organize."[22] When workers file complaints about management's "unfair practices," as Chapter 8 showed, government officials have been increasingly inclined since the early 1980s to rule against them. And when and if workers win union representation after an often tortuous, hotly contested election campaign, companies often stall and effectively refuse to negotiate a contract "in good faith"; roughly a third of workplaces in which workers vote for union representation do not achieve a collective bargaining contract with their companies.[23] "Over the past dozen years," *Business Week* concludes, "U.S. industry has conducted one of the most successful antiunion wars ever, illegally firing thousands of workers for exercising their rights to organize."[24]

One of the most important reasons nonunion members are frustrated, it would appear, stems from the American system of elections for union representation.[25] Emulating a system common and apparently effective in several Canadian provinces, we should mandate *automatic certification of union representation upon a 55-percent majority of workers signing union membership cards.*[26] This short-circuits the election process and cuts quickly to the chase. Can workers preferring union representation achieve reasonable gains and effective voice with their employers? If a majority of workers indicate their preference for union representation, let them move ahead. The Dunlop Commission agrees with the basic priority of expediting elections in order to avoid the contentiousness and litigiousness of our current system, but would favor requiring quick elections (within five days) of submission of signed petitions.[27] In either case, the basic point is to get on with it. Employers and workers have better things to do with their time, effort, energy, and money than to conduct protracted, contentious election campaigns.

A second strand of reform would aim obliquely at the top-heaviness of corporate bureaucracies. One important difference between U.S. labor law and the laws in many European countries, such as Sweden, is that many "non-production and supervisory" employees in the United States can be excluded from coverage by the National Labor Relations Act because they are "part of management." In Sweden, almost all managerial and professional employees are unionized; in the United States, virtually none are. Increasingly, one gathers, lower- and middle-level managerial personnel have grown frustrated with their status and working conditions in U.S. corporations.[28] But the National Labor Relations Board (NLRB) has recently been extending the managerial exclusion, not restricting it.

At the margin, this trend contributes to U.S. corporations' building up the ranks of their managerial personnel: if you want to limit the size of union influence, call some of the workers in a proposed collective bargaining unit "part of management." Proposal: *afford all but the highest levels of currently exempt workers—including professionals and many managerial personnel—protection under the National Labor Relations Act.* If managerial and professional employees are disgruntled and want to form unions and bargain collectively with their employers, let them have a go. My hunch—and it can only be a hunch since we have so little experience in the United States—is that this opportunity for lower- and middle-management could create substantial counter-pressures against corporate proclivities to construct top-down, top-heavy supervisory structures. All those managers and supervisors might become more trouble than they're worth.

A third strand of reform aims at expanding the range of options for worker representation. In all advanced European countries except the United Kingdom and Ireland, not only are workers entitled to belong to labor unions but firms are mandated to establish "works councils," democratically-representative participatory organizations that seek to articulate and present workers' views within the enterprise.[29] There is a kind of division of labor between unions and works councils, with the latter focusing more on issues of shop and office floor management and participation. The purpose of the works councils, Joel Rogers and Wolfgang Streeck write, "is to give workers a voice in the governance of the shop floor and the firm, and to facilitate communication and cooperation between management and labor on production-related matters, more or less free of direct distributive conflicts over wages."[30] These works councils hold one of the keys to the kind of "cooperative" success story reviewed in Chapter 6. Proposal: *Congress should mandate the formation of "employee participation councils" in all workplaces (with twenty-five employees or more)—with representatives to be elected by employees. The councils would be empowered to deliberate with management about all decisions affecting the organization of production and labor relations at the workplace.*[31] This would extend to millions of workers the kinds of contractual guarantees recently negotiated by those at the Magma Copper Corporation, which we first met in Chapter 2.[32]

Millions of workers would appear to favor such a step. In the recent Worker Representation and Participation Survey, directed by Richard Freeman and Joel Rogers, 63 percent reported they want more say in workplace decisions and roughly three-quarters of workers thought establishment of a committee to meet with management to "discuss the problems employees have as a group" would be a more effective way to ensure voice than the present system.[33] Reacting to the present existence of various kinds of "quality circles" and "employee involvement" programs, the vast majority of respondents (82 percent) agreed that "if employees, as a group, had more say in how these programs are run" they would be more effective.[34]

Nonetheless many companies and some unions are wary of this kind of proposal. "Low-road" firms want to run their own shows and don't want to bother with employee representation; in the recent survey, a majority of managers favored employee representation only if management, rather than an outside arbitrator, "has the final say in disputes."[35]

Many trade union leaders are concerned about these proposals on specific and general grounds. Specifically, for good historical reasons, unions are wary that such participation councils would devolve into "company unions."[36] But enabling Congressional legislation for such councils can make clear that workers must elect their own representatives to the councils and that section 8(a)(2) of the National Labor Relations Act, which bans company unions, still stands.[37] In dissenting from the Dunlop Commission's wording on this kind of proposal, former UAW president Douglas Fraser emphasized that "the kind of 'participation' and 'cooperation' that should be encouraged is *democratic* participation and cooperation *between equals.*"[38] Employee participation councils can begin to help foster that kind of "democratic participation and cooperation" provided that they are mandated by outside legislation—not set up by management—and that workers control the councils' election and organizational machinery.

Unions are also concerned more generally that such councils would undermine the efficacy and appeal of labor unions. The councils cannot be a substitute for unions, with which employers are legally obligated to negotiate on key issues affecting workers. And establishment of councils must not serve as an excuse for postponing some of the kinds of labor law reform already proposed; roughly 40 percent of working Americans either now belong to unions or would prefer to join them, and their preferences must not be blocked. But, at the same time, most of the other three-fifths of workers want and need a "voice" over conditions affecting their working lives. And, given the review of the "low-road" and "high-road" options in Chapter 6, we all will benefit from stronger macroeconomic performance if they achieve such voice. *Both* effective councils *and* strong unions can help nip and nudge U.S. corporations toward the high road.

Flexible, Not "Disposable" Work

Part of the problem with the emergence of the "disposable" worker is that the potential advantages of true "flexibility" at work have been compromised. Employers can benefit from some leeway in how they schedule their workforce. And many employees, especially those with children, can benefit from choice and discretion in scheduling their own working time. But disposability is not flexibility. As a result of recent trends, part-time and more contingent work is becoming a sentence, not an opportunity. Workers are losing rights, choice, and benefits.

As already noted, changing our systems of health insurance and payroll taxation would help break down the artificial distinction between regular and contingent employees. What else can be done to enhance the benefits of flexibility and reduce the penalties of disposability?

"Part of the worktime problem," Juliet Schor writes, "is that we are still operating with a 'male' model of employment—full-time hours and full-time dedication to the job." She continues:[39]

> [This is] a take-it-or-leave-it option. As women have entered the workforce in large numbers, they have had to conform to this model to succeed. But this causes serious problems, because women still retain primary responsibility for and attachment to child care and household work. And increasingly, men want time off the job too, often to be with their children.

When employers seek to avoid paying benefits for new employees, for example, they force present employees to work overtime rather than opening up jobs for others who need them. To avoid benefit costs for new workers, a *New York Times* reporter concluded, "employers have been stretching the workweek, not cutting it back."[40] Compulsion, not choice.

In our current system, employers have discretion to shift their employees around virtually any way they would like. We should reduce their temptation to do this exploitatively by altering the environment affecting worktime decisions. Proposal: *Amend the Fair Labor Standards Act to prohibit mandatory overtime; to substitute compensatory time as an optional alternative to voluntary overtime premia; to include salaried (in addition to hourly) workers within its coverage; and to mandate three-weeks vacation, rising to four weeks after an interim period of (say) 5–10 years, for all wage-and-salary employees.*

Each of these steps would help deal with the "disposable" worker problem and would help pressure employers away from their low-cost, low-road approach. A ban on *mandatory* overtime would enhance flexibility for employees, since they could still *choose* to work overtime when asked, and it could push employers to open up employment to more workers who would nonetheless retain regular rights and benefits. Substituting compensatory time as an alternative to time-and-a-half for overtime—meaning that workers would be able to work less some other day if they worked extra hours today—would provide further flexibility for workers in juggling their work and family lives. Extending worktime coverage and regulations to salaried workers would help protect one of the largest concentrations of "contingent" workers, the college-educated, mostly professional workers who, as noted in Chapter 8, are especially prone to contingent work relations. Universally mandated vacation time, finally, would also contribute to breaking down the artificial distinctions that now prevail between full-time and part-time employees. My proposal on vacation time seeks to move us in the direction of the high road in two steps: first to extend the current average vacation time for American workers to everyone, in order to help reduce the incentives for employers to depend on "disposable" employees; and then later raise the mandated minimum to four weeks, a level equivalent to many of the cooperative countries (although others provide a minimum mandate of five).[41]

Over the longer run these steps would probably contribute to a more productive and innovative economy, encouraging real flexibility and permitting workers to integrate their working, family, and community lives much more effectively. They would also probably help reduce the problem of the "overworked" American. As noted in Chapter 4, American workers now work many more hours per year than their counterparts in Europe. In 1990, for example, full-time manufacturing workers in the United States logged an average of 1,904 hours for the whole year while their German equivalents clocked only 1,643—the equivalent of more than six weeks less a year (at the average American working week).[42] And American workers to some extent "prefer" these longer hours, when compared with European employees. Linda Bell and Richard Freeman argue that one of the principal reasons Americans prefer to work more hours a years is that inequality is so much greater in the

United States than in most European countries:[43] U.S. workers face the risk of stagnating and declining earnings, of falling behind in their struggle to stay in place; opting for longer hours is a natural response to these fears and risks and, as Chapter 4 showed, one of the few ways that U.S. workers have been able to protect family incomes against the wage squeeze. With pressures on corporations to move toward the high road and, potentially, less inequality, working Americans may finally begin to savor some of the leisure time they now forsake.

A Carrot for Cooperative Workplaces

Not only do we need to pressure corporations to abandon the Stick but we should also provide them with incentives for it. In the current U.S. context, firms are provided virtually no material encouragement to make the commitments and investments that adopting the Carrot Strategy involves. Some economists refer to this as a "market failure": for many firms it would be profitable to adopt the Carrot Strategy, but they either cannot afford or cannot gain access to the funds that would be necessary to move in that direction.[44] Proposal: *establish a National Cooperative Investment Bank that would provide investment credits and subsidies to firms with cooperative and democratic organizational structures.*

Governments in the United States at the federal, state, and local levels have long subsidized certain kinds of economic activities they have wanted to encourage—think of the vast subsidies provided for private home ownership in the postwar period. But we have never sought to provide direct incentives for firms that practice cooperative work relations. We can and should begin to do so.

There are many precedents for specific trusts or investment banks aimed at encouraging targeted investment projects. For example, the Community Development Financial Institutions (CDFI) Fund, enacted by Congress and signed into law by President Clinton in 1994, has been established to provide financial assistance for community-based banks and organizations in community development projects.[45] The Southern Finance Project has called for a complementary fund, a National Reinvestment Fund constructed with assessments on nonbank lenders, to help capitalize the growth of the CDFIs supported by the federal government.[46]

We need to apply these kinds of instruments to direct support for more cooperative enterprises. Firms that can establish that they provide worker ownership or substantial and effective worker participation or control in organizing production could receive low-interest loans to help finance reorganization and expansion. As with any investment support, from banks or from the government, the firms would need to be monitored periodically to ensure that their claims of "cooperative" practices were not mere window dressing. U.C.-Berkeley economist David I. Levine suggests, for example, that firms might receive special government support if they could show that they had allotted employees at least one seat on the board of directors; featured an elected employee relations committee in each establishment; also featured a health and safety committee at each establishment; maintained some kind of profit-sharing plan; and sustained some kind of formal procedure for dispute resolution.[47] One can imagine other practicable variations on the same basic theme. The essential point is that this kind of federal subsidy involves an opportunity, not a constraint. Firms would be free to seek the incentive or to eschew it. If we would all benefit from taking the "high road," surely we can afford to provide some carrots for firms that are trying to move in that direction.

Training and Assistance for Cooperation

Two additional barriers impede movement to the high road. Neither managers nor workers are in the habit of relating cooperatively in production. And it's expensive to provide the training and assistance to help them shake their established habits. Magma Copper, as we saw in Chapter 3, invested $3 million and 300,000 person hours in retooling for life on the high road. It's paid off for the company over the longer haul, but why should we sit back and wait for corporations and unions to demonstrate the kind of foresightedness and commitment that Magma exercised? This is another example of a kind of "market failure." If, as I suggested in Chapter 6, it would be profitable for many firms to undertake the high road *except for the initial investment and training costs required to institutionalize a more cooperative labor-relations system,* and if it would also bring benefits to the aggregate economy if and when more firms adopted the Carrot Strategy, then it would make sense on pure efficiency grounds for the government to help subsidize those initial investment costs and help expedite the institutional transformations involved. Proposal: *establish a National Cooperative Training and Assistance Agency to help workers and managers acquire the skills and habits necessary for more cooperative labor relations.*

Many have noted that U.S. firms provide remarkably little training for their employees—especially when compared to leading competitors such as Germany.[48] More important, U.S. firms tend to concentrate their training on higher-level employees, leaving less-skilled production workers to fend for themselves in an increasingly turbulent marketplace.[49] This practice neglects precisely those employees whose contributions to more productive and cooperative enterprises can prove most crucial. One clear finding from surveys of participation experiments in the United States is that they lead to increased investment in education and training of the workforce.[50] We need to establish training instruments and funds that will help ensure that thousands of U.S. firms engage in the kind of intensive retraining that Magma Copper undertook. Managers and workers can't just stumble toward the high road; they need to be carefully taught.

Bucking Business

Table 9.1 pulls together this five-step program. Taken on its own terms, the proposals are tangible, practicable, easily legislated.

But that doesn't mean, of course, that these proposals will be enacted as soon as the 105th Congress convenes in January 1997. Most of these proposals don't sit well with the political agenda of either established political party or with most business leadership in this country.

Take the fate of the minimum wage. Presidential candidate Bill Clinton proposed raising the minimum wage, in particular vowing to increase it "to keep pace with inflation."[51] His new Labor Secretary Robert Reich strongly believed in the necessity of raising the wage floor and proposed a modest in-

TABLE 9.1

Five Steps Toward the High Road

Steps	Provisions
1. Raising the wage floor	Increasing minimum wage to $6.50 by year 2000
	Indexing minimum wage to consumer price index
2. More effective worker voice	Automatic union certification with 55% signature cards
	Extend NLRA protection to most nonproduction and supervisory employees
	Mandate employee participation councils in most workplaces
3. Flexible, not disposable work	Amend Fair Labor Standards Act to
	—prohibit mandatory overtime
	—substitute comp time for overtime premia
	—extend working time regulation to salaried employees
	—mandate universal 3-weeks vacation, rising to 4 weeks
4. Carrots for cooperative firms	Investment subsidies for cooperative and democratic firms
5. Training, assistance for cooperation	National Cooperative Training and Assistance Agency

crease in October 1993. No sooner had he spoken, however, when he back-pedaled "after some White House officials had grown uneasy" about his proposal.[52] By the end of the month, Reich had backtracked completely. "White House officials warned him immediately after [his initial proposal]," the *New York Times* reported, "that such a move would be unwise because it could antagonize business leaders at a time when President Clinton needs them for his health care and trade proposals." Wait until after we win on NAFTA debate, the White House insisted. Reich promised to "revisit the issue next year."[53]

"Next year" came and went. NAFTA had passed, with massive support for the Clinton team from Republicans and business leadership. Debts had been accrued, back-scratching exchanged. But the entire year of 1994 passed without so much as a peep from the White House about putting a minimum-wage hike back on the table.

Suddenly, in early 1995, with the Republicans now firmly in control of the 104th Congress, Clinton found his voice. In his January 1995 State of the Union address he proposed a minimum-wage hike—with full knowledge that the GOP-dominated Congress would resist the idea until hell freezes over. "President Clinton is in no hurry to send minimum-wage legislation to Congress," the *Wall Street Journal* reported, "hoping first to interest lawmakers in the proposal, officials said."[54] Symbolic endorsement was fine, since the President could clearly win political points with his liberal and union allies by endorsing a minimum-wage increase. But where was the White House when the idea actually had a chance on the Capitol floor?

The Clinton Administration's catering to its business allies on the minimum-wage issue was typical of its first term. In his campaign and in his first State of the Union message, the President had strongly stressed the importance of public investment in infrastructure, dramatically expanded skills training, and economic stimulus. By the end of his first summer in office, virtually all of those proposals had been shredded to satisfy business and centrist obsessions about cutting the budget.[55]

Clinton was simply learning the lessons of political interest and influence the hard way. Since the mid-1970s, corporations have moved more and more aggressively to control the political agenda in Washington (and around the country) and to fight to advance their relatively narrow interests.[56] "Merely changing the party that occupies the White House," Thomas Ferguson and Joel Rogers note, " [does] not reverse the current drift of U.S. public policy."[57] In *Arrogant Capital* Kevin Phillips reflects on Mr. Clinton Going to Washington:[58]

The accusations [Clinton] had made in his 1992 campaign that "the last twelve years were nothing less than an extended hunting season for high-priced lobbyists and Washington influence peddlers" almost certainly had sprung from an element of belief as well as politics. But by the end of his first year in office, he had found that the season had been further extended, and that his programs would have been defeated if he hadn't abandoned his election-year populism and started cutting deals—on taxes, trade, and health—with representatives of corporate and financial interests. . . . The Permanent Washington . . . now has a centrist cast which comes from a mixture of the nation's own ideological shift, the spending constraints of accumulating budget deficits, and the upper-bracket connections and raw self-interest of its pinstriped hierarchs. . . . This is the ultimate triumph of Washington's interest-group ascendancy: the party of the people can no longer *be* the party of the people.

This excursion through the imperatives of Washington politics matters for the five-step program proposed here precisely because we should expect business interests to oppose nearly every plank in the program. Corporations love to say that they favor the "high performance workplace" and prefer cooperation over conflict, but they hardly favor relinquishing either their control over their own kingdoms or their influence over politics. Corporate participants in the discussions of the Dunlop Commission smiled about enhancing workplace participation, but where will they be if labor law reform legislation with teeth makes its way through the Congressional corridors?

And so we face a fairly stark political choice in the United States as we confront the wage squeeze and corporate bloat: Do we continue to allow U.S. corporations to exercise an effective veto over public policy, condemning us to continued travels along the low road? Or do we seek to challenge and overcome business opposition? "Absent a sudden upsurge from below," Ferguson and Rogers write, "the new, more conservative party system will be maintained. Democrats and Republicans will squabble and maneuver. The costs to the population will rise. But the basic structure of the party system will remain unchanged. America will continue its right turn."[59]

Most of the U.S. citizenry understands the starkness of this choice better than established elites. In an August 1995 *New York Times*/CBS poll, four-fifths—"the highest figure in several decades"—said that "the Government is run by a few big interests looking out for themselves" and three-fifths that "people like themselves don't have much say in what the Government does." Logical conclusion? As other recent polls have also revealed, people are ready for a new party. More than half agreed that "the country needs a new political party to compete with the Republicans and Democrats."[60]

This kind of political movement requires more than a figurehead, a charismatic independent leader like Ross Perot or Colin Powell or Jesse Jackson to articulate popular discontent. It requires persistent, clear-headed continuing mobilization in support of specific policies and priorities—all of which take time.

This endurance test should hardly surprise us. The cooperative economies did not acquire their labor-management systems overnight. Business interests initially bristled at some of the proposals for cooperation, codetermination, and power-sharing. Partly through union mobilization, partly through independent citizens' initiatives, the German, Japanese, and Swedish systems were constructed over decades.[61] Roy J. Adams reviews this experience: "In Sweden, Germany, and Japan, agreements that in retrospect had very positive effects were initially entered into only grudgingly. . . . The experience of these countries also suggests that agreements once reached cannot be considered safely done. Agreements have to be worked out continually and fundamental understandings must be respected or the overall structure can collapse."[62]

U.S. corporations are fat and mean. We all bear the costs of their commitment to the low road. We cannot expect those corporations to change their ways either easily or willingly. We need to change the environment in which they operate and to push and pull them, no matter how deeply they dig in their heels, in order to overcome the wage squeeze and corporate bloat. It will take time and it will take power. "So [said the good doctor at the end of *Portnoy's Complaint*]. Now vee may perhaps to begin. Yes?"[63]

NOTES

Frequently Cited References

Because of their frequent citation, simplified references are used for the following sources:

President's Council of Economic Advisers, *Economic Report of the President* (Washington, D.C.: U.S. Government Printing Office, various years); referred to as *Economic Report of the President*.

U.S. Bureau of the Census, *Statistical Abstract of the United States* (Washington, D.C.: U.S. Government Printing Office, various years); referred to as *Statistical Abstract*.

U.S. Department of Commerce, Bureau of Economic Analysis, *The National Income and Product Accounts of the United States, 1929–82* (Washington, D.C.: U.S. Government Printing Office, September 1986), and "The U.S. National Income and Product Accounts: Revised Estimates," *Survey of Current Business,* July of various years; referred to as *National Income and Product Accounts.*

U.S. Department of Labor, Bureau of Labor Statistics, *Employment and Earnings,* various issues; referred to as *Employment and Earnings.*

Introduction

1. For some of the data which support this interpretation of the 1992 election see, for example, Stanley B. Greenberg, *Middle Class Dreams: The Politics and Power of the New American Majority* (New York: Times Books, 1995), pp. 12ff.

2. See exit polling results in "Portrait of the Electorate: Who Voted for Whom in the House," *New York Times,* November 13, 1994, p. 24.

3. For a useful reading of the 1992 and 1994 election results which stresses these economic factors, see Ruy A. Teixeira and Joel Rogers, "Who Deserted the Democrats in 1994?" *American Prospect,* No. 23 (Fall 1995), 73–77. In his recent book *Values Matter Most,* Ben J. Wattenberg argues that shifts in values affected the 1994 elections more than economic factors, but Teixeira and Rogers provide some data, especially citing the polling results reported in the text here, which effectively counter Wattenberg's argument. (Wattenberg, *Values Matter Most: How Republicans or Democrats or a Third Party Can Win and Renew the American Way of Life* (New York: The Free Press, 1995), especially Chapter 4.)

4. Quoted in Matthew Cooper with Dorian Friedman, "The Rich in America," *U.S. News & World Report,* November 18, 1991, p. 35.

5. Richard Rorty, "Sex, Lies and Virginia's Voters," *New York Times* Op-Ed Page, October 13, 1994, p. A27.

6. Greenberg, *Middle Class Dreams,* pp. 284–285.

7. Quoted in John Cassidy, "Who Killed the Middle Class?" *The New Yorker*, October 16, 1995, p. 124.

8. R. W. Apple, Jr., "Poll Shows Disenchantment with Politicians and Politics," *New York Times*, August 12, 1995, p. 1.

9. Kevin Phillips, *Arrogant Capital: Washington, Wall Street, and the Frustration of American Politics* (Boston: Little, Brown, 1994).

10. Some may read too much into the juxtaposition of my title with that of a recent book by Bennett Harrison, *Lean and Mean: The Changing Landscape of Corporate Power in the Age of Flexibility* (New York: BasicBooks, 1994), inferring that by choice of titles I am directly challenging his arguments. In fact, however, Harrison and I focus on different aspects of corporate structure. He pays more attention to changes in the way that corporations organize the *circulation* of products and technologies among and within themselves. I pay primary attention to corporate strategies for organizing *production*. Though our titles suggest opposition, our arguments are actually potentially complementary. Compare, in particular, his Chapter 9 with my Chapters 1, 3, and 4.

11. Hedrick Smith, *Rethinking America* (New York: Random House, 1995), p. xxii.

12. See, for example, the discussion in Thomas A Kochan, Harry C. Katz, and Robert B. McKersie, *The Transformation of American Industrial Relations* (Ithaca, NY: Cornell ILR Press, 1994).

13. Quoted in Aaron Bernstein, "Why America Needs Unions But Not the Kind It Has Now," *Business Week*, May 23, 1994, p. 82.

14. James Q. Wilson, "Capitalism and Morality," *The Public Interest*, Fall 1995, pp. 59–60.

15. Based on continuous Louis Harris poll results, cited in Greenberg, *Middle Class Dreams*, p. 287.

16. 1995 results from *New York Times*/CBS News poll reported in Apple, "Poll Shows Disenchantment with Politicians and Politics," p. 8; historical data for a comparable kind of question from American National Election Studies, cited in Greenberg, *Middle Class Dreams*, p. 286.

Chapter 1

1. Dirk Johnson, "Family Struggles to Make Do After Fall From Middle Class," *New York Times*, March 11, 1994, p. A1.

2. Aaron Bernstein, "The Wage Squeeze," *Business Week*, July 17, 1995, p. 55.

3. Louis Uchitelle, "Flat Wages Seen as Issue in '96 Vote," *New York Times*, August 13, 1995, p. 26.

4. William Greider, "Middle-Class Funk," *Rolling Stone*, November 2, 1995, p. 35.

5. Robert D. Hershey Jr., "U.S. Wages Up 2.7% in Year, A Record Low," *New York Times*, November 1, 1995, p. A1.

6. Robert D. Hershey Jr., "Wage Increases Are Small, But Confidence Jumps," *New York Times*, April 27, 1994, p. D1.

7. Quoted in "A 4.3% Gain for Workers," *New York Times*, January 29, 1992, p. D8.

8. Executive Office of the President, "A Vision of Change for America," February 17, 1993, p. 8.

9. For the early series see U.S. Bureau of Labor Statistics, *Employment and Earnings, United States, 1909–78*, Bulletin 1312–11, July 1979, pp. 914–929.

10. See our original proposal in Samuel Bowles, David M. Gordon, and Thomas E. Weisskopf, *Beyond the Waste Land* (Garden City, NY: Anchor Press/Doubleday, 1983), p. 24; and a full methodological presentation and justification in Thomas E. Weisskopf, "Use of Hourly Earnings Proposed to Revive Spendable Earnings Series," *Monthly Labor Review*, November 1984, pp. 38–43. Although our original index relied on the traditional version of the Consumer Price Index (CPI) for all urban consumers (CPI-U), the index presented here in the text

and the figures and tables switches over to the now-preferred modification of the CPI known felicitously as CPI-U-X1. The full data series on real spendable hourly earnings is maintained by and available from the author.

11. For one unofficial critical response to our proposal by a Bureau of Labor Statistics economist, see Paul O. Flaim, "Proposed Spendable Earnings Series Retains Basic Faults of Earlier One," *Monthly Labor Review*, November 1984, pp. 43–44.

12. See *Employment and Earnings*, January 1995, Tables 48–49.

13. Some economists have questioned the usefulness of these categories, arguing that they contain too much "noise" and mix together too many different kinds of occupations into single definitional receptacles. See, for example, Edward E. Leamer, "Trade, Wages, and Revolving Door Ideas," National Bureau of Economic Research, Working Paper No. 4716, April 1994. For this reason, I am careful in both this chapter and the next to compare conclusions derived for these categories with those derived for more determinate occupational groupings identified in the government's regular household surveys.

14. The value for 1994 is provisional, pending final available data on effective tax rates.

15. Here and throughout this book, where appropriate, data comparisons are made from one business cycle *peak* to the next in order to control for short-term fluctuations over the business cycle; 1948, 1966, 1973, 1989 were all peak years in the cycle. I identify business-cycle peak years by looking at the ratio of actual gross national product (GNP) to the corresponding "potential" GNP; potential GNP is an estimate of what the economy was capable of producing with what is somewhat arbitrarily termed "full utilization" of available resources. The ratio of actual to potential GNP reaches a cyclical peak at the stage of an expansion when the economy's productive potential is most *fully* utilized and is thus described as a measure of aggregate capacity utilization. The procedure for estimating potential output follows a method developed by the Council of Economic Advisers during the 1970s. For presentation and discussion of that method, see Peter K. Clark, "Potential GNP in the United States, 1948–80," *Review of Income and Wealth* Series 25:2 (June 1979), 141–165. For further documentation on the actual construction of the series for aggregate capacity utilization used here, see Samuel Bowles, David M. Gordon, and Thomas E. Weisskopf, "Business Ascendancy and Economic Impasse: A Structural Retrospective on Conservative Economics," *Journal of Economic Perspectives* 3(1) (Winter 1989), Data Appendix.

16. GDP per capita from *Economic Report of the President, 1995*, Tables B-2, B-32.

17. Sylvia Nasar, "Statistics Reveal Bulk of New Jobs Pay Over Average," *New York Times*, October 17, 1994, p. A1.

18. Ben J. Wattenberg, *Values Matter Most: How Republicans or Democrats or a Third Party Can Win and Renew the American Way of Life* (New York: The Free Press, 1995), p. 78.

19. Ibid., pp. 79, 81 [emphasis in original].

20. In 1993 the official government poverty line for a family of four was $14,763. U.S. Bureau of the Census, "Income, Poverty, and Valuation of Noncash Benefits: 1993," *Current Population Reports*, Series P-60, No. 188, February 1995, Table A-1.

21. I first came across this designation in Tamar Lewin, "Low Pay and Closed Doors Confront Young Job Seekers," *New York Times*, March 10, 1994, p. B12. The author defines McJobs as "jobs that pay $6 an hour or less, and offer little in the way of a career path."

22. Quoted in Stanley B. Greenberg, *Middle Class Dreams: The Politics and Power of the New American Majority* (New York: Times Books, 1995), p. 168.

23. Quoted in Greenberg, *Middle Class Dreams*, p. 169.

24. Gallup Poll News Service, "Recession Shakes Faith in American Dream," News Release, February 2, 1992.

25. *Los Angeles Times*, "Los Angeles Times Poll: Study #317, National Politics," July 15, 1993, p. 1.

26. *Los Angeles Times*, "Los Angeles Times Poll: Employment," November 15, 1993, p. 7.

27. Michael R. Kagay, "From Coast to Coast, From Affluent to Poor, Poll Shows Anxiety Over Jobs," *New York Times*, March 11, 1994, p. A14.

28. "Portrait of an Anxious Public," *Business Week*, March 13, 1995, p. 80 [emphases added].

29. Lewin, "Low Pay and Closed Doors Confront Young Job Seekers," p. B12.

30. Quoted in *New York Times*, March 31, 1994, p. A18.

31. All data in the following discussion are based on the author's tabulations from the outgoing rotation samples of the Current Population Survey for March 1979 and March 1993. The 1979 earnings figures were converted to 1993 dollars by the CPI-U-X1 price index.

32. Lawrence Mishel and Jared Bernstein, *The State of Working America, 1994–95* (Armonk, NY: M. E. Sharpe, 1994), Table 3.9.

33. Louis Uchitelle, "Trapped in the Impoverished Middle Class," *New York Times*, November 17, 1991, Sec. 3, p. 1.

34. U.S. Bureau of Labor Statistics, Office of Productivity and Technology, "Output per Hour, Hourly Compensation, and Unit Labor Costs in Manufacturing, Twelve Economies, 1950–1993," unpublished tables, February 1995, Table 13.

35. U.S. Bureau of Labor Statistics, "International Comparisons of Hourly Compensation Costs for Production Workers in Manufacturing, 1975–1994," Report No. 893, May 1995, Table 2. Trade weights are based on trade shares for 1992.

The reader should note that these comparative wage data do not permit direct comparisons of the *purchasing power* of wages in the respective countries, since they are computed at product-price exchange rates and thus measure the relative wage costs faced by manufacturers, not the relative buying power of those wages in local currencies. (For those comparisons, we would need to use *purchasing-price-parity* indices for comparison.) Still, these are the appropriate comparative wage data to use in evaluating the argument about competitive pressure discussed in the text.

36. This kind of comparison need not be limited solely to the case of manufacturing. The other comparison we can make, using OECD data, is for real annual compensation per employee in the business sector, measured in dollars. In this comparison, too, U.S. workers lag considerably behind most of the other advanced countries in compensation level and behind all of them in wage growth. See Organization for Economic Cooperation and Development, *Economic Outlook*, June 1995, Historical Tables.

37. Richard B. Freeman and Lawrence F. Katz, "Rising Wage Inequality: The United States vs. Other Advanced Countries," in *Working Under Different Rules,* edited by Richard B. Freeman (New York: Russell Sage, 1994), p. 39.

38. Richard B. Freeman, "How Labor Fares in Advanced Economies," in *Working Under Different Rules,* edited by Richard B. Freeman (New York: Russell Sage, 1994), p. 13.

39. Trade figures based on Organization for Economic Cooperation and Development, *National Accounts: Main Aggregates*, Vol. I (Paris: OECD, 1994), pp. 118–119.

40. David Moberg, "Prairie Fires," *In These Times,* July 25, 1994, p. 21.

41. Quoted in Greenberg, *Middle Class Dreams,* p. 165.

42. Quoted in Bernstein, "The Wage Squeeze," p. 55.

Chapter 1 Appendix

1. Estimation of the average tax burden involves three steps. (See Thomas E. Weisskopf, "Use of Hourly Earnings Proposed to Revive Spendable Earnings Series," *Monthly Labor Review,* November 1984, pp. 38–43 for full detail on the method used.) First, and least problematic, average payroll taxes borne by production and nonsupervisory workers are calculated at the official social security tax rate since in no year during the postwar period did average hourly earnings (if earned full-time year-round) place this class of employees above the annual income cut-off beyond which social security taxes no longer applied. Second, federal personal income tax burdens were estimated by interpolating effective income tax rates within the category in which workers

earning at their hourly rate full-time year-round would fall. Third, state and local personal income tax burdens were estimated by multiplying the estimated federal income tax rate times the ratio of state and local personal income tax revenues to federal personal income tax revenues, effectively assuming that state and local incidence schedules had the same slope as the corresponding federal schedules. This third step is obviously the most approximate; since the state and local component was consistently the smallest of the three components over this period, however, inaccuracies from this step are unlikely to distort the series very dramatically .

2. Direct measures of compensation for production/nonsupervisory workers are hard to come by. My index of real hourly compensation is obtained by multiplying real hourly earnings by the ratio of compensation to earnings for all employees. This method effectively assumes—forced by the hard facts of data availability—that the benefit ratio is the same for production and non-production workers. Since both unionized workers among production workers and most managerial employees among the non-production group are likely to receive substantial benefit packages, this assumption may not be too far off.

To the extent that it's off, however, I have probably overstated the level of the benefits rate for production workers, since if anything they probably receive fewer benefits per dollar of wages than do supervisory workers. And I've probably also overstated the *growth* in the benefits portion for production workers as well, since unionization rates declined and many benefits packages were squeezed for lower-waged workers over the past fifteen years. So, while my estimate is a reasonable approximation, it probably makes the drop in real compensation for production workers look a little less severe than it actually was.

3. Lawrence Mishel and Jared Bernstein, *The State of Working America 1994–95* (Armonk, NY: M.E. Sharpe, 1994), Table 3.2.

4. Mishel and Bernstein, *The State of Working America 1994–95*, pp. 114–115.

Chapter 2

1. "The Ailing Economy: Diagnoses and Prescriptions," *New York Times*, April 4, 1982, p. 4E.

2. Some of these early studies are reported in Mark Green and John F. Berry, *The Challenge of Hidden Profits: Reducing Corporate Bureaucracy and Waste* (New York: William Morrow, 1985).

3. "The Ailing Economy," p. 4E.

4. Based on an analysis of *The Economist* data in Lawrence Mishel and Jared Bernstein, *The State of Working America 1994–95* (Armonk, NY: M.E. Sharpe, 1994), Table 3.52. Figure for production workers' real hourly take-home pay from series on real spendable hourly earnings presented in Chapter 1.

5. "Paychecks of America's 800 Top Chief Executives," *Forbes*, May 23, 1994, pp. 190–191, 172–173.

6. Joani Nelson-Horchler, "CEO Pay," *Industry Week*, April 15, 1991, p. 13.

7. Bill Clinton and Al Gore, *Putting People First: How We Can All Change America* (New York: Times Books, 1992), p. 5.

8. Derek Bok, *The Cost of Talent: How Executives and Professionals Are Paid and How It Affects America* (New York: The Free Press, 1993), p. 95.

9. *Employment and Earnings*, January 1995, Tables 48–49.

10. Total government employment from *Employment and Earnings*, January 1995, Table 48. State and county populations from *Statistical Abstract, 1993*, Tables 31, 1375.

11. Based on median height of about 5'7"-5'8" for weighted combination of men and women, ages 36–64. *Statistical Abstract, 1993*, Table 216.

12. Data for total compensation paid to nonproduction and supervisory employees are not directly available. But I have been able to estimate it from standard government sources by making a few reasonable assumptions:

One begins with hourly earnings received by private nonfarm production and nonsupervisory (P&NS) employees [*Employment and Earnings*, January 1995, Table B-2]. Then, assuming that the ratio of earnings to compensation is the same for these employees as for all private nonfarm employees [*National Income and Product Accounts*, Tables 6.4–6.5], one extrapolates average hourly compensation for private nonfarm production and nonsupervisory employees. (This seems a fairly reasonable assumption, since many P&NS workers are unionized and enjoy healthy benefits. But, if anything, as noted in Chapter 1, it probably slightly overstates P&NS compensation which ends up understating nonproduction and supervisory [NP&S] compensation, giving me a conservative estimate of the numbers reported in the text.) Then, assuming that private nonfarm P&NS workers have the same average weekly hours worked as all private nonfarm employees and work all paid overtime hours reported in the manufacturing sector [*Employment and Earnings*, Table B-2], we can get an estimate of total annual hours worked by private nonfarm P&NS workers. (The assumption about average weekly hours seems reasonable—once again because many P&NS workers are unionized and therefore enjoy limits on straight-time hours. But, as with the ratio of earnings to compensation, this assumption is probably a slight underestimate of P&NS hours and therefore, in the end, also results in a conservative estimate of the NP&S compensation estimates.) Then, multiplying hours by hourly compensation, we get an estimate of total private nonfarm P&NS annual compensation. Subtracting this from total private nonfarm compensation (*National Income and Product Accounts*, Table 6-5), the residual provides an estimate of total private nonfarm nonproduction and supervisory employee compensation.

13. All figures for these comparisons come from the *National Income and Product Accounts*.

14. See Peter G. Peterson and Neil Howe, *On Borrowed Time: How the Growth in Entitlement Spending Threatens America's Future* (New York: ICS Press, 1988).

15. See Robert B. Reich, *The Work of Nations: Preparing Ourselves for 21st-Century Capitalism* (New York: Vintage Books, 1992), especially pp. 177–180.

16. U.S. Bureau of Labor Statistics, *Handbook of Methods*, Bulletin 2282, April 1988, p. 77 [emphasis in the original].

17. It is largely for this reason, indeed, that some economists have recently criticized reliance on these establishment survey categories. (See Chapter 1, note 13.) It is exactly for this reason that I continually check conclusions drawn from the establishment data against the more detailed breakdowns available in the BLS household surveys.

18. These data for the household surveys are based on the author's own tabulations from the Current Population Surveys microdata samples for March 1993, including only private nonfarm wage-and-salary employees. For this tabulation I include all those from the general category of "executive, administrative, and managerial" and all those in specific categories, scattered throughout the census occupational codes, designated as one kind of "supervisor" or another.

19. All the following data are based on the author's own tabulations from the 1991 U.S. survey organized under the auspices of Erik Olin Wright's Comparative Project on Class Structure and Class Consciousness. The survey was conducted by the Survey Research Center of the University of California–Berkeley under the direction of Michael Hout, Erik Olin Wright, and Martin Sanchez-Jankowski. For an introductory background to the data and their methodological purposes, see Erik Olin Wright, *Classes* (London: Verso Books, 1985). For a more recent discussion, including both a discussion of the survey methodology and an overview of the results from the 1991 survey, see Erik Olin Wright, *Class Counts: Comparative Studies in Class Analysis* (New York: Cambridge University Press, 1996), especially Ch. 2.

20. See the detailed discussion of the representative character of the surveys in Wright, *Class Counts*, Ch. 2.

21. Elinor Langer, "The Women of the Telephone Company," *New York Review of Books*, March 12, 1970, p. 16.

22. Robert M. Tomasko, *Downsizing: Reshaping the Corporation for the Future* (New York: American Management Association, 1987), p. 21.

23. Robert H. Hayes and Steven C. Wheelwright, *Restoring Our Competitive Edge: Competing Through Manufacturing* (New York: John Wiley & Sons, 1984), pp. 62–63.

24. Tomasko, *Downsizing*, p. 14.

25. Towers Perrin, Inc., "1991 Worldwide Total Remuneration," 1991, p. 12.

26. International Labour Organization, *Yearbook of Labour Statistics, 1994* (Geneva: ILO, 1994), Table 3.

27. In 1989, there were 14.8 million "administrative and managerial" employees tallied for the United States in the ILO compilation. This exactly equaled the total number of "executive, administrative, and managerial" employees identified in the BLS tabulations from the 1989 household surveys (*Employment and Earnings*, January 1990).

28. The Swedish percentage is an approximation. 1984 was the last year in which administrative and managerial employment was separated from clerical employment. To estimate the 1989 percent, the 1984 share of administrative and managerial employment within the aggregation of administrative, managerial, clerical, and related workers was applied to that composite category for 1989 in order to estimate the number of managerial and administrative employees; that number was then calculated as a percent of total nonfarm employment. Although this is an approximation, it is unlikely to distort the figure presented in the graph very much since these shares had been fairly stable in Sweden in previous years.

29. For a useful presentation of these three alternative models, see Eileen Appelbaum and Rosemary Batt, *The New American Workplace: Transforming Work Systems in the United States* (Ithaca, NY: Cornell University ILR Press, 1994), Ch. 3.

30. ILO, *Yearbook of Labour Statistics, 1994*, Table 2C.

31. There is also a survey for Japan, but it covers only Tokyo and its environs, which leads Erik Olin Wright to worry about its comparability with the other surveys. See Wright, *Class Counts*, Chapter 2 and Appendix II.

32. For some brief but useful speculation about precisely these dimensions of difference between the United States and Sweden, see Gösta Esping-Andersen, *The Three Worlds of Welfare Capitalism* (Princeton: Princeton University Press, 1990), pp. 202–203.

33. Wright, *Class Counts*, Chapter 2, p. 42.

34. For these occupational comparisons, see *Statistical Abstract, 1991*, Table 652.

35. The idea of this kind of reallocation of managerial and supervisory employees is discussed in further detail in Samuel Bowles, David M. Gordon, and Thomas E. Weisskopf, *After the Waste Land: A Democratic Economics for the Year 2000* (Armonk, NY: M.E. Sharpe, 1990), pp. 176–179.

36. For an account of this dynamic in the period of the postwar boom, see Bowles, Gordon, and Weisskopf, *After the Waste Land*, Chapter 5.

37. See Bowles, Gordon, and Weisskopf, *After the Waste Land*, Chapter 5 for documentation of these features of the "limited capital-labor accord."

38. Data for production and total employees in manufacturing establishments from U.S. Bureau of the Census, *Census of Manufactures, 1992* (Washington, D.C.: U.S. Government Printing Office, 1994), Vol. I, Table 1; and *Census of Manufactures, 1987* (Washington, D.C.: U.S. Government Printing Office, 1991), Vol. I, Table 1.

39. Richard E. Caves and Matthew B. Krepps, "Fat: The Displacement of Nonproduction Workers from U.S. Manufacturing Industries," *Brookings Papers on Economic Activity—Microeconomics*, 1993:2, 227–273.

40. From data for the Annual Survey of Manufactures, reported in *Census of Manufactures, 1992* and *Census of Manufactures, 1987*, Vol. I, Table 1 respectively.

41. Thomas A. Kochan, Harry C. Katz, and Robert B. McKersie, *The Transformation of American Industrial Relations* (Ithaca, NY: Cornell ILR Press, 1994), p. 47.

42. Quoted in Green and Berry, *The Challenge of Hidden Profits*, p. 18.

43. Quoted in Green and Berry, *The Challenge of Hidden Profits*, p. 49.

44. Barry Bluestone and Irving Bluestone, *Negotiating the Future: A Labor Perspective on American Business* (New York: BasicBooks, 1992), p. 131.

45. Quoted in Tomasko, *Downsizing*, p. 2.

46. Wright, *Class Counts,* Chapter 3, Table 3, 1980b and 1990 distributions.

47. Bruce Nussbaum, "Downward Mobility: Corporate Castoffs are Struggling Just to Stay in the Middle Class," *Business Week*, March 23, 1992, p. 57.

48. Cited in Amacom Briefings & Surveys, *Responsible Reductions in Force: An American Management Association Research Report on Downsizing and Outplacement* (New York: American Management Association, 1987), p. 55.

49. Tomasko, *Downsizing*.

50. Nussbaum, "Downward Mobility," p. 57.

51. U.S. Bureau of Labor Statistics, "Employment in Perspective: Earnings and Job Growth," Report No. 877, August 1994, Table 2; and *Employment and Earnings*, January 1990, January 1995.

52. U.S. Bureau of Labor Statistics, "Employed and experienced unemployed persons by detailed occupation, . . . , 2nd Quarter 1995," unpublished tables, 1995.

53. Reports of "downsizing" began earlier than in 1989. Would my results look different if I began with earlier years than the business cycle peak of 1989? Apparently not, since the share of managers (excluding those in public administration) in nonfarm employment increased more or less steadily for every year from 1983, when the new occupational categories begin, to 1989. (Based on detailed occupational tabulations in *Employment and Earnings*, January issue, various years.)

54. *Employment and Earnings*, January 1990; BLS, "Employed and experienced unemployed persons, . . . 2nd Quarter 1995." Two extrapolative assumptions needed to be made for this comparison. First, I assumed that the portion of the total category of "sales supervisors and proprietors" who worked as nonfarm private sales supervisory wage-and-salary employees was the same in 1989 and the second quarter of 1995 as it had been in my tabulations from the 1993 CPS. Second, I assumed that the percentage of personal service employees working as supervisors was the same in 1989 as in the published data for 1994.

55. For a careful and useful study of some other ways in which the term "lean and mean" may make sense, see Bennett Harrison, *Lean and Mean: The Changing Landscape of Corporate Power in the Age of Flexibility* (New York: BasicBooks, 1994).

56. American Management Association, "1994 AMA Survey on Downsizing," News Release, November 1994.

57. Jennifer M. Gardner, "Worker Displacement: A Decade of Change," U.S. Bureau of Labor Statistics, Report No. 2464, July 1995.

58. Gardner, "Worker Displacement," Appendix A.

59. Ibid., p. 4. Following data citations are from Tables 3, D-5, and D-7 respectively.

60. Green and Berry, *The Challenge of Hidden Profits*, p. 46.

61. Gardner, "Worker Displacement," Table D-7.

62. Katherine S. Newman, *Falling from Grace: The Experience of Downward Mobility in the American Middle Class* (New York: The Free Press, 1988), p. 48.

63. Stephen J. Rose, *Declining Job Security and the Professionalization of Opportunity* (Washington, D.C.: National Commission for Employment Policy, May 1995), Research Report No. 95–04, Table A-3.

64. Anthony Carnevale, "Preface," in Stephen J. Rose, *Declining Job Security and the Professionalization of Opportunity*, p. vi.

65. Newman, *Falling from Grace*, p. 94.

66. Alex Markels, "Restructuring Alters Middle-Manager Role But Leaves It Robust," *Wall Street Journal*, September 25, 1995, p. A1.

67. Quoted in Mary Lord, "Where You Can't Get Fired," *U.S. News & World Report*, January 14, 1991, p. 48.

68. James R. Emshoff and Teri E. Demlinger, *The New Rules of the Game* (New York: HarperCollins, 1991), p. x.

69. Hedrick Smith, *Rethinking America* (New York: Random House, 1995), p. 410.

70. Survey results summarized in The Editor, "Corporate Surveys Can't Find A Productivity Revolution, Either," *Challenge*, November-December 1995, 31–34.

71. Survey quote from Smith, *Rethinking America*, p. 411; results on morale from "Corporate Surveys Can't Find a Productivity Revolution," p. 32.

72. Quoted in Lord, "Where You Can't Get Fired," p. 48.

Chapter 3

1. Unless otherwise cited the information and quotes in this vignette about Caterpillar come from an excellent five-part series by Barry Bearak, "Cat on Strike: The Waning Power of Unions," *Los Angeles Times*, May 14–18, 1995.

2. Quoted in Jennifer Reingold, "CEO of the Year," *Financial World*, March 28, 1995, p.72.

3. Quoted in Reingold, "CEO of the Year," p. 72.

4. Quoted in Reingold, "CEO of the Year," p. 67.

5. Quoted in Bearak, "Cat on Strike," May 18, 1995, p. A13.

6. For a brief and favorable review of the Ford experience, see Hedrick Smith, *Rethinking America* (New York: Random House, 1995), Ch. 9.

7. Reported in Mark Green and John F. Berry, *The Challenge of Hidden Profits: Reducing Corporate Bureaucracy and Waste* (New York: William Morrow, 1985), p. 104.

8. Quoted in Hedrick Smith, *Rethinking America* (New York: Random House, 1995), p. 220.

9. For a compact discussion of some of the principal differences among these three countries in their systems of labor management, see Eileen Appelbaum and Rosemary Batt, *The New American Workplace: Transforming Work Systems in the United States* (Ithaca, NY: Cornell University ILR Press, 1994), Chapter 3.

10. For a useful review of these kinds of differences, including a survey of much of the relevant literature, see Roy J. Adams, *Industrial Relations Under Liberal Democracy: North America in Comparative Perspective* (Columbia, SC: University of South Carolina Press, 1995). See also Jukka Pekkarinen, M. Pohjola, and Bob Rowthorn, eds.. *Social Corporatism: A Superior Economic System?* (Oxford: Oxford University Press, 1992).

11. Thomas A Kochan, Harry C. Katz, and Robert B. McKersie, *The Transformation of American Industrial Relations* (Ithaca, NY: Cornell ILR Press, 1994), p. viii.

12. For analysis of this general trend, see Samuel Bowles, David M. Gordon, and Thomas E. Weisskopf, *Beyond the Waste Land: A Democratic Alternative to Economic Decline* (Garden City, NY: Anchor Press/Doubleday, 1983), Chapters 3–4; and David M. Gordon, Richard Edwards, and Michael Reich, *Segmented Work, Divided Workers: The Historical Transformation of Labor in the United States* (New York: Cambridge University Press, 1982), Chapter 5.

13. Quoted in Bearak, "Cat on Strike," May 17, 1995, p. A10.

14. Quoted in Bearak, "Cat on Strike," May 14, 1995, p. A14.

15. For those who want to reflect on the more formal logic of the ideas presented here, this comment amounts to the hypothesis that workers are more concerned about *changes* in their earnings than about the absolute level of those earnings. This is the model of "worker motivation" introduced in Thomas E. Weisskopf, Samuel Bowles, and David M. Gordon, "Hearts and Minds: A Social Model of U.S. Productivity Growth," *Brookings Papers on Economic Activity*, 1983:2, 381–441. The emphasis on *changes* in conditions as a motivational imperative is supported by the interesting studies reported by Daniel Kahneman, "New Challenges to the Rationality Assumption," *Journal of Institutional and Theoretical Economics*, 150:1 (March 1994), 18–36.

16. David Soskice, "Reinterpreting Corporatism and Explaining Unemployment: Co-ordinated and Non-co-ordinated Market Economies," in *Labour Relations and Economic Performance,* edited by R. Brunetta and C. Dell'Aringa (New York: New York University Press, 1990), pp. 198–199.

17. Soskice, "Reinterpreting Corporatism," pp. 190–191.

18. Quoted in Maryann Keller, *Rude Awakening: The Rise, Fall, and Struggle for Recovery of General Motors* (New York: William Morrow, 1989), p. 129.

19. The theoretical foundations of this kind of argument have been well laid in the recent economics literature. See, for example, Samuel Bowles, "The Production Process in a Competitive Economy: Walrasian, Neo-Hobbesian, and Marxian Models," *American Economic Review,* 75:1 (March 1985),16–36.

20. Gösta Esping-Andersen, *The Three Worlds of Welfare Capitalism* (Princeton: Princeton University Press, 1990), p. 203.

21. Keller, *Rude* Awakening, p. 124.

22. Quoted in Smith, *Rethinking America,* p. 220.

23. David Montgomery, *Workers' Control in America: Studies in the History of Work, Technology, and Labor Struggles* (Cambridge: Cambridge University Press, 1979), pp. 163–164.

24. Quoted in David Brody, *Workers in Industrial America* (New York: Oxford University Press, 1993), 2nd ed., p. 165.

25. Brody, ibid., p. 169.

26. On the logic and dynamics of this period, again, see Bowles, Gordon, and Weisskopf, *Beyond the Waste Land;* and Gordon, Edwards, and Reich, *Segmented Work, Divided Workers.*

27. Based on data for production and nonsupervisory worker real output per hour and real hourly compensation for the nonfarm business sector. Data for real nonfarm business output from *National Income and Product Accounts,* Table 1.8; for production and nonsupervisory hours from *Employment & Earnings,* various years, adjusted by ratio of production and nonsupervisory to total employment; and for production and nonsupervisory real hourly compensation based on same sources as for row [3], Table 1A above in Chapter 1 Appendix.

28. Quoted in Keith Bradsher, "Productivity Is All, But It Doesn't Pay Well," *New York Times,* June 25, 1995, Week in Review, Section 4, p. 4.

29. Jennifer M. Gardner, "Worker Displacement: A Decade of Change," U.S. Bureau of Labor Statistics, Report No. 2464, July 1995, pp. 1–2.

30. Stephen J. Rose, *Declining Job Security and the Professionalization of Opportunity* (Washington, D.C.: National Commission for Employment Policy, May 1995), Table 2.

31. Peter Gottschalk and Robert Moffitt, "The Growth of Earnings Instability in the U.S. Labor Market," *Brookings Papers on Economic Activity,* 1994:2, 241.

32. Rose, *Declining Job Security,* Table 3.

33. Anthony Carnevale, "Preface," in Rose, *Declining Job Security,* p. viii. A contrasting view of job stability has been put forward in a number of other articles. See, for example, Francis X. Diebold, David Neumark, and Daniel Polsky, "Job Stability in the United States," National Bureau of Economic Research Working Paper No. 4859, September 1994; the authors argue that "job retention rates have remained stable" (Abstract). But almost all of these other studies rely on the Current Population Survey, which provides snapshots of workers at a single point in time. Longitudinal data of the sort mobilized by Rose probably provide a much more accurate view of job stability than the intermittent panel data on which Diebold *et al.* rely.

34. Based on author's tabulations from the Class Structure Surveys. See full citation for these survey data in Chapter 2.

35. Edward D. Jones, *The Administration of Industrial Enterprises* (New York: Longmans, Green, 1925), 2nd edition (originally published in 1916), p. 392. For additional discussion of this problem, see Gordon, Edwards, and Reich, *Segmented Work, Divided Workers,* Ch. 4; and

Sanford M. Jacoby, *Employing Bureaucracy: Managers, Unions, and the Transformation of Work in American Industry, 1900–1945* (New York: Columbia University Press, 1985).

36. See Richard Edwards, *Contested Terrain: The Transformation of the Workplace in the Twentieth Century* (New York: Basic Books, 1979), especially Chapter 8.

37. Edwards, *Contested Terrain*, pp. 139, 142.

38. Quoted in Smith, *Rethinking America*, p. 220.

39. Michel Crozier, *The Bureaucratic Phenomenon* (Chicago: University of Chicago Press, 1964), pp. 189, 190.

40. David M. Gordon, "Bosses of Different Stripes: Monitoring and Supervision across the Advanced Economies," *American Economic Review*, 84:2 (May 1994), 375–379. A longer version with data appendix is available as Working Paper No. 46, New School for Social Research, February 1994.

41. This index is actually the sum of country scores on two independent factors apparently capturing two different dimensions of variation in the characteristics of labor-management systems. See "Bosses of Different Stripes" for details.

42. In "Bosses of Different Stripes," I further test this hypothesis with multivariate analysis. See the summary in Chapter 8.

43. Considered more systematically, the graph could actually be interpreted in two alternative ways: On the one hand, we could view the connection between cooperation and the bureaucratic burden as reflecting a *continuous* relationship across countries, with each country's individual dot on the graph indicating its own unique combination of these two dimensions of economic life. In this case, in testing for an association between labor relations and corporate bureaucracies, we would look at the simple correlation coefficient between the Cooperation Index and the Bureaucratic Burden. As already noted in the text, the correlation between the two variables is –0.72 (statistically significant at 1%).

On the other hand, rather than seeing these variables as varying continuously across the countries, we could view the graph as revealing two *clusters* of countries, one grouping featuring relatively more conflictual relations and the other more cooperative. The more adversarial cluster lies in the upper left corner of the graph, including the United States, Canada, and the United Kingdom. The more cooperative cluster occupies the lower right corner of the graph, including Germany, Japan, Sweden, and the other six countries in the sample. What matters more, from this vantage point, is the close proximity of the points *within* the two groupings, especially within the cooperative cluster, rather than the detailed differences across the individual countries.

Either way we view the relationship, the same conclusion emerges: Cooperative systems don't seem to need so many bosses.

44. Reported in James O'Toole, *Making America Work: Productivity and Responsibility* (New York: Continuum, 1981), p. 115.

45. Green and Berry, *The Challenge of Hidden Profits*, pp. 25–26.

46. Robert M. Tomasko, *Downsizing: Reshaping the Corporation for the Future* (New York: American Management Association, 1987), p. 22.

47. Lester Thurow, *Head to Head: The Coming Economic Battle among Japan, Europe, and America* (New York: William Morrow, 1992), pp. 171–172.

48. Oliver E. Williamson, "A Model of Rational Managerial Behavior," in *A Behavioral Theory of the Firm*, edited by Richard M. Cyert and James G. March (Englewood Cliffs, NJ: Prentice-Hall, 1963), p. 242 [emphasis in the original].

49. Georges Duby, *Rural Economy and Country Life in the Medieval West* (Columbia, SC: University of South Carolina Press, 1968), trans. from the French by Cynthia Postan, pp. 35–6.

50. Quoted in Green and Berry, *The Challenge of Hidden Profits*, p. 30.

51. For a brief but useful review of the possible reasons for corporations' building up "excessive" managerial employment, viewed from the vantage point of internal firm dynamics, see

Richard E. Caves and Matthew B. Krepps, "Fat: The Displacement of Nonproduction Workers from U.S. Manufacturing Industries," *Brookings Papers on Economic Activity—Microeconomics*, 1993:2, pp. 236–238.

52. Keller, *Rude Awakening*, p. 106.

53. Quoted in Green and Berry, *The Challenge of Hidden Profits*, p. 27.

54. Peter F. Drucker, *Managing in Turbulent Times* (New York: Harper & Row, 1980), p. 48.

55. Tomasko, *Downsizing*, p. 13.

56. Ibid., p. 20.

57. H. Alan Raymond, *Management in the Third Wave* (Glenview, IL: Scott, Foresman and Co., 1986), p. 16.

58. See, for two studies surveying these debates and pursuing careful empirical studies of the balance of power, David M. Kotz, *Bank Control of Large Corporations in the United States* (Berkeley, CA: University of California Press, 1978); and Edward S. Herman, *Corporate Control, Corporate Power* (New York: Cambridge University Press, 1981).

59. Williamson, "A Model of Rational Managerial Behavior," p. 241.

60. Louis R. Pondy, "Effects of Size, Complexity, and Ownership on Administrative Intensity," *Administrative Science Quarterly*, March 1969.

61. See discussion in Caves and Krepps, "Fat: The Displacement of Nonproduction Workers," *passim*.

62. Michael Useem, "Corporate Restructuring and Organizational Behavior," in *Transforming Organisations*, edited by Thomas A. Kochan and Michael Useem (New York: Oxford University Press, 1992), pp. 55–56.

63. Caves and Krepps, "Fat: The Displacement of Nonproduction Workers," Table 5 and pp. 251–254.

64. H. Alan Raymond, *Management in the Third Wave*, p. 6.

65. *Economic Report of the President, 1995*, Table B-13.

66. Ibid., Tables B-17, B-1.

67. For construction of these estimates of the NFCB before-tax profit rate, see Samuel Bowles, David M. Gordon, and Thomas E. Weisskopf, "Business Ascendancy and Economic Impasse: A Structural Retrospective on Conservative Economics," *Journal of Economic Perspectives*, 3:1 (Winter 1989), Data Appendix.

68. The method for computing the respective shares of compensation is described in Chapter 2, note #12.

69. Based on data from the Annual Survey of Manufactures. See U.S. Bureau of the Census, *Census of Manufactures, 1992* (Washington, D.C.: U.S. Government Printing Office, 1994), Vol. I, Table 1; and *Census of Manufactures, 1987* (Washington, D.C.: U.S. Government Printing Office, 1989), Vol. I, Table 1.

70. Quoted in Bradsher, "Productivity Is All, But It Doesn't Pay Well," p. 4.

71. I am grateful to my colleague John Eatwell for discussions about the British case. For some of his views on this period in England, see John Eatwell, *What Ever Happened to Britain? The Economics of Decline* (London: Duckworth, 1982).

72. "The Fortune 500," *Fortune*, May 15, 1995.

73. The following vignette is based on the useful, if also breathlessly admiring book by Richard Preston, *American Steel: Hot Metal Men and the Resurrection of the Rust Belt* (New York: Prentice Hall Press, 1991).

74. Quoted in Preston, *American Steel*, p. 87. Subsequent quotes from pp. 87, 83, 83, 84, 137, and 88. [emphasis in original].

75. On the NUMMI venture, see Clair Brown and Michael Reich, "When Does Cooperation Work? A Look at NUMMI and Van Nuys," *California Management Review*, 31:3 (Sum-

mer 1989), 26–44; and Hedrick Smith, *Rethinking America* (New York: Random House, 1995), pp. 63ff.

76. Unless otherwise noted, this vignette draws primarily from William H. Miller, "Metamorphosis in the Desert," *Industry Week*, March 16, 1992, 27–34; Marj Charlier, "Magma Copper Heals Its Workplace and Bottom Line," *Wall Street Journal*, April 6, 1992, p. B4; and J. Burgess Winter, "Magma: A High Performance Company," speech presented at the Copper 95–Cobre 95 International Conference, Santiago, Chile, November 1995. I am grateful to William Janeway for helping steer me to the Magma example.

77. "The 1000 Ranked within Industries," *Fortune*, May 15, 1995, p. F-57.

78. Quoted in Miller, "Metamorphosis in the Desert," p. 34.

79. "A Boom Ahead in Company Profits," *Fortune*, April 6, 1992, p. 82.

80. Miller, "Metamorphosis in the Desert," p. 30 [emphasis in the original].

81. Ibid., p. 33.

82. Winter, "Magma: A High Performance Company," p. 1.

83. "The 1000 Ranked within Industries," p. F-57.

84. Smith, *Rethinking America*, p. 253.

85. Charlier, "Magma Copper Heals Its Workplace and Bottom Line," p. B4.

86. Winter, "Magma: A High Performance Company," pp. 5ff. [emphases added].

87. Quoted in Charlier, "Magma Copper Heals Its Workplace," p. B4.

88. Quoted in Miller, "Metamorphosis in the Desert," p. 34.

89. William E. Halal, *The New Capitalism* (New York: John Wiley & Sons, 1986), p. 8.

90. Keith H. Hammonds *et al.*, "The New World of Work," *Business Week*, October 17, 1994, p. 76.

91. Edward E. Lawler, III, Susan A. Mohrman, and Gerald Ledford Jr., *Employee Involvement and Total Quality Management: Practice and Results in Fortune 1000 Companies* (San Francisco: Jossey-Bass, 1992).

92. Paul Osterman, "How Common Is Workplace Transformation and Who Adopts It?" *Industrial and Labor Relations Review*, 47:2 (January 1994), 173–188.

93. Eileen Appelbaum and Rosemary Batt, *The New American Workplace: Transforming Work Systems in the United States* (Ithaca, NY: Cornell University ILR Press, 1994), p. 68.

94. Susan Parks, "Improving Workplace Performance: Historical and Theoretical Contexts," *Monthly Labor Review*, May 1995, p. 26.

95. Kochan, Katz, and McKersie, *The Transformation of American Industrial Relations*, p. xi [emphasis in original].

96. "New Work Order," *The Economist*, April 9, 1994, p. 76.

97. Appelbaum and Batt, *The New American Workplace*, p. 70.

98. Harry C. Katz, Thomas A. Kochan, and Mark R. Weber, "Assessing the Effects of Industrial Relations Systems and Efforts to Improve the Quality of Working Life on Organizational Effectiveness," *Academy of Management Journal*, 28:3 (September 1985), p. 522.

99. Appelbaum and Batt, *The New American Workplace*, p. 131.

100. Ibid., p. 12.

101. Hammonds *et al.*, "The New World of Work," p. 87.

102. Janice A. Klein, "Why Supervisors Resist Employee Involvement," *Harvard Business Review*, 62:5 (September–October 1984), 88.

103. Appelbaum and Batt, *The New American Workplace*, p. 151.

104. Kochan, Katz, and McKersie, *The Transformation of American Labor Relations*, p. xiv.

105. Quoted in Aaron Bernstein, "Why America Needs Unions But Not the Kind It Has Now," *Business Week*, May 23, 1994, p. 71.

106. Ibid., p. 71.

107. Kochan, Katz and McKersie, *The Transformation of American Labor Relations*, p. xii.

108. Bennett Harrison, *Lean and Mean: The Changing Landscape of Corporate Power in the Age of Flexibility* (New York: BasicBooks, 1994), p. 213.

109. "New Work Order," *Economist*, p. 76.

Chapter 4

1. Rosabeth Moss Kanter, "A Key Fit: Employability Security," *Boston Globe*, March 13, 1994, p. 75.

2. John E. Schwarz and Thomas J. Volgy, *The Forgotten Americans* (New York: W. W. Norton, 1992), p. 20.

3. Schwarz and Volgy, *The Forgotten Americans*, pp. 23–24.

4. *Employment and Earnings*, May 1995, Table B-2.

5. This is calculated at the average working week for private nonfarm workers of 34.6 hours per week. *Employment and Earnings*, May 1995, Table B-2.

6. This is calculated at the estimated tax rate for the average production and nonsupervisory worker. For method, see the Appendix to Chapter 1.

7. This and other expenditure patterns for the hypothetical family are based on average patterns of household expenditures as represented in the most recent available Consumer Expenditure Survey. In order to focus on households typically dependent on hourly income, I've used the average expenditure patterns for the bottom four quintiles of the before-tax income distribution. See U.S. Bureau of Labor Statistics, *Consumer Expenditure Survey, 1990–91*, Bulletin 2425, September 1993, Table 1.

8. They were engaging in one kind of saving, of course, since a significant portion of their taxes was going into social security and they may have been contributing to a private pension fund. But once they received their paychecks, saving was out of the question. And, further, those who owned their own homes were building equity as they made payments on their mortgages.

9. This figure is the income level at the top of the 2nd quintile of the income distribution, or at the 40th percentile, which is the equivalent to the median for the bottom 80 percent. U.S. Bureau of the Census, "Income, Poverty, and Valuation of Noncash Benefits: 1993," *Current Population Reports*, Series P-60, No. 188, February 1995, Table 10.

10. John E. Schwarz and Thomas J. Volgy, in their recent book *The Forgotten Americans*, provide several detailed case studies of precisely these kinds of families—typical, not extreme. See Schwarz and Volgy, *The Forgotten Americans*.

11. U.S. Bureau of the Census, "Income, Poverty, and Valuation of Noncash Benefits: 1993," Table A-1.

12. U.S. Bureau of the Census, "Income, Poverty, and Valuation of Noncash Benefits: 1993," Table 8; and *Statistical Abstract, 1993*, Table 735.

13. Timothy Smeeding, Barbara Boyle Torrey, and Martin Rein, "Patterns of Income and Poverty: The Economic Status of Children and the Elderly in Eight Countries," in J. Palmer *et al.*, eds., *The Vulnerable* (Washington, D.C.: Urban Institute Press, 1988), Table 5.2.

14. For detailed discussion of the issues involved in defining a poverty threshold, and illustrations of the different estimates of poverty derived with different poverty definitions, see Patricia Ruggles, *Drawing the Line: Alternative Poverty Measures and Their Implications for Public Policy* (Washington, D.C.: Urban Institute Press, 1990), *passim* and especially Table 3.4.

15. This question was asked for years (through 1987) by the Gallup Polling organization and the results are available in the annual volumes of the *Gallup Report*.

16. Tabulations based on Gallup Poll in Schwarz and Volgy, *The Forgotten Americans*, Table 2.

17. U.S. Bureau of the Census, "Income, Poverty, and Valuation of Noncash Benefits: 1993," Fig. 1.

18. See, for example, Edward N. Wolff, *Top Heavy: A Study of the Rising Inequality of Wealth in America* (New York: The Twentieth Century Fund Press, 1995), Fig. 3–3. See also Edward M. Gramlich, Richard Kasten, and Frank Sammartino, "Growing Inequality in the 1980s: The Role of Federal Taxes and Cash Transfers," in *Uneven Tides: Rising Inequality in America,* edited by Sheldon Danziger and Peter Gottschalk (New York: Russell Sage Foundation, 1994), pp. 225–250.

19. Wolff, *Top Heavy,* Fig. 3–3.

20. Study results reported in Keith Bradsher, "Widest Gap in Incomes? Research Points to U.S.," *New York Times,* October 27, 1995, p. D2.

21. Wolff, *Top Heavy,* previous quote, p. 13; this quote, p. 21.

22. Michael Novak, "The Inequality Myth: What Wealth Gap?" *Wall Street Journal,* July 11, 1995, p. A16.

23. Marist Institute for Public Opinion, "Americans: Making Ends Meet?" March 1995, pp. 1–2.

24. Richard Sennett, "Back to Class Warfare," *New York Times,* December 27, 1994, p. A21.

25. Quoted in Louis Uchitelle, "Three Decades of Dwindling Hope for Prosperity," *New York Times,* May 9, 1993, Section 4, p. 1.

26. Quoted in Louis Uchitelle, "Moonlighting Plus: 3–Job Families on the Rise," *New York Times,* August 16, 1994, p. A1.

27. *Economic Report of the President, 1995,* Table B-31.

28. Juliet B. Schor, *The Overworked American: The Unexpected Decline of Leisure* (New York: Basic Books, 1991).

29. *Employment and Earnings,* June 1995, Table A-35.

30. Schor, *The Overworked American,* p. 31.

31. For the historic data, see Edward S. Sekscenski, "Women's Share of Moonlighting Nearly Doubles During 1969–79," *Monthly Labor Review,* May 1980, 36–42; and John F. Stinson, Jr., "Multiple Job Holding Up Sharply in the Eighties," *Monthly Labor Review,* July 1990, 3–10.

32. Stinson, "Multiple Job Holding Up Sharply in the Eighties," Table 3.

33. *Economic Report of the President, 1995,* Tables B-45, B-40.

34. Quoted in Schor, *The Overworked American,* p. 31.

35. Walecia Konrad, "Much More than a Day's Work—For Just a Day's Pay?" *Business Week,* September 23, 1991, p. 40.

36. Quoted in Konrad, "Much More than a Day's Work," p. 40.

37. Kevin G. Salwen, "Food Lion to Pay Big Settlement in Labor Case," *Wall Street Journal,* August 3, 1993, p. A3.

38. Lawrence Mishel and Jared Bernstein, *The State of Working America, 1994–95* (Armonk, NY: M.E. Sharpe, 1994), Table 3.16.

39. In most European countries, mandated employee paid vacation time is four to five weeks. In the United States, there is no mandate and the average per worker is about three. See Mishel and Bernstein, *The State of Working America, 1994–95,* Table 8.18.

40. U.S. Bureau of Labor Statistics, *Employment and Training Report of the President, 1981* (Washington, D.C.: U.S. Government Printing Office, 1981), Table B-2; and *Employment and Earnings,* January 1995.

41. Schor, *The Overworked American,* Table 2.1 and Appendix.

42. Mishel and Bernstein, *The State of Working America, 1994–95,* Table 3.1.

43. The variable is defined as the ratio of the total hours worked by the labor force to the total U.S. population. The former comes from *National Income and Product Accounts,* 6.9C:1; the latter comes from *Economic Report of the President, 1995,* Table B-32.

44. Mishel and Bernstein, *The State of Working America, 1994–95*, Table 4.12.

45. See, for example, Ronald G. Ehrenberg, Pamela Rosenberg, and Jeanne Li, "Part-time Employment in the United States," in Robert A. Hart, ed., *Employment, Unemployment, and Labor Utilization* (Boston: Unwin Hyman, 1988), pp. 256–287; and Chris Tilly, *Short Hours, Short Shrift: Causes and Consequences of Part-time Work* (Washington, D.C.: Economic Policy Institute, 1990).

46. Schor, *The Overworked American*, pp. 34ff.

47. Barbara Vobejda and D'Vera Cohn, "Today, a Father's Place Is in the Home," *Washington Post*, May 20, 1994, p. A1.

48. Ellen Galinsky, James T. Bond, and Dana E. Friedman, *The Changing Workforce: Highlights of the National Study* (New York: Families and Work Institute, 1993), Table 5.

49. Cited in Schor, *The Overworked American*, p. 22.

50. David W. Moore and Leslie McAneny, "Workers Concerned They Can't Afford to Retire," *Gallup Poll Monthly*, May 1993, p. 21.

51. Barbara Brandt, "Less Is More: A Call for Shorter Work Hours," *Utne Reader*, July/August 1991, p. 81.

52. This is the standard neoclassical view of the wage elasticity of labor demand; for a complete review of the literature, see Daniel S. Hamermesh, *Labor Demand* (Princeton: Princeton University Press, 1993). Economists of post-Keynesian striping are skeptical of this view; see, for example, Tom Michl, "Is There Evidence for a Marginalist Demand for Labour?" *Cambridge Journal of Economics*, 11:4, December 1987, 361–373. In my own work on labor demand, building on Marxian and structuralist perspectives, I find strong negative wage elasticities of labor demand even after taking into account a number of factors not considered by standard neoclassical or post-Keynesian approaches. For a brief summary, see David M. Gordon, "Putting Heterodox Macro to the Test: Comparing Post-Keynesian, Marxian, and Social Structuralist Macroeconometric Models of the Postwar U.S. Economy," in *Competition, Technology, and Money: Comparing Classical and Post-Keynesian Views*, edited by Mark Glick and E.K. Hunt (Aldershot, England: Edward Elgar, 1994), pp. 143–185.

53. See John Pencavel, "Labor Supply of Men: A Survey," in *Handbook of Labor Economics*, edited by O. Ashenfelter and R. Layard (Amsterdam: North-Holland, 1986), Vol. I, pp. 3–102.

54. See Mark R. Killingsworth and James J. Heckman, "Female Labor Supply: A Survey," in *Handbook of Labor Economics*, edited by O. Ashenfelter and R. Layard (Amsterdam: North-Holland, 1986), Vol. I, pp. 103–204.

55. Peter T. Kilborn, "More Women Take Low-Wage Jobs Just So Their Families Can Get By," *New York Times*, March 13, 1994, p. A24.

56. Quoted in Kilborn, "More Women Take Low-Wage Jobs . . . ," p. A24.

57. Quoted in Maryann Keller, *Rude Awakening: The Rise, Fall, and Struggle for Recovery of General Motors* (New York: William Morrow, 1989), p. 128.

58. The question on job satisfaction asked respondents to rate how much they liked their job on a scale from one to five, with one indicating "I hate my job" and five that "I love my job." For the comparisons in the text, I've taken scores of four and five as measures of "high levels" of job satisfaction.

59. There does not appear to be the same kind of monotonic relationship between frequency of supervision and job satisfaction among the group of managerial and supervisory employees. Referring to the same three categories of intensity of being supervised as in the text, the percentages for managers and supervisors are 82, 68, and 75 percent respectively. This is probably because there are other, stronger influences on satisfaction for this group.

60. Galinsky *et al.*, *The Changing Workforce*, p. 20.

61. Graham Staines, "Is Worker Dissatisfaction Rising?" *Challenge*, May-June 1979, pp. 38–45.

62. Michael R. Cooper, "Early Warning Signals: Growing Discontent Among Managers" *Business*, January–February 1980.

63. William A. Schiemann, ed., *Managing Human Resources: 1985 and Beyond* (Princeton: Opinion Research Corporation, 1984).

64. Alan Farnham, "The Trust Gap," *Fortune*, December 4, 1989, pp. 56–78. Quotes from pp. 56, 57, 58, 57 respectively.

65. Polling data by Roper Starch Worldwide, Inc., reported in "Satisfaction with Work," *The American Enterprise*, January/February 1995, p. 105.

66. Moore and McAneny, "Workers Concerned They Can't Afford to Retire," p. 21.

67. Ibid., p. 19.

68. Hedrick Smith, *Rethinking America* (New York: Random House, 1995), p. 412.

69. Quoted in Keith H. Hammonds *et al.*, "The New World of Work," *Business Week*, October 17, 1994, p. 84.

70. Bob Herbert, "In America, The Issue Is Jobs," *New York Times*, May 6, 1995, p. 19.

Chapter 5

1. Ben J. Wattenberg, *Values Matter Most: How Republicans or Democrats or a Third Party Can Win and Renew the American Way of Life* (New York: The Free Press, 1995), p. 13 [emphasis in original].

2. Ibid., p. 95.

3. Dan Quayle, "The Family Comes First: We Cannot Take Orders from the Special Interests," *Vital Speeches of the Day*, 58:23 (September 15, 1992), p. 712.

4. U.S. Bureau of the Census, "Household and Family Characteristics: March 1993," *Current Population Reports*, Series P-20, No. 477, June 1994, Table A-2.

5. On men's negative reactions to these trends, see Barbara Ehrenreich, *The Hearts of Men: American Dreams and the Flight from Commitment* (Garden City, NJ: Anchor Press, 1983); and Susan Faludi, *Backlash: The Undeclared War against Women* (New York: Crown, 1991).

6. For a less nostalgic and more balanced view of this history, see Stephanie Coontz, *The Way We Never Were: American Families and the Nostalgia Trap* (New York: BasicBooks, 1992).

7. Jennifer Kunz, "The Effects of Divorce on Children," in Stephen J. Bahr, ed. *Family Research: A Sixty-Year Review, 1930–1990* (New York: Lexington Books, 1991), p. 353.

8. Andrew J. Cherlin *et al.*, "Longitudinal Studies of Effects of Divorce on Children in Great Britain and the United States," *Science*, 252:5011 (June 7, 1991), p. 1388.

9. David H. Demo and Lawrence H. Ganong, "Divorce," in *Families and Change: Coping with Stressful Events*, edited by Patrick C. McKenry and Sharon J. Price (Thousand Oaks, CA: Sage Publications, 1994), p. 206.

10. Cherlin *et al.*, "Longitudinal Studies of Effects of Divorce," p. 1388.

11. Don L. Boroughs *et al.*, "Love and Money," *U.S. News & World Report*, October 19, 1992, p. 54.

12. Ibid., p. 54.

13. See Elaine McCrate, "Trade, Merger, and Employment: Economic Metaphors for Marriage," *Review of Radical Political Economics*, 19:1 (Spring 1987), 73–89; and "Accounting for the Slowdown in the Divorce Rate in the 1980s: A Bargaining Perspective," *Review of Social Economy*, 50(4) (Winter 1992), 404–419.

14. Elaine McCrate, "The Growth of Nonmarriage Among U.S. Women, 1954–1983," unpublished Ph.D. dissertation, University of Massachusetts—Amherst, 1985.

15. Mark Lino, "Mothers' Perceptions of Their Lives After Divorce," paper presented at the annual meeting of the Population Association, 1994, Figs. 2,6,3.

16. McCrate, "Trade, Merger, and Employment," pp. 85–86.

17. For an application of this kind of analysis to the leveling off and then decline of divorce rates in the 1980s, see McCrate, "Accounting for the Slowdown in the Divorce Rate."

18. Rush H. Limbaugh III, *The Way Things Ought to Be* (New York: Pocket Books, 1992), p. 197.

19. Kathleen Gerson, *No Man's Land: Men's Changing Commitments to Family and Work* (New York: BasicBooks, 1993), p. 141.

20. For a useful discussion of the policy implications of this kind of perspective, see Nancy Folbre, *Who Pays for the Kids? Gender and the Structures of Constraint* (New York: Routledge, 1994), Chapter 7.

21. U.S. Bureau of Justice Statistics, "Violence against Women: Estimates from the Redesigned Survey," *National Crime Victimization Survey*, Report No. NCJ-154348, August 1995.

22. Don Colburn, "Domestic Violence," *The Washington Post*, June 28, 1994, Health Section, p. 10.

23. Don Colburn, "When Violence Begins at Home," *The Washington Post*, March 15, 1994, Health Section, p. 7.

24. Quoted in Colburn, "When Violence Begins at Home," Health Section, p. 7.

25. Here, much of the crucial work has been developed and surveyed by Harvey M. Brenner. See, for example, Harvey M. Brenner, "Estimating the Effect of Economic Change on National Mental Health and Social Well-Being," Report for the Subcommittee on Economic Goals and Intergovernmental Policy, Joint Economic Committee, U.S. Congress, 1984.

26. Rudy Fenwick and Mark Tausig, "The Macroeconomic Context of Job Stress," *Journal of Health and Social Behavior*, 35:3 (September 1994), p. 278.

27. Ibid., p. 278.

28. See, in particular, Melvin L. Kohn and Carmi Schooler, *Work and Personality: An Inquiry into the Impact of Social Stratification* (Norwood, NJ: Ablex, 1983).

29. Alice M. Atkinson, "Stress Levels of Family Day Care Providers, Mothers Employed Outside the Home, and Mothers at Home," *Journal of Marriage and the Family*, 54:2 (May 1992), p. 383.

30. Ardis L. Olson and Lisa A. DiBrigida, "Depressive Symptoms and Work Role Satisfaction in Mothers of Toddlers," *Pediatrics*, 94:3 (September 1994), 363–367.

31. C. E. Ross, J. Mirowsky, and K. Goldsteen, "The Impact of the Family on Health: The Decade in Review," *Journal of Marriage and the Family*, 52:4 (November 1990), 1059–1078.

32. See, for example, Jennifer Glass and Tetsushi Fujimoto, "Housework, Paid Work, and Depression Among Husbands and Wives," *Journal of Health and Social Behavior*, 35:2 (June 1994), 179–191.

33. Ellen Galinsky, James T. Bond, and Dana E. Friedman, *The Changing Workforce: Highlights of the National Study* (New York: Families and Work Institute, 1993), Figure 8 and p. 72.

34. Ibid., p. 101.

35. Charles Murray, "The Coming White Underclass," *Wall Street Journal*, October 29, 1993, p. A14.

36. Wattenberg, *Values Matter Most*, pp. 175–176.

37. *Statistical Abstract, 1993*, Tables 93, 101.

38. Ibid.

39. Eileen White Read, "For Poor Teenagers, Pregnancies Become New Rite of Passage," *Wall Street Journal*, March 17, 1988, p. 1.

40. See Elaine McCrate, "Expectations of Adult Wages and Teenage Childbearing," *International Review of Applied Economics*, 6(3) (September 1992), 309–328; "The Effect of Schooling and Labor Market Expectations on Teenage Childbearing," *Review of Radical Political Economics*, 20(2&3) (Spring/Summer 1988), 203–207; and "Labor Market Segmentation and Relative Black/White Teenage Birth Rates," *Review of Black Political Economy*, 18(4) (Winter/Spring 1990), 37–53.

41. Greg J. Duncan and Saul D. Hoffman, "Teenage Underclass Behavior and Subsequent Poverty: Have the Rules Changed?", in *The Urban Underclass,* edited by Christopher Jencks and Paul E. Peterson (Washington, D.C.: The Brookings Institution, 1991), 155–174.

42. McCrate, "Expectations of Adult Wages and Teenage Childbearing," pp. 325, 326.

43. McCrate, "Labor Market Segmentation and Relative Black/White Teenage Birth Rates," p. 50.

44. Quoted in Jason DeParle, "In Debate on U.S. Poverty, 2 Studies Fuel an Argument on Who Is to Blame," *New York Times,* October 29, 1991, p. A20.

45. Christopher Jencks and Kathryn Edin, "Do Poor Women Have a Right to Bear Children?" *The American Prospect,* Winter 1995, p. 46.

46. See Roberta Spalter-Roth *et al., Welfare That Works: The Working Lives of AFDC Recipients* (Washington, D.C.: Institute for Women's Policy Research, 1995).

47. Roberta Spalter-Roth, "Welfare That Works: Increasing AFDC Mothers' Employment and Income," Testimony before the Subcommittee on Human Resources, Committee on Ways and Means, U.S. House of Representatives, February 2, 1995 (revised March 1995), p. 1.

48. Based on summary of Lein and Edin findings in Jencks and Edin, "Do Poor Women Have a Right to Bear Children?", p. 50.

49. Spalter-Roth, "Welfare That Works: Increasing AFDC Mothers' Employment and Income," p. 3.

50. Ibid., p. 2 [emphasis in the original].

51. Author's tabulations from March 1993 outgoing rotation sample of Current Population Survey.

52. Jencks and Edin, "Do Poor Women Have a Right to Bear Children?", p. 52.

53. Jason DeParle, "Welfare Mothers Find Jobs Are Easier to Get Than Hold," *New York Times,* October 24, 1994, p. A1.

54. Jason DeParle, "Better Work Than Welfare. But What If There's Neither?" *New York Times Magazine,* December 18, 1994.

55. Ibid., pp. 44, 46.

56. It was perhaps Ken Auletta who contributed most to making the term "underclass" an integral part of public discourse. See his original articles, "The Underclass," *The New Yorker,* November 16, 23, 30, 1981, subsequently collected in *The Underclass* (New York: Random House, 1982).

57. Richard John Neuhaus, *America Against Itself: Moral Vision and the Public Order* (Notre Dame: University of Notre Dame Press, 1992), p. 89.

58. Shelby Steele, *The Content of Our Character: A New Vision of Race in America* (New York: Harper Perennial, 1991), p. 173.

59. Christopher Jencks, "Is the American Underclass Growing?" in *The Urban Underclass,* edited by Christopher Jencks and Paul E. Peterson (Washington, D.C.: The Brookings Institution, 1991), p. 96.

60. William Julius Wilson, *The Truly Disadvantaged: The Inner City, the Underclass, and Public Policy* (Chicago: University of Chicago Press, 1987), p. 8.

61. Jencks, "Is the American Underclass Growing?", Table 3.

62. For a useful review of many of these trends, see Philip Moss and Chris Tilly, *Why Black Men Are Doing Worse in the Labor Market: A Review of Supply-Side and Demand-Side Explanations* (New York: Social Science Research Council, 1992), pp. 16–20.

63. See, on the IQ issue, the controversial book by Richard J. Herrnstein and Charles Murray, *The Bell Curve: Intelligence and Class Structure in American Life* (New York: The Free Press, 1994); and, for one set of responses to it, Steven Fraser, ed., *The Bell Curve Wars: Race, Intelligence and the Future of America* (New York: Basic Books, 1995).

64. See, for example, Jencks, "Is the American Underclass Growing?", Table 8.

65. Ibid., Table 10; and, for the underlying data, U.S. Department of Education, National Center for Education Statistics, *Digest of Education Statistics, 1994*, Table 106.

66. See *Digest of Education Statistics*, Tables 8, 106.

67. John Bound and Richard B. Freeman, "What Went Wrong? The Erosion of the Relative Earnings and Employment of Young Black Men in the 1980s," *Quarterly Journal of Economics*, 107:1 (February 1992), p. 223.

68. Ibid., p. 215.

69. Jencks, "Is the American Underclass Growing?", p. 57.

70. Richard B. Freeman, "Employment and Earnings of Disadvantaged Young Men in a Labor Shortage Economy," in *The Urban Underclass*, edited by Christopher Jencks and Paul E. Peterson (Washington, D.C.: The Brookings Institution, 1991), p. 119.

71. Paul Osterman, "Gains from Growth? The Impact of Full Employment on Poverty in Boston," in *The Urban Underclass*, edited by Christopher Jencks and Paul E. Peterson (Washington, D.C.: The Brookings Institution, 1991), p. 124.

72. Ibid., pp. 130, 131.

73. Marta Tienda and Haya Stier, "Joblessness and Shiftlessness: Labor Force Activity in Chicago's Inner City," in *The Urban Underclass*, edited by Christopher Jencks and Paul E. Peterson (Washington, D.C.: The Brookings Institution, 1991), p. 137.

74. Tienda and Stier, "Joblessness and Shiftlessness," p. 151.

75. Ibid., p. 143.

76. One general discussion of some of these issues is provided by Elliott Currie, *Confronting Crime* (New York: Pantheon, 1985). For summary of the complex character of the relationship between unemployment and property crime, see John Hagan, "The Social Embeddedness of Crime and Unemployment," *Criminology*, 31(4) (1993), 465–491.

77. Robert J. Bursik, Jr. and Harold G. Grasmick, "Economic Deprivation and Neighborhood Crime Rates, 1960–1980," *Law & Society Review*, 27:2 (1993), 263–283. For similar results, see also E. Britt Patterson, "Poverty, Income Inequality, and Community Crime Rates," *Criminology*, 29:4 (November 1991), 755–776.

78. U.S. Department of Justice, Federal Bureau of Investigation, *Uniform Crime Reports for the United States, 1993* (Washington, D.C.: U.S. Government Printing Office, 1994), p. 58.

79. U.S. Department of Justice, Bureau of Justice Statistics, *Criminal Victimization in the United States, 1973–92 Trends*, A National Crime Victimization Survey Report, NCJ-147006, July 1994.

80. For a review of the available data, which suggests that actual drug use may not have been increasing as much as drug arrest rates, see Diana R. Gordon, *The Return of the Dangerous Classes: Drug Prohibition and Policy Politics* (New York: W.W. Norton, 1994), Chapter 2.

81. On limited returns to most street property crimes, see for example W. Kip Viscusi, "The Risks and Rewards of Criminal Activity: A Comprehensive Test of Criminal Deterrence," *Journal of Labor Economics* 4:3 (July 1986), 317–340.

82. Robert MacCoun and Peter Reuter, "Are the Wages of Sin $30 an Hour? Economic Aspects of Street-Level Drug Dealing," *Crime & Delinquency*, 38:4 (October 1992), 477–491.

83. Ibid., p. 487.

84. Ibid., p. 488.

85. Mercer L. Sullivan, *"Getting Paid": Youth Crime and Work in the Inner City* (Ithaca, NY: Cornell University Press, 1989), p. 207.

86. Ann Dryden Witte and Helen Tauchen, "Work and Crime: An Exploration Using Panel Data," National Bureau of Economic Research Working Paper No. 4794, July 1994.

87. Bound and Freeman, "What Went Wrong?" p. 225.

88. For heuristic estimates of this kind of effect, see Bound and Freeman, "What Went Wrong?" p. 228.

89. Mike Davis, "Hell Factories in the Field," *Nation*, February 20, 1995, p. 229.

90. U.S. Bureau of Justice Statistics, *Sourcebook of Criminal Justice Statistics, 1993* (Washington, D.C.: U.S. Government Printing Office, 1994), Tables 6.29, 6.18 and *Sourcebook, 1984,* 6.19.

91. Tracy L. Snell, *Correctional Populations in the United States, 1992,* U.S. Bureau of Justice Statistics, NCJ-146413, January 1995.

92. *Economic Report of the President, 1995,* Tables B-44, B-86.

93. The Criminal Justice Institute, *The Corrections Yearbook,* South Salem, NY, various years.

94. *Statistical Abstract, 1982–83,* Table 651; *Employment and Earnings,* January 1995, Table 11.

95. Adam Walinsky, "The Crisis of Public Order," *Atlantic Monthly,* July 1995, p. 40.

96. *Statistical Abstract, 1993,* Table 645.

97. Marc Mauer, "Americans Behind Bars: The International Use of Incarceration, 1992–93," The Sentencing Project, Washington, D.C., September 1994, Table 1.

98. Based on data reported in Mauer, "Americans Behind Bars," pp. 8–9 and Table 1.

99. For a discussion of the interplay of these different factors, see Diana R. Gordon, *The Justice Juggernaut: Fighting Street Crime, Controlling Citizens* (New Brunswick, NJ: Rutgers University Press, 1991).

100. Wendy Kaminer, "Federal Offense," *Atlantic Monthly,* June 1994, p. 103.

101. Snell, *Correctional Populations in the United States, 1992,* U.S. Bureau of Justice Statistics, NCJ-146413, January 1995. Table 1.2.

102. Study by the Sentencing Project cited in Andrew Hacker, "The Crackdown on African-Americans," *The Nation,* July 10, 1995, p. 48.

103. Study by the Sentencing Project reported in Fox Butterfield, "More Blacks in Their 20's Have Trouble with the Law," *New York Times,* October 5, 1995, p. A18.

104. Quoted and cited in Butterfield, "More Blacks in Their 20's Have Trouble with the Law," p. A18.

105. Hacker, "The Crackdown on African-Americans," p. 48.

106. Ibid., p. 48.

107. Data for bureaucratic burden from Chapter 2. Data for incarceration rates from Mauer, "Americans Behind Bars," Table 1.

Chapter 6

1. Aaron Bernstein, "The Global Economy," *Business Week,* August 10, 1992, p. 53.

2. Paul Krugman, *Peddling Prosperity: Economic Sense and Nonsense in the Age of Diminished Expectations* (New York: W. W. Norton, 1994), p. 56.

3. The idea of the Carrot Strategy is actually a kind of composite. As Eileen Appelbaum and Rosemary Batt observe, different countries relying largely on the cooperative approach have many of their own distinctive features; the German system differs from the Swedish model and both contrast markedly with the Japanese system. But all tend, at least in contrast to the conflictual model characteristic of the United States, to share the features of the Carrot Strategy listed in the text. See Appelbaum and Batt, *The New American Workplace: Transforming Work Systems in the United States* (Ithaca, NY: ILR Press, 1994), especially Ch. 4.

4. David I. Levine and Laura D'Andrea Tyson, "Participation, Productivity and the Firm's Environment," in *Paying for Productivity: A Look at the Evidence,* edited by Alan S. Blinder (Washington, D.C.: Brookings Institution, 1990), p. 203.

5. Ibid., p. 204.

6. Ibid., pp. 205ff. See also Appelbaum and Batt, *The New American Workplace,* pp. 144ff.

7. See Aaron Bernstein, "Why America Needs Unions But Not the Kind It Has Now," *Business Week,* May 23, 1994, p. 82.

8. Ibid., p. 82.

9. See, for example, Roy J. Adams, *Industrial Relations Under Liberal Democracy: North America in Comparative Perspective* (Columbia, SC: University of South Carolina Press, 1995), Chapter 6; Carlo Dell'Aringa and Manuela Samek Lodovici, "Industrial Relations and Economic Performance," in *Participation in Public Policy-Making: The Role of Trade Unions and Employers' Associations,* edited by Tiziano Treu (Berlin: Walter deGruyter, 1992), pp. 26–58; and my own classification in David M. Gordon, "Bosses of Different Stripes: Monitoring and Supervision across the Advanced Economies," *American Economic Review,* 84:2 (May 1994), 375–379.

10. Throughout this chapter, the comparisons for the 1973–89 period actually involve averages of levels for the years 1974–89, to avoid counting an extra peak, and averages of rates of change for 1974–89 as well. In the text as well as the figures, I continue to use the dates 1973–89 in order to refer to the peak dates demarcating the cycles.

11. Based on data for business sector output per employee from the OECD data set: Organization for Economic Cooperation and Development, *Economic Outlook,* June 1995, country historical tables. Group figures are unweighted averages of country average annual arithmetic rates of change.

12. Based on data for output per hour in manufacturing from U.S. Bureau of Labor Statistics, Office of Productivity and Technology, "Output per Hour, Hourly Compensation and Unit Labor Costs in Manufacturing, Twelve Economies," unpublished tables, February 1995, Table 1. Group figures are unweighted averages of country average annual arithmetic rates of change. Data for the United States for 1973–76 are extrapolated based on ratio of manufacturing to business sector productivity growth rates for 1978–88; data from *Economic Report of the President, 1995,* Table B-47.

13. Very few comparative studies of productivity growth pay attention to the effects of labor relations. For one which focuses primarily on technological factors, see William J. Baumol, Sue A. B. Blackman, and Edward N. Wolff, *Productivity and American Leadership: The Long View* (Cambridge, MA: MIT Press, 1989). For studies exploring the impact of labor-management systems, among other institutions, on macro performance in general—but not including productivity growth—see several of the chapters in Renato Brunetta and Carlo Dell'Aringa, eds., *Labour Relations and Economic Performance* (New York: New York University Press, 1990).

14. Robert Buchele and Jens Christiansen, "Industrial Relations and Productivity Growth: A Comparative Perspective," *International Contributions to Labour Studies,* 2, 1992, 77–97.

15. Ibid., p. 95.

16. This important dimension to the cooperative approach is stressed by David I. Levine, "Demand Variability and Work Organization," in *Markets and Democracy: Participation, Accountability and Efficiency,* edited by Samuel Bowles, Herbert Gintis and Bo Gustafsson (New York: Cambridge University Press, 1993), pp. 159–175.

17. In more technical terms, I take the regression coefficients from individual country time-series regressions of productivity growth rates on the rate of change of the fixed-capital/employee ratio for 1967–89. Each regression is estimated with the same specifications: a one-period lag on the independent variable (since, in order to avoid exaggerating the result, this was the lag in which the coefficient was uniformly highest for the conflictual cases) and a first-order moving-average correction for autocorrelation. Data for the dependent variable is the measure for the business sector already documented in footnote #11 above. Data for the dependent variable is the measure for capital per employee documented in footnote #39 below. The group averages reported in text and figure are the unweighted averages of the respective individual-country regression coefficients.

18. Adams, *Industrial Relations Under Liberal Democracy,* pp. 137–138.

19. Thomas E. Weisskopf, "The Effect of Unemployment on Labour Productivity: An International Comparative Analysis," *International Review of Applied Economics,* 1:2 (June 1987), 127–151.

20. Weisskopf, "The Effect of Unemployment on Labour Productivity," p. 150.

21. Buchele and Christiansen, "Industrial Relations and Productivity Growth," p. 95.

22. McKinsey Global Institute, *Manufacturing Productivity* (Washington, D.C.: McKinsey Global Institute, October 1993), "Synthesis," p. 10.

23. Alan S. Blinder, "Introduction," in *Paying for Productivity: A Look at the Evidence,* edited by Alan S. Blinder (Washington, D.C.: Brookings Institution, 1990), p. 4.

24. See, for example, the very tentative conclusions reached in the careful study by David I. Levine, Gerald E. Ledford Jr., Edward E. Lawler III, and Susan Albers Mohrman, "The Effects of Employee Involvement on Large U.S. Employers," paper presented to a conference on "What Works at Work: Human Resource Policies and Organizational Performance," Washington, D.C., January 5, 1995.

25. Mark A. Huselid and Brian E. Becker, "The Strategic Impact of Human Resources: Evidence from a Panel Study," paper presented to a conference on "What Works at Work: Human Resource Policies and Organizational Performance," Washington, D.C., January 5, 1995, p. 13.

26. Cited in Mark Green and John F. Berry, *The Challenge of Hidden Profits: Reducing Corporate Bureaucracy and Waste* (New York: William Morrow, 1985), p. 390.

27. David I. Levine, "Public Policy Implications of Imperfections in the Market for Worker Participation," *Economic and Industrial Democracy* 13(3) (May 1992), 197.

28. Bennett Harrison, *Lean and Mean: The Changing Landscape of Corporate Power in the Age of Flexibility* (New York: BasicBooks, 1994), p. 213 [emphasis added].

29. This point is stressed by Levine, "Demand Variability and Workplace Organization."

30. Harrison, *Lean and Mean,* p. 213.

31. Appelbaum and Batt, *The New American Workplace,* p. 13.

32. Lester Thurow, *Head to Head: The Coming Economic Battle among Japan, Europe, and America* (New York: William Morrow, 1992), p. 167.

33. Thomas A. Kochan, Harry C. Katz, and Robert B. McKersie, *The Transformation of American Industrial Relations* (Ithaca, NY: Cornell ILR Press, 1994), p. xiii.

34. See Ruth Milkman, *Japan's California Factories: Labor Relations and Economic Globalization* (Los Angeles: Institute of Industrial Relations, University of California, 1991).

35. Kochan, Katz, and McKersie, *The Transformation of American Industrial Relations,* p. xiv.

36. See, for example, Smith, *Rethinking America, passim,* for numerous success stories.

37. Cited in W. Edwards Deming, *Out of the Crisis* (Cambridge, MA: MIT, 1986), p. 148.

38. The investment share is measured as fixed investment, business sector, divided by GDP. The data come from the OECD data set. The group figures are unweighted period averages of individual country ratios for the years 1974–89.

39. Author's tabulations from OECD data. The capital-labor ratio is defined as the gross fixed nonresidential capital stock for the business sector divided by business sector employment. The group figures are unweighted country averages of the individual country average annual arithmetic rates of growth in the capital/labor ratio over the period 1974–89.

40. For a recent and comprehensive review, see Robert S. Chirinko, "Business Fixed Investment Spending: Modeling Strategies, Empirical Results, and Policy Implications," *Journal of Economic Literature,* 31:4 (December 1993), 1875–1911.

41. Some studies that integrate all three effects into an analysis of aggregate investment include Martin Feldstein, "Inflation, Tax Rules and Investment: Some Econometric Evidence," *Econometrica,* 50:4 (July 1982), 825–62; M. Catinat et al., "Investment Behavior in Europe: A Comparative Analysis," *Recherches Economiques de Louvain,* 54, 1988, 277–324; and David M. Gordon, Thomas E. Weisskopf, and Samuel Bowles, "Power, Profits, and Investment: The Postwar Social Structure of Accumulation and the Stagnation of U.S. Net Investment since the Mid-1960s," New School for Social Research, December 1995.

42. Two useful essays making this kind of argument, which has evolved into what's known as the "U-curve hypothesis," are Lars Calmfors and John Driffill, "Bargaining Structure, Corporatism and Macroeconomic Performance," *Economic Policy: A European Forum*, No. 6 (April 1988), 13–61; and Heikki Paloheimo, "Between Liberalism and Corporatism: The Effect of Trade Unions and Governments on Economic Performance in Eighteen OECD Countries," in *Labour Relations and Economic Performance*, edited by R. Brunetta and C. Dell'Aringa (New York: New York University Press, 1990), pp. 114–136. See also Richard B. Freeman, "Labour Market Institutions and Economic Performance," *Economic Policy: A European Forum*, No. 6 (April 1988), 64–80.

43. Based on author's calculations from OECD data. The productivity measure is for real business sector per employee, while the wage rate is annual business-sector compensation per employee. Group figures are unweighted averages of individual country average annual arithmetic growth rates for the years 1974–89.

44. See discussion of this dynamic in Samuel Bowles, David M. Gordon, and Thomas E. Weisskopf, *After the Waste Land: A Democratic Economics for the Year 2000* (Armonk, NY: M.E. Sharpe, 1990), pp. 209ff.

45. It is possible, of course, that the causation runs in the opposite direction, from changes in capital intensity to wage growth rather than the other way around: If the capital-labor ratio increases rapidly, so will productivity growth, creating room for rapid wage growth. The consistency of the advantages which the cooperative economies appear to have enjoyed makes it likely that causation runs in both directions, creating a "virtuous cycle" for those traveling the high road.

46. Harrison, *Lean and Mean*, p. 213.

47. Author's tabulations from OECD data. The rate of inflation is defined as the rate of change of the GDP deflator. Group figures are unweighted averages of individual country average annual arithmetic rates of change.

48. Juliet B. Schor, *The Overworked American: The Unexpected Decline of Leisure* (New York: BasicBooks, 1991).

49. Averages based on individual country data for average annual hours worked in manufacturing in U.S. Bureau of Labor Statistics, Office of Productivity and Technology, "Output per Hour, Hourly Compensation, and Unit Labor Costs in Manufacturing, Twelve Economies, 1950–1993," unpublished tables, February 1995, Table 6.

50. Based on data for unit labor costs in manufacturing, national currency basis, from U.S. Bureau of Labor Statistics, Office of Productivity and Technology, "Output per Hour, Hourly Compensation, and Unit Labor Costs in Manufacturing, Twelve Economies, 1950–1993," unpublished tables, February 1995, Table 9. Group averages are unweighted country averages for the average annual change from 1979 to 1989.

51. Jonathan Peterson, "Economists Play 'Happy Days' as Many Sing Blues," *Los Angeles Times*, February 21, 1994.

52. James C. Cooper, "The New Golden Age of Productivity," *Business Week*, September 16, 1994, p. 62.

53. See Robert J. Gordon, "The Jobless Recovery: Does It Signal a New Era of Productivity-led Growth?", *Brookings Papers on Economic Activity*, 1993:1, 271–316; and Stephen D. Oliner and Daniel E. Sichel, "Computers and Output Growth Revisited: How Big Is the Puzzle?," *Brookings Papers on Economic Activity*, 1994:2, 273–334.

54. Stephen D. Oliner and Daniel E. Sichel, "Is a Productivity Revolution Under Way in the United States?," *Challenge*, November-December 1995, pp. 28–29.

55. This paragraph draws on the same sources as for the comparisons for 1973–89 in the earlier sections of this chapter.

56. Charles R. Bean, "European Unemployment: A Survey," *Journal of Economic Literature*, 32(2) (June 1994), p. 573.

57. Quoted in Jane A. Sasseen, "The Winds of Change Blow Everywhere," *Business Week*, October 17, 1994, p. 92.

58. Richard B. Freeman, "How Labor Fares in Advanced Economies," in *Working Under Different Rules*, edited by Richard B. Freeman (New York: Russell Sage, 1994), p. 14.

59. As is standard in these kinds of cross-country comparisons, the unemployment rates for Germany are those for the former West Germany only, in order to avoid distortions from the integration of the former East Germany. For our purposes here, this practice is especially important, since analysts would refer only to labor relations in western Germany as reflecting historically cooperative structures.

60. Based on standardized unemployment rates, Organization for Economic Cooperation and Development, *OECD Economic Outlook*, 57 (June 1995), Annex Table 22. Group averages are unweighted average annual rates for the respective periods.

61. The underlying framework generating the expectations of a trade-off between unemployment on the one hand and wage and productivity growth on the other may also be inadequate, since it largely builds on assumptions of perfectly competitive labor markets. For a careful analysis which, in spite of its predictions, fails to find evidence of the expected trade-off between unemployment growth and productivity growth among the G-7 economies, see Robert J. Gordon, "Is There a Tradeoff between Unemployment and Productivity Growth?" in *Unemployment Policy*, edited by Dennis J. Snower and Guillermo de la Dehesa (forthcoming 1996).

62. Organization for Economic Cooperation and Development, *The OECD Jobs Study* (Paris: OECD, June 1994), Vol. I, Chart 1.14.

63. Andrew Glyn, "Social Democracy and Full Employment," *New Left Review*, No. 211 (May/June 1995), p. 54.

Chapter 7

1. This anecdote and the quotes included in it come from Jon Pattee, "Sprint and the Shutdown of La Conexion Familiar," *Labor Research Review*, No. 23, 1995, 13–22.

2. Quoted in Katherine S. Newman, *Declining Fortunes: The Withering of the American Dream* (New York: BasicBooks, 1993), p. 3 [emphasis in the original].

3. J. David Richardson, "Income Inequality and Trade: How to Think, What to Conclude," *Journal of Economic Perspectives*, 9(3) (Summer 1995), p. 34.

4. I am heavily indebted in this section to the recent work of my colleague at the New School for Social Research, David Howell. See, in particular, David R. Howell, "Collapsing Wages and Rising Inequality," *Challenge* (January–February 1995), 27–35; "The Skills Myth," *American Prospect* (Summer 1994), 81–89; "The Collapse of Low-Skill Earnings in the U.S.: Skill Mismatch or Shifting Wage Norms?", Policy Brief of the Jerome Levy Institute, July 1995; and, with Maury B. Gittelman, "Changes in the Structure and Quality of Jobs in the United States: Effects by Race and Gender, 1973–1990," *Industrial and Labor Relations Review*, 48:3 (April 1995): 420–440.

5. Keith Bradsher, "Productivity Is All, But It Doesn't Pay Well," *New York Times*, June 25, 1995, News of the Week in Review, p. 4.

6. Robert B. Reich, "Workers of the World, Get Smart," *New York Times*, July 20, 1993, p. A19.

7. See, for example, the conclusions in Marvin H. Kosters, "Wages and Demographics," in *Workers and Their Wages: Changing Patterns in the United States*, edited by Marvin H. Kosters (Washington, D.C.: AEI Press, 1991), 1–32.

8. Bradsher, "Productivity Is All," p. 4.

9. Martin Neil Baily, Gary Burtless, and Robert E. Litan, *Growth with Equity: Economic Policymaking for the Next Century* (Washington, D.C.: The Brookings Institution, 1993), p. 12.

10. For one review of these trends, see Maury Gittelman, "Earnings in the 1980's: An Occupational Perspective," *Monthly Labor Review*, July 1994, 16–27.

11. Based on author's tabulations from March 1993 outgoing rotation sample of the Current Population Survey.

12. McKinley L. Blackburn, David E. Bloom, and Richard B. Freeman, "The Declining Economic Position of Less Skilled American Men," in Gary Burtless, ed., *A Future of Lousy Jobs? The Changing Structure of U.S. Wages* (Washington, D.C.: The Brookings Institution, 1990), p. 53.

13. Some analysts place emphasis on the relative slowdown from the 1970s to the 1980s in the growth of college graduates, suggesting that this can help explain the rising relative wages of those with a college degree or better. But this does not help in tracing the declining absolute real wages of the vast majority of workers, the major focus of this study. Nor does it provide much assistance in explaining the decline in the real earnings of college graduates after the mid-1980s, to which we turn below. For emphasis on the sluggish supply of college graduates and its effects, see Lawrence F. Katz and Kevin M. Murphy, "Changes in Relative Wages, 1963–1987: Supply and Demand Factors," *Quarterly Journal of Economics*, 107:1 (February 1992): 35–78.

14. Sheldon Danziger and Peter Gottschalk, "Introduction," in *Uneven Tides: Rising Inequality in America,* edited by Sheldon Danziger and Peter Gottschalk (New York: Russell Sage Foundation, 1994), p. 11.

15. Kevin M. Murphy and Finis Welch, "Industrial Change and the Rising Importance of Skill," in *Uneven Tides: Rising Inequality in America,* edited by Sheldon Danziger and Peter Gottschalk (New York: Russell Sage Foundation, 1994), p. 114 [emphasis added].

16. Danziger and Gottschalk, "Introduction," p. 12.

17. John Bound and George Johnson, "Changes in the Structure of Wages During the 1980's: An Evaluation of Alternative Explanations," *American Economic Review*, 82:3 (June 1992), p. 371.

18. One influential study is Eli Berman, John Bound, and Zvi Griliches, "Changes in the Demand for Skilled Labor within U.S. Manufacturing: Evidence from the Annual Survey of Manufactures," *Quarterly Journal of Economics*, 109:2 (May 1994), 367–397. The study which has looked most closely at the use of computers themselves is Alan B. Krueger, "How Computers Have Changed the Wage Structure: Evidence from Microdata, 1984–1989," *Quarterly Journal of Economics*, 108:1 (February 1993): 33–60. Since Krueger's analysis is limited to changes over a short interval in the 1980s, it is difficult to judge the general implications of his findings that those working with computers, if other things are equal, tend to earn more than those who don't.

19. John Bound and George Johnson, "What Are the Causes of Rising Wage Inequality in the United States?" *Federal Reserve Bank of New York Economic Policy Review*, 1:1 (January 1995), p. 13.

20. Berman, Bound, and Griliches, "Changes in the Demand for Skilled Labor," p. 368.

21. Kevin M. Murphy and Finis Welch, "Industrial Change and the Rising Importance of Skill," p. 131.

22. Bound and Johnson, "What Are the Causes of Rising Wage Inequality," pp. 13–14.

23. Ibid., p. 14 [emphasis added].

24. See Howell, "Collapsing Wages and Rising Inequality," pp. 28ff.

25. See, for example, Lynn A. Karoly, "The Trend in Inequality Among Families, Individuals, and Workers in the United States: A Twenty-Five Year Perspective," in *Uneven Tides: Rising Inequality in America,* edited by Sheldon Danziger and Peter Gottschalk (New York: Russell Sage Foundation, 1994), Table II.B.2.; and Gittelman and Howell, "Changes in the Structure and Quality of Jobs in the United States," Table 3.

26. Howell, "Collapsing Wages and Rising Inequality"; "The Skills Myth"; and Howell and Susan S. Wieler, "Trends in Computerization, Skill Composition and Low Earnings: Implications for Education and Training Policy," unpublished paper, New School for Social Research, October 1994.

27. See Lawrence Mishel and Jared Bernstein, *The State of Working America, 1994–95* (Armonk, NY: M. E. Sharpe, 1994), Table 3.19.

28. Ibid., p. 143.

29. The flow of men earning bachelor's degrees from institutions of higher education in the United States were no higher in the late 1980s and early 1990s than they were in the late 1970s and early to mid-1980s. See U.S. Department of Education, National Center for Education Statistics, *Digest of Education Statistics, 1994*, October 1994, Table 254.

30. For two important analyses of this disjuncture between what's learned in school and what's required on the job, see Richard Edwards, "Individual Traits and Organizational Incentives: What Makes a 'Good' Worker?" *Journal of Human Resources*, 11:1 (Winter 1976), 51–68; and David R. Howell and Edward N. Wolff, "Trends in the Growth and Distribution of Skills in the U.S. Workplace, 1960–85," *Industrial and Labor Relations Review*, 44:3 (April 1991): 486–502.

31. U.S. Department of Labor, *Dictionary of Occupational Titles* (Washington, D.C.: U.S. Government Printing Office, various editions).

32. Howell and Wolff, "Trends in the Growth and Distribution of Skills in the U.S. Workplace, 1960–85," Table 5.

33. Susan Sheehan Wieler, "Can Technological Change Explain Increasing Inequality within Age, Schooling, and Gender Groups," paper presented to the Eastern Economics Association, March 1994. For further arguments pointed in this direction, see also Ruy A. Teixeira and Lawrence Mishel, "Whose Skills Shortage: Workers or Management?" *Issues in Science and Technology*, 9:4 (Summer 1993): 69–74.

34. See, for example, Peter Cappelli, "Are Skill Requirements Rising? Evidence from Production and Clerical Jobs," *Industrial and Labor Relations Review*, 46:3 (April 1993), Table 1.

35. Cappelli, "Are Skill Requirements Rising?", Table 2.

36. Jeffrey H. Keefe, "Numerically Controlled Machine Tools and Worker Skills," *Industrial and Labor Relations Review*, 44:3 (April 1991), p. 515. See also Cappelli, "Are Skill Requirements Rising?", p. 51; and Howell and Wieler, "Trends in Computerization," p. 8.

37. Cappelli, "Are Skill Requirements Rising?", Table 1.

38. Howell and Wieler, "Trends in Computerization," p. 11.

39. See, for example, the data and analysis in Robert J. Gordon, "The Jobless Recovery: Does It Signal a New Era of Productivity-led Growth?", *Brookings Papers on Economic Activity*, 1993(1): 271–316.

40. Steven J. Davis and Robert H. Topel, "Comment," *Brookings Papers on Economic Activity*, 1993:2, p. 219.

41. Robert Topel, "What Have We Learned from Empirical Studies of Unemployment and Turnover?", *American Economic Review*, 83:2 (May 1993), p. 110.

42. Howell and Wolff, "Trends in the Growth and Distribution of Skills," Table 2 and pp. 489–490.

43. Ibid., p. 500.

44. Wieler, "Can Technological Change Explain Increasing Inequality Within Age, Schooling, and Gender Groups," Table 3.

45. Steven G. Allen, "Technology and the Wage Structure," unpublished paper, North Carolina State University, October 1993, p. 22 [emphasis added]. Similarly, David A. Brauer and Susan Hickok find a positive relationship between their measures of technological change in wage changes for high-skill workers, but "a much weaker connection at lower skill levels." Brauer and Hickok, "Explaining the Growing Inequality in Wages across Skill Levels," *Federal Reserve Bank of New York Economic Policy Review*, 1:1 (January 1995), p. 69.

46. Keefe, "Numerically Controlled Machine Tools and Worker Skills," Table 5.

47. Howell, "The Skills Myth," p. 85.

48. Gittelman and Howell, "Changes in the Structure and Quality of Jobs in the United States," p. 430 [emphasis added].

49. Lawrence Mishel and Jared Bernstein, "Is the Technology Black Box Empty? An Empirical Examination of the Impact of Technology on Wage Inequality and the Employment Structure," unpublished paper, Economic Policy Institute, 1994.

50. Mishel and Bernstein, "Is the Technology Black Box Empty?", p. 37.

51. Frank Levy and Richard Murnane, "U.S. Earnings Levels and Earnings Inequality: A Review of Recent Trends and Proposed Explanations," *Journal of Economic Literature*, 30:3 (September 1992), p. 1373 [emphasis in original].

52. *Economic Report of the President, 1995*, Tables B-105, B-2; and *Survey of Current Business*, April 1995, Table C-5.

53. Vernon M. Briggs, Jr., "Mass Immigration, Free Trade, and the Forgotten American Worker," *Challenge*, May-June 1995, pp. 41–42.

54. For a popular book with many stories of individual workers feeling the brunt of global competition, see Donald L. Barlett and James B. Steele, *America: What Went Wrong?* (Kansas City: Andrews and McMeel, 1992).

55. *Economic Report of the President, 1995*, Table B-44.

56. Based on summaries of employment for full- and part-time employees by two-digit industry in *National Income and Product Accounts*, Table 6.4B.

57. Quoted in Michael Janofsky, "Trade Pact Casts Shadow for Garment Workers," *New York Times*, December 12, 1994, p. A14.

58. Data based on author's tabulations from Current Population Survey samples for March 1979 and March 1993. Earnings for 1979 are converted to 1993 dollars by the CPI-U-X1.

59. Aaron Bernstein, "The Global Economy," *Business Week*, August 10, 1992, pp. 48–49.

60. Adrian Wood, *North-South Trade, Employment and Inequality* (Oxford: Clarendon Press, 1994).

61. Others who have paid special attention to the trade-and-wages connection, particularly for the United States, include Edward E. Leamer, "Wage Effects of a U.S.-Mexico Free Trade Agreement," in *The Mexico-U.S. Free Trade Agreement*, edited by Peter M. Garber (Cambridge, MA: MIT Press, 1993), pp. 57–162; Kevin M. Murphy and Finis Welch, "The Role of International Trade in Wage Differentials," in *Workers and Their Wages: Changing Patterns in the United States*, edited by Marvin Kosters (Washington, D.C.: AEI Press, 1991), pp. 39–69; and George J. Borjas and Valerie A. Ramey, "Foreign Competition, Market Power, and Wage Inequality: Theory and Evidence," National Bureau of Economic Research Working Paper No. 4556, December 1993.

62. Wood, *North-South Trade*, p. 1.

63. Ibid., p. 4.

64. I first formulated some of these arguments in David M. Gordon, "The Global Economy: New Edifice or Crumbling Foundations?" *New Left Review*, No. 168 (March-April 1988), 24–64.

65. Nominal hourly wages by sector come from *Employment & Earnings*, June 1995, Table B-2. They are deflated by the CPI-U-X1 price index, from *Economic Report of the President, 1995*, Table B-61.

66. Bernstein, "The Global Economy," p. 48.

67. *Economic Report of the President, 1995*, Tables B-122, B-44, B-106.

68. Jeffrey D. Sachs and Howard J. Shatz, "Trade and Jobs in U.S. Manufacturing," *Brookings Papers on Economic Activity*, 1994:1, p. 29. Sachs and Shatz present the figure for the percent loss; the conversion to absolute employment losses is based on 1978 production-worker employment in manufacturing from U.S. Bureau of the Census, *Census of Manufactures* (Washington, D.C.: U.S. Government Printing Office, 1994), Vol. I, Table 1.

69. George J. Borjas, Richard B. Freeman, and Lawrence F. Katz, "On the Labor Market Effects of Immigration and Trade," in *Immigration and the Work Force: Economic Consequences*

for the United States and Source Areas, edited by George J. Borjas and Richard B. Freeman (Chicago: University of Chicago Press, 1992), Table 7.6.

For a similar estimate, based on different methodology, see Brauer and Hickok, "Explaining the Growing Inequality in Wages," Table 3, in which less than ten percent of the widening wage differential between high school graduates and college graduates is attributable to intensifying import competition.

70. More technically, the elasticity of relative wages with respect to relative labor supplies is derived from an equation in which there are two independent variables, relative labor supplies and a linear time trend. (Borjas, Freeman, and Katz, "Labor Market Effects of Immigration and Trade," note #18.) The authors could argue that the linear time trend proximately captures other influences such as declining union densities, but this is no substitute for more direct estimates.

71. A number of other studies indeed arrive at lower quantitative estimates of the effects of trade on wages. See, for example, Berman, Bound, and Griliches, "Changes in the Demand for Skilled Labor"; and Bound and Johnson, "Changes in the Structure of Wages in the 1980s."

72. Gary Burtless, "International Trade and the Rise in Earnings Inequality," *Journal of Economic Literature*, 33:2 (June 1995), pp. 813–814.

73. Richard B. Freeman, "Are Your Wages Set in Beijing?", *Journal of Economic Perspectives*, 9(3) (Summer 1995), p. 30.

74. Sachs and Shatz, "Trade and Jobs in U.S. Manufacturing," p. 44.

75. Robert Z. Lawrence, "Trade, Multinationals, and Labor," National Bureau of Economic Research Working Paper No. 4836, August 1994, Table 5.

76. Lawrence, "Trade, Multinationals, and Labor," Table 5.

77. Ibid., Table 5 and p. 25.

78. For an effort at a balanced assessment of impact of globalization which shares, in the end, my skepticism about the magnitudes of those effects, see Freeman, "Are Your Wages Set in Beijing?"

79. See, for example, Paul Krugman, *Peddling Prosperity* (New York: W.W. Norton, 1994) Ch. 10; and Krugman and Robert Z. Lawrence, "Trade, Jobs, and Wages," National Bureau of Economic Research Discussion Paper No. 4478, September 1993.

80. Richard B. Freeman, "Is Globalisation Impoverishing Low Skill American Workers?" Urban Institute, Session on Policy Responses to an International Labor Market, November 17, 1993, p. 2.

81. Kuttner, *The End of Laissez-Faire*, p. 24.

82. Krugman, *Peddling Prosperity*, p. 234.

83. Peter Passell, "An Immigration Puzzle," *New York Times*, September 6, 1994, p. D3.

84. Voting results cited in *Newsweek*, November 21, 1994, p. 57; and *Time*, November 21, 1994, p. 73.

85. David W. Moore, "Americans Feel Threatened by New Immigrants," *Gallup Poll Monthly*, July 1993, p. 10.

86. Ibid., p. 10.

87. Briggs, "Mass Immigration, Free Trade, and the Forgotten American Worker," pp. 43–44.

88. U.S. Immigration and Naturalization Service, *Statistical Yearbook of the Immigration and Naturalization Service, 1992* (Washington, D.C.: U.S. Government Printing Office, 1993), pp. 27–28.

89. Steven A. Holmes, "Surprising Rise in Immigration Stirs Up Debate," *New York Times*, August 30, 1995, p. A1.

90. George J. Borjas, "Assimilation and Changes in Cohort Quality Revisited: What Happened to Immigrant Earnings in the 1980s?" National Bureau of Economic Research Working Paper No.4866, September 1994, Table 2.

91. Borjas, Freeman, and Katz, "On the Labor Market Effects of Immigration and Trade," p. 238.

92. Ibid., p. 242. The authors only present, in their Table 7.8, the combined effects of trade and immigration; my estimate of immigration effects comes from multiplying their estimate of the combined effect of 42 percent from Table 7.8 by the relative proportion of immigration to changes in skill levels presented in Table 7.7.

93. Howell and Wolff, "Trends in the Growth and Distribution of Skills," p. 500.

94. Rachel M. Friedberg and Jennifer Hunt, "The Impact of Immigrants on Host Country Wages, Employment and Growth," *Journal of Economic Perspectives*, 9:2 (Spring 1995), p. 42.

95. Gregory DeFreitas, "Immigration, Inequality, and Policy Alternatives," Hofstra University, October 1995, p. 24.

96. See the essays in *How Labor Markets Work: Reflections on Theory and Practice*, edited by Bruce E. Kaufman, (Lexington, MA: Lexington Books, 1988).

97. One introduction to these more recent views is provided in a symposium of papers presented at the annual meetings of the American Economic Association in January 1995. See the trio of papers collected on "Unconventional Views of the Labor Market," *American Economic Review*, 85:2 (May 1995).

98. David Card and Alan B. Krueger, *Myth and Measurement: The New Economics of the Minimum Wage* (Princeton: Princeton University Press, 1995), p. 384.

99. Katherine S. Newman, *Declining Fortunes: The Withering of the American Dream* (New York: BasicBooks, 1993), p. 18.

Chapter 8

1. This account of those meetings is based on Leonard Silk and David Vogel, *Ethics and Profits: The Crisis of Confidence in American Business* (New York: Simon and Schuster, 1976).

2. Ibid., pp. 79, 70.

3. Ibid., p. 189.

4. Ibid., p. 76.

5. Douglas Fraser, letter of resignation from the Labor-Management Advisory Committee, July 19, 1978, circulated by the United Automobile Workers Union.

6. For definition and sources on this measure of the after-tax corporate rate of profit, see Samuel Bowles, David M. Gordon, and Thomas E. Weisskopf, "Business Ascendancy and Economic Impasse: A Structural Retrospective on Conservative Economics," *Journal of Economic Perspectives* 3(1) (Winter 1989), Data Appendix.

7. This argument is developed in detail in Samuel Bowles, David M. Gordon, and Thomas E. Weisskopf, *Beyond the Waste Land: A Democratic Alternative to Economic Decline* (Garden City, NY: Anchor Press/Doubleday, 1983), Chs. 4–6; and "Power and Profits: The Social Structure of Accumulation and the Profitability of the Postwar U.S. Economy," *Review of Radical Political Economics*, 18:1&2 (Spring & Summer 1986), 132–167.

8. Quoted in Jeremy Brecher, *Strike!* (San Francisco: Straight Arrow Books, 1972), pp. 266–67.

9. On the broader economic background to this offensive, see Bowles, Gordon, and Weisskopf, *Beyond the Waste Land*, Chapters 4–5.

10. For accounts of the anti-union drive, see Richard B. Freeman and James L. Medoff, *What Do Unions Do?* (New York: Basic Books, 1984), Ch. 15; and Michael Goldfield, *The Decline of Organized Labor in the United States* (Chicago: University of Chicago Press, 1987), Part 3.

11. Michael L. Wachter and William H. Carter, "Norm Shifts in Union Wages: Will 1989 Be a Replay of 1969?" *Brookings Papers on Economic Activity*, 1989:2, Table 6.

12. Ibid., pp. 251, 252.

13. From a blurb by Financial Management Associates, cited in Goldfield, *The Decline of Organized Labor*, p. 193.

14. See Thomas A. Kochan, Harry C. Katz, and Robert B. McKersie, *The Transformation of American Industrial Relations* (Ithaca, NY: Cornell ILR Press, 1994), Chapter 3.

15. For a summary, see Ibid., Chapter 4.

16. Ibid., p. 79.

17. See Audrey Freedman, *Managing Labor Relations* (New York: The Conference Board, 1979); and *The New Look in Wage Policy and Employee Relations* (New York: The Conference Board, 1985).

18. Freedman, *The New Look in Wage Policy*, pp. 1–14 and p. iv.

19. For an analysis of the Conference Board data, see Thomas A. Kochan, Robert B. McKersie, and John Chalykoff, "Corporate Strategy, Workplace Innovation, and Union Members," *Industrial and Labor Relations Review*, 39:3 (July 1986), 487–501; and summary in Kochan, Katz, and McKersie, *The Transformation of American Labor Relations*, pp. 62–64.

20. Kochan, Katz, and McKersie, *The Transformation of American Labor Relations*, p. 64.

21. Freedman, *The New Look in Wage Policy*, pp. 13–14.

22. See Wachter and Carter, "Norm Shifts in Union Wages," Table 5.

23. See especially Wachter and Carter, Tables 5,6.

24. Daniel J. B. Mitchell, "Shifting Norms in Wage Determination," *Brookings Papers on Economic Activity*, 1985:2, p. 589.

25. For one account of this intensified effort, see David Vogel, *Fluctuating Fortunes: The Political Power of Business in America* (New York: Basic Books, 1989), especially Chapter 7.

26. Vogel, *Fluctuating Fortunes*, p. 154.

27. Fraser, July 1978 letter.

28. Thomas Ferguson and Joel Rogers, *Right Turn: The Decline of the Democrats and the Future of American Politics* (New York: Hill and Wang, 1986), Table 4.2.

29. See Mitchell, "Shifting Norms in Wage Determination."

30. Wachter and Carter, "Norm Shifts in Union Wages," especially Tables 6, 7.

31. For a careful study through early 1995, see Dean Baker, "Trends in Corporate Profitability: Getting More for Less?", unpublished paper, Economic Policy Institute, July 31, 1995.

32. Aaron Bernstein, "The Wage Squeeze," *Business Week*, July 17, 1995, p. 56.

33. In Figure 8.1 and in the discussion in the text, the nominal value of the federal minimum wage is taken from the *Statistical Abstract*, 1993, Table 675, and is deflated by the CPI-U-X1 from *Economic Report of the President, 1995*, Table B-61.

34. See, for example, Silk and Vogel, *Ethics and Profits*, on the initial impetus for this intensified political effort; and Vogel, *Fluctuating Fortunes*.

35. The average production-worker's wage in manufacturing is taken from U.S. Bureau of Labor Statistics, *Employment and Earnings, United States, 1909–78*, Bulletin 1312–11 (July 1979); and *Economic Report of the President, 1995*, Table B-45.

36. Bob Herbert, "City Job, Minimum Wage," *New York Times*, July 28, 1995, p. A27.

37. Richard B. Freeman and Lawrence F. Katz, "Rising Wage Inequality: The United States vs. Other Advanced Countries," in *Working Under Different Rules*, edited by Richard B. Freeman (New York: Russell Sage, 1994), p. 49.

38. Based on the author's tabulations from the outgoing-rotation sample of the Current Population Survey for March 1993.

39. Eleanor Clift and Rich Thomas, "It's Sacred—But Is It Smart?", *Newsweek*, April 17, 1989, p. 24 [emphasis added].

40. Lawrence Mishel and Jared Bernstein, *The State of Working America 1994–95* (Armonk, NY: M.E. Sharpe, 1994), Table 3.44.

41. David Card and Alan B. Krueger, *Myth and Measurement: The New Economics of the Minimum Wage* (Princeton: Princeton University Press, 1995), pp. 14, 165–166.

42. Based on tabulations from the March 1993 CPS outgoing rotation sample for private nonfarm wage-and-salary employees. In 1993, 4.3 percent of that group earned at or below $4.25, the nominal level of the minimum wage, and 18.9 percent earned at or below $5.66, the real value (in 1993 dollars) of the 1979 minimum wage. For the ripple effect, I take Card and Krueger's estimate that in 1989–91 it affected those earning in the range from $4.25 to $4.50—or up to 5.9 percent above the level of the minimum wage itself. If we apply this assumption to the decline from 1979, this would suggest that the wages of those earning up to 5.9 percent above the 1979 minimum wage (in 1993 dollars), or up to $6.00, would also be likely to have been negatively affected by its subsequent decline. In 1993, 23.5 percent of private nonfarm wage-and-salary employees earned below $6.00 (in 1993 dollars).

43. Card and Krueger, *Myth and Measurement*, p. 277.

44. Based on author's tabulations from March 1993 outgoing rotation sample from the Current Population Survey.

45. See Card and Krueger, *Myth and Measurement*, Table 9.1; and Mishel and Bernstein, *The State of Working America, 1994–95*, Table 3.45.

46. Families and Work Institute, *Women: The New Providers* (New York: Families and Work Institute, May 1995), Table 9.

47. Herbert, "City Job, Minimum Wage," p. A27.

48. Card and Krueger, *Myth and Measurement*, p. 297.

49. John DiNardo, Nicole M. Fortin, and Thomas Lemieux, "Labor Market Institutions and the Distribution of Wages, 1973–1992: A Semiparametric Approach," unpublished paper, University of California at Irvine, March 1994.

50. Ibid., Tables 3, 4.

51. Mishel and Bernstein, *The State of Working America, 1994–95*, Table 3.46.

52. Ibid., p. 178.

53. Quoted in Don Nichols, "The Management Revolution and Loss of Union Clout," *Management Review*, February 1988, p. 26.

54. On the union wage premium, see Richard B. Freeman and James L. Medoff, *What Do Unions Do?* (New York: Basic Books, 1984), Chapter 3; and H. Gregg Lewis, *Union Relative Wage Effects: A Survey* (Chicago: University of Chicago Press, 1986).

55. For documentation and sources for estimates of unionized workers as percent of nonfarm employment, see Bowles, Gordon, and Weisskopf, "Business Ascendancy and Economic Impasse," Data Appendix.

56. See tabulations in DiNardo, Fortin, and Lemieux, "Labor Market Institutions and the Distribution of Wages," Table 2.

57. DiNardo, Fortin, and Lemieux, "Labor Market Institutions and the Distribution of Wages," Table 2.

58. See, for example, Mitchell, "Shifting Norms in Wage Determination."

59. Linda A. Bell, "Union Concessions in the 1980s," *Federal Reserve Bank of New York Quarterly Review*, Summer 1990, p. 46.

60. Richard B. Freeman, "How Much Has De-Unionization Contributed to the Rise in Male Earnings Inequality?", in *Uneven Tides: Rising Inequality in America*, edited by Sheldon Danziger and Peter Gottschalk (New York: Russell Sage, 1994), pp. 133–163.

61. Ibid., Table 4.6.

62. See David Card, "The Effect of Unions on the Distribution of Wages: Redistribution or Relabelling?", National Bureau of Economic Research, Working Paper No. 4195, October 1992; and DiNardo, Fortin, and Lemieux, "Labor Market Institutions and the Distribution of Wages."

63. Mishel and Bernstein, *The State of Working America, 1994–95*, p. 170.

64. Daniel J. B. Mitchell, "Wage Pressures and Labor Shortages: The 1960s and 1980s," *Brookings Papers on Economic Activity*, 1989:2, Table 14.

65. Based on author's regressions for private nonfarm wage-and-salary employees in the bottom 80 percent of the wage distribution. The dependent variable is the hourly wage in 1993 dollars. Control variables include the standard demographic variables, part-time status, education, and experience.

66. Freeman and Katz, "Rising Wage Inequality," p. 48.

67. Card, "The Effect of Unions on the Distribution of Wages," p. 40.

68. Bernstein, "The Wage Squeeze," p. 56.

69. Freeman, "How Much Has De-Unionization Contributed to Earnings Inequality?", p. 159.

70. See very helpful discussion on this trend in Phillip Mattera, *Prosperity Lost* (New York: Addison-Wesley, 1990), Ch. 5.

71. Quoted in "Where Will the Jobs Come From?" *Fortune*, October 19, 1992, p. 59.

72. Lance Morrow, "The Temping of America," *Time*, March 29, 1993, pp. 40–41.

73. Janice Castro, "Disposable Workers," *Time*, March 29, 1993, pp. 43–44.

74. Mishel and Bernstein, *The State of Working America, 1994–95*, Table 4.12.

75. Based on author's regressions for private nonfarm wage-and-salary employees in the bottom 80 percent of the wage distribution. The dependent variable is the hourly wage in 1993 dollars. Control variables include the standard demographic variables, union membership, education, and experience.

76. Estimate of 1.7 million from Mishel and Bernstein, *The State of Working America, 1994–95*, Table 4.24.

77. Castro, "Disposable Workers," p. 43.

78. Mishel and Bernstein, *The State of Working America, 1994–95*, Table 4.24.

79. Study citation and quote are both from Mattera, *Prosperity Lost*, pp. 87–88.

80. Richard S. Belous, "How Human Resource Systems Adjust to the Shift Toward Contingent Workers," *Monthly Labor Review*, March 1989, 7–12.

81. Belous, *Ibid.*, p. 10.

82. Castro, "Disposable Workers," p. 44.

83. U.S. Bureau of Labor Statistics, "New Data on Contingent and Alternative Employment Examined by BLS," USDL Release 95–318, August 17, 1995.

84. If workers expected to leave their jobs for personal reasons, such as returning to school, the job was still defined as contingent "if they would continue working at that job were it not for that personal reason" but they did not expect it to last beyond one year. In this way, the survey usefully focuses on the character of the job, not the personal situation of the employee.

85. *Employment and Earnings*, March 1995, Table A-20.

86. This estimate is derived from the survey's definition #3, which drops the condition that "contingent" workers should have been on their present job for one year or less. The total for estimate #3 is reduced by the total number of farm and government contingent workers and adjusted to remove the self-employed.

87. I take the total number of part-time contingent employees already included in the first row and estimate those who are part-time for economic reasons by multiplying this number by the percent of contingent workers who would "prefer a noncontingent arrangement"—the closest equivalent to the voluntary/involuntary split we have in the BLS contingent employment survey. I then subtract this group from total (private nonfarm wage-and-salary) part-time workers for economic reasons in order to avoid double-counting.

88. This estimate is derived by taking the total number in these "alternative" arrangements who are *not* already included as "contingent" employees, in order to avoid double-counting, and then multiplying the remaining group by the percentage in that category who would prefer a "traditional" employment arrangement. There may be some double-counting between this group and those involuntary part-time noncontingent workers included in the second row

of the table, but the numbers in this category are small enough that the total is not likely to be significantly affected.

89. I assume that four-fifths of the emergence of disposable employment occurred between 1979 and 1995, roughly the rate at which temporary-help employment has expanded. And I assume that the wage penalty for disposable employees was 23.6 percent, the estimate presented above from my 1993 regression estimates for involuntary part-time employees [see above, note #75].

90. For further detail on the conditions of contingent workers, see Roberta Spalter-Roth and Heidi Hartmann, "Contingent Work: Its Consequences for Economic Well-Being, the Gendered Division of Labor, and the Welfare State," in *Contingent Work: From Entitlement to Privilege,* edited by Kathleen Barker and Kathleen Christensen (forthcoming, 1996).

91. Quoted in Castro, "Disposable Workers," p. 46.

92. DiNardo, Fortin, and Lemieux, "Labor Market Institutions and the Distribution of Wages," Tables 3, 6.

93. Ibid., pp. 36–37.

94. John DiNardo and Thomas Lemieux, "Diverging Male Wage Inequality in the United States and Canada, 1981–1988: Do Unions Explain the Difference?", unpublished paper, University of California at Irvine, 1994.

95. Ibid., p. 33.

96. The analysis is based on a time series regression for 1952 through 1989. The dependent variable is the rate of change of real (before-tax) production workers' wages in the private nonfarm sector. The equation has a first-order moving-average correction for serial correlation. The minimum wage and union density measures are as defined in this chapter. The supervisory compensation index is a measure of the share of nonproduction and supervisory employees' compensation in total employee compensation in the nonfarm business sector. The R&D and technology measures are explained and documented in David M. Gordon, "What Makes Epochs? A Comparative Analysis of Technological and Social Explanations of Long Economic Swings," in *Technological and Social Factors in Long-Term Fluctuations,* edited by R. Goodwin *et al.* (New York: Springer-Verlag, 1989), pp. 267–304. The import competition measure is the adjusted share of imports as explained and documented in Bowles, Gordon, and Weisskopf, "Business Ascendancy and Economic Impasse," Data Appendix.

97. Bowles, Gordon, and Weisskopf, "Business Ascendancy and Economic Impasse."

98. Mattera, *Prosperity Lost,* p. 96.

99. BLS, "New Data on Contingent and Alternative Employment," Table 4. I use the industrial distribution for their estimate #3, which is the estimate on which I build in Table 8.2.

100. Richard B. Freeman, "Is Globalisation Impoverishing Low Skill American Workers?" Urban Institute, Session on Policy Responses to an International Labor Market, November 17, 1993, p. 20.

101. Based on author's tabulations from March 1993 outgoing rotation sample of the Current Population Survey.

102. BLS, "New Data on Contingent and Alternative Employment," Tables 3,4.

103. More formally, within manufacturing it appears that changes in import exposure and changes in union density were insignificantly associated during the 1980s, with a simple correlation coefficient of –0.01. Union shares by industry based on author's tabulations from the March 1983 and March 1993 outgoing rotation samples of the Current Population Survey. Change in imports divided by shipments between 1979 and 1985—with the lag in imports introduced because it is being considered as potentially exogenous to changes in union density—from Jane Sneddon Little, "Exchange Rates and Structural Change in U.S. Manufacturing Employment," *New England Economic Review,* March/April 1989, Table 5.

104. Richard B. Freeman and Lawrence F. Katz, "Introduction and Summary," in *Differences and Changes in Wage Structures,* edited by Freeman and Katz (Chicago: University of Chicago Press, 1995), Table 2.

105. Freeman, "How Much Has De-Unionization Contributed to the Rise in Male Earnings Inequality?", pp. 158–159.

106. "A Comparison of Changes in the Structure of Wages in Four OECD Countries," in *Differences and Changes in Wage Structures,* edited by Richard B. Freeman and Lawrence F. Katz (Chicago: University of Chicago Press, 1995), pp. 25–65.

107. Katharine G. Abraham and Susan N. Houseman, "Earnings Inequality in Germany," in *Differences and Changes in Wage Structures,* edited by Richard B. Freeman and Lawrence F. Katz (Chicago: University of Chicago Press, 1995), pp. 371–403.

108. Francine D. Blau and Lawrence M. Kahn support this comparative interpretation in their analysis of patterns of gender inequality across the advanced countries. Gender earnings inequality is higher in the United States than in most other countries. See "The Gender Earnings Gap: Some International Evidence," in *Differences and Changes in Wage Structures,* Richard B. Freeman and Lawrence F. Katz (Chicago: University of Chicago Press, 1995), pp. 105–144. Blau and Kahn find that differences in labor market institutions are crucial in explaining these patterns. They note in particular that the structure of wage-setting institutions in the United States imposes a much higher relative penalty on those toward the bottom of the earnings distribution, where disproportionate numbers of female workers are lodged, than is true in other economies.

109. This represents a simplified version, for the purposes of illustration in this book, of the time-series analysis in David M. Gordon, "Who Bosses Whom? The Intensity of Supervision and the Discipline of Labor," *American Economic Review,* 80:2 (May 1990); and a longer, fuller version available as Working Paper No. 16, New School for Social Research, January 1991.

110. Thomas E. Weisskopf, Samuel Bowles, and David M. Gordon, "Hearts and Minds: A Social Model of U.S. Productivity Growth," *Brookings Papers on Economic Activity,* 1983:2, 381–441.

111. The analysis is based on a time series regression for 1952 through 1989. The dependent variable is the rate of change of the percentage of nonproduction and supervisory workers in total private nonfarm employment. The equation has a first-order moving-average correction for serial correlation. The cyclical effect is captured by the rate of change of an index of capacity utilization in the nonfarm business sector (see documentation in Bowles, Gordon, and Weisskopf, "Business Ascendancy and Economic Impasse," Data Appendix). The capital intensity effect is measured by the rate of change of the ratio of the real nonfinancial corporate capital stock to total nonfarm business production-worker employment. The supervisory-wage effect is represented by the rate of change of the real hourly wage for nonproduction and supervisory employees in the nonfarm business sector. The cost of job loss measures the "employer control" effect. (These three variables are all documented in Gordon, "Who Bosses Whom?", Data Appendix.) The worker motivation hypothesis is tested by the rate of change of real spendable hourly earnings, as documented in Chapter 1 of this book.

112. More precisely, the F-test for the exclusion of those variables from the equation is statistically significant at less than 1%.

113. On the trends and implications of the decline in the cost of job loss during this period, see Bowles, Gordon, and Weisskopf, *Beyond the Waste Land,* Chapters 4, 6.

114. Richard E. Caves and Matthew B. Krepps, "Fat: The Displacement of Nonproduction Workers from U.S. Manufacturing Industries," *Brookings Papers on Economic Activity—Microeconomics,* 1993:2, 227–273.

115. I use the same modified measure of import competition as used in the simple time-series wage analysis reviewed earlier in this chapter; see Bowles, Gordon, and Weisskopf, "Business Ascendancy and Economic Impasse," Data Appendix. I used a piece-wise regression term to test for differential impact during the 1980s.

116. See David M. Gordon, "Bosses of Different Stripes: Monitoring and Supervision across the Advanced Economies," *American Economic Review,* 84:2 (May 1994), 375–379. A

more detailed version with Data Appendix is available under the same title as Working Paper No. 46, Department of Economics, New School for Social Research, February 1994.

117. See the longer working-paper version of Gordon, "Bosses of Different Stripes" for a report of these tests. Data are not available to test directly the effect of the percent of a country's corporations that are multinational, so the indirect country-size and trade involvement measures must serve as proxies.

Chapter 9

1. Aaron Bernstein, "The Wage Squeeze," *Business Week*, July 17, 1995.

2. Ibid., pp. 57, 55.

3. Ibid., p. 62.

4. James Q. Wilson, "Capitalism and Morality," *The Public Interest*, Fall 1995, p. 59.

5. Rosabeth Moss Kanter, "A Key Fit: Employability Security," *Boston Globe*, March 13, 1994, p. 75.

6. Wilson, "Capitalism and Morality," p. 60.

7. Quoted in John Cassidy, "Who Killed the Middle Class?" *The New Yorker*, October 16, 1995, p. 113.

8. Aaron Bernstein, "Why America Needs Unions But Not the Kind It Has Now," *Business Week*, May 23, 1994, p. 71.

9. Quoted in Bernstein, "The Wage Squeeze," p. 62.

10. *Employment and Earnings*, January 1995, Table B-2.

11. For a comparison of minimum wage standards across countries, see David Card and Alan B. Krueger, *Myth and Measurement: The New Economics of the Minimum Wage* (Princeton: Princeton University Press, 1995), Table 8.1.

12. Ibid., *passim*.

13. Card and Krueger are careful not to generalize beyond the immediate experiences they have studied. But their analysis and results lead one to feel reasonably confident that something like a four-year increase to $6.50 remains within bounds of that experience.

14. See Card and Krueger, *Myth and Measurement*, pp. 394–395 for a discussion of this issue. As also noted in Chapter 1, others may worry about inflationary biases in the CPI as currently constructed. But that suggests we ought to consider possible revisions in the CPI, not that we shouldn't peg the minimum wage to it.

15. Ibid., p. 272.

16. See, for example, highly critical reviews by Daniel S. Hamermesh and by Finis Welch in a symposium in *Industrial and Labor Relations Review*, 48:4 (July 1995), 827–849.

17. Richard B. Freeman, "Comment" in "Review Symposium," *Industrial and Labor Relations Review*, 48:4 (July 1995), p. 834.

18. For pieces of this debate, see Richard B. Freeman and James L. Medoff, *What Do Unions Do?* (New York: Basic Books, 1984); William T. Dickens and Jonathan S. Leonard, "Accounting for the Decline in Union Membership, 1950–1980," *Industrial and Labor Relations Review*, 38(2) (April 1985), 323–334; and Henry S. Farber and Allan B. Krueger, "Union Membership in the United States": The Decline Continues," in Bruce E. Kaufman and Morris M. Kleiner, eds., *Employee Representation: Alternatives and Future Directions* (Madison, WI: Industrial Relations Research Association, 1993), 105–134.

19. Richard Freeman and Joel Rogers, "Worker Representation and Participation Survey: First Report of Findings," December 5, 1994.

20. This estimate comes from multiplying 32 percent times total private-sector employment in 1994 (from *Economic Report of the President, 1994*, Table B-44*).

21. See, for example, discussions in Michael Goldfield, *The Decline of Organized Labor in the United States* (Chicago: University of Chicago Press, 1987), Part III; and Paul C. Weiler,

Governing the Workplace: The Future of Labor and Employment Law (Cambridge, MA: Harvard University Press, 1990), Chapter 3.

22. Commission on the Future of Worker-Management Relations, *Report and Recommendations*, U.S. Departments of Labor and Commerce, December 1994, p. 19.

23. Ibid., p. 18.

24. Bernstein, "Why America Needs Unions," p. 71.

25. Commission on the Future of Worker-Management Relations, *Report and Recommendations*, p. 18.

26. For brief reviews of the Canadian system, its variations, and its advantages, see Gary N. Chaison and Joseph B. Rose, "The Canadian Perspective on Workers' Rights to Form a Union and Bargain Collectively"; and Peter G. Bruce, "On the Status of Workers' Rights to Organize in the United States and Canada," in *Restoring the Promise of American Labor Law*, edited by Sheldon Friedman *et al.* (Ithaca, NY: ILR Press, 1994), pp. 241–249 and 273–284 respectively.

27. Commission on the Future of Worker-Management Relations, *Report and Recommendations*, pp. 18–20. See also similar comments in *Governing the Workplace: The Future of Labor and Employment Law*, edited by Paul C. Weiler (Cambridge, MA: Harvard University Press, 1990), pp. 253ff.

28. See some of the poll results reported in Alan Farnham, "The Trust Gap," *Fortune*, December 4, 1989.

29. See Joel Rogers and Wolfgang Streeck, "Workplace Representation Overseas: The Works Councils Story," in *Working Under Different Rules*, edited by Richard B. Freeman (New York: Russell Sage, 1994), 97–156; and Rogers and Streeck, in *Works Councils: Consultation, Representation, and Cooperation in Industrial Relations* (Chicago: University of Chicago Press, 1996). See also Richard B. Freeman and Joel Rogers, "Who Speaks for Us? Employee Representation in a Nonunion Labor Market," in *Employee Representation: Alternatives and Future Directions*, edited by Bruce E. Kaufman and Morris M. Kleiner (Madison, WI: Industrial Relations Research Association, 1993), 13–80.

30. Rogers and Streeck, "Workplace Representation Overseas," p. 97.

31. The term "employee participation council" is close to that suggested by Weiler, *Governing the Workplace*, pp. 284ff., and this discussion draws substantially on his formulations, which cover in detail some of the administrative and legal requirements for such councils.

32. For considerable further detail see Freeman and Rogers, "Who Speaks for Us?"

33. Freeman and Rogers, "Worker Representation and Participation Survey," p. 9.

34. Commission on the Future of Worker-Management Relations, *Report and Recommendations*, p. 64.

35. Freeman and Rogers, "Worker Representation and Participation Survey," p. 15.

36. On the historical background to this concern, see, for example, David Brody, "Section 8(a)(2) and the Origins of the Wagner Act," in *Restoring the Promise of American Labor Law*, edited by Sheldon Friedman *et al.* (Ithaca, NY: ILR Press, 1994), pp. 29–44.

37. Clear Congressional directives could thus help clear up the current legal morass about whether employee participation groups are in violation of the "company unions" ban or not.

38. Commission on the Future of Worker-Management Relations, *Report and Recommendations*, p. 13 [emphasis in original].

39. Juliet Schor, "A Sustainable Economy for the 21st Century," *Open Magazine Pamphlet Series*, Pamphlet #31, p. 9.

40. Peter T. Kilborn, "U.S. Unions Back Shorter Week, But Employers Seem Reluctant," *New York Times*, November 22, 1993, p. A6.

41. For mandated vacation times in other countries, see Lawrence Mishel and Jared Bernstein, *The State of Working America, 1994–95* (Armonk, NY: M.E. Sharpe, 1994), Table 8.18.

42. Linda Bell and Richard Freeman, "Why Do Americans and Germans Work Different Hours?" National Bureau of Economic Research, Working Paper No. 4808, July 1994, Table 2.

43. Ibid., pp. 21–24 and Tables 11–12.

44. This argument is developed effectively by David I. Levine, "Public Policy Implications of Imperfections in the Market for Worker Participation," *Economic and Industrial Democracy*, 13:3 (May 1992), 184–206.

45. Riegle Community Development and Regulatory Improvement Act of 1994, Public Law 103–325, 103rd Congress, September 23, 1994.

46. Southern Finance Project, "Reinvestment Reform in an Era of Financial Change," Philomont, VA, April 1995.

47. Levine, "Public Policy Implications of Imperfections in the Market for Worker Participation," p. 198.

48. See Lisa M. Lynch, "Payoffs to Alternative Training Strategies at Work," in *Working Under Different Rules*, edited by Richard B. Freeman (New York: Russell Sage, 1994), 63–96; and Lisa M. Lynch, ed., *Training and the Private Sector: International Comparisons* (Chicago: University of Chicago Press, 1994).

49. See Peter B. Doeringer *et al.*, *Turbulence in the American Workplace* (New York: Oxford University Press, 1991), especially Chapters 9–10.

50. Commission on the Future of Worker-Management Relations, "Employee Participation and Labor-Management Cooperation in American Workplaces," *Challenge*, September-October 1995, p. 45.

51. Bill Clinton and Al Gore, *Putting People First: How We Can All Change America* (New York: Times Books, 1992), p. 127.

52. Steven Greenhouse, "Labor Secretary to Urge Clinton to Propose Minimum Wage Rise," *New York Times*, October 13, 1993, p. A18.

53. Steven Greenhouse, "Labor Official Retreats on Higher Minimum Wage," *New York Times*, October 30, 1993, p. 9.

54. "Clinton Seeks to Interest Congress in Wage Proposal," *Wall Street Journal*, January 26, 1995, p. A2.

55. On the paramount importance of deficit reduction, see Bob Woodward, *The Agenda: Inside the Clinton White House* (New York: Simon and Schuster, 1994).

56. On the history of this growing political influence in the 1970s and 1980s, see, for example, Thomas Ferguson and Joel Rogers, *Right Turn: The Decline of the Democrats and the Future of American Politics* (New York: Hill and Wang, 1986).

57. Ferguson and Rogers, *Right Turn*, p. 219.

58. Kevin Phillips, *Arrogant Capital: Washington, Wall Street, and the Frustration of American Politics* (Boston: Little, Brown, 1994), pp. 43–44 [emphasis in the original].

59. Ferguson and Rogers, *Right Turn*, p. 219.

60. R. W. Apple Jr., "Poll Shows Disenchantment with Politicians and Politics," *New York Times*, August 12, 1995, pp. 1, 8.

61. See, for example, Roy J. Adams, *Industrial Relations Under Liberal Democracy: North America in Comparative Perspective* (Columbia, SC: University of South Carolina Press, 1995), especially Chapter 7.

62. Adams, *Industrial Relations Under Liberal Democracy*, pp. 162, 163.

63. Philip Roth, *Portnoy's Complaint* (New York: Random House, 1969), p. 274.

BIBLIOGRAPHY

Abraham, Katharine G., "The Consumer Price Index: What Does It Measure?" *Challenge*, May–June 1995: 59–62.

Abraham, Katharine G. and Susan N. Houseman, "Earnings Inequality in Germany," in *Differences and Changes in Wage Structures*, edited by Richard B. Freeman and Lawrence F. Katz. Chicago: University of Chicago Press, 1995. Pp. 371–403.

Adams, Roy J., *Industrial Relations Under Liberal Democracy: North America in Comparative Perspective*. Columbia, SC: University of South Carolina Press, 1995.

AFL-CIO Research Department, "Trashing the CPI," Report No. 83, June 1995.

"A 4.3% Gain for Workers," *New York Times*, January 29, 1992.

"The Ailing Economy: Diagnoses and Prescriptions," *New York Times*, April 4, 1982.

Allen, Steven G., "Technology and the Wage Structure," unpublished paper, North Carolina State University, October 1993.

Amacom Briefings & Surveys, *Responsible Reductions in Force: An American Management Association Research Report on Downsizing and Outplacement*. New York: American Management Association, 1987.

American Management Association, "1994 AMA Survey on Downsizing," News Release, November 1994.

Appelbaum, Eileen and Rosemary Batt, *The New American Workplace: Transforming Work Systems in the United States*. Ithaca, NY: Cornell University ILR Press, 1994.

Apple, R.W. Jr., "Poll Shows Disenchantment with Politicians and Politics," *New York Times*, August 12, 1995.

Atkinson, Alice M., "Stress Levels of Family Day Care Providers, Mothers Employed Outside the Home, and Mothers at Home," *Journal of Marriage and the Family* 54(2) (May 1992): 379–386.

Auletta, Ken, *The Underclass*. New York: Random House, 1982.

Baily, Martin Neil, Gary Burtless, and Robert E. Litan, *Growth with Equity: Economic Policymaking for the Next Century*. Washington, D.C.: The Brookings Institution, 1993.

Baker, Dean, "Trends in Corporate Profitability: Getting More for Less?", unpublished paper, Economic Policy Institute, July 31, 1995.

Barlett, Donald L. and James B. Steele, *America: What Went Wrong?* Kansas City: Andrews and McMeel, 1992.

Baumol, William J., Sue A. B. Blackman, and Edward N. Wolff, *Productivity and American Leadership: The Long View*. Cambridge, MA: MIT Press, 1989.

Bean, Charles R., "European Unemployment: A Survey," *Journal of Economic Literature* 32(2) (June 1994): 573–619.

Bearak, Barry, "Cat on Strike: The Waning Power of Unions," *Los Angeles Times*, May 14–18, 1995.

Becker, Gary, *Human Capital.* Chicago: National Bureau of Economic Research, 1975. 2nd edition.

Bell, Linda A., "Union Concessions in the 1980s," *Federal Reserve Bank of New York Quarterly Review,* Summer 1990.

Bell, Linda A. and Richard Freeman, "Why Do Americans and Germans Work Different Hours?" National Bureau of Economic Research, Working Paper No. 4808, July 1994.

Belous, Richard S., "How Human Resource Systems Adjust to the Shift Toward Contingent Workers," *Monthly Labor Review,* March 1989: 7–12.

Berman, Eli, John Bound, and Zvi Griliches, "Changes in the Demand for Skilled Labor within U.S. Manufacturing: Evidence from the Annual Survey of Manufactures," *Quarterly Journal of Economics* 109(2) (May 1994): 367–397.

Bernstein, Aaron, "The Global Economy," *Business Week,* August 10, 1992.

———, "Why America Needs Unions But Not the Kind It Has Now," *Business Week,* May 23, 1994.

———, "The Wage Squeeze," *Business Week,* July 17, 1995.

Bhagwati, Jagdish, "Trade and Wages: Choosing Among Alternative Explanations," *Federal Reserve Bank of New York Economic Policy Review* 1(1), January 1995: 42–47.

Blackburn, McKinley L., David E. Bloom, and Richard B. Freeman, "The Declining Economic Position of Less Skilled American Men," in *A Future of Lousy Jobs? The Changing Structure of U.S. Wages,* edited by Gary Burtless. Washington, D.C.: The Brookings Institution, 1990. Pp. 31–76.

Blau, Francine D. and Lawrence M. Kahn, "The Gender Earnings Gap: Some International Evidence," in *Differences and Changes in Wage Structures,* edited by Richard B. Freeman and Lawrence F. Katz. Chicago: University of Chicago Press, 1995. Pp. 105–144.

———, "International Differences in Male Wage Inequality: Institutions versus Market Forces," National Bureau of Economic Research, Working Paper No. 4678, March 1994.

Blinder, Alan S., "Introduction," in *Paying for Productivity: A Look at the Evidence,* edited by Alan S. Blinder. Washington, D.C.: Brookings Institution, 1990. Pp.1–13.

Bluestone, Barry and Irving Bluestone, *Negotiating the Future: A Labor Perspective on American Business.* New York: BasicBooks, 1992.

Bok, Derek, *The Cost of Talent: How Executives and Professionals Are Paid and How It Affects America.* New York: The Free Press, 1993.

"A Boom Ahead in Company Profits," *Fortune,* April 6, 1992.

Borjas, George J., "Assimilation and Changes in Cohort Quality Revisited: What Happened to Immigrant Earnings in the 1980s?" National Bureau of Economic Research, Working Paper No.4866, September 1994.

Borjas, George J., Richard B. Freeman, and Lawrence F. Katz, "On the Labor Market Effects of Immigration and Trade," in *Immigration and the Work Force: Economic Consequences for the United States and Source Areas,* edited by George J. Borjas and Richard B. Freeman. Chicago: University of Chicago Press, 1992. Pp. 213–244.

Borjas, George J. and Valerie A. Ramey, "Foreign Competition, Market Power, and Wage Inequality: Theory and Evidence," National Bureau of Economic Research, Working Paper No. 4556, December 1993.

Boroughs, Don L. *et al.,* "Love and Money," *U.S. News & World Report,* October 19, 1992.

Bound, John and Richard B. Freeman, "What Went Wrong? The Erosion of the Relative Earnings and Employment of Young Black Men in the 1980s," *Quarterly Journal of Economics* 107(1) (February 1992): 201–232.

Bound, John and George Johnson, "Changes in the Structure of Wages During the 1980's: An Evaluation of Alternative Explanations," *American Economic Review* 82(3) (June 1992): 371–392.

————, "What Are the Causes of Rising Wage Inequality in the United States?" *Federal Reserve Bank of New York Economic Policy Review* 1(1) (January 1995): 9–17.

Bowles, Samuel, "The Production Process in a Competitive Economy: Walrasian, Neo-Hobbesian, and Marxian Models," *American Economic Review* 75(1)(March 1985): 16–36.

Bowles, Samuel, David M. Gordon, and Thomas E. Weisskopf, *Beyond the Waste Land: A Democratic Alternative to Economic Decline.* Garden City, NJ: Anchor Press/Doubleday, 1983.

————, "Power and Profits: The Social Structure of Accumulation and the Profitability of the Postwar U.S. Economy," *Review of Radical Political Economics* 18(1&2) (Spring & Summer 1986): 132–167.

————, "Business Ascendancy and Economic Impasse: A Structural Retrospective on Conservative Economics," *Journal of Economic Perspectives* 3(1) (Winter 1989): 107–134.

————, *After the Waste Land: A Democratic Economics for the Year 2000.* Armonk, NY: M.E. Sharpe, 1990.

Bradsher, Keith, "Productivity Is All, But It Doesn't Pay Well," *New York Times,* June 25, 1995.

————, "Widest Gap in Incomes? Research Points to U.S.," *New York Times,* October 27, 1995.

Brandt, Barbara, "Less Is More: A Call for Shorter Work Hours," *Utne Reader,* July/August 1991.

Brauer, David A. and Susan Hickok, "Explaining the Growing Inequality in Wages across Skill Levels," *Federal Reserve Bank of New York Economic Policy Review* 1(1) (January 1995): 61–75.

Brecher, Jeremy, *Strike!* San Francisco: Straight Arrow Books, 1972.

Brenner, Harvey M., "Estimating the Effect of Economic Change on National Mental Health and Social Well-Being," Report for the Subcommittee on Economic Goals and Intergovernmental Policy, Joint Economic Committee, U.S. Congress, 1984.

Briggs, Vernon M. Jr., "Mass Immigration, Free Trade, and the Forgotten American Worker," *Challenge,* May–June 1995: 37–44.

Brody, David, *Workers in Industrial America.* New York: Oxford University Press, 1993. 2nd ed.

————, "Section 8(a)(2) and the Origins of the Wagner Act," in *Restoring the Promise of American Labor Law,* edited by Sheldon Friedman *et al.* Ithaca, NY: ILR Press, 1994. Pp. 29–44.

Brown, Clair and Michael Reich, "When Does Cooperation Work? A Look at NUMMI and Van Nuys," *California Management Review* 31(3) (Summer 1989): 26–44.

Bruce, Peter G., "On the Status of Workers' Rights to Organize in the United States and Canada," in *Restoring the Promise of American Labor Law,* edited by Sheldon Friedman *et al.* Ithaca, NY: ILR Press, 1994. Pp. 273–284.

Brunetta, Renato and Carlo Dell'Aringa, eds., *Labour Relations and Economic Performance.* New York: New York University Press, 1990.

Buchele, Robert and Jens Christiansen, "Industrial Relations and Productivity Growth: A Comparative Perspective," *International Contributions to Labour Studies* 2, 1992: 77–97.

Bursik, Robert J. Jr. and Harold G. Grasmick, "Economic Deprivation and Neighborhood Crime Rates, 1960–1980," *Law & Society Review* 27(2), 1993: 263–283.

Burtless, Gary, "International Trade and the Rise in Earnings Inequality," *Journal of Economic Literature* 33(2) (June 1995): 800–816.

Butterfield, Fox, "More Blacks in Their 20's Have Trouble with the Law," *New York Times,* October 5, 1995.

Calmfors, Lars and John Driffill, "Bargaining Structure, Corporatism and Macroeconomic Performance," *Economic Policy: A European Forum,* No. 6, April 1988: 13–61.

Cappelli, Peter, "Are Skill Requirements Rising? Evidence from Production and Clerical Jobs," *Industrial and Labor Relations Review* 46(3) (April 1993): 515–530.

Card, David, "The Effect of Unions on the Distribution of Wages: Redistribution or Relabelling?", National Bureau of Economic Research, Working Paper No. 4195, October 1992.

Card, David and Alan B. Krueger, *Myth and Measurement: The New Economics of the Minimum Wage.* Princeton: Princeton University Press, 1995.

Carnevale, Anthony, "Preface," in Stephen J. Rose, *Declining Job Security and the Professionalization of Opportunity.* Washington, D.C.: National Commission for Employment Policy, May 1995. Pp. i–xi.

Cassidy, John, "Who Killed the Middle Class?" *The New Yorker*, October 16, 1995.

Castro, Janice, "Disposable Workers," *Time*, March 29, 1993.

Catinat, M. *et al.*, "Investment Behavior in Europe: A Comparative Analysis," *Recherches Economiques de Louvain* 54, 1988: 277–324.

Caves, Richard E. and Matthew B. Krepps, "Fat: The Displacement of Nonproduction Workers from U.S. Manufacturing Industries," *Brookings Papers on Economic Activity— Microeconomics* 1993(2): 227–273.

Chaison, Gary N. and Joseph B. Rose, "The Canadian Perspective on Workers' Rights to Form a Union and Bargain Collectively," in *Restoring the Promise of American Labor Law*, edited by Sheldon Friedman *et al.* Ithaca, NY: ILR Press, 1994. Pp. 241–249.

Charlier, Marj, "Magma Copper Heals Its Workplace and Bottom Line," *Wall Street Journal*, April 6, 1992.

Cherlin, Andrew J. *et al.*, "Longitudinal Studies of Effects of Divorce on Children in Great Britain and the United States," *Science*, June 7, 1991: 1386–1389.

Chirinko, Robert S., "Business Fixed Investment Spending: Modeling Strategies, Empirical Results, and Policy Implications," *Journal of Economic Literature* 31(4) (December 1993): 1875–1911.

Clark, Peter K., "Potential GNP in the United States, 1948–80," *Review of Income and Wealth* Series 25(2) (June 1979): 141–165.

Clift, Eleanor and Rich Thomas, "It's Sacred—But Is It Smart?", *Newsweek*, April 17, 1989.

Clinton, Bill and Al Gore, *Putting People First: How We Can All Change America.* New York: Times Books, 1992.

Cohen, Susan and Mary Fainsod Katzenstein, "The War over the Family Is Not over the Family," in *Feminism, Children, and the New Families*, edited by Sanford M. Dornbusch and Myra H. Strober. New York: Guilford Press, 1988. Pp. 25–46.

Colburn, Don, "Domestic Violence," *The Washington Post*, June 28, 1994.

———, "When Violence Begins at Home," *The Washington Post*, March 15, 1994.

Commission on the Future of Worker-Management Relations, *Report and Recommendations.* U.S. Departments of Labor and Commerce, December 1994.

———, "Employee Participation and Labor-Management Cooperation in American Workplaces," *Challenge*, September–October 1995: 41–45.

Commission on the Skills of the American Workforce, *America's Choice: High Skills or Low Wages.* Rochester, NY: National Center on Education and the Economy, 1990.

Coontz, Stephanie, *The Way We Never Were: American Families and the Nostalgia Trap.* NY: BasicBooks, 1992.

Cooper, James C., "The New Golden Age of Productivity," *Business Week*, September 16, 1994.

Cooper, Matthew with Dorian Friedman, "The Rich in America," *U.S. News & World Report*, November 18, 1991.

Cooper, Michael R., "Early Warning Signals: Growing Discontent Among Managers" *Business*, January–February 1980.

Crozier, Michel, *The Bureaucratic Phenomenon.* Chicago: University of Chicago Press, 1964.

The Criminal Justice Institute, *The Corrections Yearbook.* South Salem, NY: Criminal Justice Institute, various years.

Currie, Elliott, *Confronting Crime.* New York: Pantheon, 1985.

Danziger, Sheldon and Peter Gottschalk, "Introduction," in *Uneven Tides: Rising Inequality in America*, edited by Sheldon Danziger and Peter Gottschalk. New York: Russell Sage Foundation, 1994. Pp. 3–17.

————, eds., *Uneven Tides: Rising Inequality in America*. New York: Russell Sage Foundation, 1994.

Davis, Mike, "Hell Factories in the Field," *Nation*, February 20, 1995.

Davis, Steven J. and Robert H. Topel, "Comment," *Brookings Papers on Economic Activity* 1993(2): 214–221.

DeFreitas, Gregory, "Immigration, Inequality, and Policy Alternatives," Hofstra University, October 1995.

Dell'Aringa, Carlo and Manuela Samek Lodovici, "Industrial Relations and Economic Performance," in *Participation in Public Policy-Making: The Role of Trade Unions and Employers' Associations*, edited by Tiziano Treu. Berlin: Walter deGruyter, 1992. Pp. 26–58.

Deming, W. Edwards, *Out of the Crisis*. Cambridge, MA: MIT Press, 1986.

Demo, David H. and Lawrence H. Ganong, "Divorce," in *Families and Change: Coping with Stressful Events*, edited by Patrick C. McKenry and Sharon J. Price. Thousand Oaks, CA: Sage Publications, 1994. Pp. 197–218.

DeParle, Jason, "In Debate on U.S. Poverty, 2 Studies Fuel an Argument on Who Is to Blame," *New York Times*, October 29, 1991.

————, "Welfare Mothers Find Jobs Are Easier to Get Than Hold," *New York Times*, October 24, 1994.

————, "Better Work Than Welfare. But What If There's Neither?" *New York Times Magazine*, December 18, 1994.

Dickens, William T. and Jonathan S. Leonard, "Accounting for the Decline in Union Membership, 1950–1980," *Industrial and Labor Relations Review*, 38(2) (April 1985): 323–34.

Diebold, Francis X., David Neumark, and Daniel Polsky, "Job Stability in the United States," National Bureau of Economic Research, Working Paper No. 4859, September 1994.

DiNardo, John, Nicole M. Fortin, and Thomas Lemieux, "Labor Market Institutions and the Distribution of Wages, 1973–1992: A Semiparametric Approach," unpublished paper, University of California at Irvine, March 1994.

DiNardo, John and Thomas Lemieux, "Diverging Male Wage Inequality in the United States and Canada, 1981–1988: Do Unions Explain the Difference?", unpublished paper, University of California, Irvine, 1994.

Doeringer, Peter B. *et al.*, *Turbulence in the American Workplace*. New York: Oxford University Press, 1991.

Drucker, Peter F., *Managing in Turbulent Times*. New York: Harper & Row, 1980.

Duby, Georges, *Rural Economy and Country Life in the Medieval West*. Columbia, SC: University of South Carolina Press, 1968. Trans. by Cynthia Postan. [Originally published in French: L'Économie Rurale et la Vie des Campagnes dans l'Occident Médiéval. Paris: Aubier, Éditions Montaigne, 1962.]

Duncan, Greg J. and Saul D. Hoffman, "Teenage Underclass Behavior and Subsequent Poverty: Have the Rules Changed?", in *The Urban Underclass*, edited by Christopher Jencks and Paul E. Peterson. Washington, D.C.: The Brookings Institution, 1991. Pp. 155–174.

Eatwell, John, *What Ever Happened to Britain? The Economics of Decline*. London: Duckworth, 1982.

The Editor, "Corporate Surveys Can't Find A Productivity Revolution, Either," *Challenge*, November–December 1995.

Edwards, Richard, "Individual Traits and Organizational Incentives: What Makes a 'Good' Worker?", *Journal of Human Resources* 11(1) (Winter 1976): 51–68.

————, *Contested Terrain: The Transformation of the Workplace in the Twentieth Century*. New York: Basic Books, 1979.

———, *Rights at Work: Employment Relations in the Post-Union Era.* Washington, D.C.: The Brookings Institution, 1993.

Ehrenberg, Ronald G., Pamela Rosenberg, and Jeanne Li, "Part-time Employment in the United States," in *Employment, Unemployment, and Labor Utilization,* edited by Robert A. Hart. Boston: Unwin Hyman, 1988. Pp. 256–87.

Ehrenreich, Barbara, *The Hearts of Men: American Dreams and the Flight from Commitment.* Garden City, NJ: Anchor Press, 1983.

Emshoff, James R. and Teri E. Demlinger, *The New Rules of the Game.* New York: Harper-Collins, 1991.

Esping-Andersen, Gösta, *The Three Worlds of Welfare Capitalism.* Princeton: Princeton University Press, 1990.

Faludi, Susan, *Backlash: The Undeclared War against Women.* New York: Crown, 1991.

Families and Work Institute, *Women: The New Providers.* New York: Families and Work Institute, May 1995.

Farber, Henry S. and Alan B. Krueger, "Union Membership in the United States: The Decline Continues," in *Employee Representation: Alternatives and Future Directions,* edited by Bruce E. Kaufman and Morris M. Kleiner. Madison, WI: Industrial Relations Research Association, 1993. Pp. 105–134.

Farnham, Alan, "The Trust Gap," *Fortune,* December 4, 1989.

Feldstein, Martin, "Inflation, Tax Rules and Investment: Some Econometric Evidence," *Econometrica* 50(4) (July 1982): 825–862.

Fenwick, Rudy and Mark Tausig, "The Macroeconomic Context of Job Stress," *Journal of Health and Social Behavior* 35(3) (September 1994): 266–282.

Ferguson, Thomas and Joel Rogers, "Labor Law Reform and Its Enemies," *Nation,* January 6–13, 1979.

———, *Right Turn: The Decline of the Democrats and the Future of American Politics.* New York: Hill and Wang, 1986.

Flaim, Paul O., "Proposed Spendable Earnings Series Retains Basic Faults of Earlier One," *Monthly Labor Review,* November 1984: 43–44.

Folbre, Nancy, *Who Pays for the Kids? Gender and the Structures of Constraint.* New York: Routledge, 1994.

Folbre, Nancy and the Center for Popular Economics, *The New Field Guide to the U.S. Economy: A Compact and Irreverent Guide to Economic Life.* New York: The New Press, 1995.

"The Fortune 500," *Fortune,* May 15, 1995.

Fraser, Douglas, Letter of resignation from the Labor-Management Advisory Committee, July 10, 1978, circulated by the United Auto Workers Union.

Fraser, Steven, ed., *The Bell Curve Wars: Race, Intelligence and the Future of America.* New York: Basic Books, 1995.

Freedman, Audrey, *Managing Labor Relations.* New York: The Conference Board, 1979.

———, *The New Look in Wage Policy and Employee Relations.* New York: The Conference Board, 1985.

Freeman, Richard B., "Labour Market Institutions and Economic Performance," *Economic Policy: A European Forum,* No. 6 (April 1988): 64–80.

———, "Employment and Earnings of Disadvantaged Young Men in a Labor Shortage Economy," in *The Urban Underclass,* edited by Christopher Jencks and Paul E. Peterson. Washington, D.C.: The Brookings Institution, 1991. Pp. 103–121.

———, "Is Globalisation Impoverishing Low Skill American Workers?" Urban Institute, Session on Policy Responses to an International Labor Market, November 17, 1993.

———, "How Much Has De-Unionization Contributed to the Rise in Male Earnings Inequality?", in *Uneven Tides: Rising Inequality in America,* edited by Sheldon Danziger and Peter Gottschalk. New York: Russell Sage, 1994. Pp. 133–163.

————, "How Labor Fares in Advanced Economies," in *Working Under Different Rules,* edited by Richard B. Freeman. New York: Russell Sage, 1994. Pp. 1–28.

————, "Are Your Wages Set in Beijing?" *Journal of Economic Perspectives,* 9(3) (Summer 1995): 15–32.

Freeman, Richard B. and Lawrence F. Katz, "Rising Wage Inequality: The United States vs. Other Advanced Countries," in *Working Under Different Rules,* edited by Richard B. Freeman. New York: Russell Sage, 1994. Pp. 29–62.

————, "Introduction and Summary," in *Differences and Changes in Wage Structures,* edited by Freeman and Katz. Chicago: University of Chicago Press, 1995. Pp. 1–22.

Freeman, Richard B. and James L. Medoff, *What Do Unions Do?* New York: Basic Books, 1984.

Freeman, Richard B. and Joel Rogers, "Worker Representation and Participation Survey: First Report of Findings," December 5, 1994.

————, "Who Speaks for Us? Employee Representation in a Nonunion Labor Market," in *Employee Representation: Alternatives and Future Directions,* edited by Bruce E. Kaufman and Morris M. Kleiner. Madison, WI: Industrial Relations Research Association, 1993. Pp. 13–80.

Friedberg, Rachel M. and Jennifer Hunt, "The Impact of Immigrants on Host Country Wages, Employment and Growth," *Journal of Economic Perspectives* 9(2) (Spring 1995): 23–44.

Galinsky, Ellen, James T. Bond, and Dana E. Friedman, *The Changing Workforce: Highlights of the National Study.* New York: Families and Work Institute, 1993.

Gallup Poll News Service, "Recession Shakes Faith in American Dream," News Release, February 2, 1992.

Gardner, Jennifer M., "Worker Displacement: A Decade of Change," U.S. Bureau of Labor Statistics, Report No. 2464, July 1995.

Gerson, Kathleen, *No Man's Land: Men's Changing Commitments to Family and Work.* New York: BasicBooks, 1993.

Gittleman, Maury, "Earnings in the 1980's: An Occupational Perspective," *Monthly Labor Review,* July 1994: 16–27.

Gittleman, Maury and David R. Howell, "Changes in the Structure and Quality of Jobs in the United States: Effects by Race and Gender, 1973–1990," *Industrial and Labor Relations Review* 48(3) (April 1995): 420–440.

Glass, Jennifer and Tetsushi Fujimoto, "Housework, Paid Work, and Depression Among Husbands and Wives," *Journal of Health and Social Behavior* 35(2) (June 1994): 179–191.

Glyn, Andrew, "Social Democracy and Full Employment," *New Left Review,* No. 211, May/June 1995: 33–55.

Goldfield, Michael, *The Decline of Organized Labor in the United States.* Chicago: University of Chicago Press, 1987.

Gordon, David M., "Do We Need to Be Number 1?", *Atlantic Monthly,* April 1986.

————, "The Global Economy: New Edifice or Crumbling Foundations?" *New Left Review,* No. 168, March/April 1988: 24–64.

————, "The Un-Natural Rate of Unemployment: An Econometric Critique of the NAIRU Hypothesis," *American Economic Review* 78(2) (May 1988): 117–123.

————, "What Makes Epochs? A Comparative Analysis of Technological and Social Explanations of Long Economic Swings," in *Technological and Social Factors in Long-Term Fluctuations,* edited by R. Goodwin *et al.,* New York: Springer-Verlag, 1989. Pp. 267–304.

————, "Who Bosses Whom? The Intensity of Supervision and the Discipline of Labor," *American Economic Review* 80(2) (May 1990): 28–32.

————, "Bosses of Different Stripes: Monitoring and Supervision across the Advanced Economies," *American Economic Review* 84(2) (May 1994): 375–379.

————, "Putting Heterodox Macro to the Test: Comparing Post-Keynesian, Marxian, and Social Structuralist Macroeconometric Models of the Postwar U.S. Economy," in *Competition,*

Technology, and Money: Comparing Classical and Post-Keynesian Views, edited by Mark Glick and E. K. Hunt. Aldershot, England: Edward Elgar, 1994. Pp. 143–185.

Gordon, David M., Richard Edwards, and Michael Reich, *Segmented Work, Divided Workers:The Historical Transformation of Labor in the United States*. New York: Cambridge University Press, 1982.

Gordon, David M., Thomas E. Weisskopf, and Samuel Bowles, "Power, Profits, and Investment: The Postwar Social Structure of Accumulation and the Stagnation of U.S. Net Investment since the Mid-1960s," unpublished paper, New School for Social Research, December 1995.

Gordon, Diana R., *The Justice Juggernaut: Fighting Street Crime, Controlling Citizens*. New Brunswick, NJ: Rutgers University Press, 1991.

———, *The Return of the Dangerous Classes: Drug Prohibition and Policy Politics*. New York: W. W. Norton, 1994.

Gordon, Robert J., "The 'End-of-Expansion' Phenomenon in Short-Run Productivity Behavior," *Brookings Papers on Economic Activity* 10(2), 1979: 447–461.

———, "The Jobless Recovery: Does It Signal a New Era of Productivity-led Growth?", *Brookings Papers on Economic Activity* 1993(1): 271–316.

———, "Measurement Errors in the CPI: Causes and Consequences," Testimony before Senate Finance Committee, March 13, 1995.

———, "Is There a Tradeoff between Unemployment and Productivity Growth?" in *Unemployment Policy*, edited by Dennis J. Snower and Guillermo de la Dehesa. (forthcoming 1996).

Gottschalk, Peter and Robet Moffitt, "The Growth of Earnings Instability in the U.S. Labor Market," *Brookings Papers on Economic Activity* 1994(2): 217–272.

Greider, William, "Middle-Class Funk," *Rolling Stone*, November 2, 1995.

Green, Mark and John F. Berry, *The Challenge of Hidden Profits: Reducing Corporate Bureaucracy and Waste*. New York: William Morrow, 1985.

Greenberg, Stanley B., *Middle Class Dreams: The Politics and Power of the New American Majority*. New York: Times Books, 1995.

Greenhouse, Steven, "Labor Secretary to Urge Clinton to Propose Minimum Wage Rise," *New York Times*, October 13, 1993.

———, "Labor Official Retreats on Higher Minimum Wage," *New York Times*, October 30, 1993.

Hacker, Andrew, "The Crackdown on African-Americans," *The Nation*, July 10, 1995.

Hasan, John, "The Social Embeddedness of Crime and Unemployment," *Criminology*, 31(4), 1993.

Halal, William E., *The New Capitalism*. New York: John Wiley & Sons, 1986.

Hamermesh, Daniel S., *Labor Demand*. Princeton: Princeton University Press, 1993.

Hammonds, Keith H. *et al.*, "The New World of Work," *Business Week*, October 17, 1994.

Harrison, Bennett, *Lean and Mean: The Changing Landscape of Corporate Power in the Age of Flexibility*. New York: BasicBooks, 1994.

Hayes, Robert H. and Steven C. Wheelwright, *Restoring Our Competitive Edge: Competing Through Manufacturing*. New York: John Wiley & Sons, 1984.

Herbert, Bob, "In America, The Issue Is Jobs," *New York Times*, May 6, 1995.

———, "City Job, Minimum Wage," *New York Times*, July 28, 1995.

Herman, Edward S., *Corporate Control, Corporate Power*. New York: Cambridge University Press, 1981.

Herrnstein, Richard J. and Charles Murray, *The Bell Curve: Intelligence and Class Structure in American Life*. New York: The Free Press, 1994.

Hershey, Robert D., Jr., "Wage Increases Are Small, But Confidence Jumps," *New York Times*, April 27, 1994.

———, "U.S. Wages Up 2.7% in Year, A Record Low," *New York Times*, November 1, 1995.

Holmes, Steven A., "Surprising Rise in Immigration Stirs Up Debate," *New York Times*, August 30, 1995.

Howell, David R., "The Skills Myth," *American Prospect*, Summer 1994: 81–89.

———, "Collapsing Wages and Rising Inequality: Has Computerization Shifted the Demand for Skills?", *Challenge*, January–February 1995: 27–35.

———, "The Collapse of Low-Skill Earnings in the U.S.: Skill Mismatch or Shifting Wage Norms?", Policy Brief of the Jerome Levy Institute, July 1995.

Howell, David R. and Susan S. Wieler, "Trends in Computerization, Skill Composition and Low Earnings: Implications for Education and Training Policy," unpublished paper, New School for Social Research, October 1994.

Howell, David R. and Edward N. Wolff, "Trends in the Growth and Distribution of Skills in the U.S. Workplace, 1960–85," *Industrial and Labor Relations Review* 44(3) (April 1991): 486–502.

Huselid, Mark A. and Brian E. Becker, "The Strategic Impact of Human Resources: Evidence from a Panel Study," paper presented to a conference on "What Works at Work: Human Resource Policies and Organizational Performance," Washington, D.C., January 5, 1995.

International Labour Organization, *Yearbook of Labour Statistics*, 1994 Geneva: ILO, 1994.

Jacoby, Sanford M., *Employing Bureaucracy: Managers, Unions, and the Transformation of Work in American Industry, 1900–1945*. New York: Columbia University Press, 1985.

Janofsky, Michael, "Trade Pact Casts Shadow for Garment Workers," *New York Times*, December 12, 1994.

Jencks, Christopher, "Is the American Underclass Growing?" in Christopher Jencks and Paul E. Peterson, eds., *The Urban Underclass*. Washington, D.C.: The Brookings Institution, 1991. Pp. 28–100.

Jencks, Christopher and Kathryn Edin, "Do Poor Women Have a Right to Bear Children?" *The American Prospect*, Winter 1995: 43–52.

Johnson, Dirk, "Family Struggles to Make Do After Fall From Middle Class," *New York Times*, March 11, 1994.

Jones, Edward D., *The Administration of Industrial Enterprises*. New York: Longmans, Green, 1925. Second edition (originally published in 1916).

Kagay, Michael R., "From Coast to Coast, From Affluent to Poor, Poll Shows Anxiety Over Jobs," *New York Times*, March 11, 1994.

Kahneman, Daniel, "New Challenges to the Rationality Assumption," *Journal of Institutional and Theoretical Economics* 150(1) (March 1994): 18–36.

Kaminer, Wendy, "Federal Offense," *Atlantic Monthly*, June 1994.

Kanter, Rosabeth Moss, "A Key Fit: Employability Security," *Boston Globe*, March 13, 1994.

Karoly, Lynn A., "The Trend in Inequality Among Families, Individuals, and Workers in the United States: A Twenty-Five Year Perspective," in *Uneven Tides: Rising Inequality in America*, edited by Sheldon Danziger and Peter Gottschalk. New York: Russell Sage Foundation, 1994. Pp. 19–97.

Katz, Harry C., Thomas A. Kochan, and Mark R. Weber, "Assessing the Effects of Industrial Relations Systems and Efforts to Improve the Quality of Working Life on Organizational Effectiveness," *Academy of Management Journal* 28(3) (September 1985): 509–526.

Katz, Lawrence F. and Kevin M. Murphy, "Changes in Relative Wages, 1963–1987: Supply and Demand Factors," *Quarterly Journal of Economics* 107(1) (February 1992): 35–78.

Katz, Lawrence F., Gary W. Loveman, and David G. Blanchflower, "A Comparison of Changes in the Structure of Wages in Four OECD Countries," in *Differences and Changes in Wage Structures*, edited by Richard B. Freeman and Lawrence F. Katz. Chicago: University of Chicago Press, 1995. Pp. 25–65.

Kaufman, Bruce E., ed., *How Labor Markets Work: Reflections on Theory and Practice*. Lexington, MA: Lexington Books, 1988.

Keefe, Jeffrey H., "Numerically Controlled Machine Tools and Worker Skills," *Industrial and Labor Relations Review* 44(3) (April 1991): 503–519.

Keller, Maryann, *Rude Awakening: The Rise, Fall, and Struggle for Recovery of General Motors.* New York: William Morrow, 1989.

Kilborn, Peter T., "U.S. Unions Back Shorter Week, But Employers Seem Reluctant," *New York Times,* November 22, 1993.

———, "More Women Take Low-Wage Jobs Just So their Families Can Get By," *New York Times,* March 13, 1994.

Killingsworth, Mark R. and James J. Heckman, "Female Labor Supply: A Survey," in *Handbook of Labor Economics,* edited by O. Ashenfelter and R. Layard. Amsterdam: North-Holland, 1986. Vol. I. Pp. 103–204.

Klein, Janice A., "Why Supervisors Resist Employee Involvement," *Harvard Business Review* 62(5), September–October, 1984: 87–95.

Kochan, Thomas A., Robert B. McKersie, and John Chalykoff, "Corporate Stratregy, Workplace Innovation, and Union Members," *Industrial and Labor Relations Review* 39(3) (July 1986): 487–501.

Kochan, Thomas A., Harry C. Katz, and Robert B. McKersie, *The Transformation of American Industrial Relations.* Ithaca, NY: Cornell ILR Press, 1994.

Kohn, Melvin L. and Carmi Schooler, *Work and Personality: An Inquiry into the Impact of Social Stratification.* Norwood, NJ: Ablex, 1983.

Konrad, Walecia, "Much More than a Day's Work—For Just a Day's Pay?" *Business Week,* Semptember 23, 1991.

Kosters, Marvin H., "Wages and Demographics," in *Workers and Their Wages: Changing Patterns in the United States,* edited by Marvin H. Kosters. Washington, D.C.: AEI Press, 1991. Pp. 1–32.

Kotz, David M., *Bank Control of Large Corporations in the United States.* Berkeley, CA: University of California Press, 1978.

Krueger, Alan B., "How Computers Have Changed the Wage Structure: Evidence from Microdata, 1984–1989," *Quarterly Journal of Economics* 108(1) (February 1993): 33–60.

Krugman, Paul, *Peddling Prosperity: Economic Sense and Nonsense in the Age of Diminished Expectations.* New York: W. W. Norton, 1994.

———, "Competitiveness: A Dangerous Obsession," *Foreign Affairs,* March/April 1994: 28–44.

Krugman, Paul and Robert Lawrence, "Trade, Jobs, and Wages," National Bureau of Economic Research, Discussion Paper No. 4478, September 1993.

Kunz, Jennifer, "The Effects of Divorce on Children," in Stephen J. Bahr, ed., *Family Research: A Sixty-Year Review, 1930–1990.* New York: Lexington Books, 1991. Pp. 325–376.

Kuttner, Robert, *The End of Laissez-Faire: National Purpose and the Global Economy After the Cold War.* Philadelphia: University of Pennsylvania Press, 1992.

Langer, Elinor, "The Women of the Telephone Company," *New York Review of Books,* March 12, 1970, and March 26, 1970.

Lawler, Edward E., III, Susan A. Mohrman, and Gerald Ledford Jr., *Employee Involvement and Total Quality Management: Practice and Results in Fortune 1000 Companies.* San Francisco: Jossey-Bass, 1992.

Lawrence, Robert Z., "Trade, Multinationals, and Labor," National Bureau of Economic Research, Working Paper No. 4836, August 1994.

———, "U.S. Wage Trends in the 1980s: The Role of International Factors," *Federal Reserve Bank of New York Economic Policy Review* 1(1) (January 1995): 18–23.

Lawrence, Robert Z. and Matthew J. Slaughter, "International Trade and American Wages in the 1980s: Giant Sucking Sound or Small Hiccup?" *Brookings Papers on Economic Activity* 1993(2): 161–210.

Leamer, Edward E., "Wage Effects of of a U.S.-Mexico Free Trade Agreement," in *The Mexico-U.S. Free Trade Agreement*, edited by Peter M. Garber. Cambridge, MA: MIT Press, 1993. Pp. 57–162.

———, "Trade, Wages, and Revolving Door Ideas," National Bureau of Economic Research, Working Paper No. 4716, April 1994.

Levine, David I., "Public Policy Implications of Imperfections in the Market for Worker Participation," *Economic and Industrial Democracy* 13(3) (May 1992): 184–206.

———, "Demand Variability and Work Organization," in *Markets and Democracy: Participation, Accountability and Efficiency*, edited by Samuel Bowles, Herbert Gintis, and Bo Gustafsson. New York: Cambridge University Press, 1993. Pp. 159–175.

Levine, David I. and Laura D'Andrea Tyson, "Participation, Productivity and the Firm's Environment," in *Paying for Productivity: A Look at the Evidence*, edited by Alan S. Blinder. Washington, D.C.: Brookings Institution, 1990. Pp. 183–237.

Levine, David I., Gerald E. Ledford Jr., Edward E. Lawler III, and Susan Albers Mohrman, "The Effects of Employee Involvement on Large U.S. Employers," paper presented to a conference on "What Works at Work: Human Resource Policies and Organizational Performance," Washington, D.C., January 5, 1995.

Levy, Frank and Richard J. Murnane, "U.S. Earnings Levels and Earnings Inequality: A Review of Recent Trends and Proposed Explanations," *Journal of Economic Literature* 30(3), September 1992: 1333–1381.

Lewin, Tamar, "Low Pay and Closed Doors Confront Young Job Seekers," *New York Times*, March 10, 1994.

Lewis, H. Gregg, *Union Relative Wage Effects: A Survey*. Chicago: University of Chicago Press, 1986.

Limbaugh, Rush H., III, *The Way Things Ought to Be*. New York: Pocket Books, 1992.

Lino, Mark, "Mothers' Perceptions of Their Lives After Divorce," paper presented at the annual meeting of the Population Association, 1994.

Little, Jane Sneddon, "Exchange Rates and Structural Change in U.S. Manufacturing Employment," *New England Economic Review*, March/April 1989: 56–69.

Lord, Mary, "Where You Can't Get Fired," *U.S. News & World Report*, January 14, 1991.

Los Angeles Times, "Los Angeles Times Poll: Study #317, National Politics," July 15, 1993.

Los Angeles Times, "Los Angeles Times Poll: Employment," November 15, 1993.

Lynch, Lisa, ed., *Training and the Private Sector: International Comparisons*. Chicago: University of Chicago Press, 1994.

———, "Payoffs to Alternative Training Strategies at Work," in *Working Under Different Rules*, edited by Richard B. Freeman. New York: Russell Sage, 1994. Pp. 63–96.

MacCoun, Robert and Peter Reuter, "Are the Wages of Sin $30 an Hour? Economic Aspects of Street-Level Drug Dealing," *Crime & Delinquency* 38(4) (October 1992): 477–491.

Marist Institute for Public Opinion, "Americans Making Ends Meet?" March 1995.

Markels, Alex, "Restructuring Alters Middle-Manager Role But Leaves It Robust," *Wall Street Journal*, September 25, 1995.

Mattera, Phillip, *Prosperity Lost* (New York: Addison-Wesley, 1990),

Mauer, Marc, "Americans Behind Bars: The International Use of Incarceration, 1992–93," The Sentencing Project, Washington, D.C., September 1994.

McCrate, Elaine, "The Growth of Nonmarriage Among U.S. Women, 1954–1983," unpublished Ph.D. dissertation, University of Massachusetts—Amherst, 1985.

———, "Trade, Merger and Employment: Economic Metaphors for Marriage," *Review of Radical Political Economics* 19(1) (Spring 1987): 73–87.

———, "Expectations of Adult Wages and Teenage Childbearing," *International Review of Applied Economics* 6(3) (September 1992): 309–328.

————, "The Effect of Schooling and Labor Market Expectations on Teenage Childbearing," *Review of Radical Political Economics* 20(2&3) (Spring/Summer 1988): 203–207.

————, "Labor Market Segmentation and Relative Black/White Teenage Birth Rates," *Review of Black Political Economy,* 18(4) (Winter/Spring 1990): 37–53.

————, "Accounting for the Slowdown in the Divorce Rate in the 1980s: A Bargaining Perspective," *Review of Social Economy* 50(4)(Winter 1992): 404–419.

McKinsey Global Institute, *Manufacturing Productivity.* Washington, D.C.: McKinsey Global Institute, October 1993.

Michl, Tom, "Is There Evidence for a Marginalist Demand for Labour?" *Cambridge Journal of Economics* 11(4) (December 1987): 361–373.

Milkman, Ruth, *Japan's California Factories: Labor Relations and Economic Globalization.* Los Angeles: Institute of Industrial Relations, University of California, 1991.

Miller, William H., "Metamorphosis in the Desert," *Industry Week,* March 16, 1992.

Mishel, Lawrence and Jared Bernstein, *The State of Working America 1994–95.* Armonk, NY: M. E. Sharpe, 1994.

————, "Is the Technology Black Box Empty? An Empirical Examination of the Impact of Technology on Wage Inequality and the Employment Structure," unpublished paper, Economic Policy Institute, 1994.

Mitchell, Daniel J. B., "Shifting Norms in Wage Determination," *Brookings Papers on Economic Activity* 1985(2): 575–599.

————, "Wage Pressures and Labor Shortages: The 1960s and 1980s," *Brookings Papers on Economic Activity* 1989(2): 191–231.

Moberg, David, "Prairie Fires," *In These Times,* July 25, 1994.

Montgomery, David, *Workers' Control in America: Studies in the History of Work, Technology, and Labor Struggles.* Cambridge: Cambridge University Press, 1979.

Moore, David W., "Americans Feel Threatened by New Immigrants," *Gallup Poll Monthly,* July 1993.

Moore, David W. and Leslie McAneny, "Workers Concerned They Can't Afford to Retire," *Gallup Poll Monthly,* May 1993.

Morrow, Lance, "The Temping of America," *Time,* March 29, 1993.

Moss, Philip and Chris Tilly, *Why Black Men Are Doing Worse in the Labor Market: A Review of Supply-Side and Demand-Side Explanations.* New York: Social Science Research Council, 1992.

Murphy, Kevin M. and Finis Welch, "The Role of International Trade in Wage Differentials," in *Workers and Their Wages: Changing Patterns in the United States,* edited by Marvin Kosters. Washington, D.C.: AEI Press, 1991. Pp. 39–69.

————, "Industrial Change and the Rising Importance of Skill," in *Uneven Tides: Rising Inequality in America,* edited by Sheldon Danziger and Peter Gottschalk. New York: Russell Sage Foundation, 1994. Pp. 101–132.

Murray, Charles, "The Coming White Underclass," *Wall Street Journal,* October 29, 1993.

Nasar, Sylvia, "Statistics Reveal Bulk of New Jobs Pay Over Average," *New York Times,* October 17, 1994.

Nelson-Horchler, Joani, "CEO Pay," *Industry Week,* April 15, 1991.

"New Work Order," *The Economist,* April 9, 1994.

Neuhaus, Richard John, *America Against Itself: Moral Vision and the Public Order.* Notre Dame: University of Notre Dame Press, 1992.

Newman, Katherine S., *Falling from Grace: The Experience of Downward Mobility in the American Middle Class.* New York: The Free Press, 1988.

————, *Declining Fortunes: The Withering of the American Dream.* New York: Basic Books, 1993.

Nichols, Don, "The Management Revolution and Loss of Union Clout," *Management Review*, February 1988: 25–26.

Novak, Michael, "The Inequality Myth: What Wealth Gap?" *Wall Street Journal*, July 11, 1995.

Nussbaum, Bruce, "Downward Mobility: Corporate Castoffs are Struggling Just to Stay in the Middle Class," *Business Week*, March 23, 1992.

Oliner, Stephen D. and Daniel E. Sichel, "Computers and Output Growth Revisited: How Big is the Puzzle?," *Brookings Papers on Economic Activity*, 1994:2: 273–334.

———, "Is a Productivity Revolution Under Way in the United States?," *Challenge*, November–December 1995: 18–29.

Olson, Ardis L. and Lisa A. DiBrigida, "Depressive Symptoms and Work Role Satisfaction in Mothers of Toddlers," *Pediatrics* 94(3) (September 1994): 363–367.

Organization for Economic Cooperation and Development, *OECD Economic Outlook*, various issues.

———, *The OECD Jobs Study*. Paris: OECD, June 1994.

Osterman, Paul, "Gains from Growth? The Impact of Full Employment on Poverty in Boston," in *The Urban Underclass*, edited by Christopher Jencks and Paul E. Peterson. Washington, D.C.: The Brookings Institution, 1991. Pp. 122–134.

———, "How Common Is Workplace Transformation and Who Adopts It?" *Industrial and Labor Relations Review* 47(2) (January 1994): 173–188.

O'Toole, James, *Making America Work: Productivity and Responsibility*. New York: Continuum, 1981.

Paloheimo, Heikki, "Between Liberalism and Corporatism: The Effect of Trade Unions and Governments on Economic Performance in Eighteen OECD Countries," in R. Brunetta and C. Dell'Aringa, eds., *Labour Relations and Economic Performance*. New York: New York University Press, 1990. Pp. 114–136.

Parks, Susan, "Improving Workplace Performance: Historical and Theoretical Contexts," *Monthly Labor Review*, May 1995: 18–28.

Passell, Peter, "An Immigration Puzzle," *New York Times*, September 6, 1994.

Pattee, Jon, "Sprint and the Shutdown of La Conexion Familiar," *Labor Research Review*, No. 23, 1995: 13–22.

Patterson, E. Britt, "Poverty, Income Inequality, and Community Crime Rates," *Criminology* 29(4) (November 1991): 755–776.

"Paychecks of America's 800 Top Chief Executives," *Forbes*, May 23, 1994.

Pekkarinen, Jukka, M. Pohjola, and Bob Rowthorn, eds.. *Social Corporatism: A Superior Economic System?* Oxford: Oxford University Press, 1992.

Pencavel, John, "Labor Supply of Men: A Survey," in *Handbook of Labor Economics*, edited by O. Ashenfelter and R. Layard. Amsterdam: North-Holland, 1986. Vol. I. Pp. 3–102.

Peterson, Jonathan, "Economists Play 'Happy Days' as Many Sing Blues," *Los Angeles Times*, February 21, 1994.

Peterson, Peter G. and Neil Howe, *On Borrowed Time: How the Growth in Entitlement Spending Threatens America's Future*. New York: ICS Press, 1988.

Phillips, Kevin, *Arrogant Capital: Washington, Wall Street, and the Frustration of American Politics*. Boston: Little, Brown, 1994.

Pondy, Louis R., "Effects of Size, Complexity, and Ownership on Administrative Intensity," *Administrative Science Quarterly*, March 1969: 47–61.

"Portrait of an Anxious Public," *Business Week*, March 13, 1995.

"Portrait of the Electorate: Who Voted for Whom in the House," *New York Times*, November 13, 1994.

Preston, Richard, *American Steel: Hot Metal Men and the Resurrection of the Rust Belt*. New York: Prentice Hall Press, 1991.

Quayle, Dan, "The Family Comes First: We Cannot Take Orders from the Special Interests," *Vital Speeches of the Day* 58(23) (September 15, 1992).

———, *Standing Firm: A Vice-Presidential Memoir.* New York: HarperCollins, 1994.

Raymond, H. Alan, *Management in the Third Wave.* Glenview, IL: Scott, Foresman and Co., 1986.

Read, Eileen White, "For Poor Teenagers, Pregnancies Become New Rite of Passage," *Wall Street Journal*, March 17, 1988.

Reich, Robert B., *The Work of Nations: Preparing Ourselves for 21st-Century Capitalism.* New York: Vintage Books, 1992.

———, "Workers of the World, Get Smart," *New York Times*, July 20, 1993.

Reingold, Jennifer, "CEO of the Year," *Financial World*, March 28, 1995.

Richardson, J. David, "Income Inequality and Trade: How to Think, What to Conclude," *Journal of Economic Perspectives*, 9(3) (Summer 1995): 33–55.

Riegle Community Development and Regulatory Improvement Act of 1994, Public Law 103–325, 103rd Congress, September 23, 1994.

Rogers Joel and Wolfgang Streeck, "Workplace Representation Overseas: The Works Councils Story," in *Working Under Different Rules*, edited by Richard B. Freeman. New York: Russell Sage, 1994. Pp. 97–156.

———, eds., *Works Councils: Consultation, Representation, and Cooperation in Industrial Relations.* Chicago: University of Chicago Press, 1996.

Rorty, Richard, "Sex, Lies and Virginia's Voters," *New York Times*, October 13, 1994.

Rose, Stephen J., *Declining Job Security and the Professionalization of Opportunity.* Washington, D.C.: National Commission for Employment Policy, May 1995. Research Report No. 95–04.

Ross, C. E., J. Mirowsky, and K. Goldsteen, "The Impact of the Family on Health: The Decade in Review," *Journal of Marriage and the Family* 52(4) (November 1990): 1059–1078.

Roth, Philip, *Portnoy's Complaint.* New York: Random House, 1969.

Ruggles, Patricia, *Drawing the Line: Alternative Poverty Measures and Their Implications for Public Policy.* Washington, D.C.: Urban Institute Press, 1990.

Ryscavage, Paul, "Gender-related Shifts in the Distribution of Wages," *Monthly Labor Review*, July 1994: 3–15.

Sachs, Jeffrey D. and Howard J. Shatz, "Trade and Jobs in U.S. Manufacturing," *Brookings Papers on Economic Activity* 1994(1): 1–84.

Salwen, Kevin G., "Food Lion to Pay Big Settlement in Labor Case," *Wall Street Journal*, August 3, 1993.

Sasseen, Jane A., "The Winds of Change Blow Everywhere," *Business Week*, October 17, 1994.

"Satisfaction with Work," *The American Enterprise*, January/February 1995.

Schiemann, William A., ed., *Managing Human Resources: 1985 and Beyond.* Princeton: Opinion Research Corporation, 1984.

Schor, Juliet B., *The Overworked American: The Unexpected Decline of Leisure.* New York: Basic Books, 1991.

———, "A Sustainable Economy for the 21st Century," *Open Magazine Pamphlet Series*, Pamphlet #31.

Schwarz, John E. and Thomas J. Volgy, *The Forgotten Americans.* New York: W.W. Norton, 1992.

Sekscenski, Edward S., "Women's Share of Moonlighting Nearly Doubles During 1969–79," *Monthly Labor Review*, May 1980: 36–42.

Sennett, Richard, "Back to Class Warfare," *New York Times*, December 27, 1994.

Silk, Leonard and David Vogel, *Ethics and Profits: The Crisis of Confidence in American Business.* New York: Simon and Schuster, 1976.

Smeeding, Timothy, Barbara Boyle Torrey, and Martin Rein, "Patterns of Income and Poverty: The Economic Status of Children and the Elderly in Eight Countries," in *The Vulnerable*, edited by J. Palmer *et al.* Washington, D.C.: Urban Institute Press, 1988. Pp. 89–119.

Smith, Hedrick, *Rethinking America*. New York: Random House, 1995.

Snell, Tracy L., *Correctional Populations in the United States, 1992*, U.S. Bureau of Justice Statistics, NCJ-146413, January 1995.

Sorensen, Glorian *et al.*, "Sex Differences in the Relationship Between Work and Health: The Minnesota Heart Survey," *Journal of Health and Social Behavior* 26(4) (December 1985): 379–394.

Soskice, David, "Reinterpreting Corporatism and Explaining Unemployment: Co-ordinated and Non-co-ordinated Market Economies," in *Labour Relations and Economic Performance*, edited by R. Brunetta and C. Dell'Aringa. New York: New York University Press, 1990.

Southern Finance Project, "Reinvestment Reform in an Era of Financial Change," Philomont, VA, April 1995.

Spalter-Roth, Roberta, "Welfare That Works: Increasing AFDC Mothers' Employment and Income," Testimony before the Subcommittee on Human Resources, Committee on Ways and Means, U.S. House of Representatives, February 2, 1995 (revised March 1995).

Spalter-Roth, Roberta et al., *Welfare That Works: The Working Lives of AFDC Recipients*. Washington, D.C.: Institute for Women's Policy Research, 1995.

Spalter-Roth, Roberta and Heidi Hartmann, "Contingent Work: Its Consequences for Economic Well-Being, the Gendered Division of Labor, and the Welfare State," in *Contingent Work: From Entitlement to Privilege*, edited by Kathleen Barker and Kathleen Christensen. (forthcoming, 1996).

Staines, Graham, "Is Worker Dissatisfaction Rising?" *Challenge*, May–June 1979: 38–45.

Steele, Shelby, *The Content of Our Character: A New Vision of Race in America*. New York: Harper Perennial, 1991.

Stinson, John F. Jr., "Multiple Job Holding Up Sharply in the Eighties," *Monthly Labor Review*, July 1990: 3–10.

Sullivan, Mercer L., *"Getting Paid": Youth Crime and Work in the Inner City*. Ithaca, NY: Cornell University Press, 1989.

Teixeira, Ruy A. and Lawrence Mishel, "Whose Skills Shortage: Workers or Management?" *Issues in Science and Technology* 9(4) (Summer 1993): 69–74.

Teixeira, Ruy A. and Joel Rogers, "Who Deserted the Democrats in 1994?" *American Prospect*, No. 23 (Fall 1995): 73–77.

Thurow, Lester, *Head to Head: The Coming Economic Battle among Japan, Europe, and America*. New York: William Morrow, 1992.

Tienda, Marta and Haya Stier, "Joblessness and Shiftlessness: Labor Force Activity in Chicago's Inner City," in *The Urban Underclass*, edited by Christopher Jencks and Paul E. Peterson. Washington, D.C.: The Brookings Institution, 1991. Pp. 135–154.

Tilly, Chris, *Short Hours, Short Shrift: Causes and Consequences of Part-time Work*. Washington, D.C.: Economic Policy Institute, 1990.

Tomasko, Robert M., *Downsizing: Reshaping the Corporation for the Future*. New York: American Management Association, 1987.

Topel, Robert, "What Have We Learned from Empirical Studies of Unemployment and Turnover?", *American Economic Review* 83(2) (May 1993): 115–120.

Towers Perrin, Inc., "1991 Worldwide Total Remuneration," 1991.

Uchitelle, Louis, "Trapped in the Impoverished Middle Class," *New York Times*, November 17, 1991.

———, "Three Decades of Dwindling Hope for Prosperity," *New York Times*, May 9, 1993.

———, "Moonlighting Plus: 3–Job Families on the Rise," *New York Times*, August 16, 1994.

———, "Flat Wages Seen as Issue in '96 Vote," *New York Times*, August 13, 1995.

U.S. Bureau of the Census, *The National Income and Product Accounts of the United States, 1929–82: Statistical Tables* (Washington, D.C.: U.S. Government Printing Office, 1986).

————, *Census of Manufactures, 1987* (Washington, D.C.: U.S. Government Printing Office, 1991).

————, "Workers with Low Earnings: 1964 to 1990," *Current Population Reports*, Series P-60, No. 178, March 1992.

————, *Census of Manufactures, 1992* (Washington, D.C.: U.S. Government Printing Office, 1994).

————, "Household and Family Characteristics: March 1993," *Current Population Reports*, Series P-20, No. 477, June 1994.

————, "Income, Poverty, and Valuation of Noncash Benefits: 1993," *Current Population Reports*, Series P-60, No. 188, February 1995.

U.S. Bureau of Justice Statistics, *Sourcebook of Criminal Justice Statistics*. Washington, D.C.: U.S. Government Printing Office, various years.

U.S. Bureau of Labor Statistics, *Employment and Earnings, United States, 1909–78*, Bulletin 1312–11, July 1979.

————, *Employment and Training Report of the President*, 1981 Washington D.C.: U.S. Government Printing Office, 1981.

————, *Handbook of Methods*, Bulletin 2282, April 1988.

————, Office of Productivity and Technology, "Real Gross Fixed Capital Formation," unpublished tables, May 1991, Table II.A.

————, *Consumer Expenditure Survey, 1990–91*, Bulletin 2425, September 1993.

————, "International Comparisons of Hourly Compensation Costs for Production Workers in Manufacturing, 1975–1994," Report No. 893, May 1995.

————, "Employment in Perspective: Earnings and Job Growth," Report No. 877, August 1994.

————, "Worker Displacement During the Early 1990s," News Release USDL 94–434, September 14, 1994.

————, Office of Productivity and Technology, "Output per Hour, Hourly Compensation, and Unit Labor Costs in Manufacturing, Twelve Economies, 1950–1993," unpublished tables, February 1995.

————, "Employed and experienced unemployed persons by detailed occupation, . . . , 2nd Quarter 1995," unpublished tables, 1995.

————, "New Data on Contingent and Alternative Employment Examined by BLS," USDL Release 95–318, August 17, 1995.

U.S. Department of Commerce, National Institute of Standards and Technology, *Malcolm Baldridge National Quality Award, 1992 Award Criteria*. Gaithersburg, MD: National Institute of Standards and Technology, 1992.

U.S. Department of Education, National Center for Education Statistics, *Digest of Education Statistics, 1994*.

U.S. Department of Justice, Federal Bureau of Investigation, *Uniform Crime Reports for the United States, 1993*. Washington, D.C.: U.S. Government Printing Office, 1994.

U.S. Department of Justice, Bureau of Justice Statistics, *Criminal Victimization in the United States, 1973–92 Trends*, A National Crime Victimization Survey Report, NCJ-147006, July 1994.

————, "Violence against Women: Estimates from the Redesigned Survey," *National Crime Victimization Survey*, Report No. NCJ-154348, August 1995.

U.S. Department of Labor, *Dictionary of Occupational Titles*. Washington, D.C.: U.S. Government Printing Office, various editions.

U.S. Executive Office of the President, "A Vision of Change for America," February 17, 1993.

U.S. Immigration and Naturalization Service, *Statistical Yearbook of the Immigration and Naturalization Service, 1992*. Washington, D.C.: U.S. Government Printing Office, 1993.

Useem, Michael, "Corporate Restructuring and Organizational Behavior," in Thomas A. Kochan and Michael Useem, eds., *Transforming Organisations*. New York: Oxford University Press, 1992. Pp. 44–59.

Viscusi, W. Kip, "The Risks and Rewards of Criminal Activity: A Comprehensive Test of Criminal Deterrence," *Journal of Labor Economics* 4(3) (July 1986): 317–340.

Vobejda, Barbara and D'Vera Cohn, "Today, a Father's Place Is in the Home," *Washington Post*, May 20, 1994.

Vogel, David, *Fluctuating Fortunes: The Political Power of Business in America*. New York: Basic Books, 1989.

Wachter, Michael L. and William H. Carter, "Norm Shifts in Union Wages: Will 1989 Be a Replay of 1969?" *Brookings Papers on Economic Activity* 1989(2): 233–64.

Walinsky, Adam, "The Crisis of Public Order," *Atlantic Monthly*, July 1995.

Wattenberg, Ben J., *Values Matter Most: How Republicans or Democrats or a Third Party Can Win and Renew the American Way of Life*. New York: The Free Press, 1995.

Weiler, Paul C., *Governing the Workplace: The Future of Labor and Employment Law*. Cambridge, MA: Harvard University Press, 1990.

Weisskopf, Thomas E., "Use of Hourly Earnings Proposed to Revive Spendable Earnings Series," *Monthly Labor Review*, November 1984: 38–43.

———, "The Effect of Unemployment on Labour Productivity: An International Comparative Analysis," *International Review of Applied Economics* 1(2) (June 1987): 127–151.

Weisskopf, Thomas E., Samuel Bowles, and David M. Gordon, "Hearts and Minds: A Social Model of U.S. Productivity Growth," *Brookings Papers on Economic Activity* 1983(2): 381–441.

"Where Will the Jobs Come From?" *Fortune*, October 19, 1992.

Wieler, Susan Sheehan, "Can Technological Change Explain Increasing Inequality within Age, Schooling, and Gender Groups?", paper presented to the Eastern Economics Association, March 1994.

Williamson, Oliver E., "A Model of Rational Managerial Behavior," in Richard M. Cyert and James G. March, *A Behavioral Theory of the Firm*. Englewood Cliffs, NJ: Prentice-Hall, 1963. Pp. 237–252.

Wilson, James Q., "Capitalism and Morality," *The Public Interest*, Fall 1995.

Wilson, William Julius, *The Truly Disadvantaged: The Inner City, the Underclass, and Public Policy*. Chicago: University of Chicago Press, 1987.

Winter, J. Burgess, "Magma: A High Performance Company," speech presented at the Copper 95–Cobre 95 International Conference, Santiago, Chile, November 1995.

Witte, Ann Dryden and Helen Tauchen, "Work and Crime: An Exploration Using Panel Data," National Bureau of Economic Research, Working Paper No. 4794, July 1994.

Wolff, Edward N., *Top Heavy: A Study of the Rising Inequality of Wealth in America*. New York: The Twentieth Century Fund Press, 1995.

Wood, Adrian, *North-South Trade, Employment and Inequality*. Oxford: Clarendon Press, 1994.

Woodward, Bob, *The Agenda: Inside the Clinton White House*. New York: Simon and Schuster, 1994.

Wright, Erik Olin, *Classes*. London: Verso Books, 1985.

———, *Class Counts: Comparative Studies in Class Analysis*. New York: Cambridge University Press, 1996.

Yuskavage, Robert E., "Gross Product by Industry, 1988–91," *Survey of Current Business*, November 1993: 33–44.

INDEX

311